Simple Fondant Dress Cookies

Volume 1

Simple Fondant Dress Cookies, Volume 1

First published in the United States by
Constant Desserts Press, Selma, Alabama

Paperback ISBN 978-1-953956-34-7
Hardback ISBN 978-1-953956-35-4
eBook ISBN 978-1-953956-36-1

Library of Congress Control Number 2021909633

Printed in the United States of America

First Edition

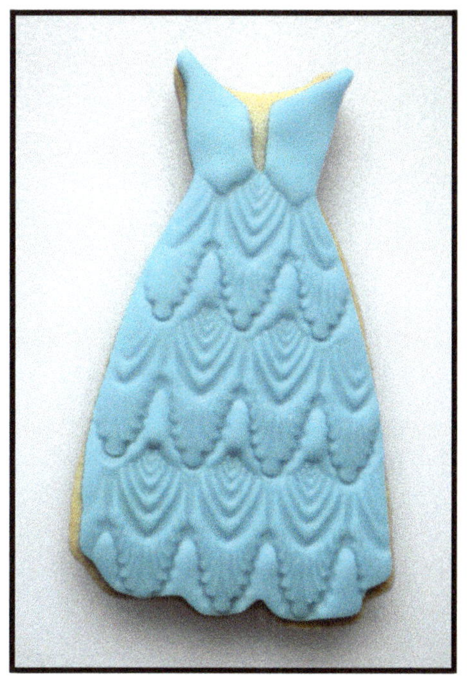

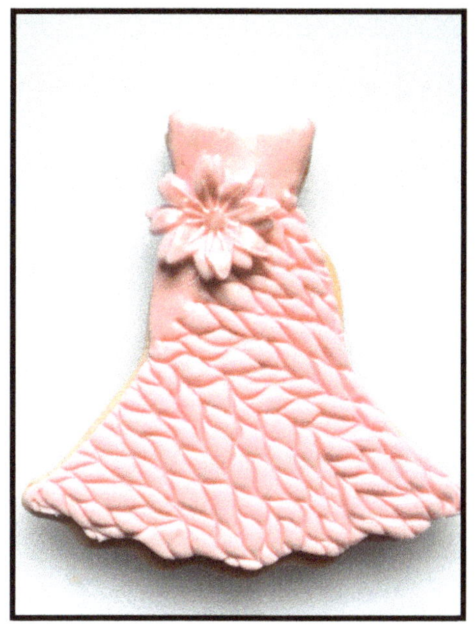

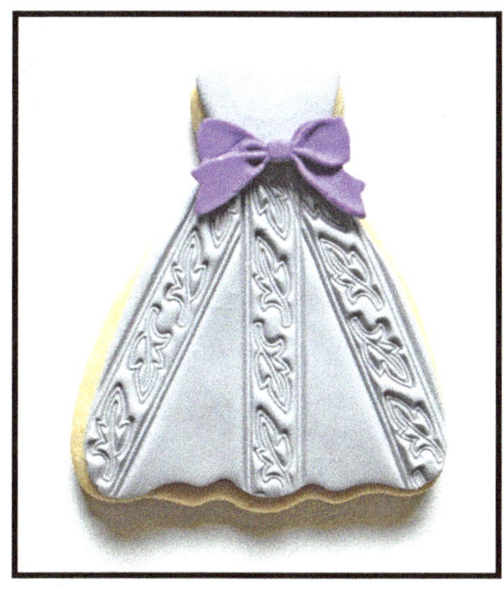

Contents

Introduction 1

**Top Tools for Beginner
Fondant Cookie Decorators** 2

How to Use this Book 4

Sugar Cookie Recipes 5

Basic Sugar Cookies 7

Chocolate Sugar Cookies 8

Carrot Cake Sugar Cookies 8

German Chocolate Sugar Cookies 9

Time to Roll Out Your
Sugar Cookie Dough 10

Using Cookie Cutters to Cut Out Your
Sugar Cookie Dough 10

**How to Use Fondant
Right Out of the Package** 12

How to Cover Sugar Cookies in Fondant 14

Instructions for Fondant-Covered
Dress Sugar Cookies with Designs
On the Cookie 14

Instructions for Fondant-Covered
Dress Sugar Cookies with Designs
Off the Cookie 16

**Fondant Decorating Tools
& Techniques** 18

Paint Brushes 18

Piping Gel.. 18

Edible Food Color Spray 19

Plunger Cutters 20

Icing Tips 20

Impression Mats 21

Luster Dusts 21

Patchwork Cutters to Emboss
Your Dress Cookie 22

Pattern Rollers & Stencils.................. 22

Sanding Sugar
or Sprinkles on Your Dress Cookies 23

Fondant Embossers 24

Cake Stamps 24

Silicone Lace Fondant Molds.................. 25

Silicone Molds for Fondant Decorations 25

Flavoring Fondant............................ 26

Fondant Troubleshooting 27

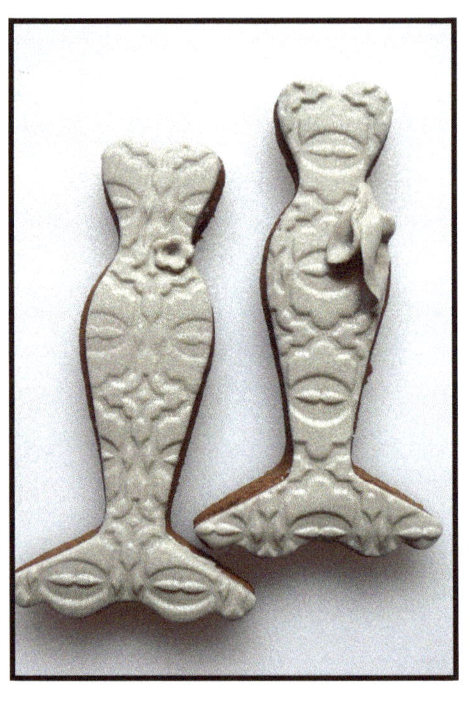

Dress Cookie Cutter Chart **28**

Black Lattice Dress Cookie.................... **29**

Coconut Dress Cookie **31**

Navy Lace Dress Cookie........................**33**

Lavender Swirl Dress Cookie **35**

White Rose Bow Dress Cookie **37**

Red Swirls Dress Cookie...................... **39**

Blue Wavy Dress Cookie **41**

Black Sparkle Dress Cookies.................. **43**

Gold Stenciled Dress Cookie....................**45**

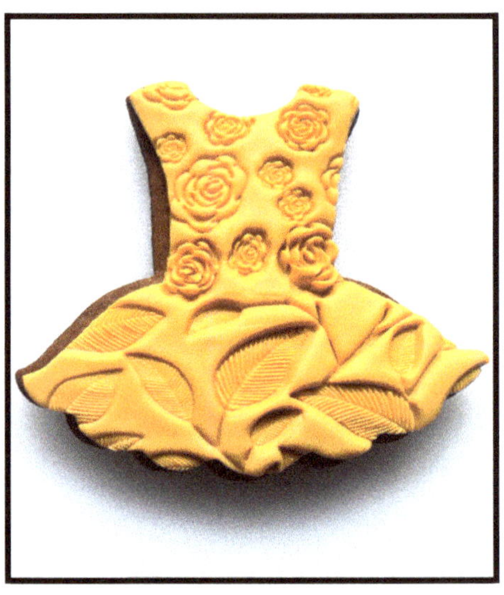

Blue Sprinkles Dress Cookie....................**47**

Green Grass Dress Cookie **49**

Coral Rose Dress Cookies **51**

Pink Pattern Dress Cookie **53**

Hot Pink & Black Dress Cookie................**55**

Green Lace Dress Cookie **57**

Navy Peach Dress Cookie **59**

Black Lace Dress Cookie **61**

Blue Hearts Dress Cookie **63**

Lavender Pattern Dress Cookie **65**

Peach Smock Dress Cookie **67**

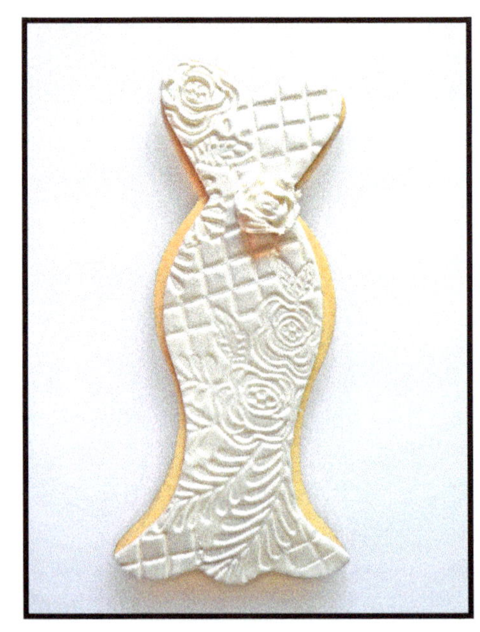

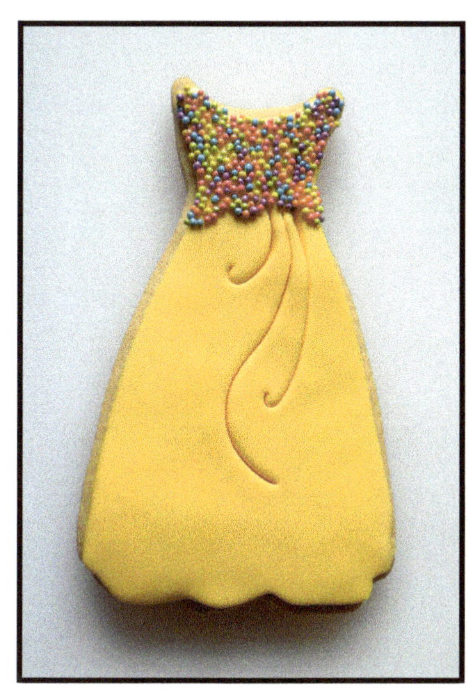

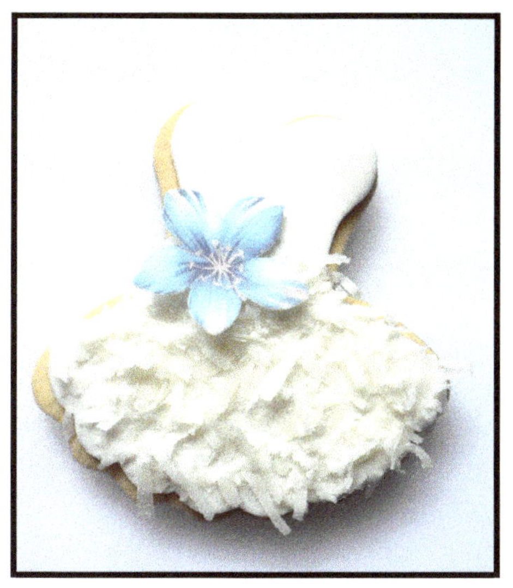

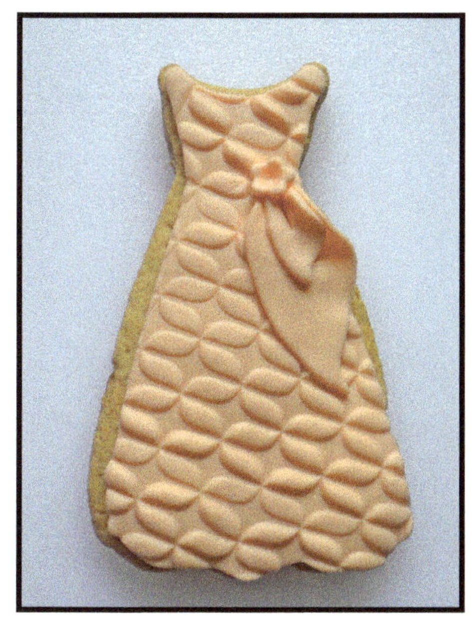

Purple Roses Dress Cookie 69

White Lace Gown Dress Cookie 71

Tan Flowers Dress Cookie 73

Marbled Swirl Dress Cookie............................... 75

Black Mini Dress Cookie 77

Blue Pattern Press Dress Cookie 79

Purple Pattern Dress Cookie.............................. 81

White Flowers Dress Cookie 83

Pink Patterns Dress Cookie................................ 85

Red Gown Dress Cookie 87

Lavender Lace Dress Cookie 89

Cream Mini Dress Cookies 91

Silver Tulip Dress Cookie 93

Orange Lace Dress Cookie 95

Metallic Gold Dress Cookie 97

Gold Pressed Dress Cookie 99

Purple Lace Dress Cookie................................... 101

Blue Imprint Dress Cookie 103

Burgundy Butterfly Dress Cookies 105

Gold Strip Dress Cookie 107

Peach Bridesmaid Dress Cookies 109

Pink Swirl Dress Cookie 111

Silver Dots Dress Cookie 113

White Lace Dress Cookie.................................... 115

Yellow Sprinkles Dress Cookie 117

Silver Pattern Dress Cookies............................... 119

Gold Sprinkles Dress Cookie 121

White Large Roses Dress Cookie........................ 123

Silver Cake Comb Dress Cookie 125

Yellow Lattice Dress Cookie 127

Lavender Black Dress Cookie.............................. 129

Chocolate Daisy Dress Cookie 131

Coral Blossom Dress Cookie.............................. 133

Lavender Tulip Dress Cookie............................ 135

Gray Ribbon Dress Cookie 137

Black Ruffle Dress Cookie 139

Burgundy Swirl Dress Cookie........................141

Final Touches 143

Drying Your Decorated
Fondant Dress Cookies 143

Packaging Your Decorated
Fondant Dress Cookies 143

Troubleshooting Packaging Problems.................. 144

Displaying Your Decorated
Fondant Dress Cookies 145

Favorite Websites/Suppliers............................ 146

Index.. 147

**About the Author
& Photographer**.. 149

**Dress Cookie
Creation Chart** 150

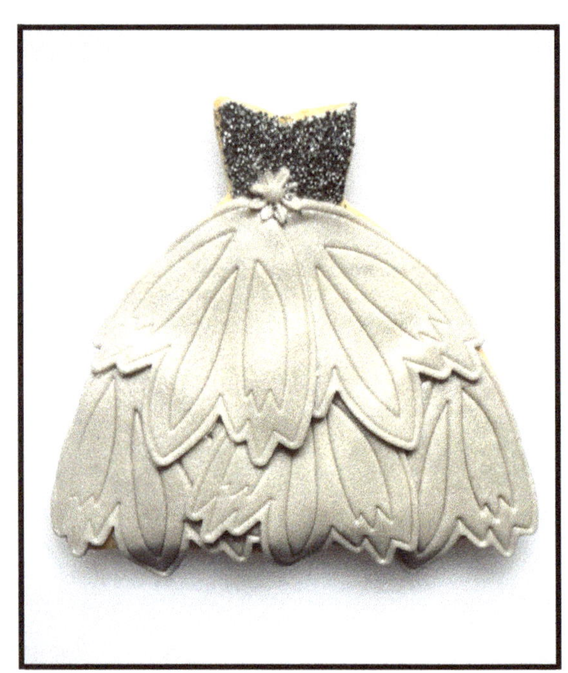

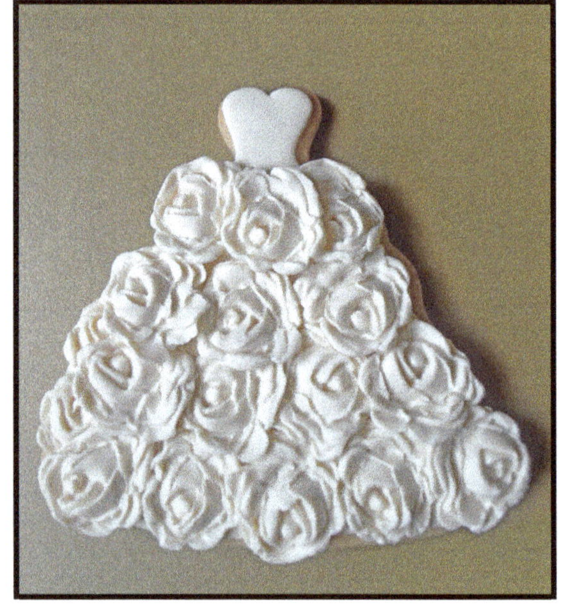

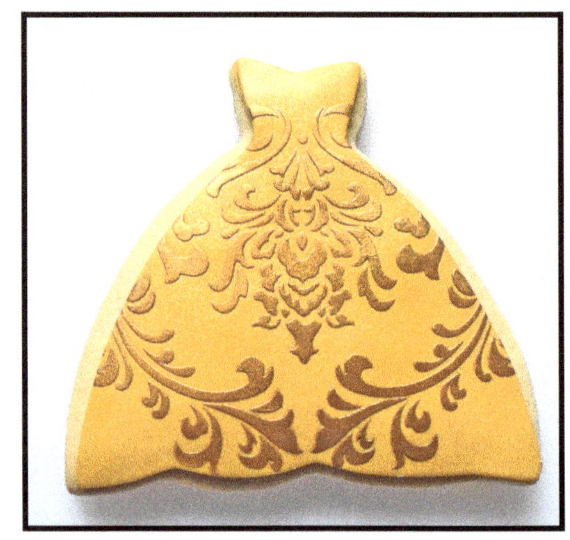

Introduction

I LOVE decorating fondant-covered sugar cookies.

It has become my passion. I have been baking fashion-related fondant sugar cookies since I met Laura Darnall of Fondarific fondant at a cake show in 2009. I believe things happen for a reason, and I have been using Fondarific fondant all these years. I believe that it is easy to work with, and the taste is amazing. I have tested my sugar cookie recipes and Fondarific fondant on family and friends for years. They keep coming back for more.

My goal in writing this book is to share some simple cookie decorating techniques with you that will give you amazing results in a short period of time. I want you to love fondant cookie decorating as much as I do, and get you in and out of the kitchen quickly. Whether you are a home baker who just bakes for family or friends or someone who has their own cookie decorating business, I believe that the simple fondant-covered dress cookie designs featured in this book will add a lot more design ideas to your sugar cookie decorating arsenal.

These fondant-covered dress cookies can be used for birthdays, milestone celebrations, bridal showers, or any other event where you want to celebrate a little girl, teenager, or grown woman. Making fondant-covered dress cookies in your recipient's favorite color will delight their heart and spirit knowing that you thought of them this way and took the time to create something spectacular for them. It is something they will never forget.

It is my wish that this Simple Fondant Dress Cookies book becomes an incredible resource that you refer to for years to come, and that your family and friends will be blown away by your fondant-covered dress cookie designs.

Please contact me through my website if you have any questions.

Happy Decorating!
Debra

www.debrajmosely.com

Top Tools for Beginner Fondant Cookie Decorators

 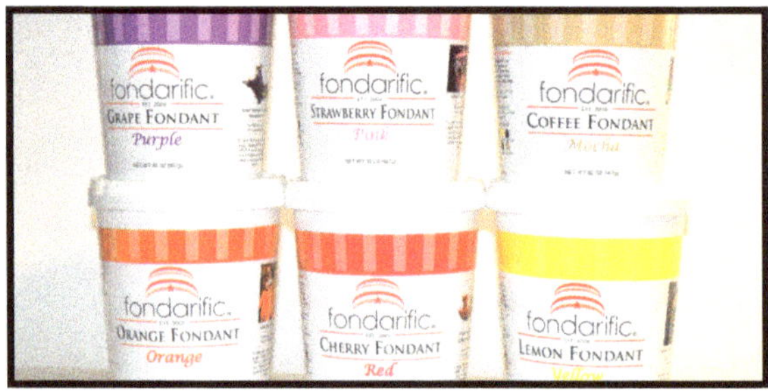

I believe Fondarific is the best brand of fondant for beginners to use. Workability time without fondant drying out is so important to new fondant cookie decorators. Taste is also important, and Fondarific has a lot of flavors.

A non-stick silicone board or mat is important for beginners to use when working with fondant. White fondant attracts everything, and you will see it on your finished dress cookie design so it is important to start with a surface you can clean thoroughly.

 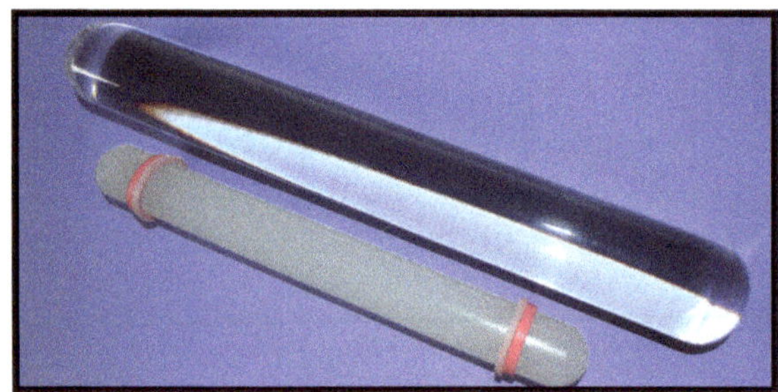

Rolling pins are extremely important in fondant sugar cookie decorating. You use a rolling pin when rolling out the sugar cookie dough, and then again when rolling out the fondant. There are also larger rolling pins on the market.

 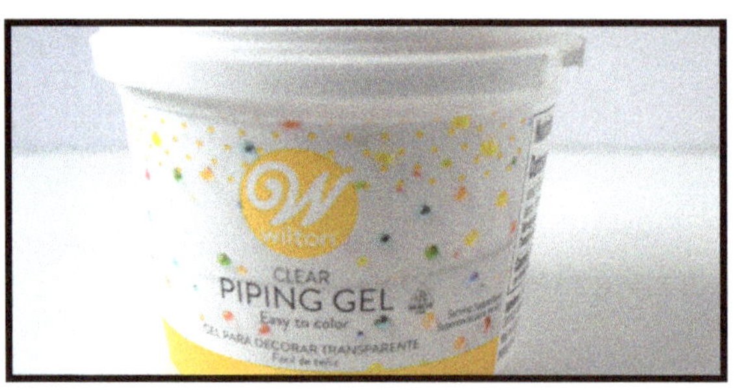

Piping gel is what I use to paint the center most part of the dress sugar cookie to secure the fondant cut-outs to the dress sugar cookie. A little goes a long way. If you use too much and the piping gel spreads to the edge of your dress cookie, it will dry shiny.

 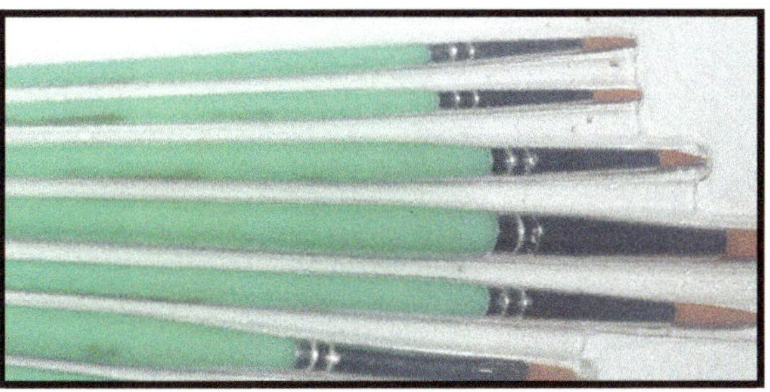

Food safe paint brushes, rather than the ones you find in the craft painting section for acrylics, are the ones you should use at home for fondant cookie decorating.

 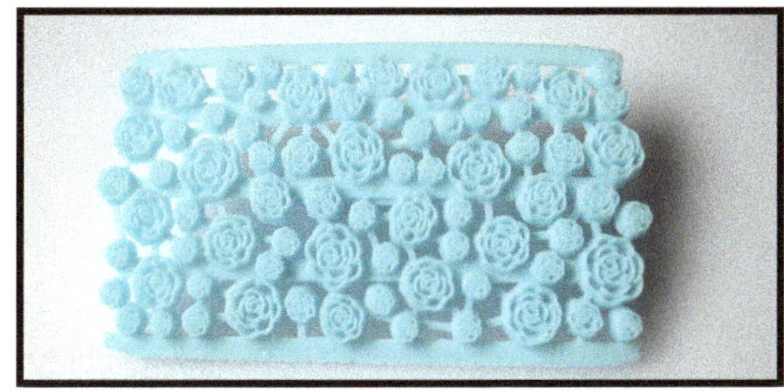

Fondant Embosser Sets are perfect for fondant dress cookie decorating. The sets come with different textures you can mix and match to use on your fondant-covered dress cookies. You can find these fondant embosser sets at your local cake decorating store or online.

 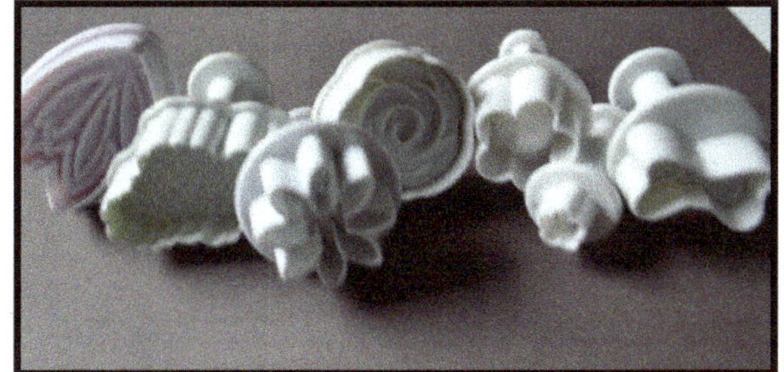

Plunger cutters are perfect for fondant-covered dress cookie decorators because they can be bought in inexpensive sets. You can use them to add accents or cover an entire fondant dress cookie quickly.

 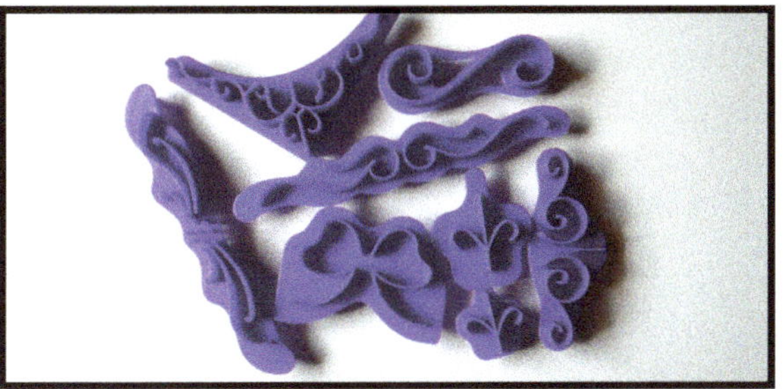

If you can find Wilton's Designer Pattern Press Set, I highly recommend it. This set makes quick work in fondant dress cookie decorating. You can imprint the fondant, and go on to something else. I wish that Wilton would release this set again.

 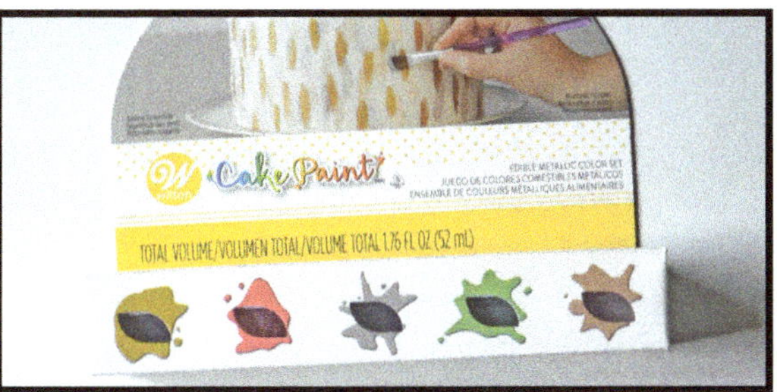

I recommend Wilton's Cake Paint for beginners because it is inexpensive and available at most cake decorating and craft stores. Once you master using this cake paint, you can move on to other brands of edible paint to decorate your fondant dress cookies.

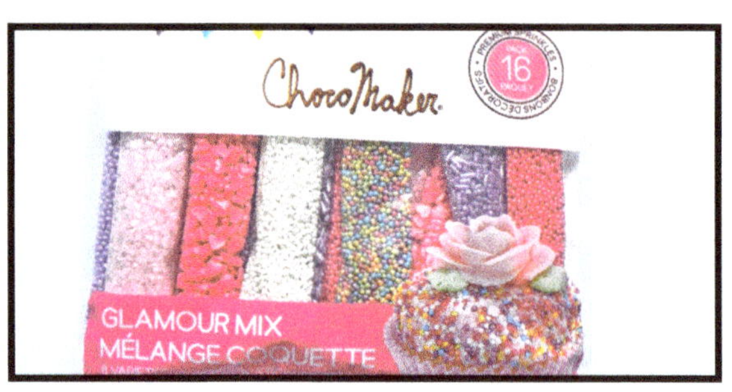

Sprinkles are great for adding accents to your fondant-covered dress cookies. You get more for your money when you purchase a mix of colors like this one. These sprinkles can be added to your fondant-covered dress cookie by painting some piping gel on the fondant-covered dress cookie, and then covering that area with sprinkles.

How to Use this Book

This book contains two pages for each decorated fondant dress sugar cookie design. One page contains the picture and all of the materials and tools required to complete the fondant-covered dress cookie design. The second page contains pictures and step-by-step instructions to guide you through the fondant-covered sugar cookie decorating process.

I want you to become as knowledgeable as you can about products on the market available for you to use in fondant sugar cookie decorating. All of the products featured in this book can speed up your cookie decorating time to get you in and out of the kitchen. Before you start buying products, read through this entire book, and then decide which decorated sugar cookies you want to make, and the tools required to create them. You can start with the fondant-covered dress cookies made with products you can find at your local craft or cake decorating store, and then add other products to your decorating arsenal as you grow. Please note that these same products can be used on your fondant-covered cakes, cupcakes, and other desserts.

Sugar Cookie Recipes

The success of your fondant decorated sugar cookie starts with a good sugar cookie base. Here are some important tips:

- Test your oven temperature for accuracy.
- Preheat your oven for 10 minutes before you add the cookie trays.
- Read both the recipe ingredients and instructions completely before starting.
- Use the best ingredients you can find. It really makes a difference in the cookie flavor.
- Please do not substitute margarine for butter in any of these recipes. They were not tested with margarine.
- All ingredients should be at room temperature. Butter that is too soft will cause your cookies to spread and not hold their shape. If your sugar cookie dough is too soft to roll out immediately, place it in a gallon-sized plastic bag, flatten the cookie dough, remove the excess air, and place in the refrigerator for a couple hours (or until firm enough to roll out). Roll it out cold.
- Please do not soften your butter in the microwave. It will lose some of its flavor and can melt resulting in a different cookie dough texture.
- All eggs listed in these recipes are large eggs.
- Vanilla extract or vanilla bean paste can be used in these recipes.
- Weigh your ingredients with a scale for accuracy.
- Line your cookie sheets with parchment paper. Cut away any excess parchment paper because cookie dough placed on the edge will bake in a warped shape and will not be flat.
- You can bake with two cookie sheets in the oven at the same time. Rotate your cookie sheets halfway through baking time for even baking.

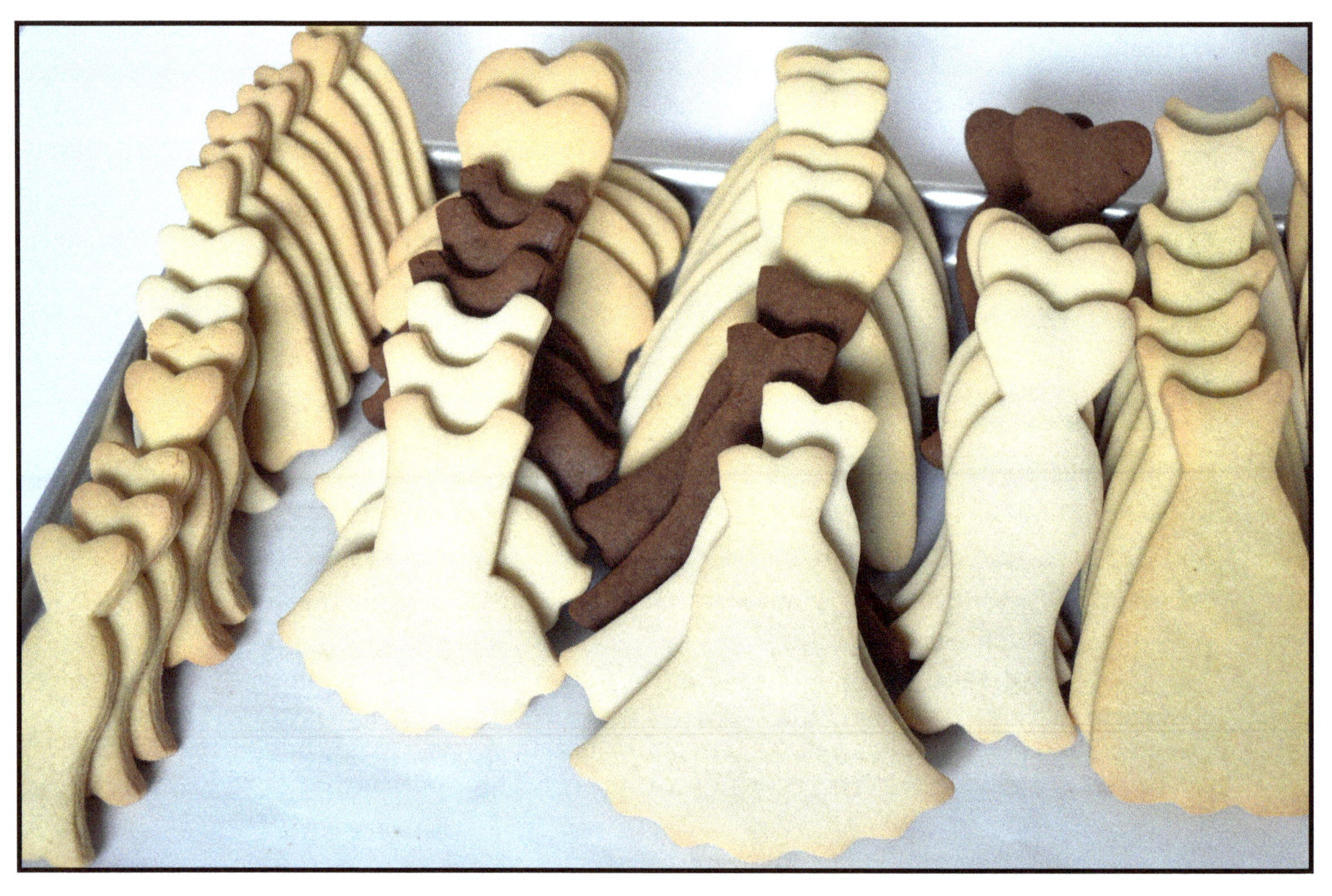

Important Tip

Use the dress cookie chart on page 28 which shows
you how much cookie dough you need to create each
dress cookie. You can use this information to calculate
how much sugar cookie dough you will need to
make the quantity of dress cookies you
want to make.

Basic Sugar Cookies

1 cup unsalted butter, softened (226g)
1 cup granulated sugar (198g)
1/2 cup confectioner's sugar (56g)
1 large egg (50g)

1 tsp pure vanilla extract (5g)
3-1/2 cups all-purpose flour (420g)
1/2 cup cake flour (60g)
1/4 tsp salt (2g)

Directions:

1. Preheat oven to 350 degrees.

2. In a large mixing bowl, blend the softened butter, granulated sugar, and confectioner's sugar together until light. Scrape down the sides of bowl.

3. Add egg and blend well. Scrape down the sides of the bowl.

4. Add vanilla extract and blend well. Scrape down the sides of the bowl. Set aside.

5. In another large mixing bowl, combine the all-purpose flour, cake flour, and salt. Use a whisk to blend dry ingredients together.

6. Add the flour mixture to the butter mixture, a little at a time, scraping down the sides of the mixing bowl until all of the flour has been incorporated. The dough should be ready to use immediately.

7. Roll out your cookie dough. If your cookie dough is extremely soft and cannot be immediately rolled out, that means your butter was too soft before blending. Refrigerate cookie dough for an hour or two before using.

8. Remove from refrigerator and let sit at room temperature for 10-15 minutes before rolling out dough. Dough should still be cold, but pliable. Cut out desired dress cookie shapes. Bake at 350 degrees for 15-18 minutes. Cool completely before decorating.

Makes 2 lbs 4.1 oz. of cookie dough (1025 grams).

Variations:
- **Champagne sugar cookies - Mix 1/2 tsp to 1 tsp of Wilton Treatology Crisp Champagne flavor into your cookie dough with the vanilla extract.**
- **Salted Caramel sugar cookies - Mix 1/2 tsp to 1 tsp of Wilton Treatology Salted Caramel flavor into your cookie dough with the vanilla extract.**

Chocolate Sugar Cookies

1 cup unsalted butter, softened (226g)
1 cup granulated sugar (198g)
1/2 cup confectioner's sugar (56g)
1 large egg (50g)
2 tsp pure vanilla extract (10g)

3 cups all-purpose flour (360g)
1/2 cup cake flour (60g)
1 tsp baking powder (3g)
2/3 cup unsweetened regular cocoa (65g)
1/2 tsp salt (2g)

Directions:

1. In a large mixing bowl, blend the softened butter, granulated sugar, and confectioner's sugar together until light. Scrape down the sides of bowl.

2. Add the egg and beat until blended. Scrape down the sides of bowl. Set aside.

3. In another medium mixing bowl, add the flour, cake flour, cocoa, baking powder, and salt. Use a whisk to blend well.

4. Add cocoa mixture to butter mixture, a little at a time, and blend well after each addition. Scrape down the sides of bowl. Chocolate sugar cookie dough should be ready for use immediately.

5. Roll out your cookie dough. If your cookie dough is extremely soft and cannot be immediately rolled out, that could mean that your butter got too soft before blending. Place chocolate sugar cookie dough into two gallon-sized plastic bags, push chocolate sugar cookie dough down to flatten, remove air, and seal bag. Place in the refrigerator for an hour.

6. Remove from refrigerator and let sit at room temperature for 10-15 minutes before rolling out dough. Preheat oven to 350 degrees. Dough should still be cold, but pliable. Cut out desired dress cookie shapes. Bake for 12-15 minutes. Cool completely before decorating.

Makes 2 lbs. 3.8 oz. of chocolate sugar cookie dough (1018g).

Carrot Cake Sugar Cookies

1 cup butter, softened (226g)
1 cup light brown sugar (213g)
1 large egg (50g)
1 tsp pure vanilla extract (5g)
1 cup freshly grated carrot (99g)

5 cups all-purpose flour (600g)
2-1/2 tsp ground cinnamon (7g)
2 tsp baking powder (8g)
1/4 tsp salt (2g)

Directions:

1. In a large mixing bowl, blend the softened butter and brown sugar together until light. Scrape down the sides of bowl.

2. Add the egg and beat until blended.

3. Add grated carrots and vanilla to this mixture. Blend well. Set aside.

4. In another large mixing bowl, combine the all-purpose flour, cinnamon, baking powder, and salt. Use a whisk to blend well.

5. Add a little of the flour mixture to the wet mixture, a little at a time, scraping down the sides until all of the flour has been incorporated.

6. Place carrot sugar cookie dough into two gallon-sized plastic bags. Press the carrot sugar cookie dough down to flatten, remove excess air, and seal bag. Place in the refrigerator for two hours.

7. Remove from refrigerator and let sit at room temperature for 10-15 minutes before rolling out dough. Preheat oven to 350 degrees. Dough should still be cold, but pliable. Cut out desired dress cookie shapes. Bake for 17-22 minutes. Cool completely before decorating.

Makes 2 lbs 4.6 oz. of carrot sugar cookie dough (1141g).

German Chocolate Sugar Cookies

1 cup unsalted butter, softened (226g)
1 cup light brown sugar (213g)
2 large eggs (100g)
4 oz. German chocolate, melted and cooled (113g)
3 Tbsp buttermilk powder

2 tsp pure vanilla extract
 or vanilla bean paste (10g)
4 cups all-purpose flour (480g)
1 cup cake flour (120g)
1 tsp baking powder (33g)
1/2 tsp salt (2g)

Directions:

1. Melt German chocolate in a microwave safe bowl. Cool completely.

2. In a large mixing bowl, blend together the softened butter and brown sugar until light. Scrape down the sides of the bowl.

3. Add eggs, one at a time, and mix until thoroughly blended. Scrape down the sides of the bowl.

4. Add the vanilla and melted German chocolate. Blend well. Scrape down the sides of the bowl. Set aside.

5. In another large mixing bowl, add the flour, cake flour, baking powder and salt. Use a whisk to blend ingredients together.

6. Add the flour mixture, a little at a time, to the butter mixture until completely blended.

7. Place German chocolate sugar cookie dough into two gallon-sized plastic bags. Press the German chocolate sugar cookie dough down to flatten, remove excess air, and seal bag. Place in the refrigerator for two hours.

8. Remove from refrigerator and let sit at room temperature for 10-15 minutes before rolling out dough. Preheat oven to 350 degrees. Dough should still be cold, but pliable. Cut out desired dress cookie shapes. Bake for 15-18 minutes. Cool completely before decorating.

Makes 2 lbs 12.1 oz. of German chocolate cookie dough (1252g).

Time to Roll Out Your Sugar Cookie Dough

Sugar cookie dough should be rolled out evenly for consistent results. You can eyeball it if you have that ability or use Perfection Strips (pictured below) which come in three colors -- red (1/8-inch or 4 mm), white (1/8-inch or 6 mm), and black (1/16-inch or 2 mm).

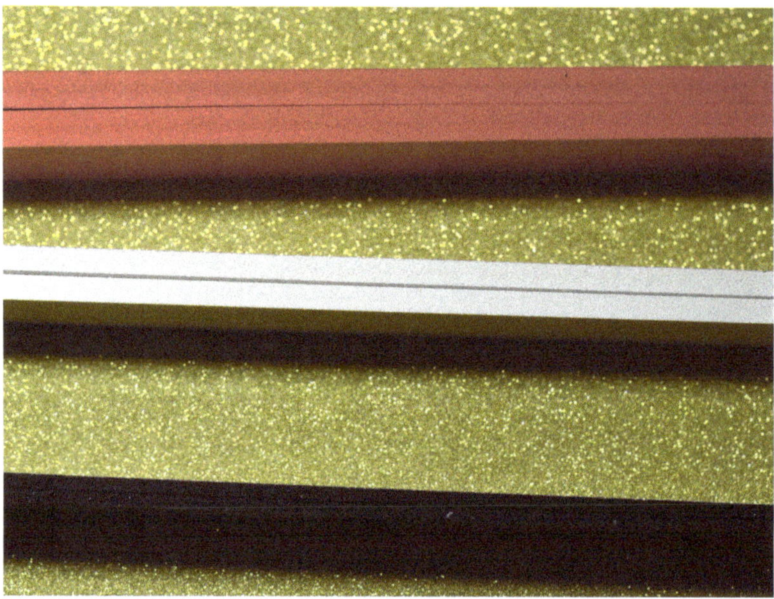

These Perfection Strips are perfect for sugar cookie dough because you can use the red strips to roll out the cookie dough. This ensures that consistent results are achieved, and all of your cookies look the same and are the same height.

Using Cookie Cutters to Cut Out Your Sugar Cookie Dough

Use firm pressure to push down the cookie cutter into the sugar cookie dough, and then wiggle the cookie cutter to get a clean cut. See the middle picture on the next page for an example. Does not matter whether you use a plastic, metal or copper cookie cutter, this technique give you a clean sugar cookie edge.

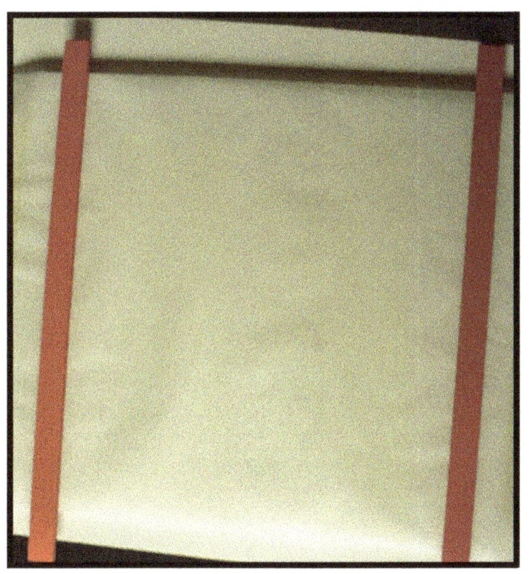

This is a silicone board covered with a sheet of parchment paper and two red Perfection Strips.

Once you place your sugar cookie dough on the parchment paper, press it down some, and then use another sheet of parchment to cover and then use a rolling pin to roll out your sugar cookie dough. This eliminates the need to add flour.

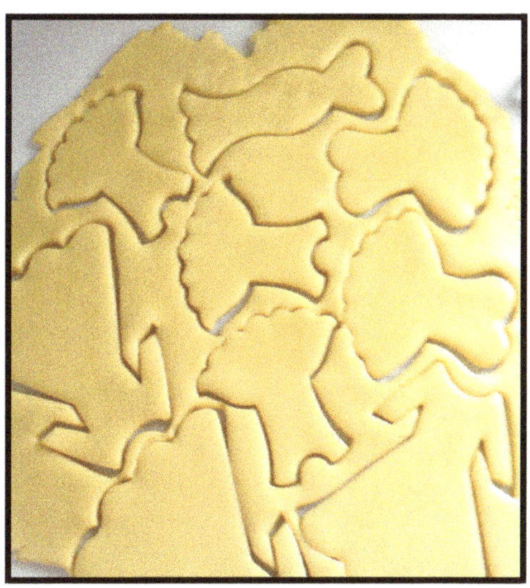

Cookie cutters should be used close together to cut out the dough. This eliminates re-rolling the dough over and over which makes your baked cookies tough. Press the cookie cutter down firmly into your cookie dough and then wiggle a little to get a clean cut. Remove cookie cutter.

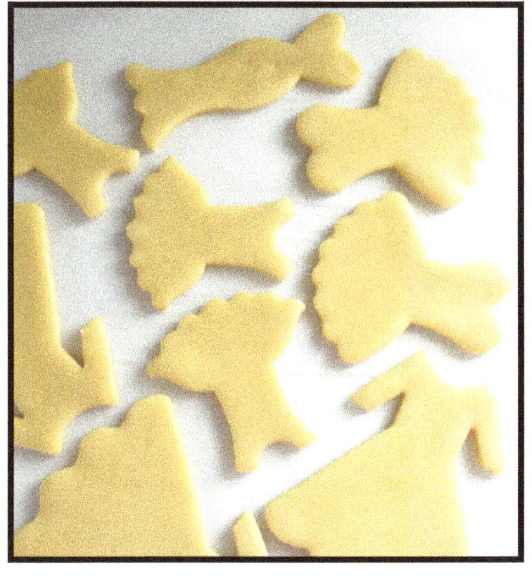

Remove the excess sugar cookie dough from around your dress cookies before using a bench scraper to transfer the cookie dough to the parchment-covered cookie sheet.

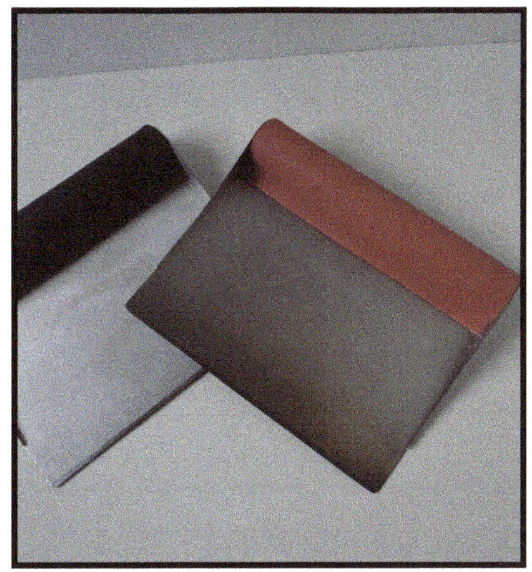

A bench scraper or a flat spatula is perfect for transferring the sugar cookie dough onto your parchment-lined cookie sheet because it does not distort the cookie dough.

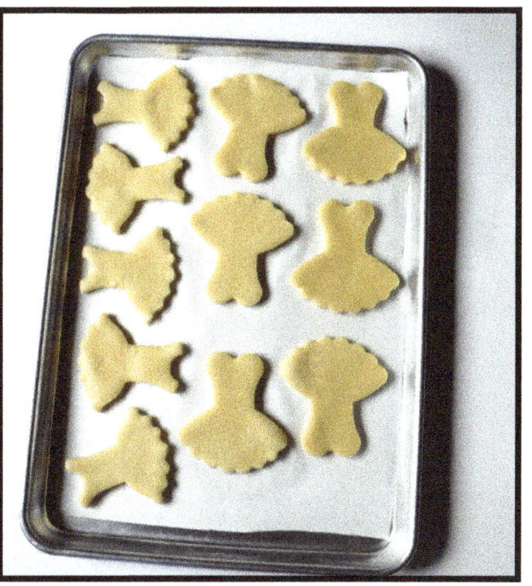

Cookies should be spaced apart on your parchment-covered cookie sheet so they don't run together as they bake. Keep the same sized sugar cookies on the same cookie sheet for even baking. Once your cookies are baked and cooled, you can stack them. At this point, your baked cookies can be frozen until you are ready to decorate them.

How to Use Fondant Right Out of the Package

The level of preparation required for using your fondant right out of the package depends on the brand of fondant you have purchased. Some brands are ready to use right out of the container after kneading, and other brands are solid and require you to prepare them for use by softening the fondant in the microwave.

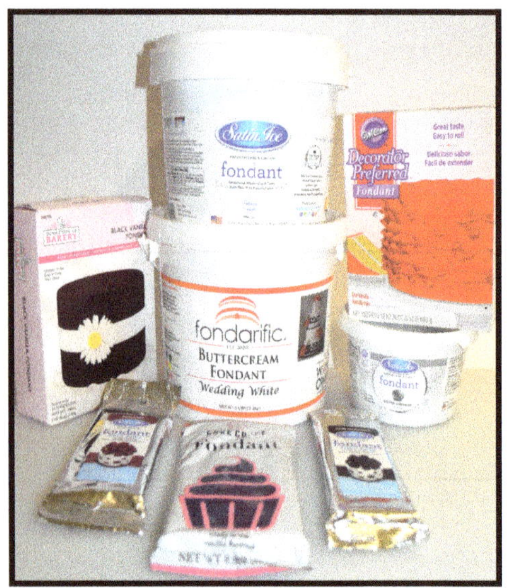

Open the package or container and look at your fondant. This is an important step. Is it firm or pliable? Pinch off a piece of fondant and test it. If it is pliable and you can roll it out, you can use it immediately.

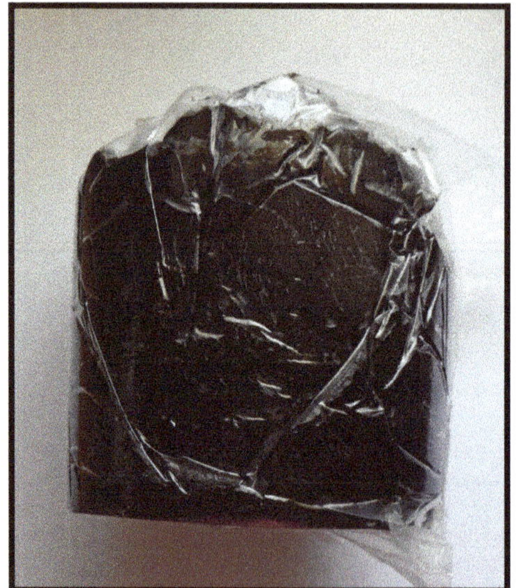

There are two ways to soften firm fondant. The first is to place the fondant into the microwave on a microwave-safe plate. Use 50% power and 10-second intervals to soften the fondant. Keep testing it by pinching the fondant. The interior will soften before the sides soften. Do not overheat.

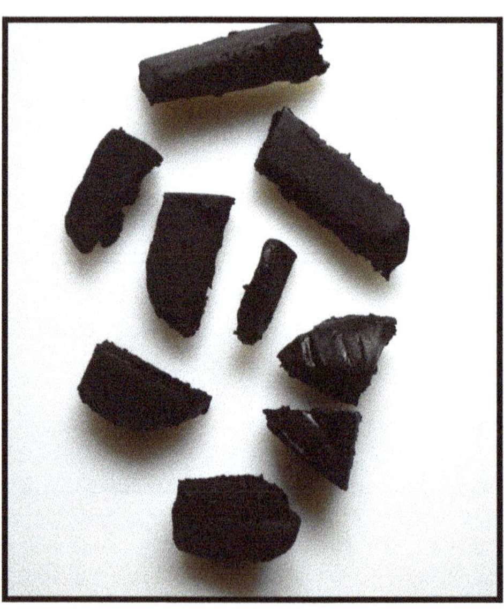

The second way to soften firm fondant is to use a bench scraper or knife to cut off small pieces of fondant.

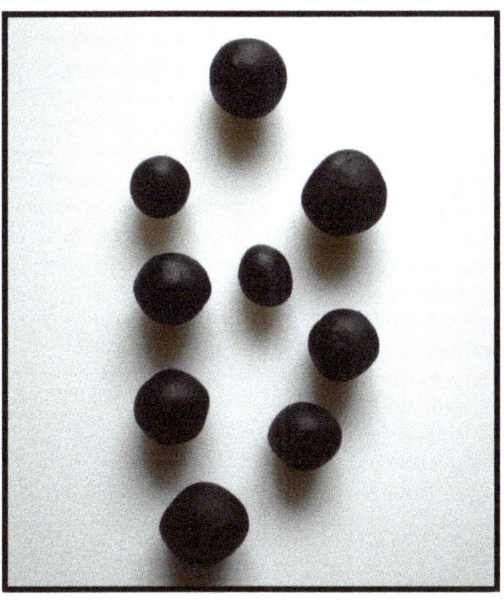

Mash each of the fondant pieces and form balls.

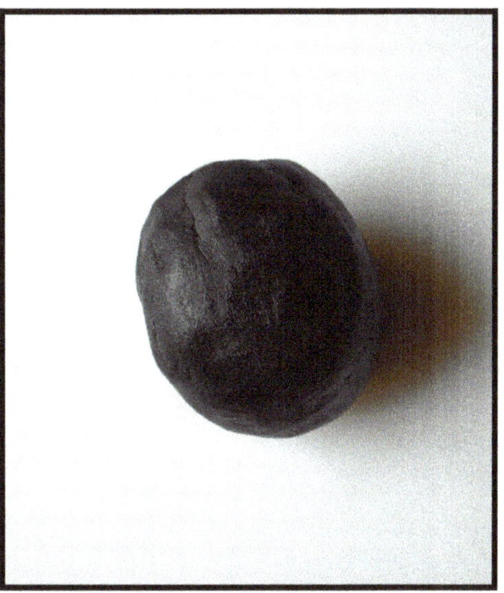

Press all of the fondant balls together and knead into a large fondant ball. Use a silicone mat or non-stick surface to roll out your fondant. Practice using a large rolling pin.

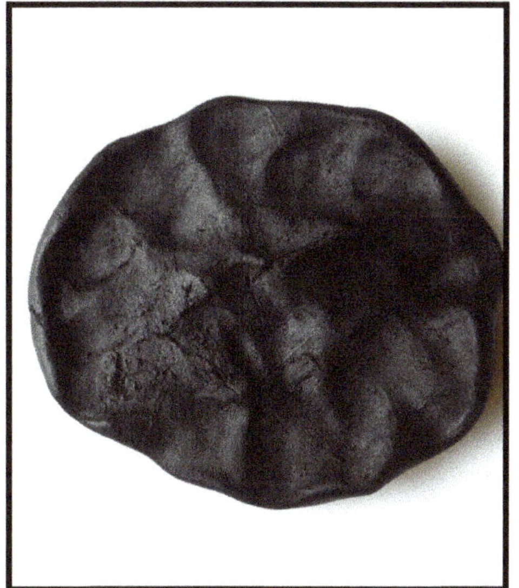

Press the fondant ball down into a fondant disc. Use your rolling pin to start rolling out this fondant. Practice using a large rolling pin. Lift your fondant up and turn after you roll it so that it does not stick to the surface. If your fondant is sticky, use a 50/50 mix of confectioner's sugar and cornstarch to knead into the fondant.

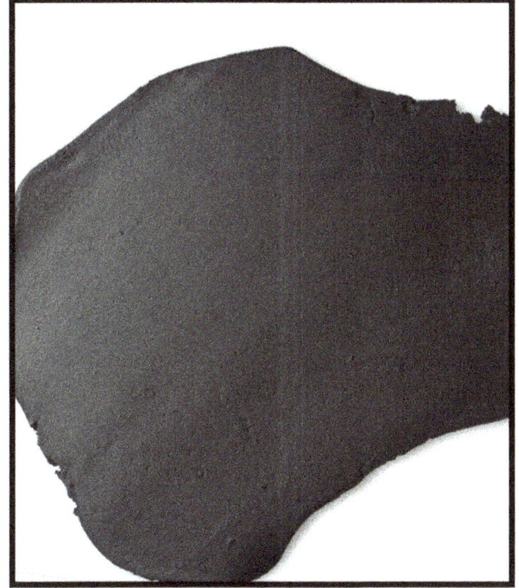

 If you end up with air bubbles, use a pin to burst them and smooth the area to release the air. Practice makes perfect. Practice to make sure that you are comfortable using your rolling pin to evenly roll out your fondant. Roll fondant to 1/8-inch thickness for fondant-covered dress cookies. Roll thinner for plunger cut-outs.

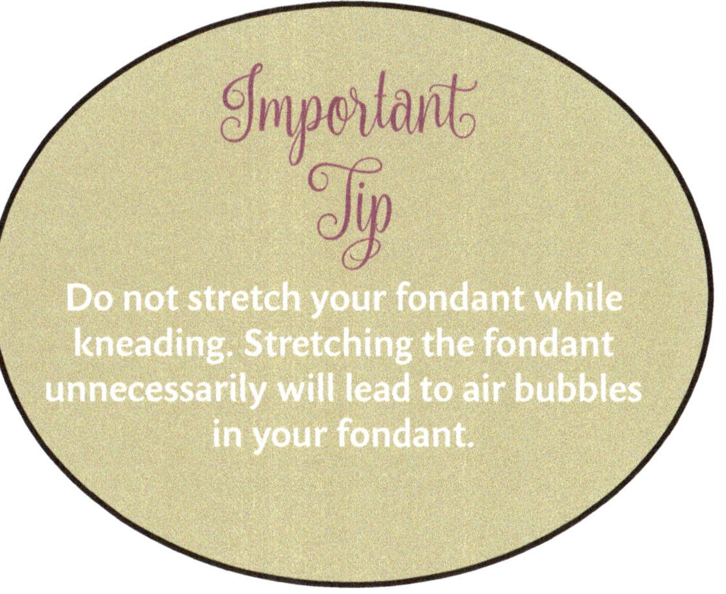

How to Cover Sugar Cookies in Fondant

Before you can start decorating your sugar cookies, I want to give you some tips I have learned over the years to make this process easier for fondant beginners.

Instructions for Fondant-Covered Dress Sugar Cookies with Designs On the Cookie

(meaning the design is added after the fondant is cut out and placed on the dress sugar cookie.)

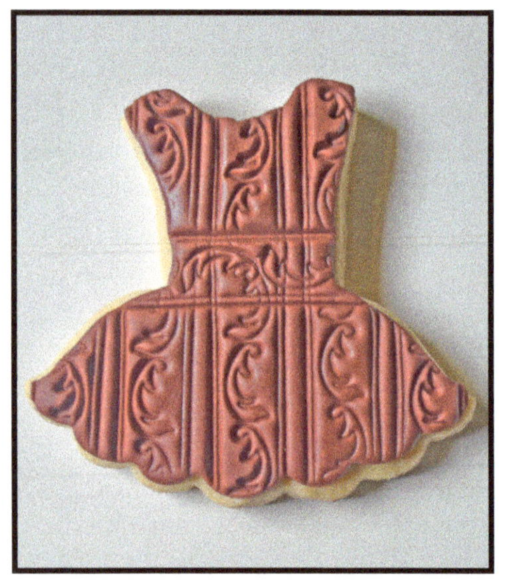
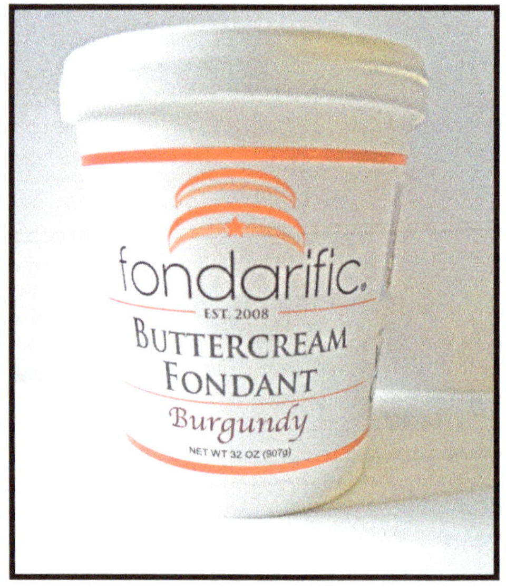

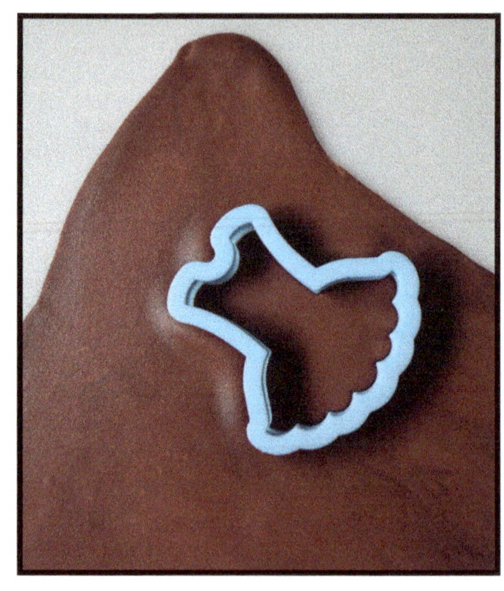

1. Decide what dress cookie design you want to create. Read the instructions completely. This fondant-covered dress cookie design requires you to decorate the fondant cut-out "on the sugar cookie."

2. Open your fondant prepare for use by using one of the techniques featured on pages 12 and 13.

3. Roll your fondant out to 1/8-inch thickness. Use the same dress cookie cutter you used to cut out the cookie dough. Make sure it is clean and dry.

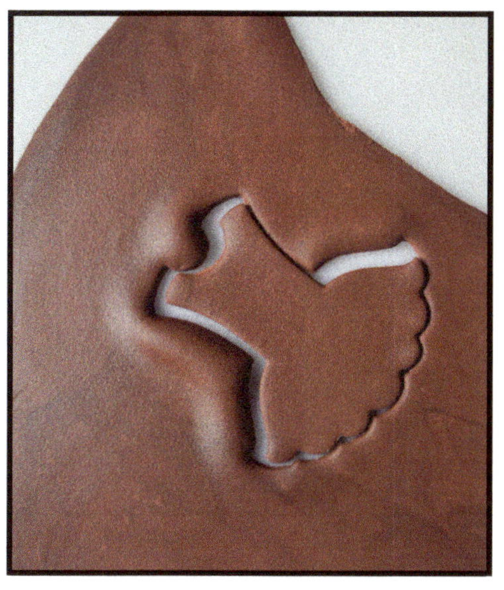

4. Press cookie cutter down firmly, wiggle to release fondant, and lift to release cookie cutter.

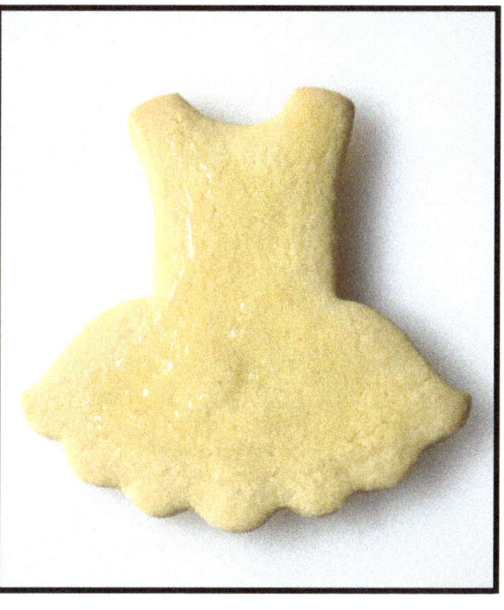

5. Use a food safe paint brush to lightly paint the center part of your dress cookie with piping gel.

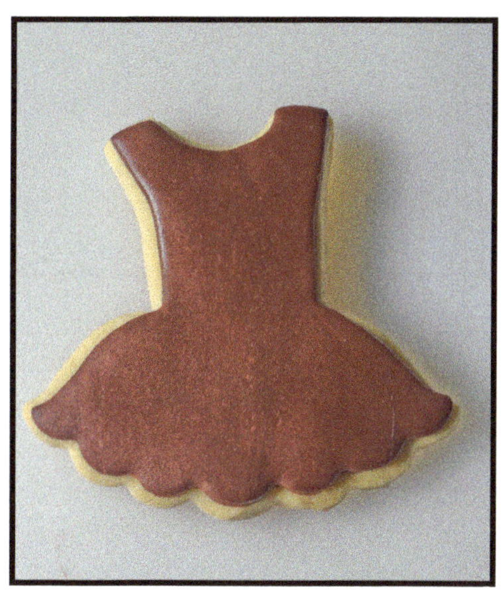

6. Place fondant cut-out on top of the dress cookie. Gently smooth the top of the fondant cut-out to secure it to the sugar cookie.

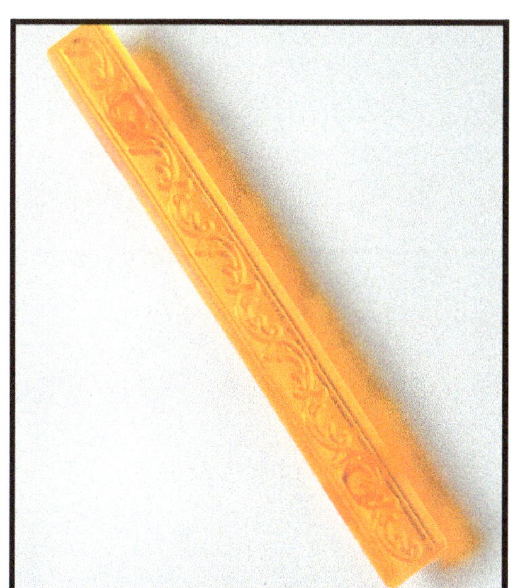

7. This is a lace embosser.

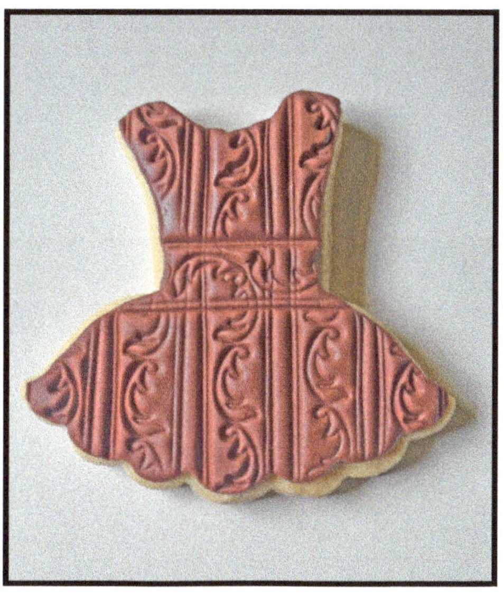

8. This fondant-covered dress sugar cookie is simple. It uses an embosser to imprint the fondant.

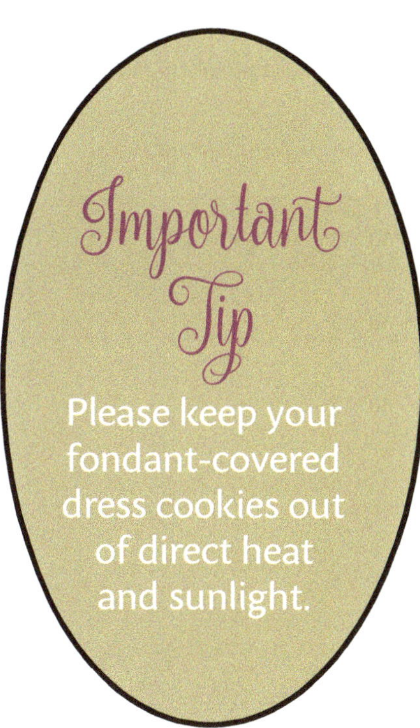

(meaning the design is added before the fondant dress is cut out and placed on the dress sugar cookie.)

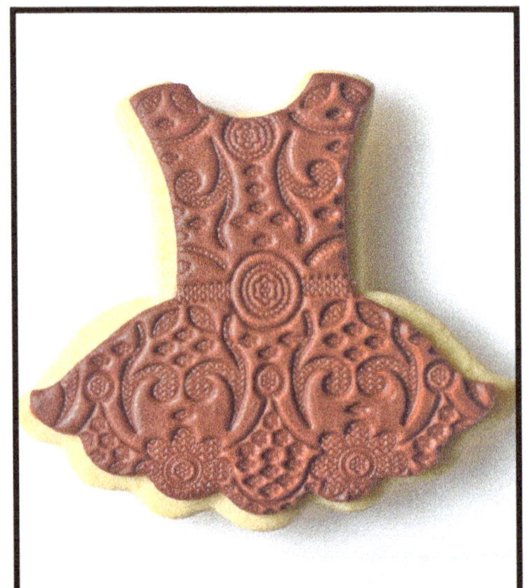

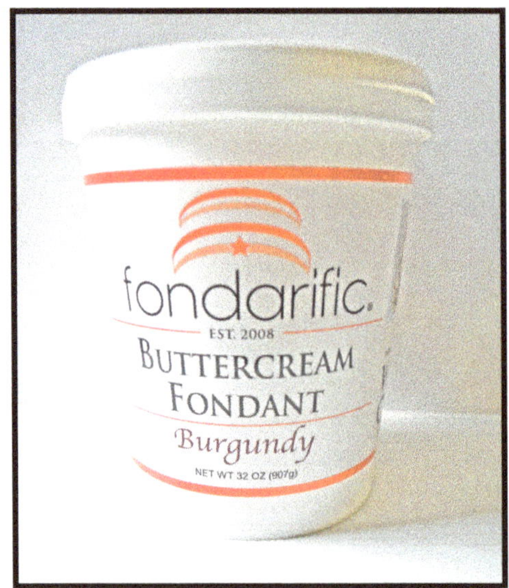

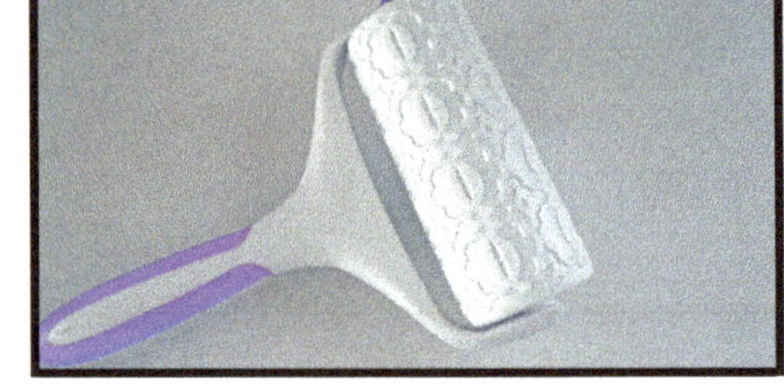

1. Decide what dress cookie design you want to create. Read the instructions completely. This fondant-covered dress cookie design requires you to start decorating the fondant cut-out "off the sugar cookie."

2. Open your fondant prepare for use by using one of the techniques featured on pages 12 and 13

3. These are two types of impression mats for fondant. There are several other impression tools used in this book to imprint fondant before cutting out your dress cookie.

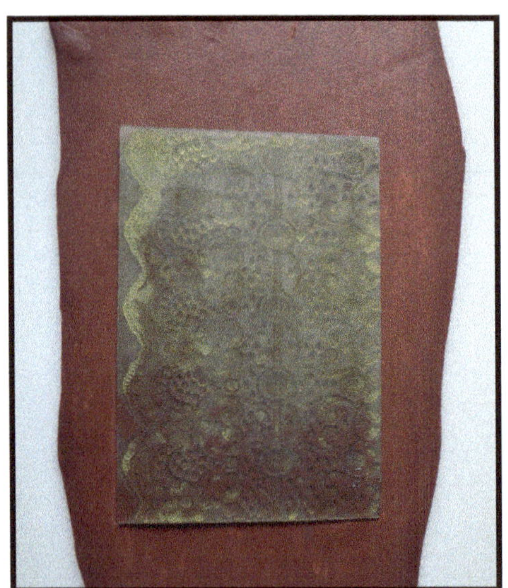

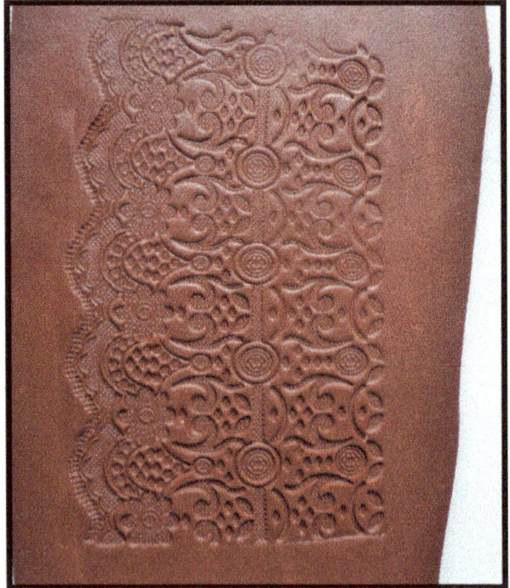

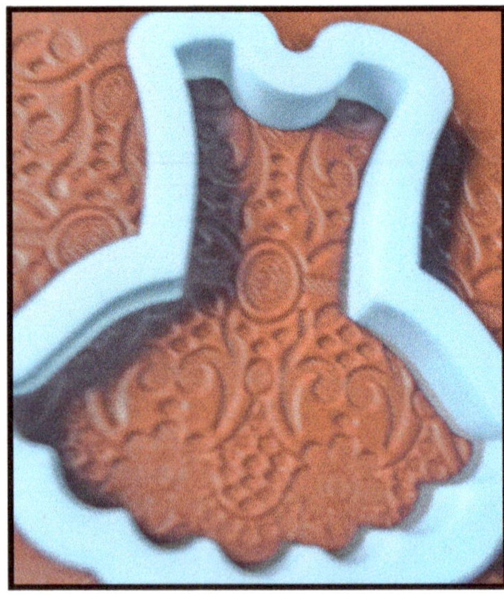

4. Roll your fondant out to 1/8-inch thickness. Use an impression mat, pattern roller, or other decorating tools to imprint the fondant.

5. This is what your fondant impression looks like. Use a bench scraper to lift fondant up and then place back on your surface.

6. Center your dress cookie cutter over the design. Press firmly into the fondant and wiggle the dress cookie cutter. Remove cookie cutter.

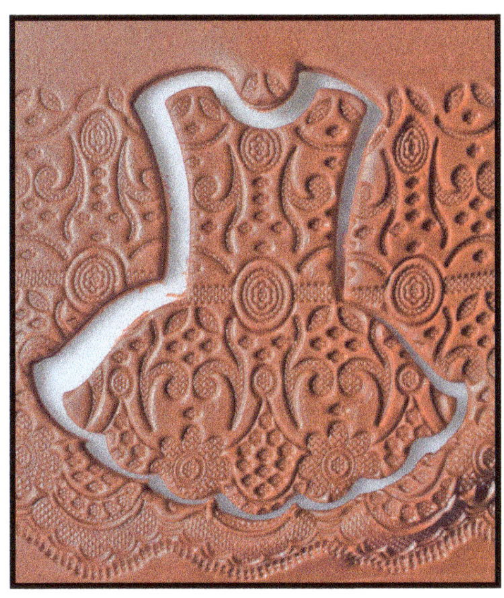 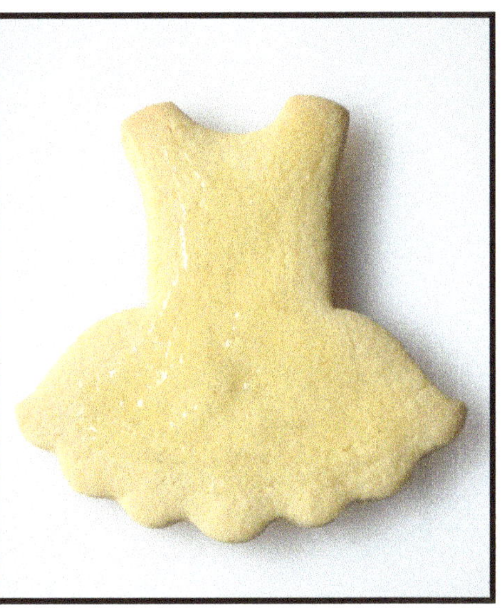 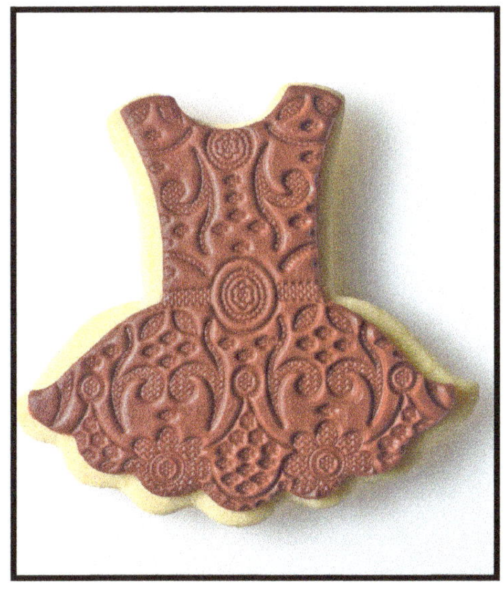

7. This fondant cut-out is the complete dress design. (*If you want, you can embellish the dress with plunger cutter flowers in other colors.*)

8. Use a food safe paint brush to lightly paint the center part of your dress cookie with piping gel.

9. Place fondant cut-out on top of the dress cookie. Gently smooth the top of the fondant cut-out to secure it to the sugar cookie. This is a very simple dress cookie design that looks elegant.

Important Tip

Please be careful when placing an embossed fondant cut-out on your piping gel-covered sugar cookie. You want to start from either the bottom or the top and gently press down to make sure it is secured to the sugar cookie. Practice this technique so that you can tell the difference in pressure required for your pattern to be clearly identified and evenly displayed across the entire cookie. If the imprint is uneven, remove the fondant cut-out from the cookie, knead it with a little more fondant, roll out again and start over. This is why it is important not to use a lot of piping gel.

Fondant Decorating Tools & Techniques

Here are some of the tools and techniques that I used in this book to create the fondant-covered dress cookies featured in this book.

Paint Brushes

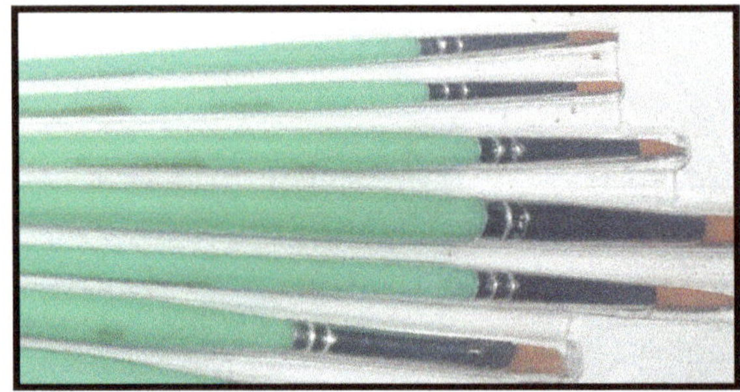

Food safe paint brushes are used to "paint" piping gel onto your dress sugar cookies. Large paint brushes can cover a lot of area quickly so you can apply sprinkles or nonpareils. Paint brushes are also used to apply luster dust paint (mixed with lemon extract) to fondant-covered dress sugar cookies.

Piping Gel

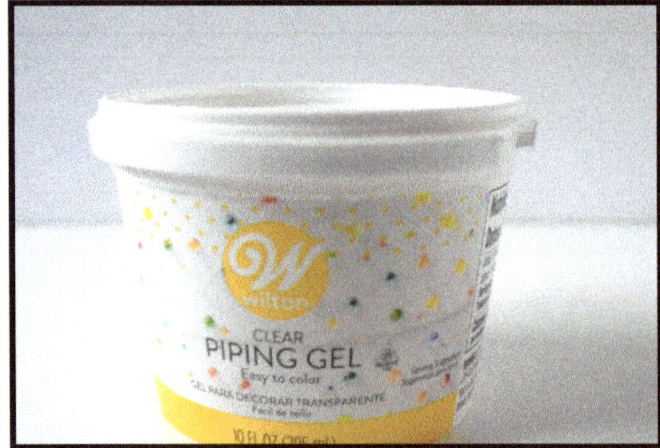

Piping gel is used to "glue" the fondant onto your sugar cookie. Putting your "glue" in the innermost part of the sugar cookie means you will have clean, professional looking edges around your dress cookie when you are finished decorating.

Edible Food Color Spray

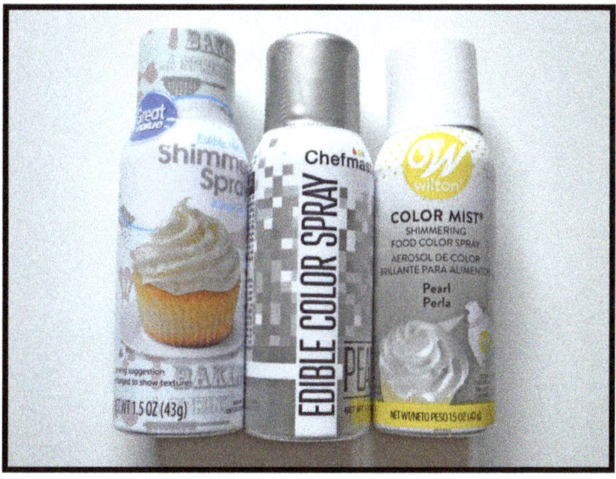

Edible spray comes in assorted colors and can be used to add a beautiful sheen to your decorated fondant-covered dress sugar cookies. Pearl spray is featured in this book. All of the brands pictured above will give you the same results. In order to avoid over spray on your dress sugar cookie, you should place your fondant dress cut-out onto a sheet of parchment paper, and then lightly spray your fondant dress cut-out with the edible food spray. Let the spray dry, and then apply the dress fondant cut-out to the piping gel-covered dress sugar cookie. Lightly press down over the fondant dress cookie surface to secure it to your dress sugar cookie. See the picture on the right below. The cookie edges are clean and free from the edible pearl spray.

This picture shows a white dress cookie without edible pearl food color spray, and then one with the edible pearl food color spray. The sheen makes the dress cookie look more dramatic. The edible pearl food spray dries quickly and does not rub off when placed in a cellophane bag.

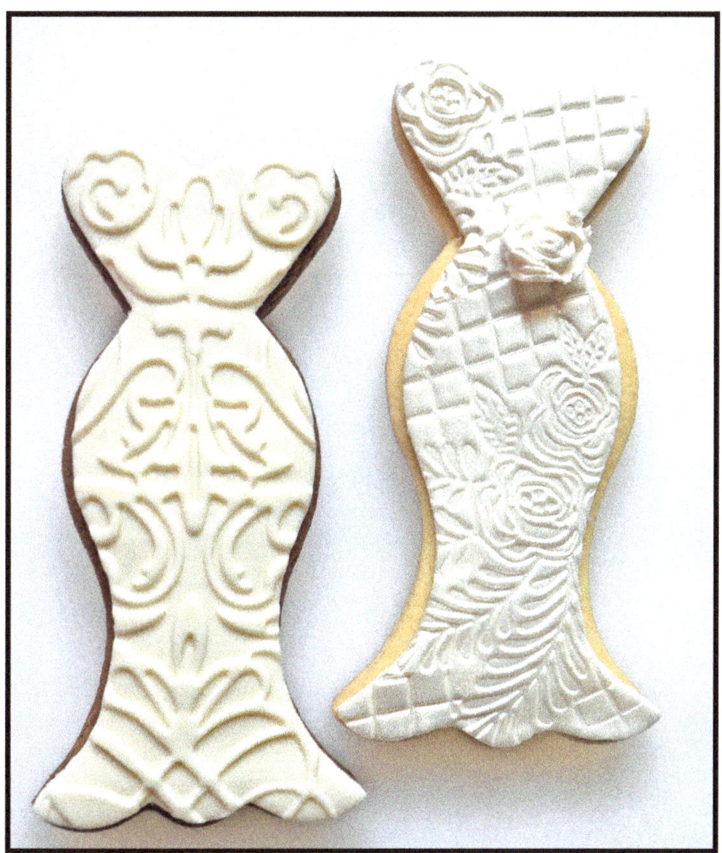

Plunger Cutters

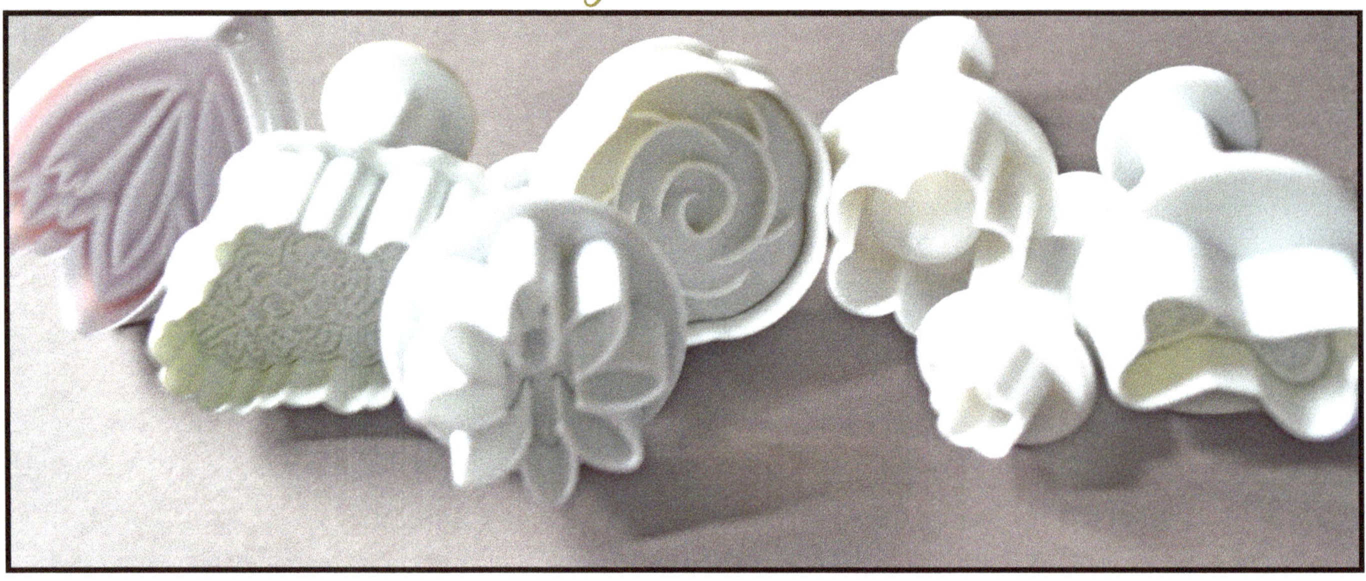

Plunger cutters come in a large variety of styles and make quick work out of creating dramatic effects on your fondant-covered dress cookies. Plunger cutters are huge time savers. Blossom, daisy, tulip, roses, bows, and lace plunger cutters are featured in this book. Other plunger cutter designs can be found in your local cake or craft stores or online retailers. The most important thing to remember with plunger cutters is that you have to roll the fondant thinner for flowers, practice pressure control in cutting out your fondant, and then again when using the plunger to press down and release the plunger cutter design. Play around with various plunger cutters. Also, try stacking various-sized plunger cutter flower designs together.

You can also make an imprint of the plunger cutter without actually cutting the fondant. Just hold the plunger button down all the way, and then press the plunger into the fondant to imprint the pattern design without cutting the fondant.

Icing Tips

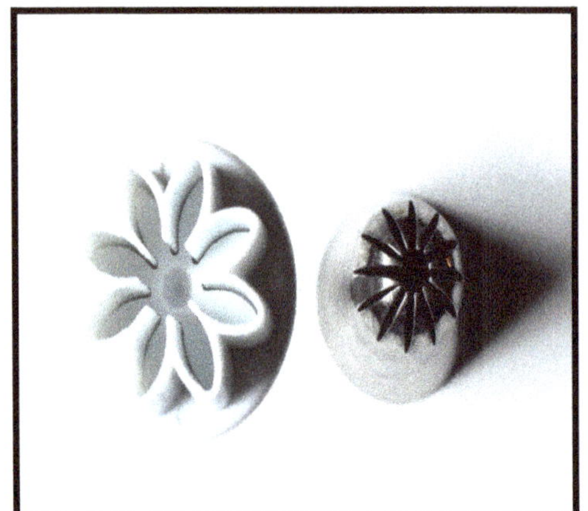
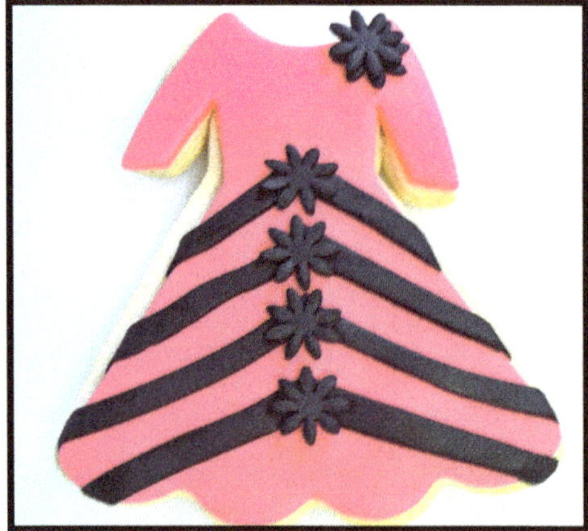
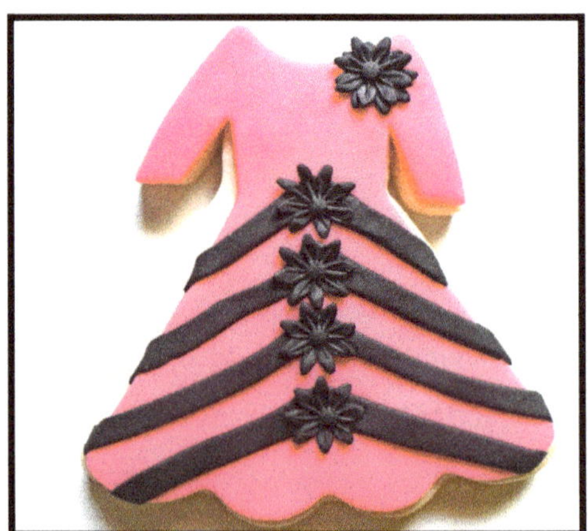

Regular icing tips can be used to imprint fondant to give it a unique design. Use tip 1C, 1D or 1E to imprint the center of a daisy flower (see picture) for a quick and easy design.

Impression Mats

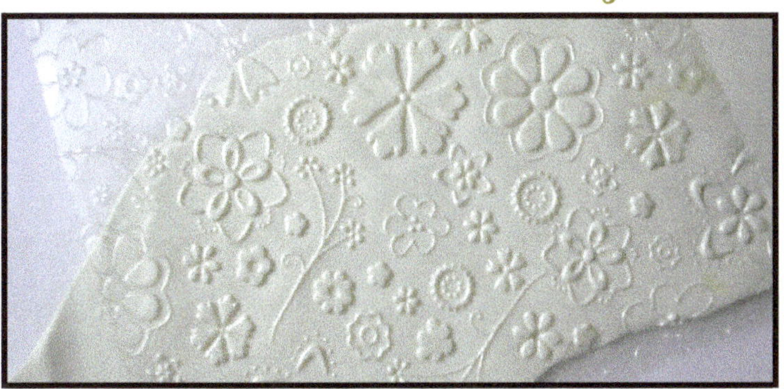 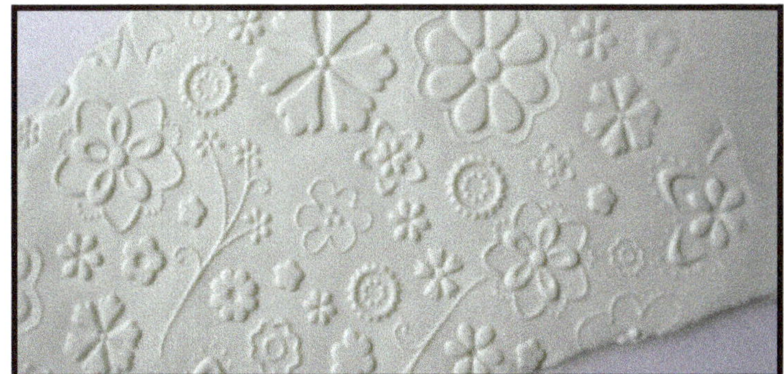

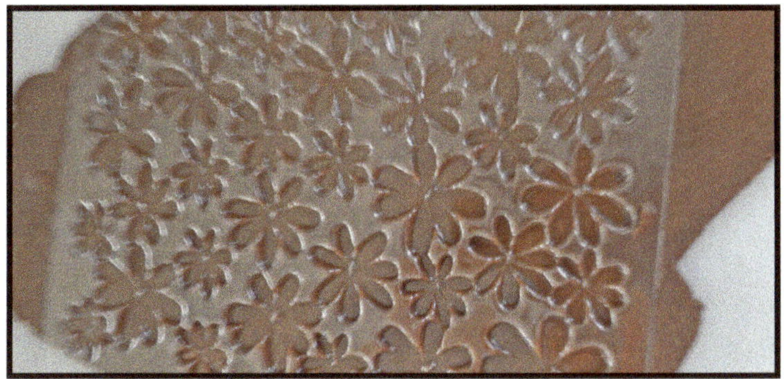 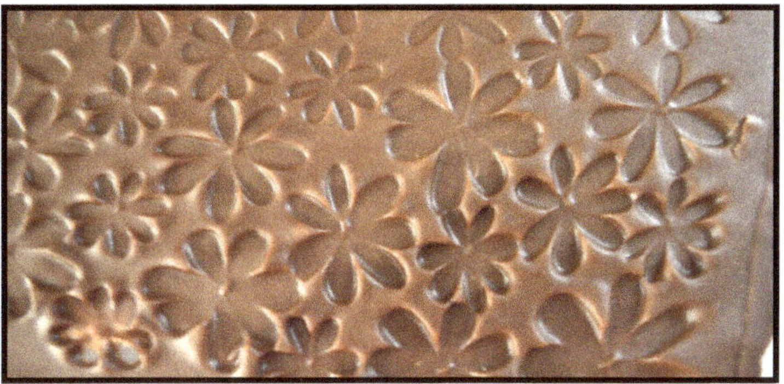

Impression mats come in many styles and sizes. Even pressure is best. Use a large rolling pin to make sure you have a good imprint. Impression mats have a raised impression on one side which imprints the fondant upward (raised design) and an indented impression on the other side which imprints the fondant downward (recessed design). This dual use gives you more design options.

Luster Dusts

Super Pearl and Pink Fairy Dust are my favorite dusts to use because they give decorated cookies a metallic sheen which makes them look expensive. Please check the label to make sure that your luster dust says "FDA approved." Otherwise, it should be used for decoration purposes only and not be eaten. You can use the luster dust right out of the container or create your own paint by mixing the luster dust with a little lemon extract to "paint" a metallic finish onto your cookie. The consistency should be like pudding. As you use it, the mixture will evaporate quickly so you have to keep adding a little lemon extract as the mixture thickens. Stir thoroughly. Once all of the liquid evaporates, the luster dust will return to its powder form. Use a small container with a top so that you can label it and reuse this luster dust for another project. Please note that luster dust will rub off when placed in cellophane bags. PME has a Clear Edible Glaze Spray that you can use to seal the luster dust to prevent it from rubbing off on your cellophane bag.

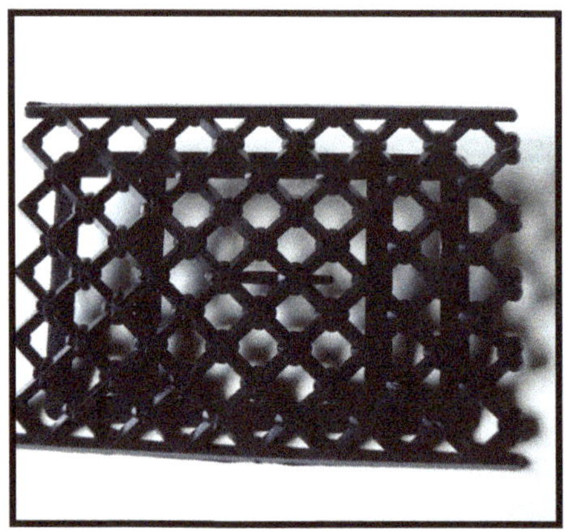 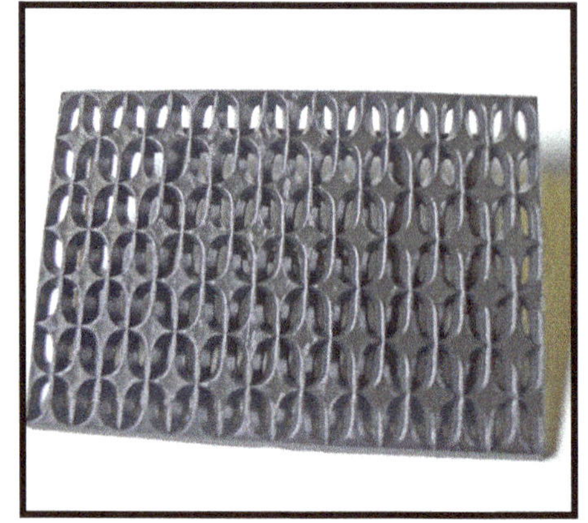

Your decorating time can be substantially cut down by using embossed cutters. Patchwork cutters can be pressed into fondant many different ways to give you quick custom designs on your fondant-covered dress sugar cookies. They come in a variety of designs and sizes and can be found at your local cake decorating stores or online retailers.

Pattern Rollers & Stencils

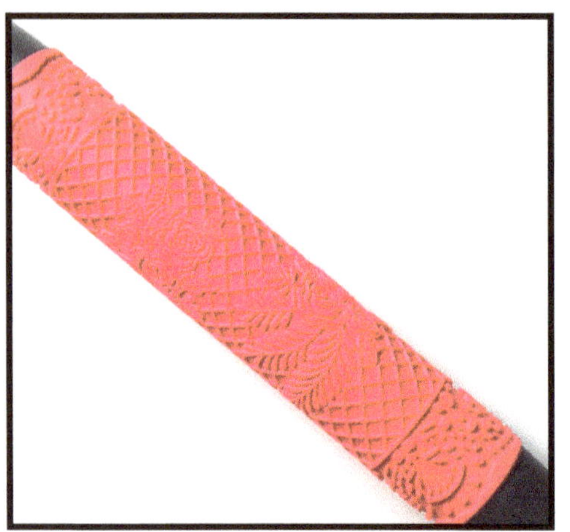 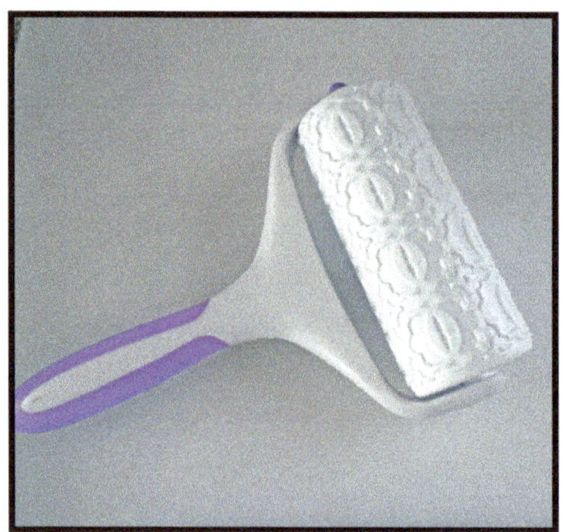 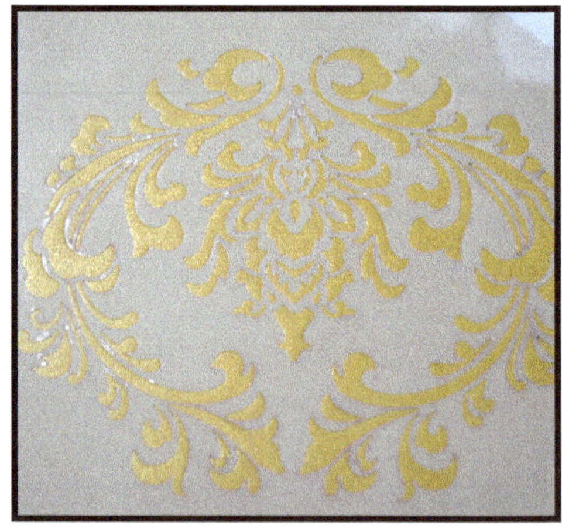

Pattern rollers and stencils come in a variety of styles and sizes, and provide you with a full base pattern for your fondant-covered dress cookies. Pattern rollers give you several different design options in one roller. This will shorten your decorating time. You can cut out shapes in one pattern or combine them with other patterns for a unique design. Practice using your pattern mats and stencils in various ways.

Stencils are also good time savers when you are decorating and give your sugar cookies a very professional, high end looking appearance. To use a stencil on fondant, roll out your fondant and place the stencil on top. Now use your rolling pin to roll over the stencil to completely secure it to the fondant. You can use edible paint or luster dust paint (made with lemon extract) on the stencil. I used several coats of edible paint, and allowed each layer to dry before adding the next layer of paint. Four layers of edible paint were used on the gold dress design featured with this stencil.

Sanding Sugar or Sprinkles on Your Dress Cookies

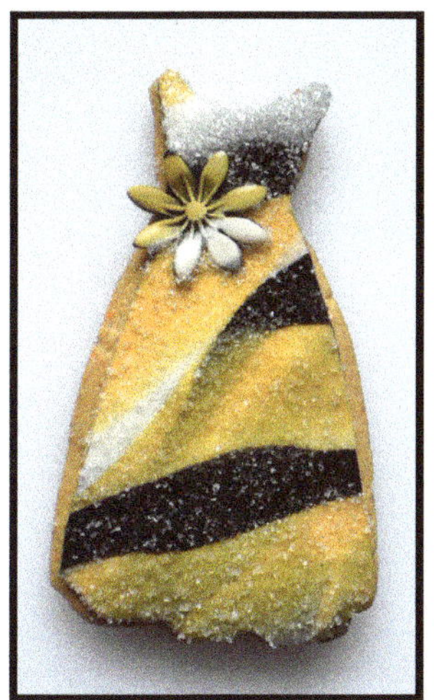 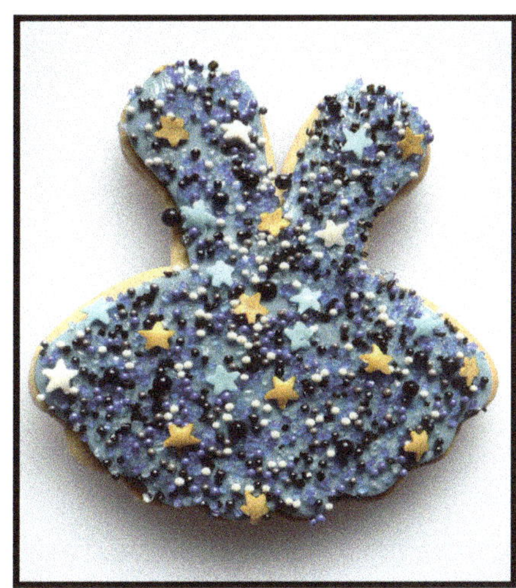 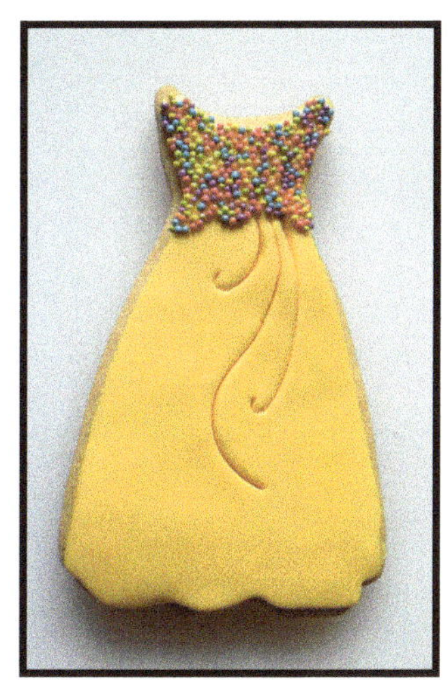

Sanding sugar and sprinkles look fabulous on decorated dress sugar cookies. They can be applied to the top of the fondant in different areas or by completely covering your fondant dress cookie. Piping gel works well as glue for sanding sugar and sprinkles. Spread a thin layer of piping gel in the area you want the sprinkles to go on top of your fondant-covered dress cookie or you can completely cover the entire fondant dress area. Now you can pour the sanding sugar or sprinkles over the piping gel area, and then remove the excess sprinkles. Use a dry paint brush to remove the excess sanding sugar or sprinkles from your dress cookie.

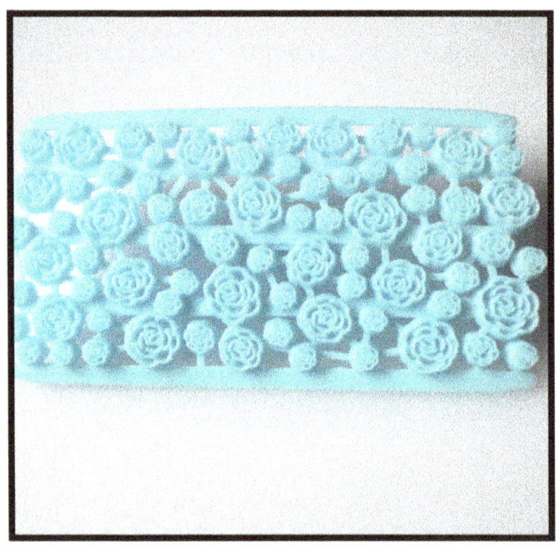
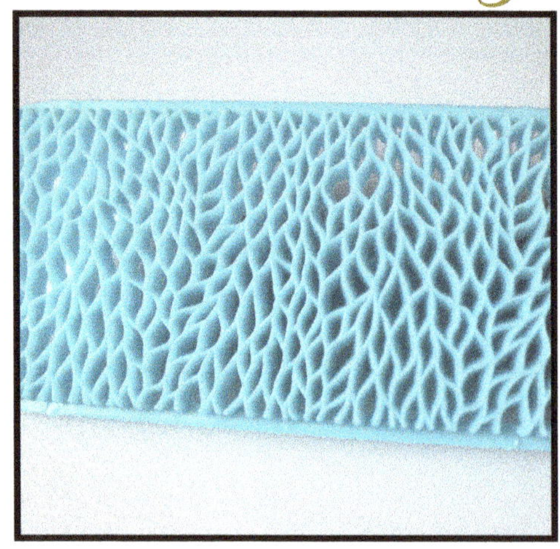
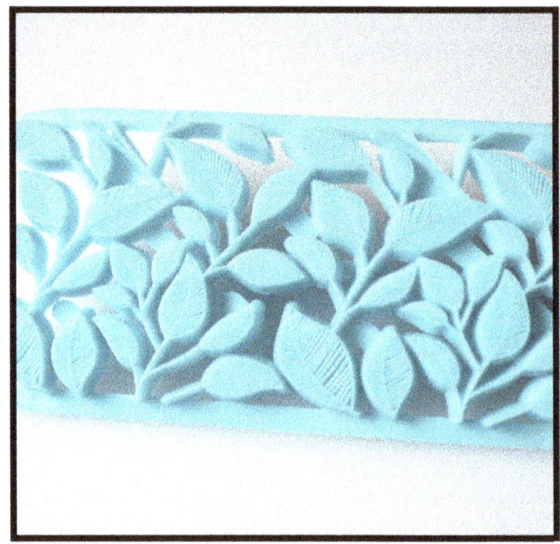

Fondant embossers are inexpensive and great for fondant dress cookie decorators. They come in different sets and can be used to quickly imprint the fondant which cuts down on decorating time. These designs can be combined together as shown in the fondant dress cookie designs in this book.

Keep experimenting with these embosser tools to create your own unique design.

Cake Stamps

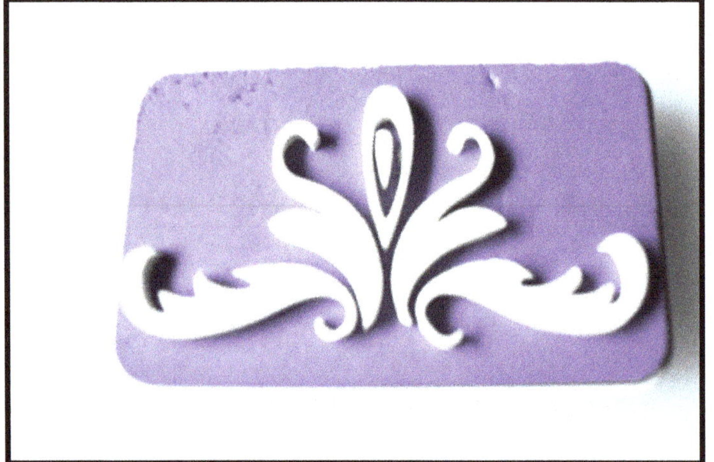
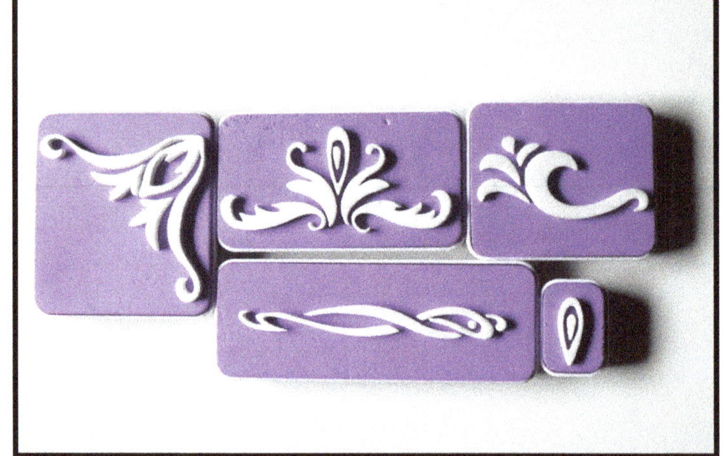

Wilton has a set of cake stamps that are perfect for embossing your fondant dress-covered sugar cookies. The one pictured above on the left side is my favorite one. Wilton has discontinued them on their website, but you can still find them online by doing a Google search or at your local cake decorating stores. These cake stamps are made of food safe sponge and can be used in different directions on your fondant. Practice even pressure for success.

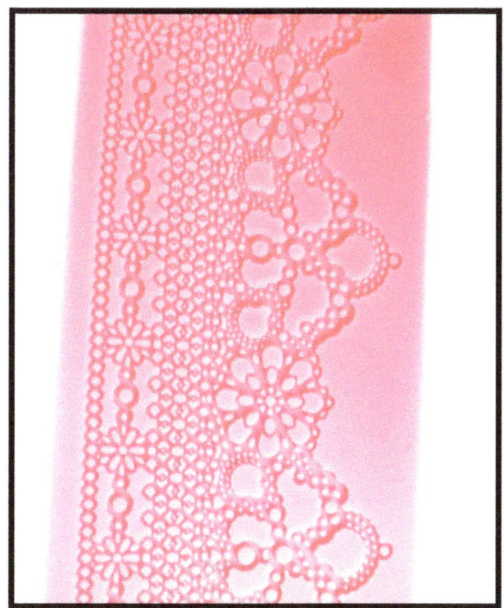
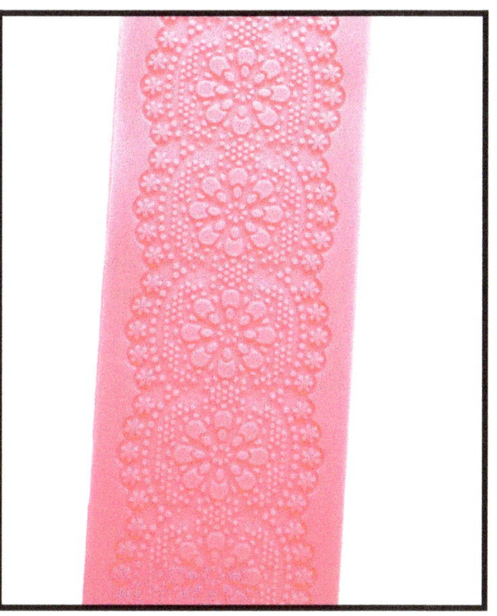
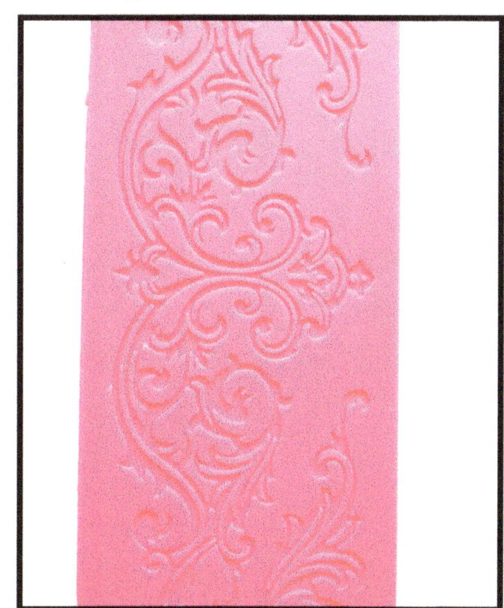

I love these inexpensive silicone lace fondant molds that I found at Hobby Lobby. They are meant to be used to create delicate lace to go on your cakes, cupcakes and cookies, but they can also be used in fondant dress cookie decorating. The only difference is that you roll out the fondant first, then place the fondant face down onto the silicone lace fondant mold, dust the top of the fondant with a 50/50 mix of confectioner's sugar and cornstarch, and then use your rolling pin to roll over the fondant to imprint the design using even pressure as you roll over the fondant. You can then lift the fondant and turn it over to reveal the fondant lace detail.

It is important to note the size of your dress cookie cutter whenever using silicone lace fondant molds. You need to leave space above and below the silicone lace fondant to cut out your fondant dress with the dress cookie cutter. If there are lines from the silicone lace fondant mold impression on your fondant cut-out, you can gently smooth them out with your finger to remove them.

Silicone Molds for Fondant Decorations

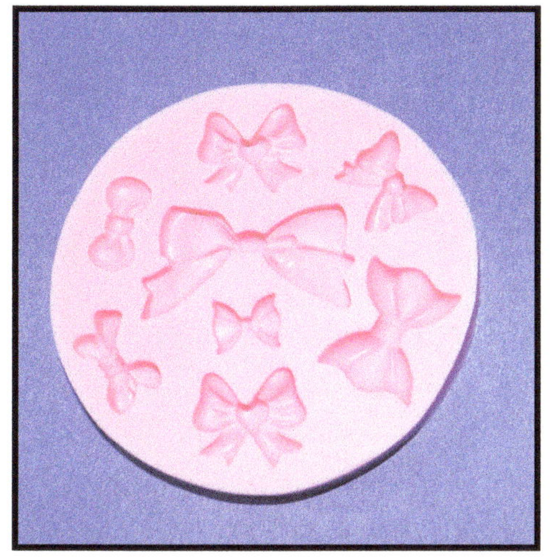
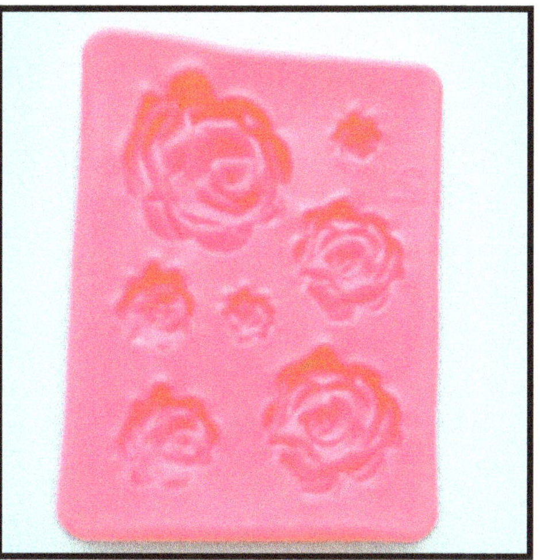
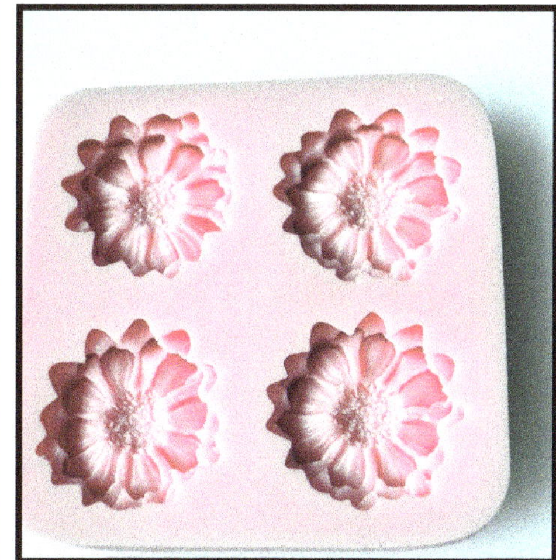

There are a lot of silicone molds on the market that are perfect for fondant decorations. You just press in the fondant, refrigerate until firm, and then unmold and add it to your fondant dress cookie.

Here are my tips for getting clean fondant decorations out of your silicone molds.

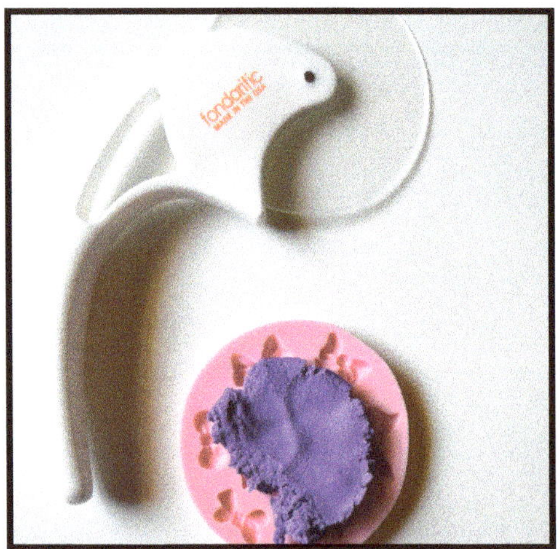 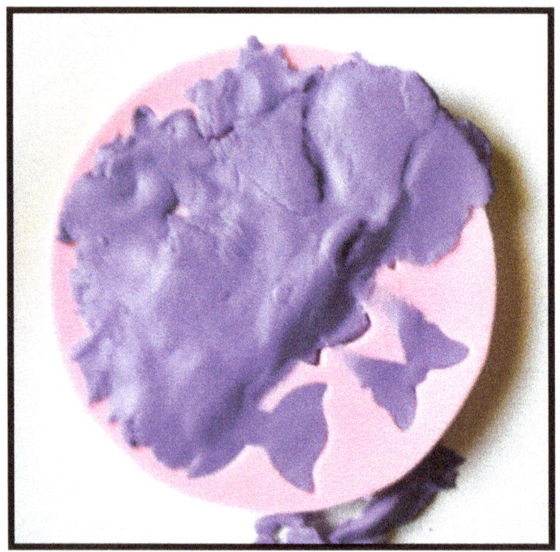 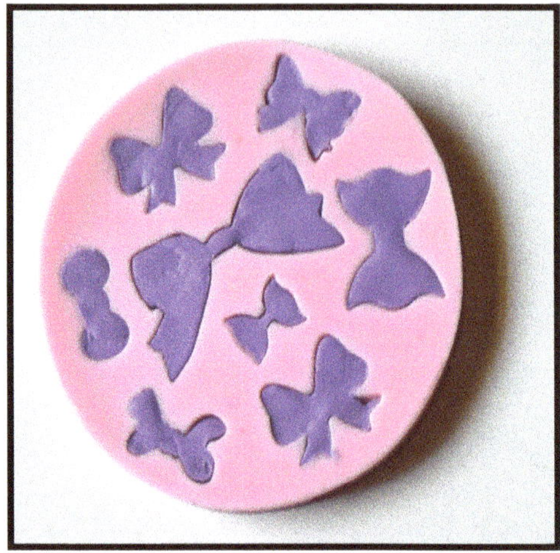

Place your fondant on top of the silicone mold. Push the fondant into the cavities using the side of a large pizza cutter. Use the pizza cutter to keep pushing the fondant into each cavity, then use the pizza cutter (at an angle) to start cutting away the excess fondant. If the fondant comes out of the cavity, use the pizza cutter to push the fondant back into the cavity. Turn the silicone mold so that you can push the fondant in and cut, turn the silicone mold, and push the fondant in the silicone mold and cut. Keep doing this until your silicone mold looks like the last one.

Flavoring Fondant

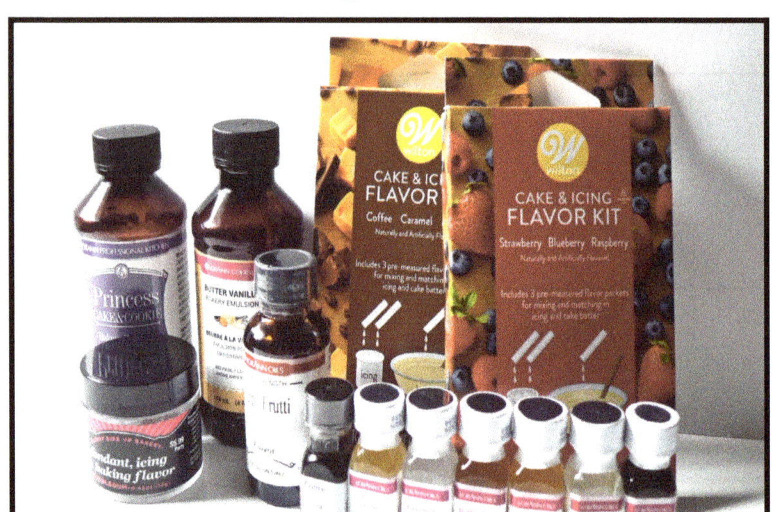

I suggest that you taste the fondant you purchase. If you do not like the flavor or you want the fondant flavor to compliment the sugar cookie flavor, you can use candy flavors by LorAnn or any of the bakery emulsions. All of them are concentrated so a little goes a long way. Start with a half teaspoon per pound of fondant. Let fondant rest, and then taste fondant again. If your fondant becomes sticky during this process, use a 50/50 mix of confectioner's sugar and cornstarch to knead into the fondant. Wilton also has a line of flavoring which can be used in cakes, cupcakes, sugar cookies, and fondant.

Fondant Troubleshooting

Problems can arise when you are working with fondant. Here are some tips to help you fix them.

My fondant is sticky. What can I do?	Use a 50/50 mixture of confectioner's sugar and cornstarch together. Knead a little at a time into the fondant until the fondant is no longer sticky.
I opened the package, and the fondant is hard. What can I do?	Look to see if there are instructions on the package. If not, follow the instructions on pages 12 and 13 for preparing your fondant for use right out of the package.
I do not like the taste of the fondant I purchased. What can I do?	Look at the Flavoring Fondant section on page 26.
I rolled out my fondant, and it is uneven in places. What do I do?	You will have to re-roll your rolling pin over your fondant. Practice rolling out your fondant with a large rolling pin with even pressure.
My fondant has a white shortening type substance on it. What can I do?	Knead your fondant so that the shortening type substance is kneaded back into your fondant. This is one of the ingredients that comes to the surface when your fondant is shipped during the summer.
Fondant has gotten wet. What can I do?	Use a food safe brush and brush a mixture of 50/50 powdered sugar and cornstarch over the wet fondant so that it can dry without a shine. Remove excess powder with a food safe brush.
It's humid in my house, and I cannot get my fondant to set. What can I do?	If you have a dehumidifier, you can use it to remove some of the humidity in your house and allow your fondant to set. If not, try using a fan.
I can see fingerprints in my fondant design. What can I do?	Gently rub your finger over the fingerprint to remove it.

Dress Cookie Cutter Chart

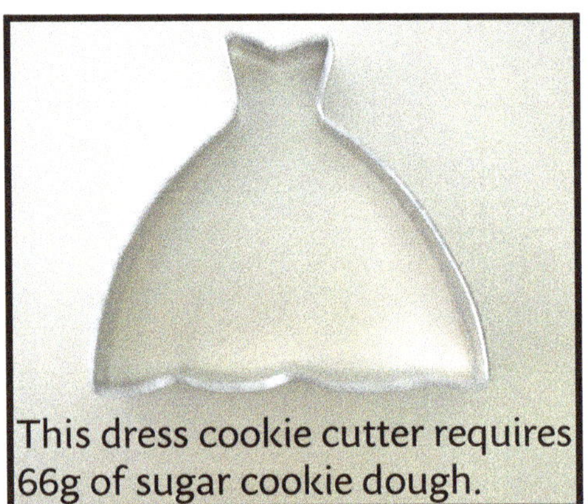

This dress cookie cutter requires 66g of sugar cookie dough.

This dress cookie cutter requires 74g of sugar cookie dough.

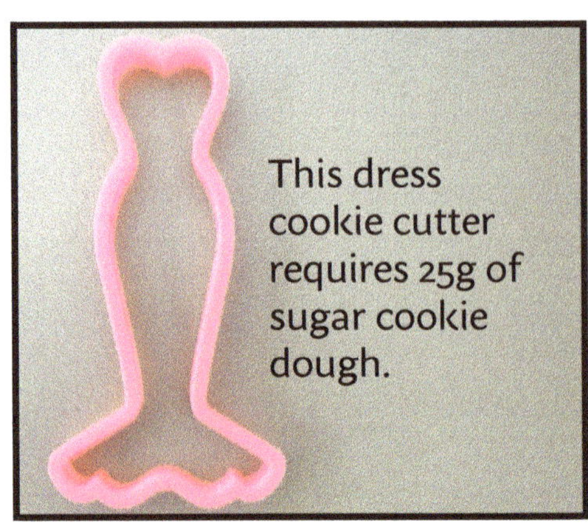

This dress cookie cutter requires 25g of sugar cookie dough.

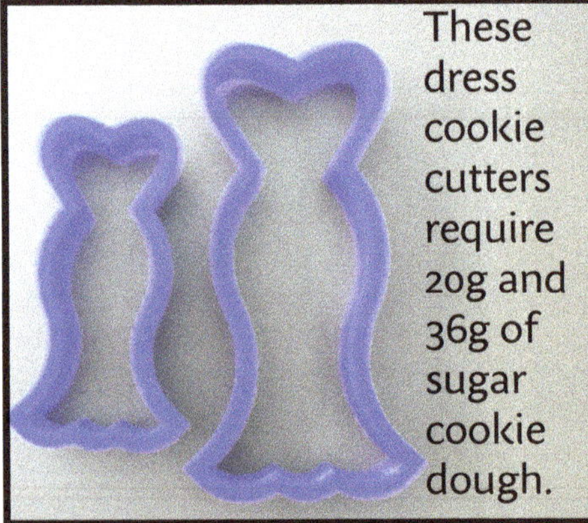

These dress cookie cutters require 20g and 36g of sugar cookie dough.

This dress cookie cutter requires 81g of sugar cookie dough.

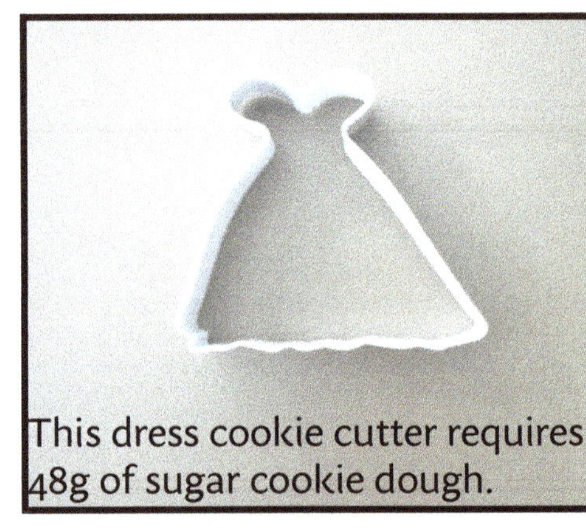

This dress cookie cutter requires 48g of sugar cookie dough.

This dress cookie cutter requires 54g of sugar cookie dough.

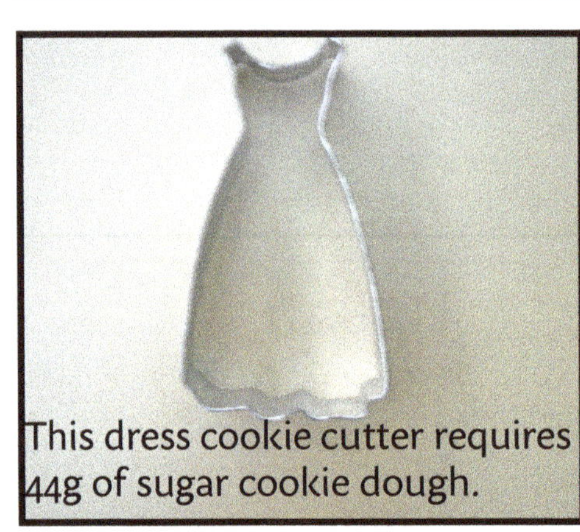

This dress cookie cutter requires 44g of sugar cookie dough.

This dress cookie cutter requires 33g of sugar cookie dough.

This dress cookie cutter requires 52g of sugar cookie dough.

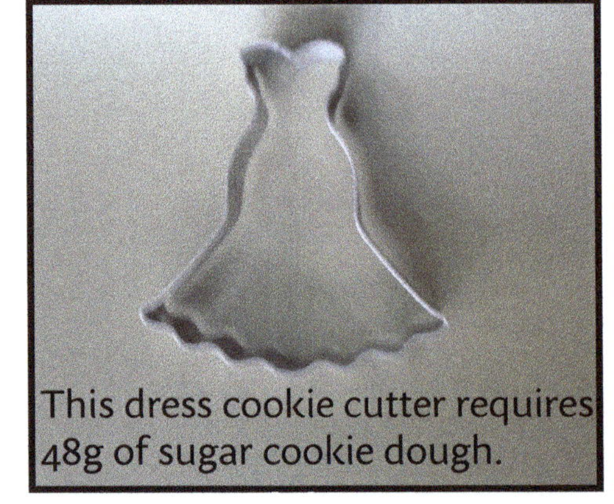

This dress cookie cutter requires 48g of sugar cookie dough.

Black Lattice Dress Cookie

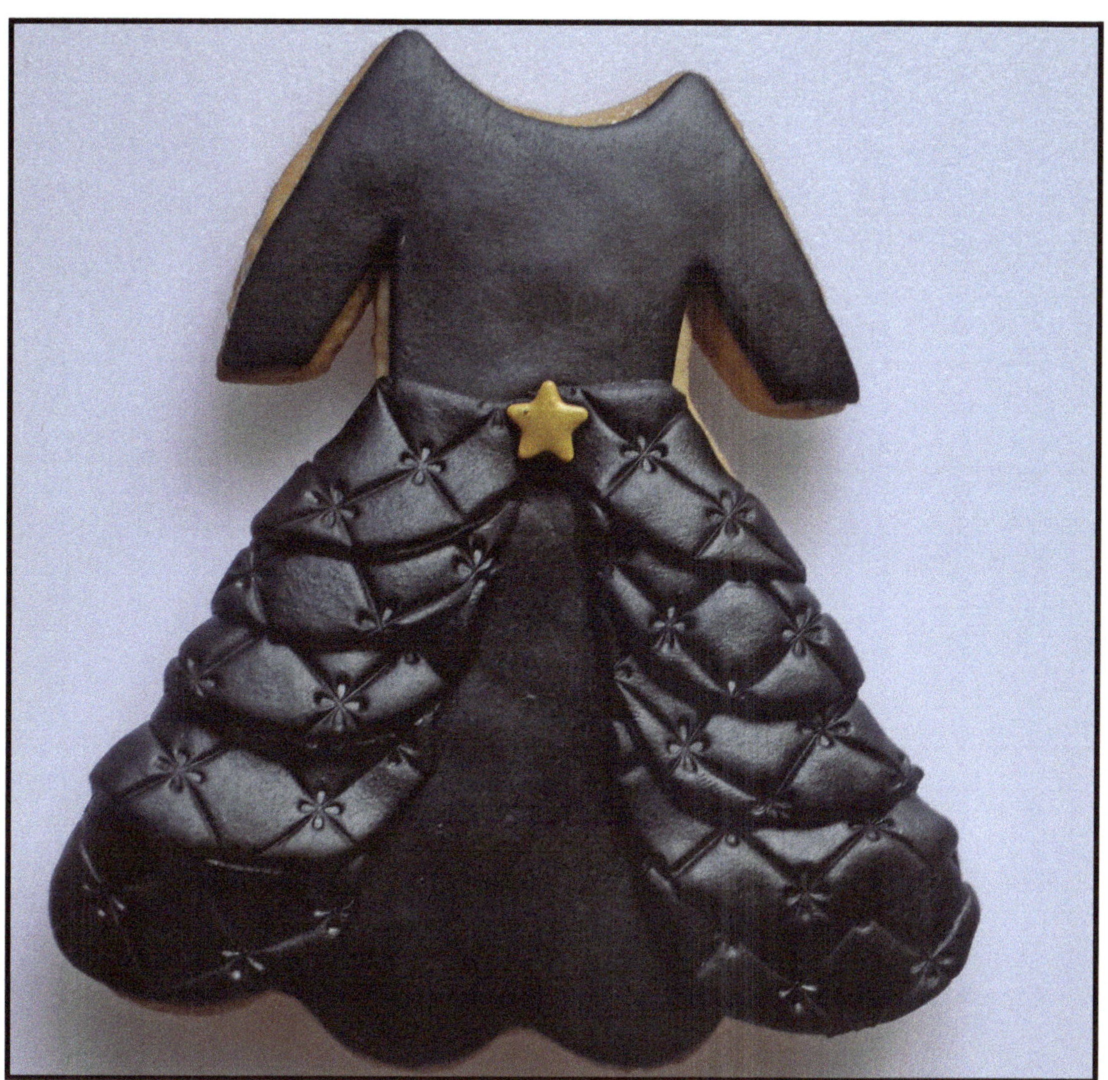

<table>
<tr>
<td valign="top">

Materials:
- **Dress cookie**
- **2.1 oz. Fondarific Black fondant**
- **2-1/2 inch circle cutter**
- **Piping gel**
- **Food safe paint brush**
- **Pizza cutter or Xacto knife**

</td>
<td valign="top">

Tools:
- **The Diane Dress Cookie Cutter (etsy.com, Sinful Cutters)**
- **Patchwork Cutters Quilting Embosser**
- **Wilton Star Sprinkles**

</td>
</tr>
</table>

Suggested cellophane bag size is 6x8 inches to package this dress cookie. Normally, this dress cookie uses a 5x7, but due to the fondant on top of this design, it requires a larger sized cellophane bag.

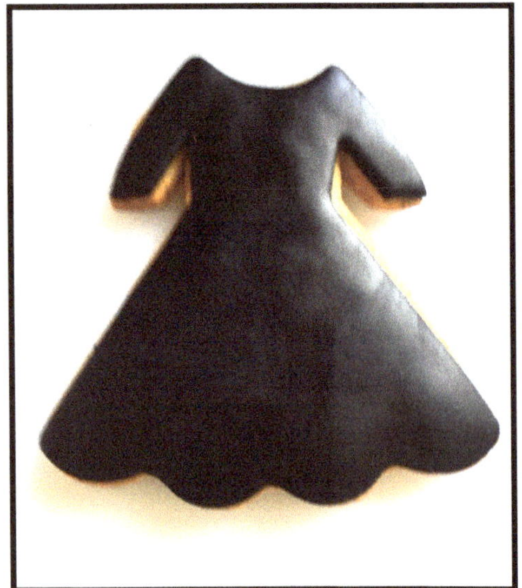

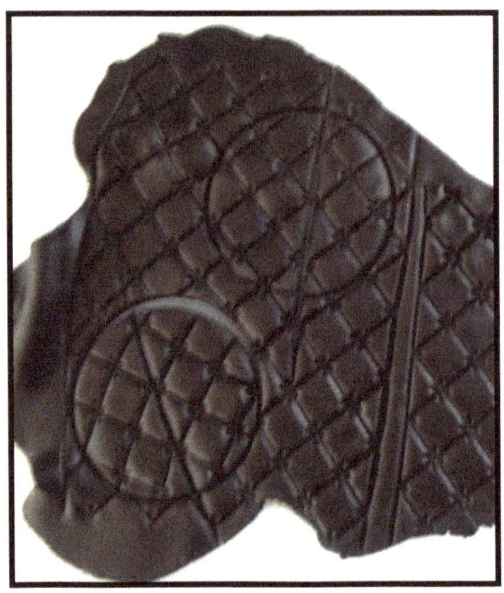

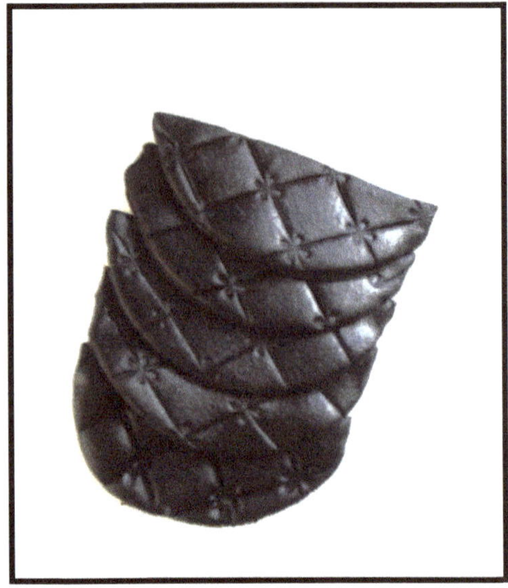

1. Roll out black fondant. Use the dress cookie cutter to cut out the black fondant dress. Use a paint brush to apply a thin layer of piping gel onto your dress cookie. Apply fondant cut-out to cookie, and gently smooth top. Set aside.

2. Re-roll black fondant. Use the quilting embosser to imprint fondant. Cut out five circles making sure you have a center section as shown in the picture above. Cut them in half through the center stitch.

3. Stack the quilted half circles on top of each other as shown above. Use a pizza cutter or Xacto knife to move the fondant up to make it even on the right side as shown above in the picture.

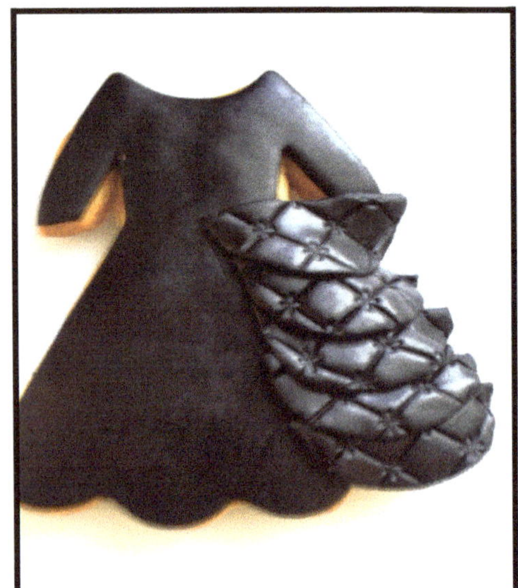

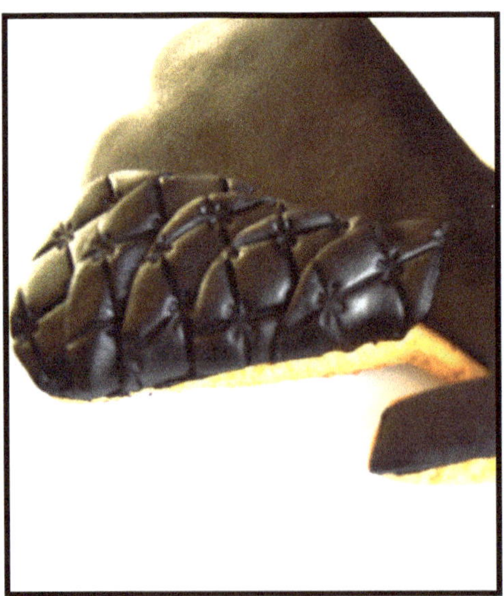

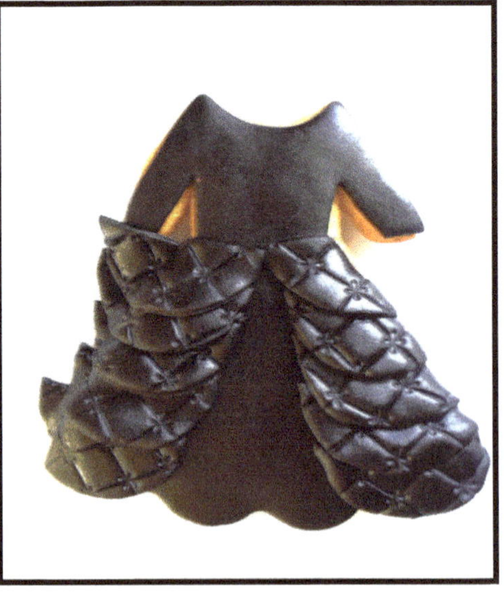

4. Place the five quilted half circles onto your dress using the waist as your top and extend the quilted half circles off the right side of the dress cookie. Use your fingers to slightly press the fondant to adhere to the dress.

5. Use your finger to press the right side of the fondant into the dress cookie. Use a paring knife or Xacto knife to follow the edge of the dress cookie and remove the excess fondant as shown.

6. Repeat steps 4 and 5 to place the quilted half circles on the left side of the dress cookie evenly spacing the quilted layers and meeting the right side of the fondant skirt at the top point. Apply gold star in center of the waist.

Coconut Dress Cookie

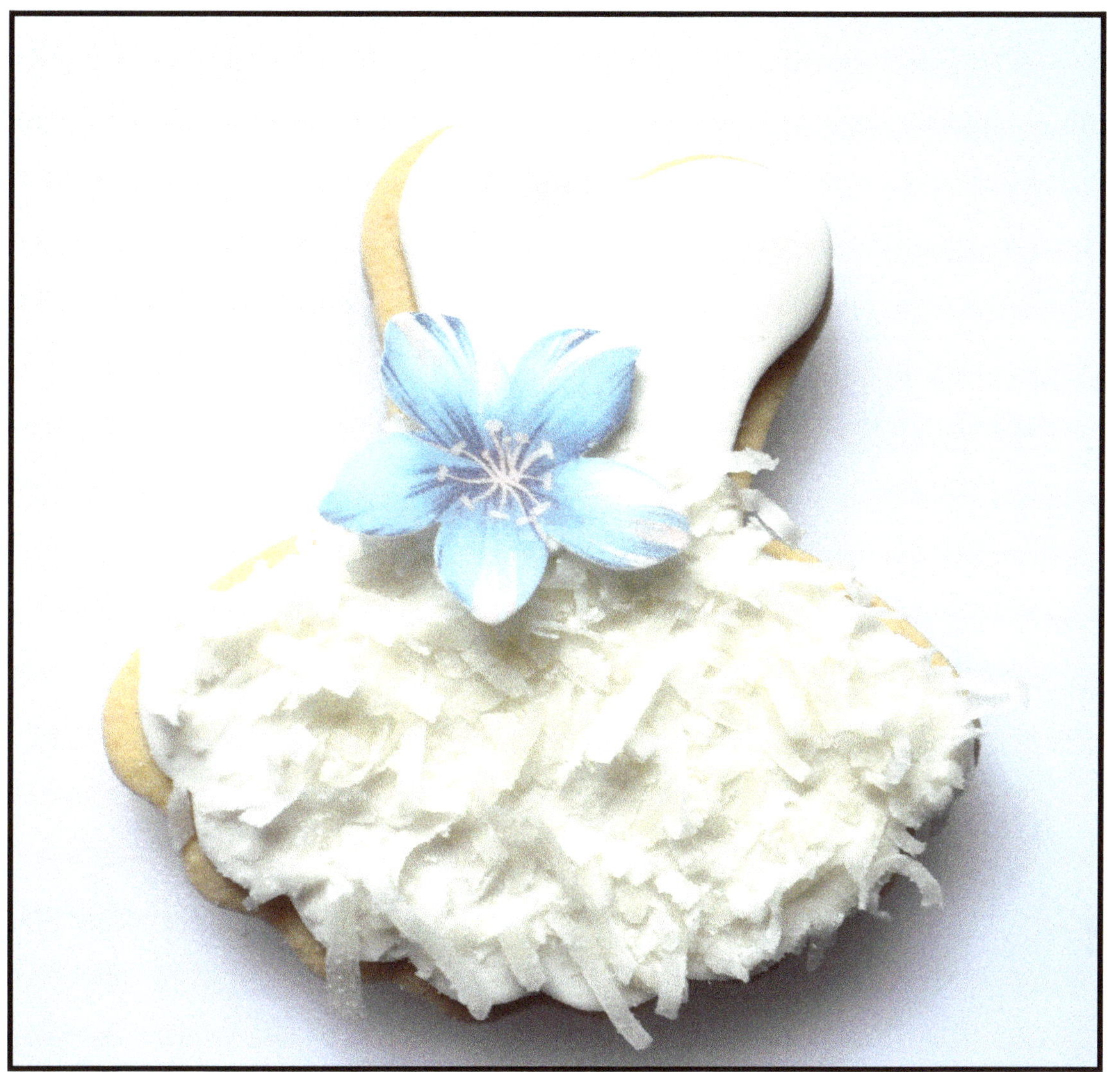

Materials:
- Dress cookie
- 0.5 oz. white fondant
- Sweetened flaked coconut
- Piping gel
- Food safe paint brush

Tools:
- Party Dress Cookie Cutter
  (etsy.com, Sinful Cutters)
- Wafer paper flowers
  (amazon.com)

Suggested cellophane bag size is 4x6 inches to package this dress cookie.

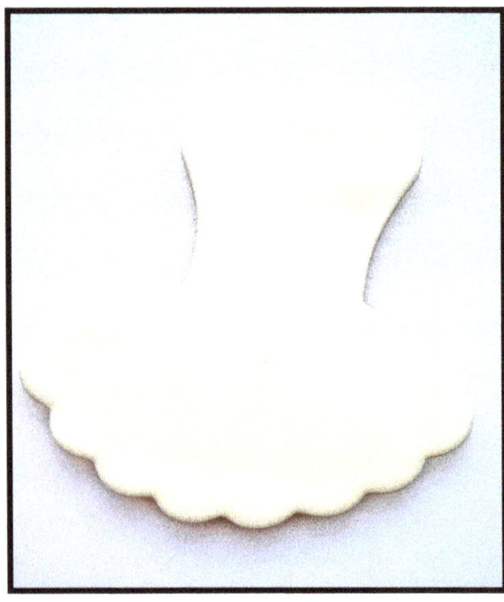

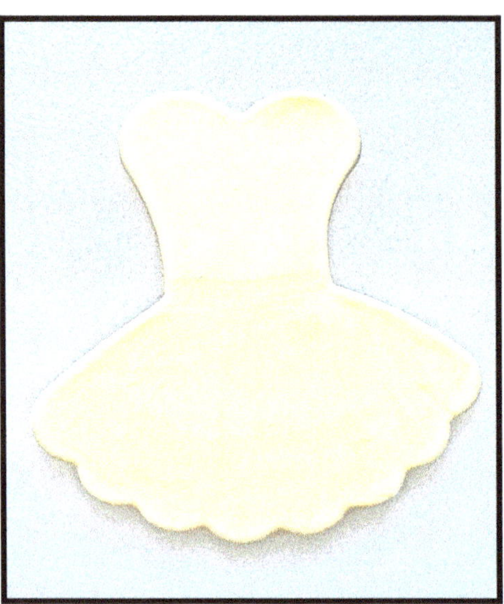

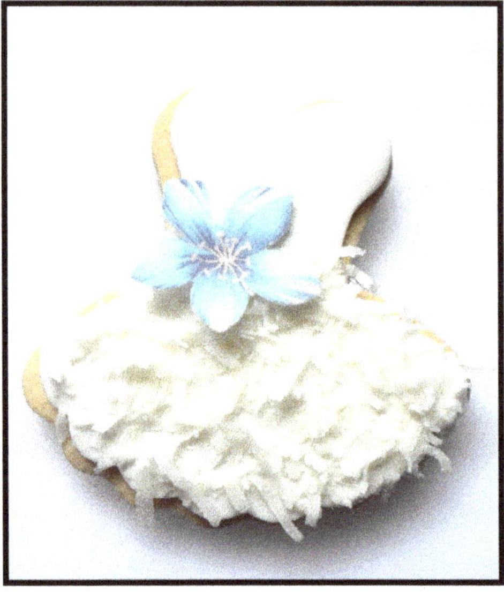

1. Roll out white fondant. Use the dress cookie cutter to cut out the white fondant dress.

2. Use a paint brush to apply a thin layer of piping gel onto the bottom section of your dress cookie. Apply coconut over the piping gel and remove excess.

3. Use a paint brush to apply a thin layer of piping gel onto your dress cookie. Gently apply your fondant cut-out to the cookie, and gently press down to secure to cookie. Add a dab of piping gel to the back of the blue wafer flower and attach to cookie waist as shown.

Important Tip

The suggested cellophane bag size is based on the cookie thickness and fondant thickness specified. If you add additional fondant embellishments to the dress cookie, you should account for that in the cellophane bag size. You can wrap the decorated dress cookie with plastic wrap, parchment paper or wax paper to help you determine what cellophane bag size you will need to package your decorated dress cookies.

Packaging your decorated dress cookies will help keep them fresh longer and sanitary. And, people will not have to ask you for something to wrap their cookie in. They can eat a little piece at a time or take their cookie home.

Navy Lace Dress Cookie

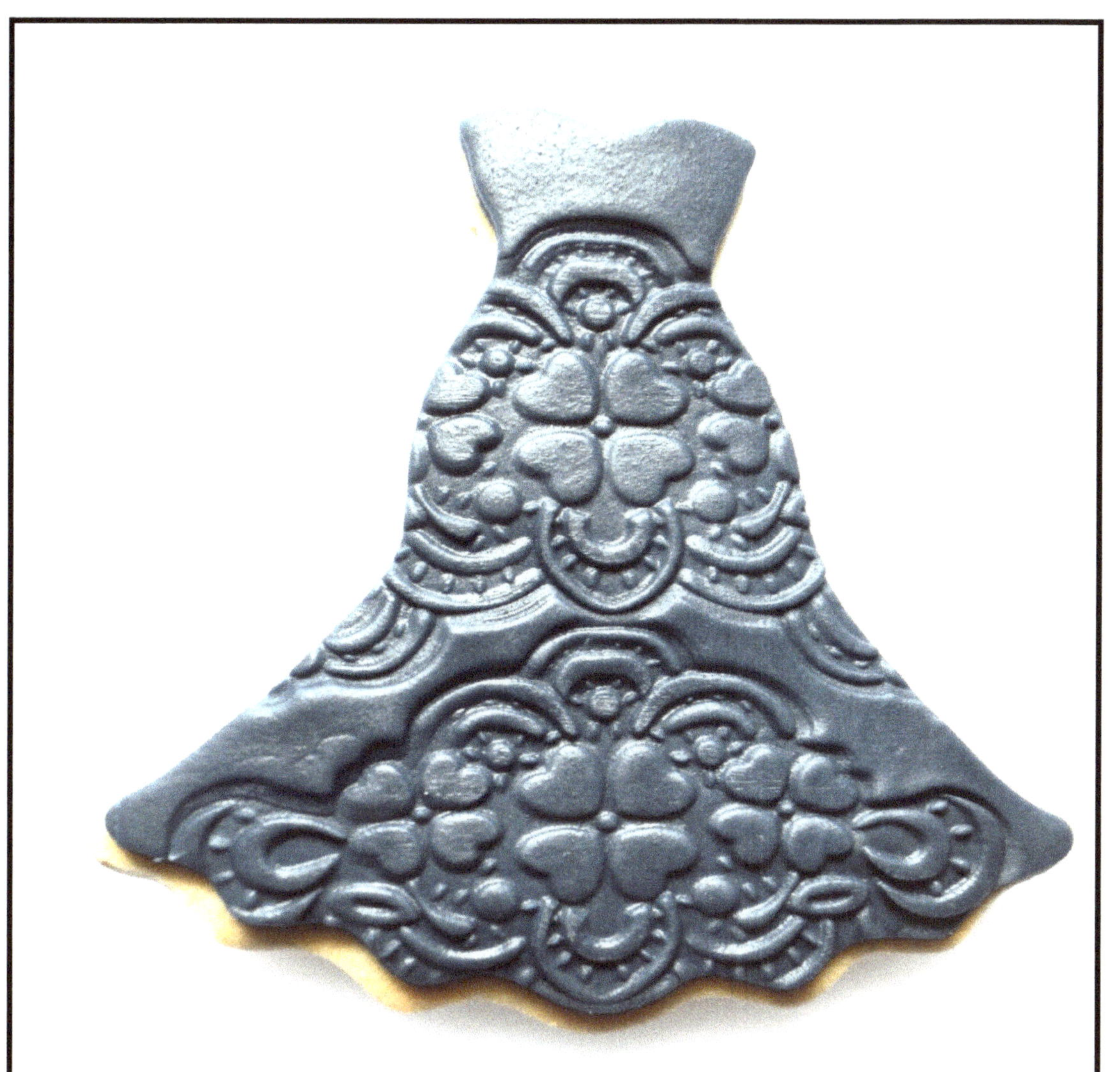

Materials:
- Dress cookie
- 0.6 oz. Fondarific Navy fondant
- Piping gel
- Food safe paint brush

Tools:
- LILIAO Wedding Dress Cookie Cutter (amazon.com)
- Fat Daddio's Lace Swag Acrylic Impression Cutter (amazon.com)

Suggested cellophane bag size is 5x7 inches to package this dress cookie.

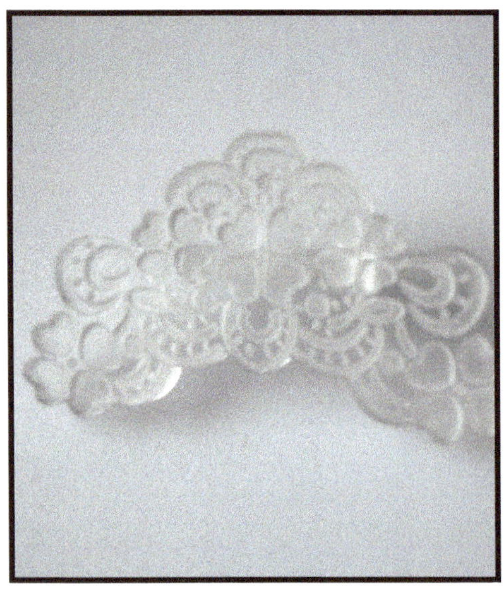

1. This is Fat Daddio's Lace Swag Acrylic Impression Cutter.

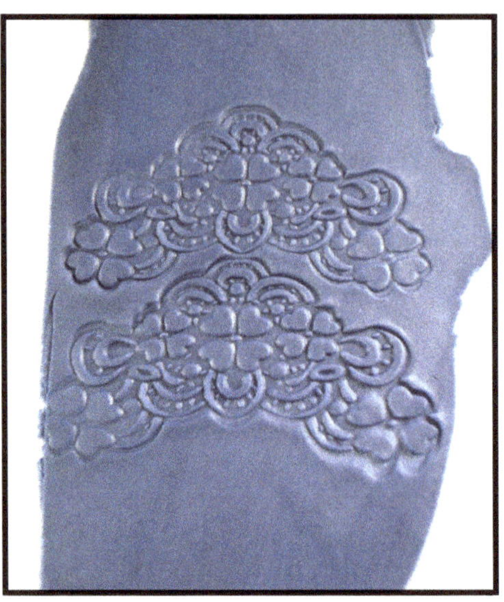

2. Roll out navy fondant and make two imprints with the lace swag acrylic impression cutter. Use a bench scraper to lift the fondant up from the surface, and then lay it back down and gently spread back it out.

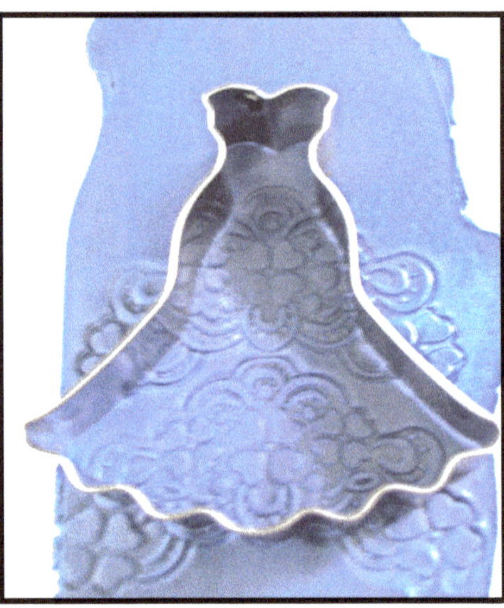

3. Center the dress cookie cutter over the fondant. Firmly press the dress cookie cutter down, and then wiggle the dress cookie cutter to release it from the fondant. Remove the dress cookie cutter.

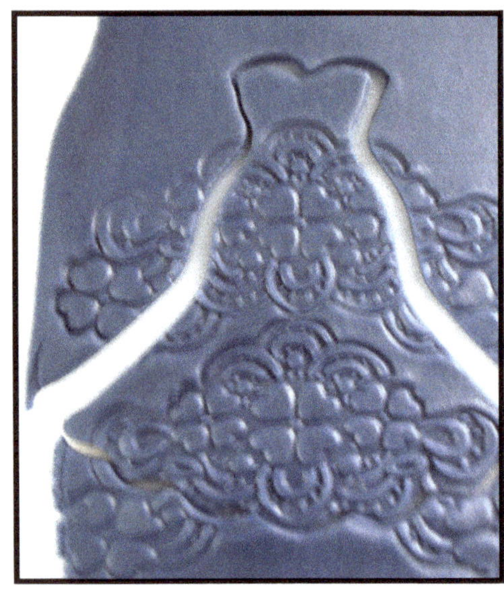

4. This is what the fondant cut-out looks like.

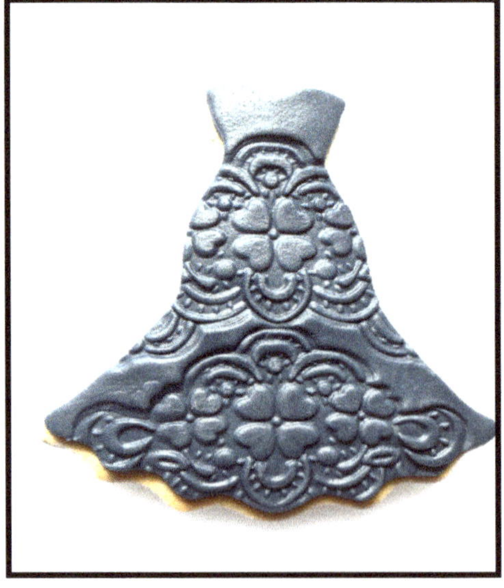

5. Use a paint brush to apply a thin layer of piping gel onto your dress cookie. Gently apply your fondant cut-out to the cookie, and gently press down to secure to cookie.

Lavender Swirl Dress Cookie

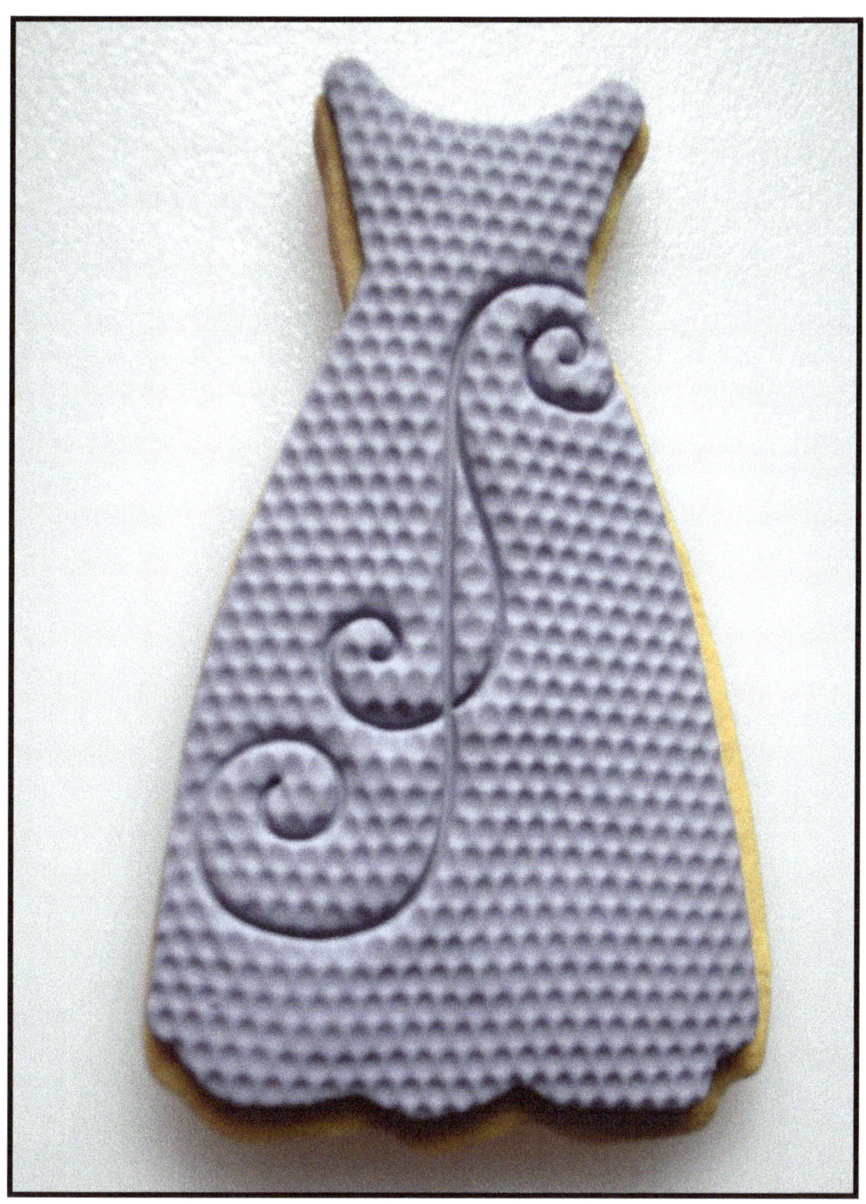

Materials:
- Dress cookie
- 0.7 oz. lavender fondant
- Piping gel
- Food safe paint brush

Tools:
- Dress Cookie Cutter (flourbox.com)
- Makin's Texture Sheets-Set B (Dots)
- Wilton Decorative Press Set

Suggested cellophane bag size is 4x6 inches to package this dress cookie.

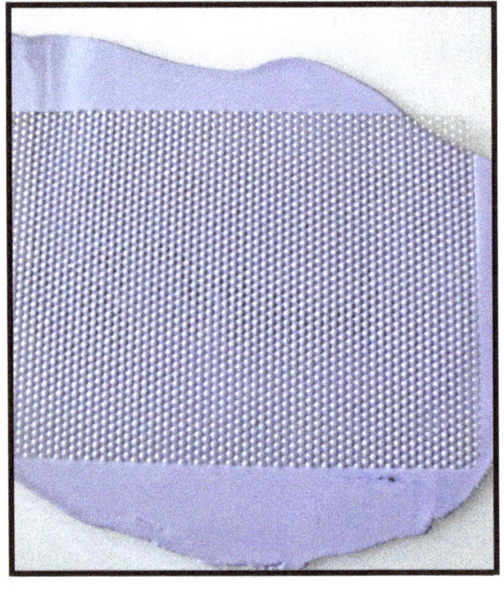

1. Use Makins dot impression mat to imprint the lavender fondant.

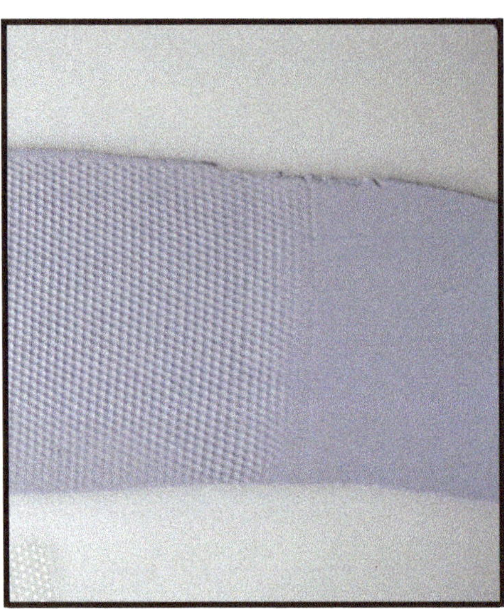

2. Remove mat.

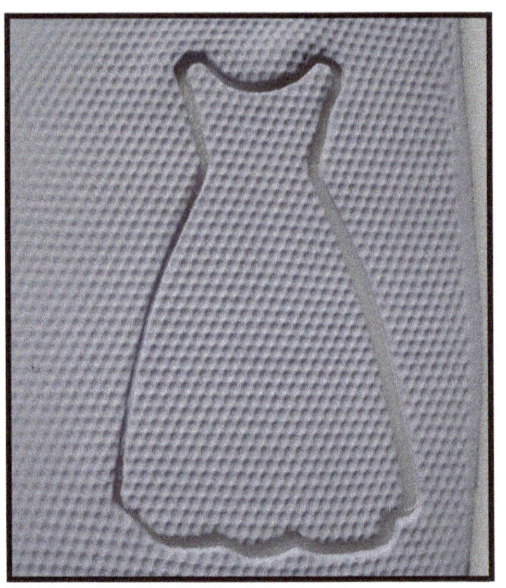

3. Press the dress cookie cutter into the fondant. Firmly press the dress cookie cutter down, and then wiggle the dress cookie cutter to release it from the fondant. Remove the dress cookie cutter. Use a paint brush to apply a thin layer of piping gel onto your dress cookie. Gently apply your fondant cut-out to the cookie, and gently press down to secure to cookie.

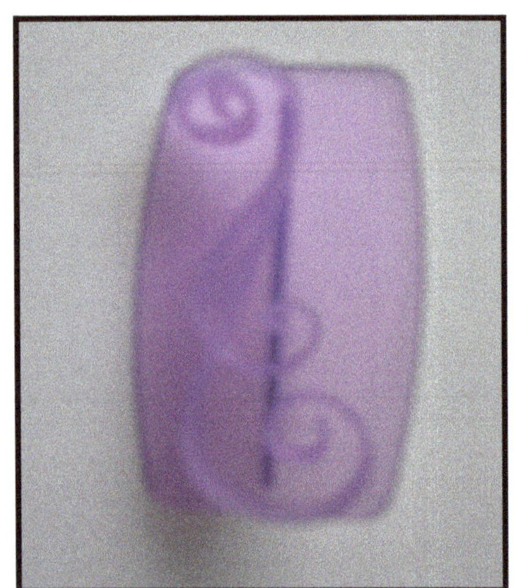

4. This is the double swirl in Wilton's Decorative Press Set.

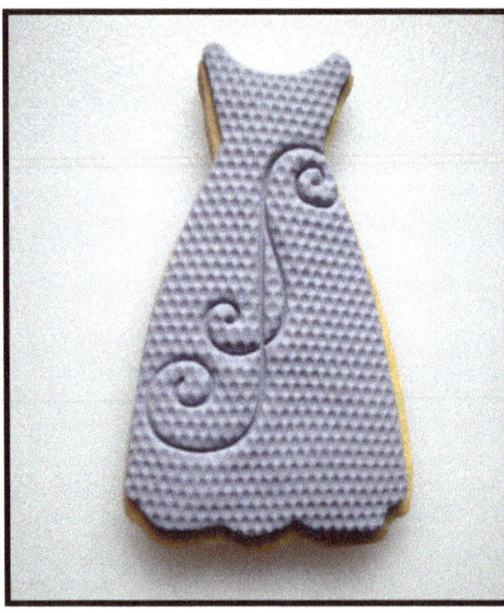

5. Press the double swirl into the fondant as shown above.

White Rose Bow Dress Cookie

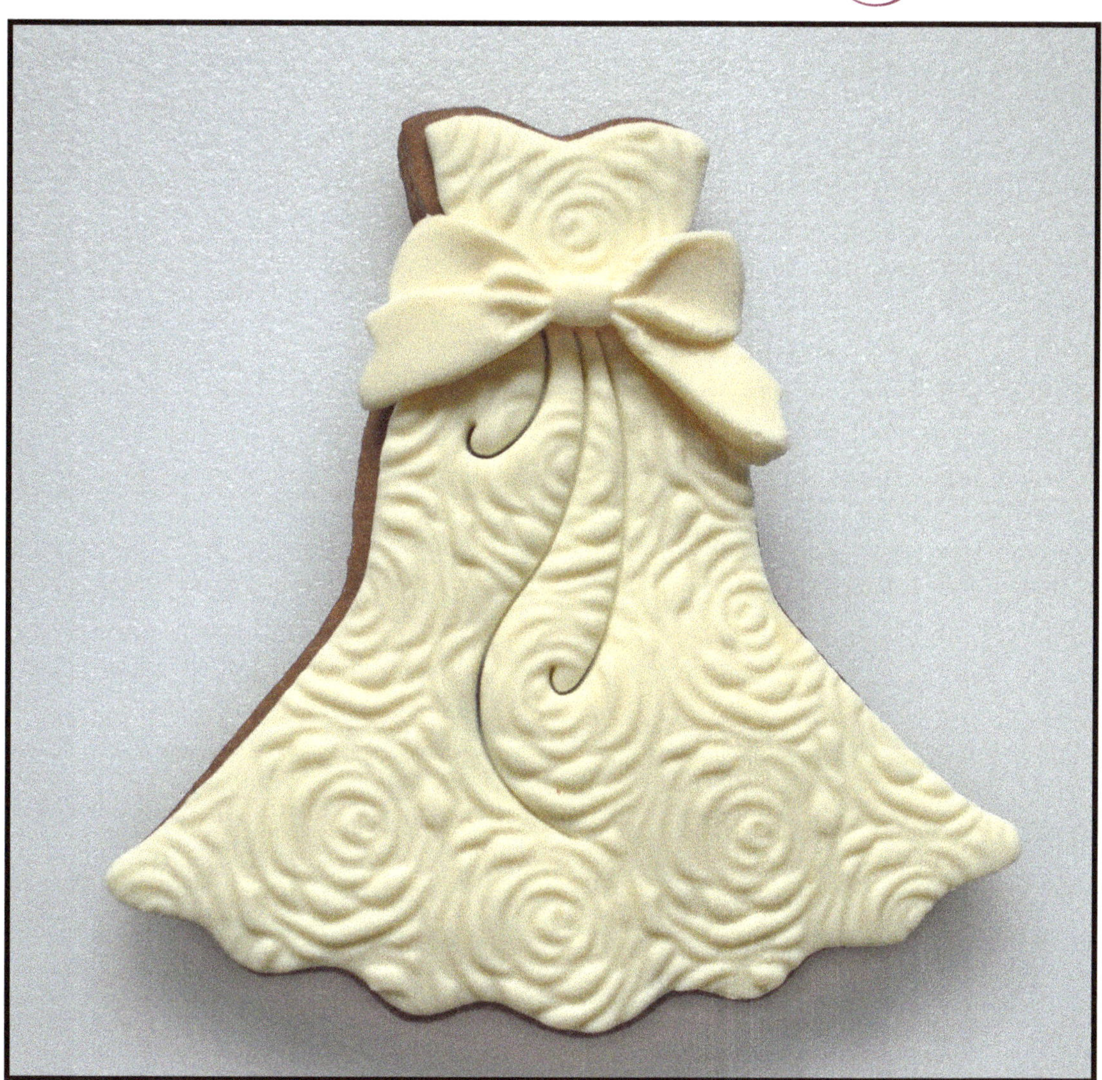

Materials:
- Dress cookie
- 0.8 oz. Fondarific Wedding White fondant
- Piping gel
- Food safe paint brush

Tools:
- LILIAO Wedding Dress Cookie Cutter (amazon.com)
- Autumn Carpenter Floral Texture Sheet Set (Roses)
- Wilton's Designer Pattern Press Set, Flower Press
- Bows silicone mold (hobbylobby.com)

Suggested cellophane bag size is 5x7 inches to package this dress cookie.

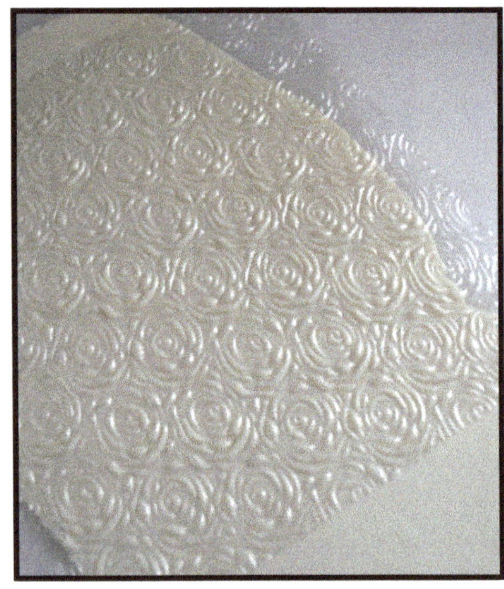

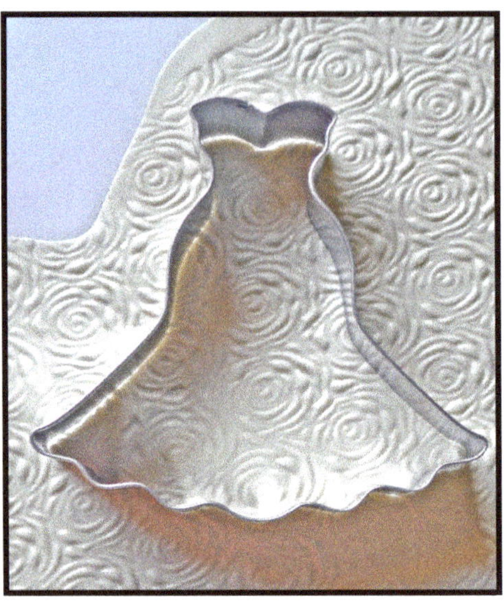

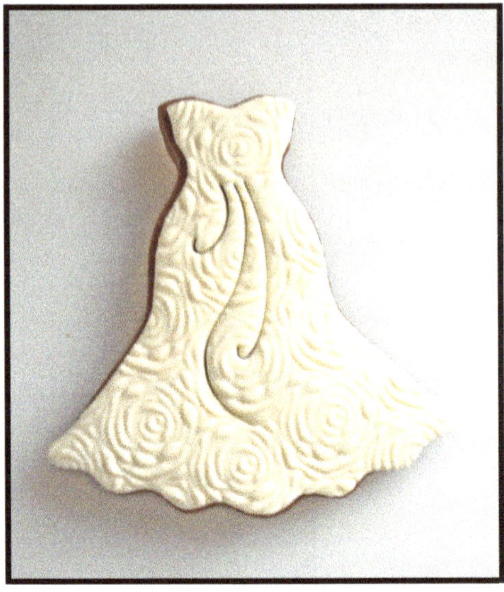

1. Roll out white fondant. Use the roses texture sheet and press over the white fondant. Use a rolling pin to roll over the texture sheet. Use your fingers to rub over the texture sheet. Remove texture sheet.

2. Press the dress cookie cutter into the fondant. Firmly press the dress cookie cutter down, and then wiggle the dress cookie cutter to release it from the fondant. Remove the dress cookie cutter.

3. Use a paint brush to apply a thin layer of piping gel onto your dress cookie. Gently apply your fondant cut-out to the cookie, and gently press down to secure to cookie. Use the flower press to imprint fondant at the waist.

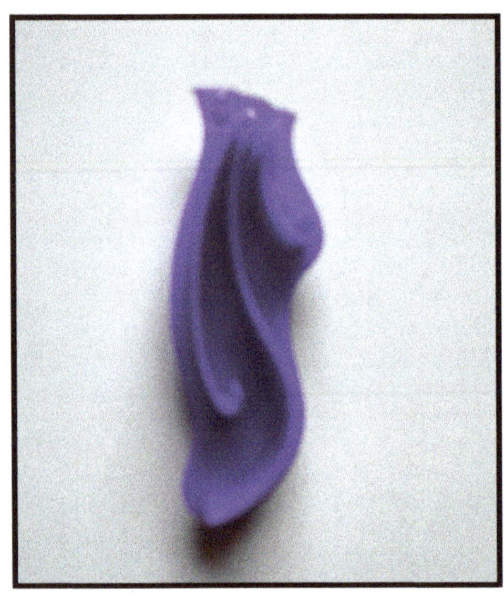

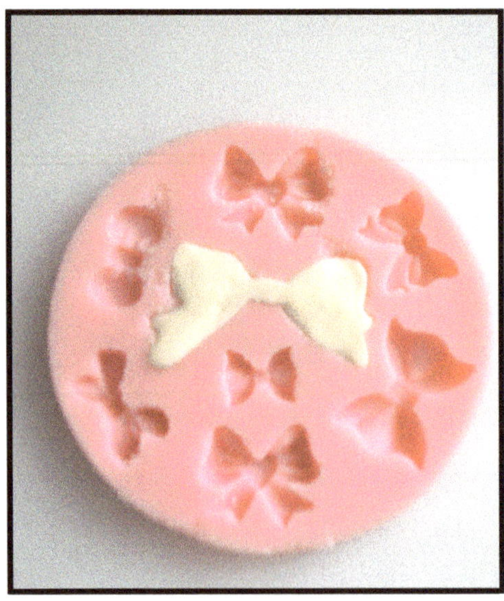

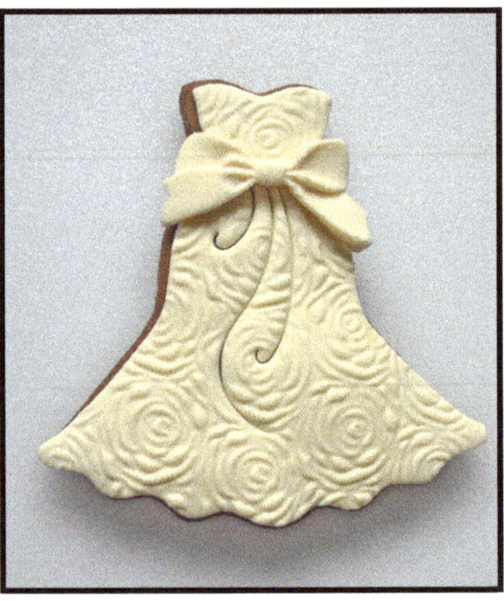

4. This is the flower press tool broken in half. One side is short, and the other side is long. Use the long side for this dress cookie.

5. Press some white fondant into the large cavity of the bow silicone mold. Refrigerate until cold, and then remove.

6. Use a dab of piping gel on the back of the large bow, and then attach to the waist as shown.

Red Swirls Dress Cookie

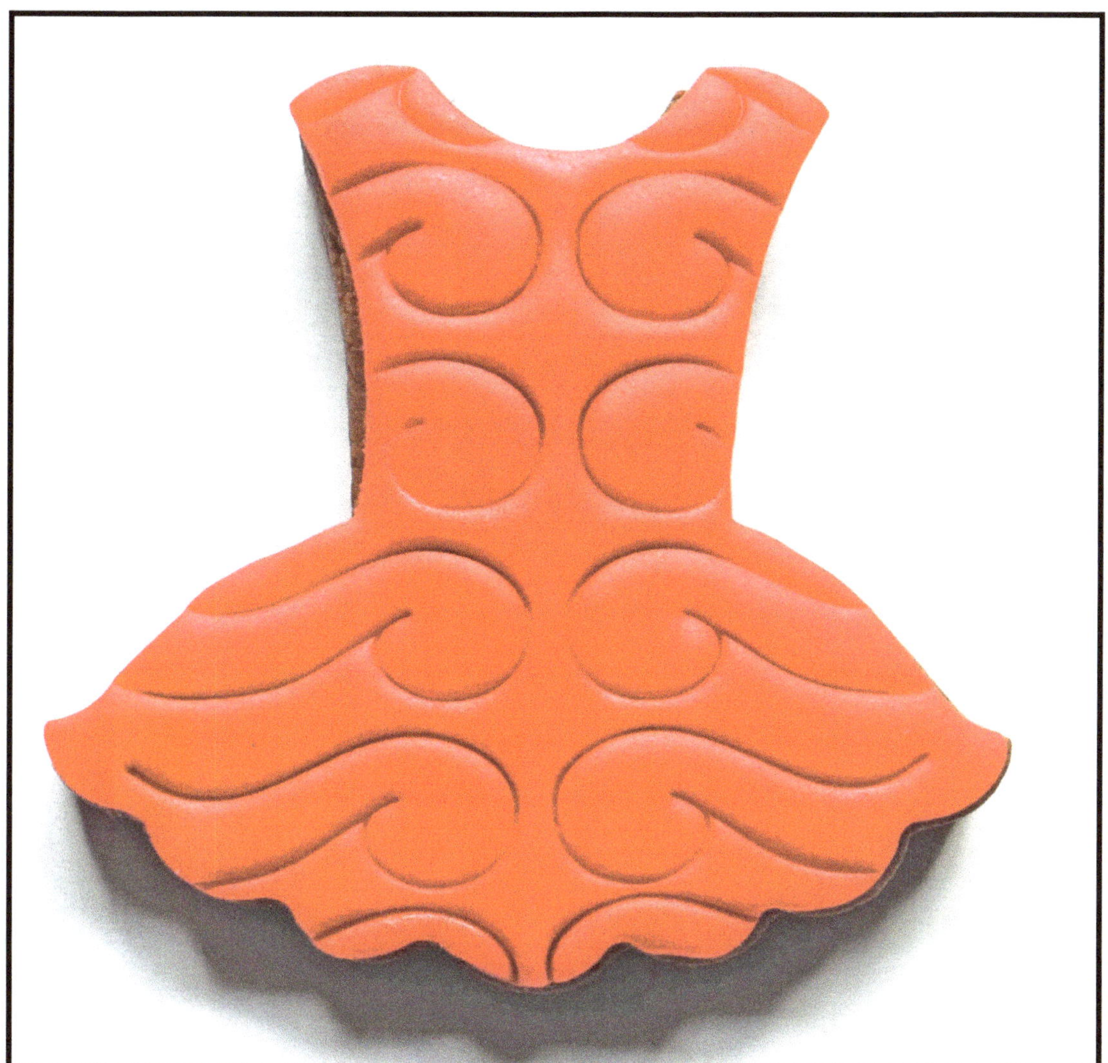

Materials:
- Dress cookie
- 0.6 oz. Fondarific Red fondant
- Piping gel
- Food safe paint brush

Tools:
- Tutu and Dress Cookie Cutter (etsy.com, WhiskedAwayCutters)
- Wilton's Designer Pattern Press Set, Symmetrical Swirl

Suggested cellophane bag size is 4x6 inches to package this dress cookie.

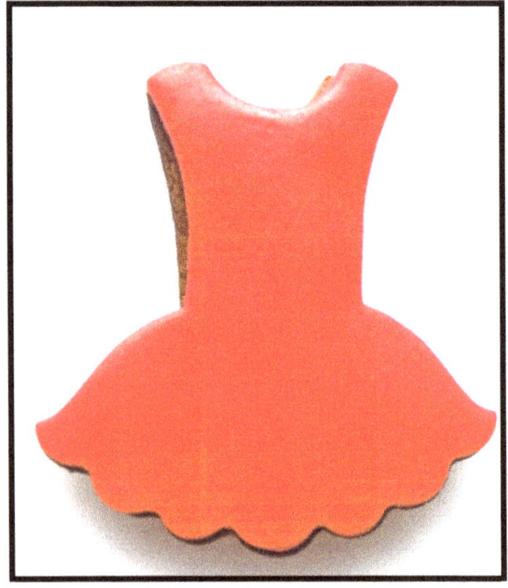

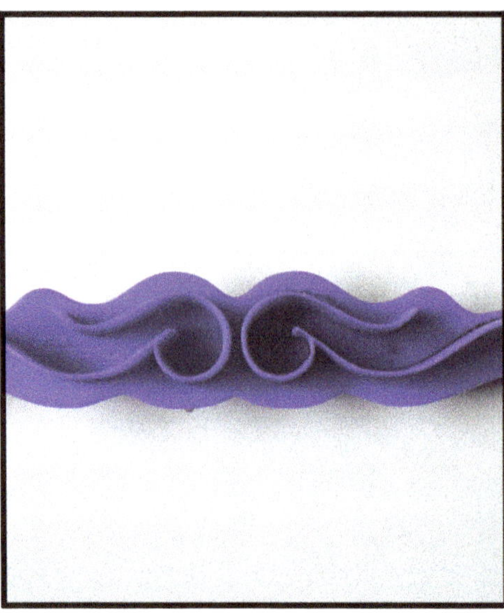

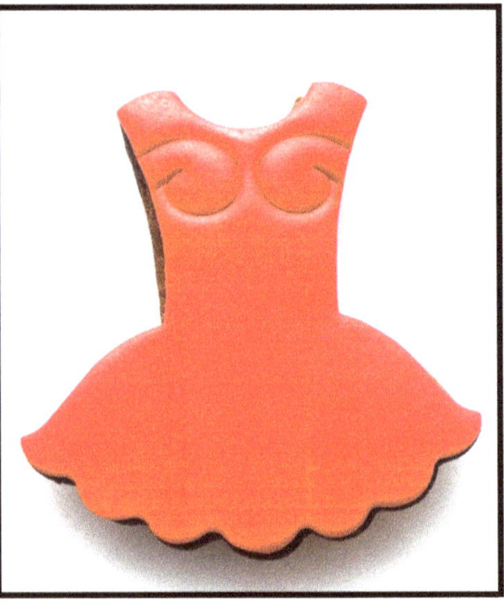

1. Roll out red fondant. Use the dress cookie cutter to cut out the red fondant dress. Use a paint brush to apply a thin layer of piping gel onto your dress cookie. Apply fondant cut-out to cookie, and gently smooth top.

2. This is the symmetrical swirl tool. One side is small, and the other side is large. Use the small side for this dress design.

3. Press the symmetrical swirl into the fondant starting from the top of the dress cookie.

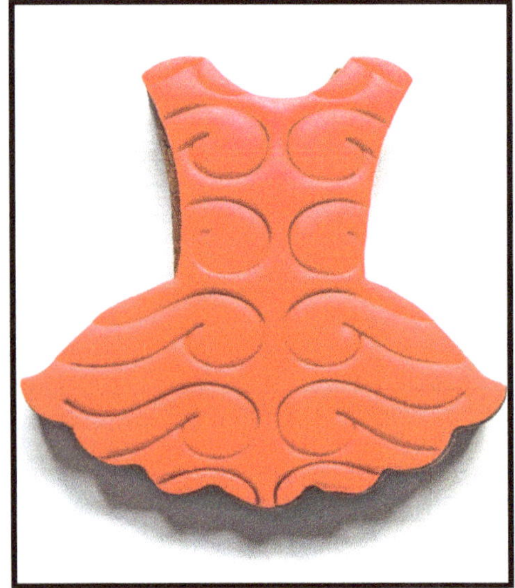

4. Continue to evenly press the symmetrical swirl tool into the fondant dress as shown above.

Blue Wavy Dress Cookie

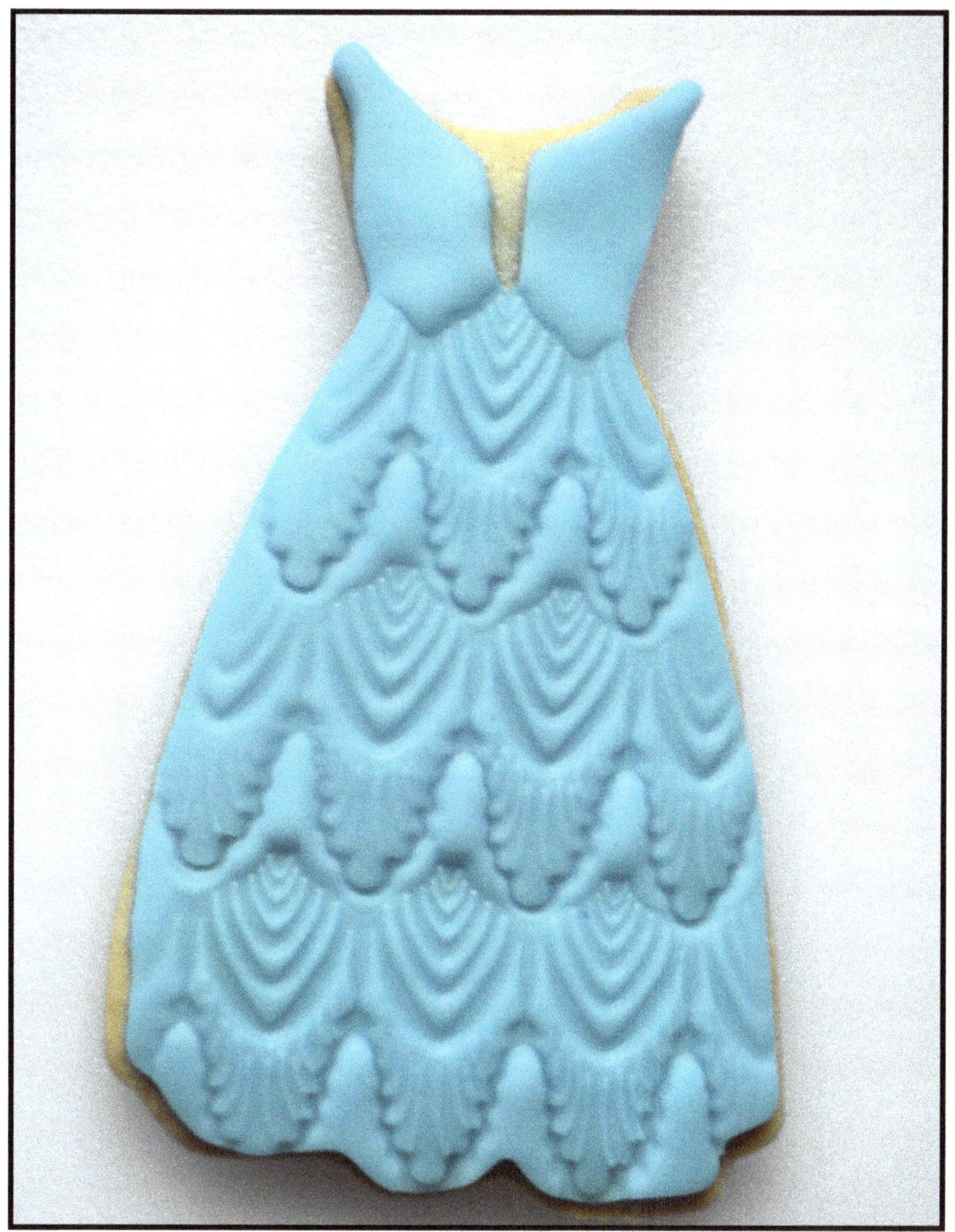

Materials:
- Dress cookie
- 0.7 oz. Fondarific Blue fondant
- Piping gel
- Food safe paint brush

Tools:
- Dress Cookie Cutter (flourbox.com)
- Fat Daddio's Fondant Impression Cutter, Paradise Border

Suggested cellophane bag size is 4x6 inches to package this dress cookie.

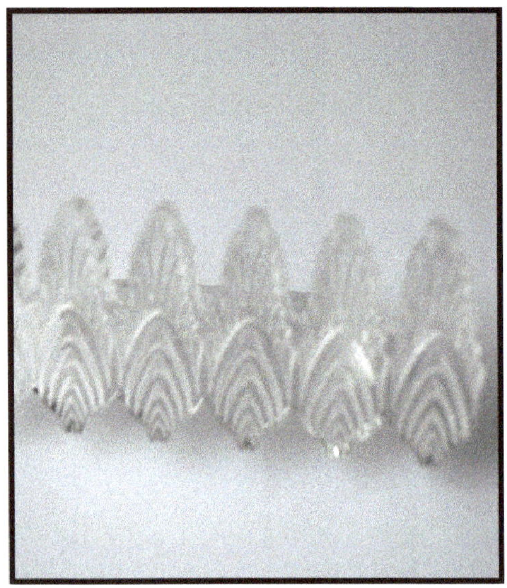

1. This is Fat Daddio's Fondant Impression Cutter, Paradise Border. Turn the impression cutter over to use.

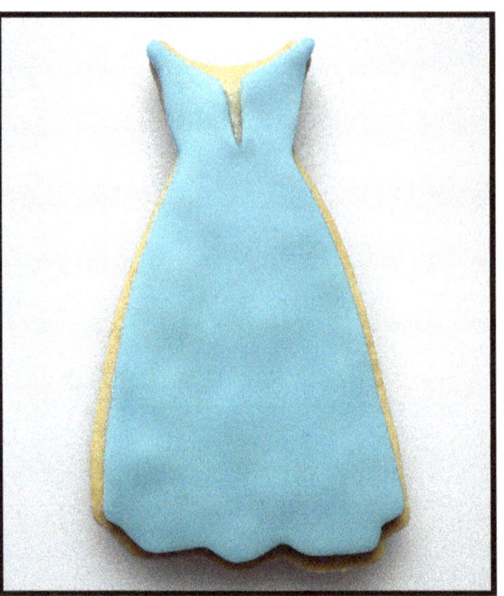

2. Roll out blue fondant. Use the dress cookie cutter to cut out the blue fondant dress. Use a paint brush to apply a thin layer of piping gel onto your dress cookie. Apply fondant cut-out to cookie, and gently smooth top. Use a knife to cut open bodice area.

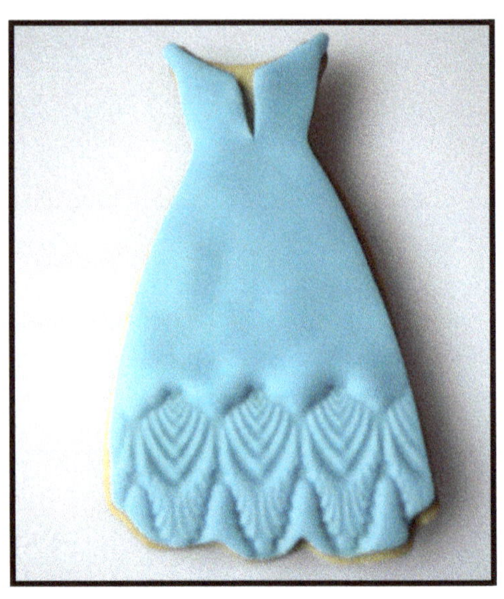

3. Gently press the impression cutter into the fondant on the dress as shown.

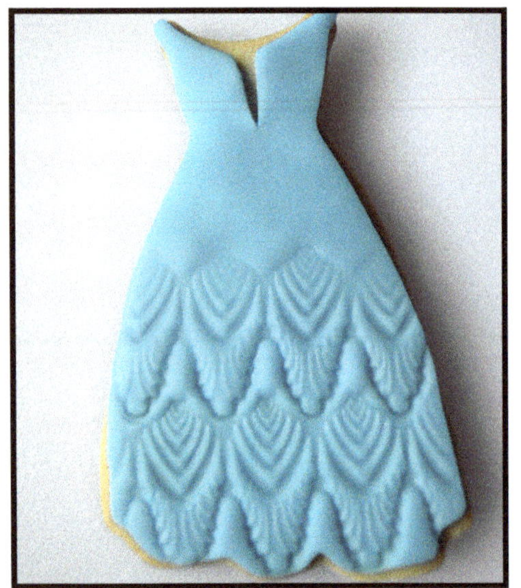

4. Center the impression tool over the dress cookie and imprint the fondant as shown above to make the second impression.

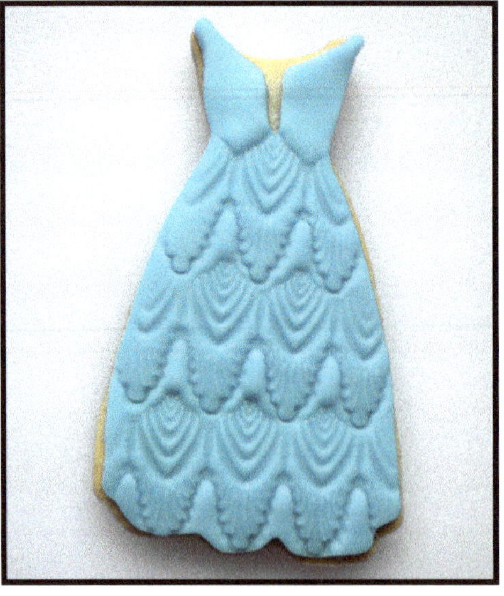

5. Center the impression tool over the dress cookie and imprint the fondant as shown above to make the third impression.

Black Sparkle Dress Cookies

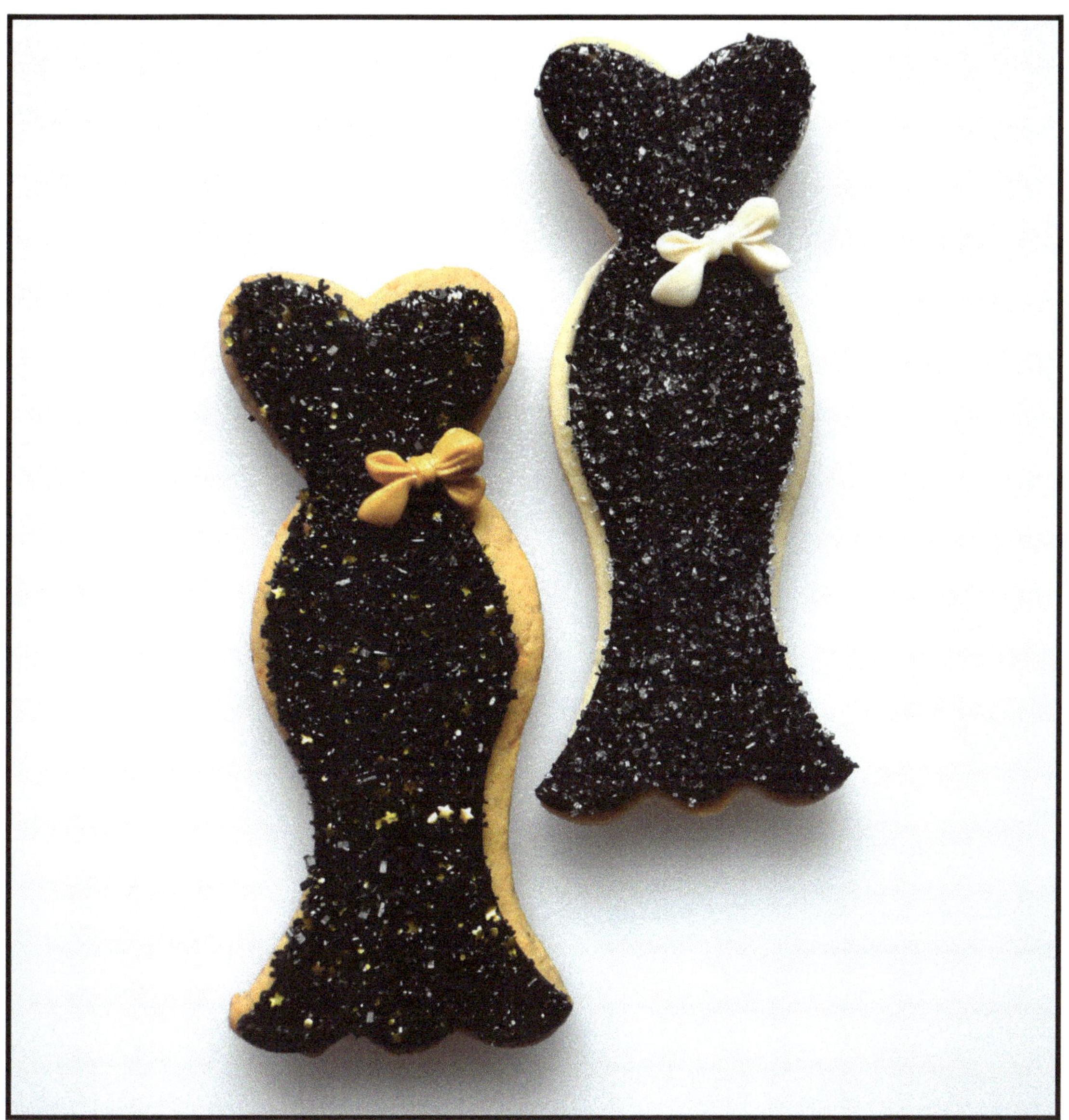

<table>
<tr>
<td>

Materials:

- Two dress cookies
- 0.8 oz. Fondarific Black fondant
- 0.1 oz. gold fondant
- Piping gel
- Food safe paint brush

</td>
<td>

Tools:

- The Marilyn Gown Cookie Cutter (etsy.com, Sinful Cutters)
- Black sanding sugar
- White sanding sugar
- Bakery Bling Glittery Black Stars
- Small bow silicone mold

</td>
</tr>
</table>

Suggested cellophane bag size is 3x8 inches to package these dress cookies.

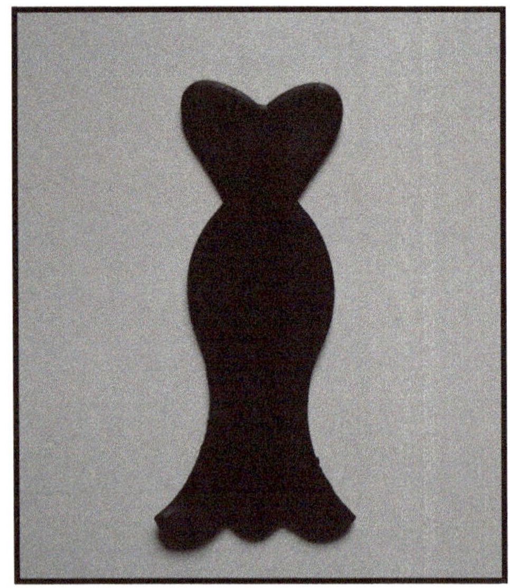 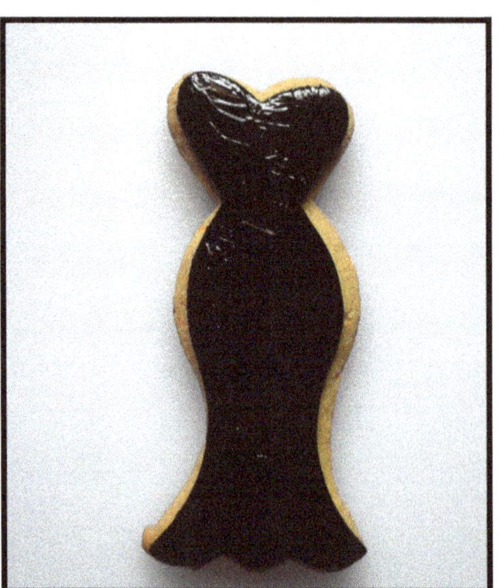 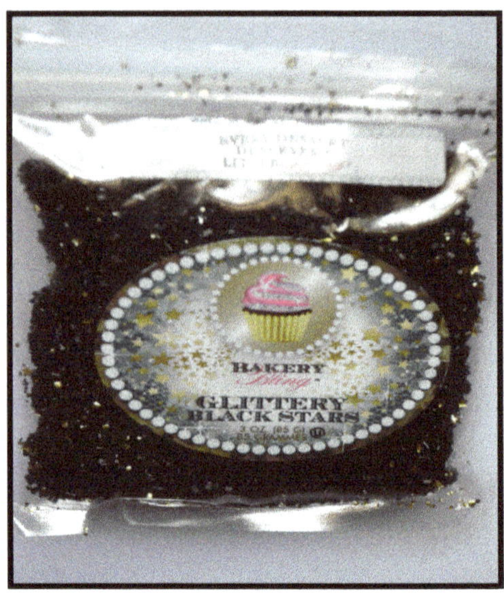

1. Roll out black fondant. Use the dress cookie cutter to cut out the black fondant dress.

2. Use a paint brush to apply a thin layer of piping gel onto your dress cookie. Apply fondant cut-out to cookie, and gently smooth top. Completely cover the black fondant area with piping gel.

3. This is the Bakery Bling Glittery Black Stars. Use a bowl to hold the dress cookie with one hand, and use the other hand to sprinkle the entire surface of the fondant dress cut-out. Gently press sprinkles into fondant to secure.

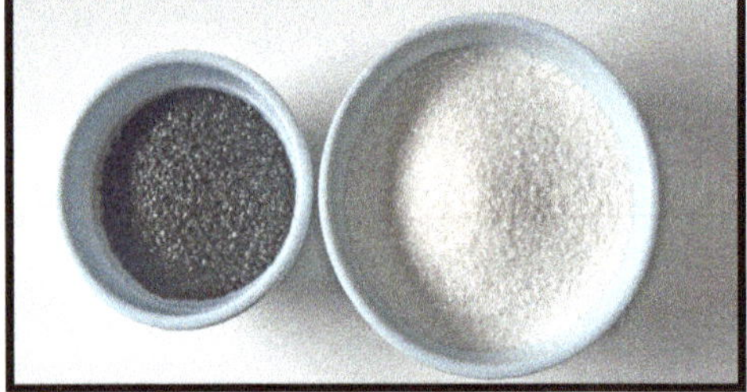

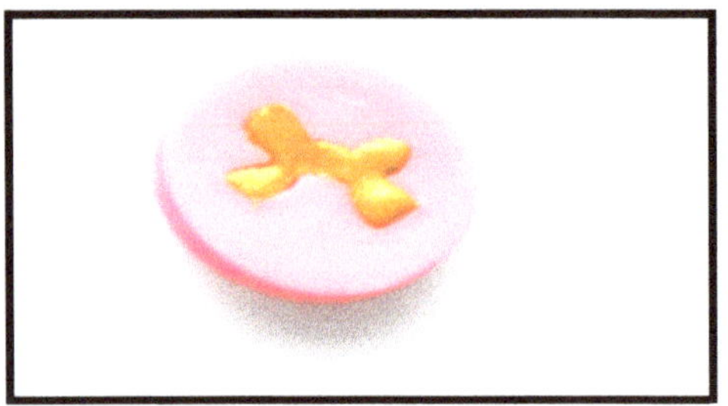

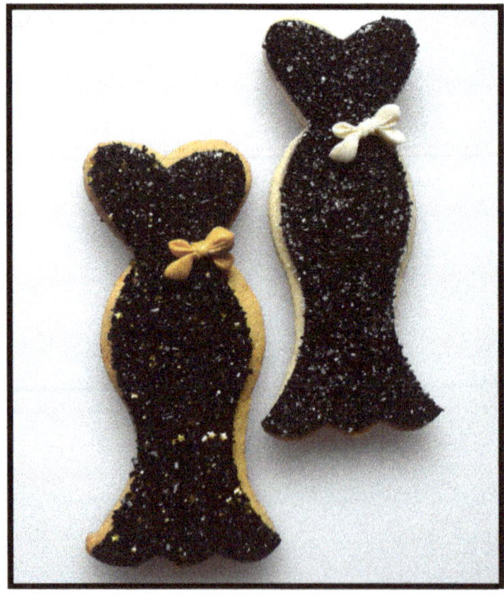

4. The black and white sprinkles are shown above. Repeat steps 1 and 2 above for the second dress cookie. Use the black sprinkles first, then use the white sprinkles to cover the fondant dress cookie. Use the small ribbon silicone mold to make both the gold and white bows. Refrigerate until firm.

5. Use a dab of piping gel on the back of the gold and white fondant bows and secure them to the waist of the dress cookies.

Gold Stenciled Dress Cookie

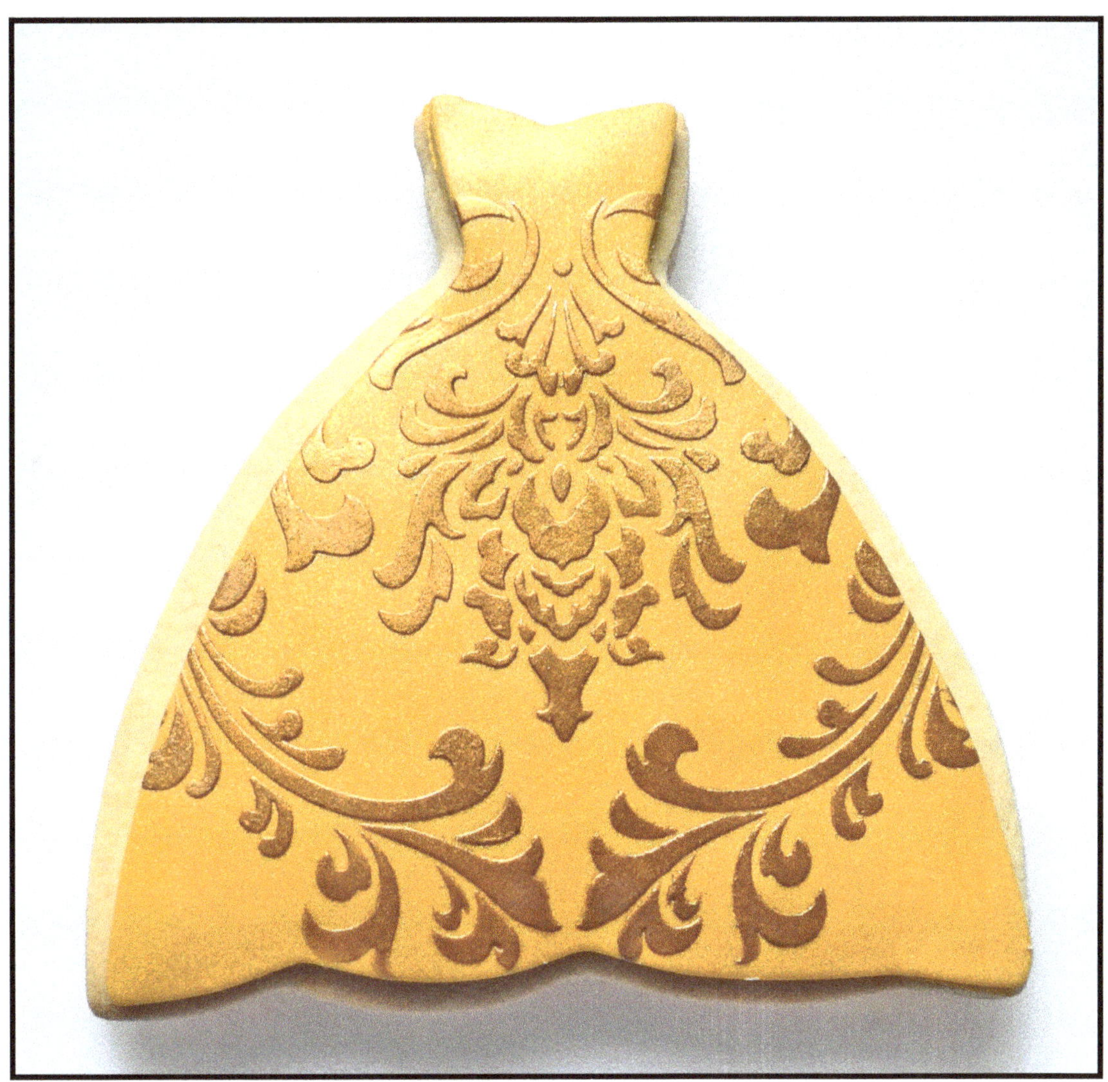

Materials:
- Dress cookie
- 1.2 oz. Sunny Side Up Bakery Gold Vanilla Fondant
- Piping gel
- Food safe paint brush

Tools:
- Ann Clark Gown Cookie Cutter (amazon.com)
- Designer Stencils, C551 (Filigree Damask Cake Stencil Tier #1) (designerstencils.com)
- Wilton-Edible-Metallic-Cake-Paint-Set (Metallic Gold)

Suggested cellophane bag size is 5x7 inches to package this dress cookie (slide decorated dress cookie in sideways).

1. Roll out gold fondant. Place Designer Stencils C551 on top of fondant. Use rolling pin to secure stencil to fondant.

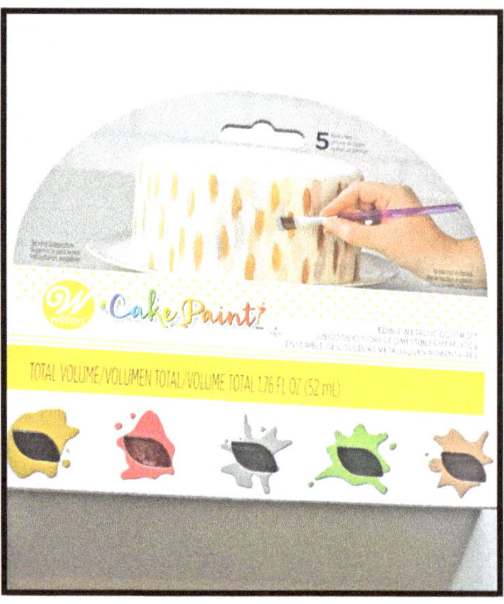

2. This is Wilton's Cake Paint. Use the metallic gold. Stir the paint to make sure it is completely blended. Use a paint brush to paint the stencil. I used four layers of paint for this dress. Let paint dry between layers.

3. Remove the stencil. This is what the finished fondant design looks like.

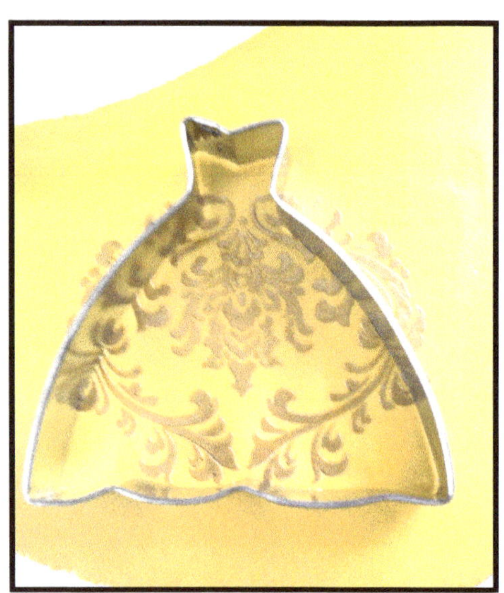

4. Center the dress cookie cutter over the painted area on the gold fondant, and then press firmly down into the fondant. Wiggle the cookie cutter to release the cookie cutter from the fondant.

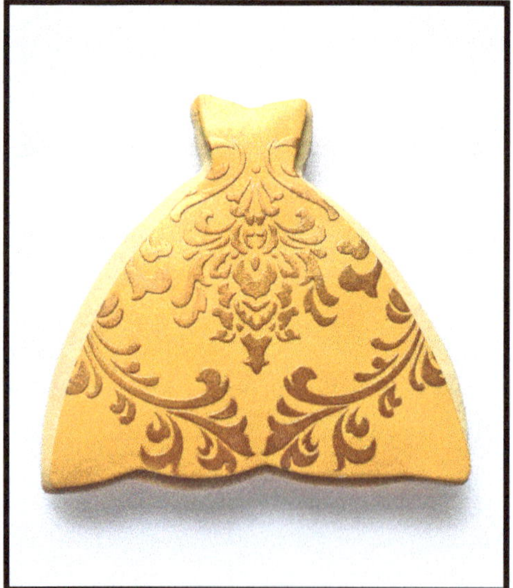

5. Use a paint brush to apply a thin layer of piping gel onto your dress cookie. Apply fondant cutout to cookie, and gently smooth top.

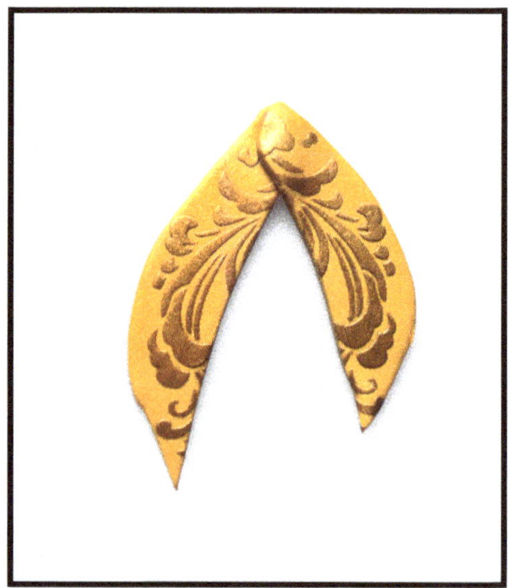

6. Remove the excess stencil from the gold fondant so you can reuse the fondant.

Blue Sprinkles Dress Cookie

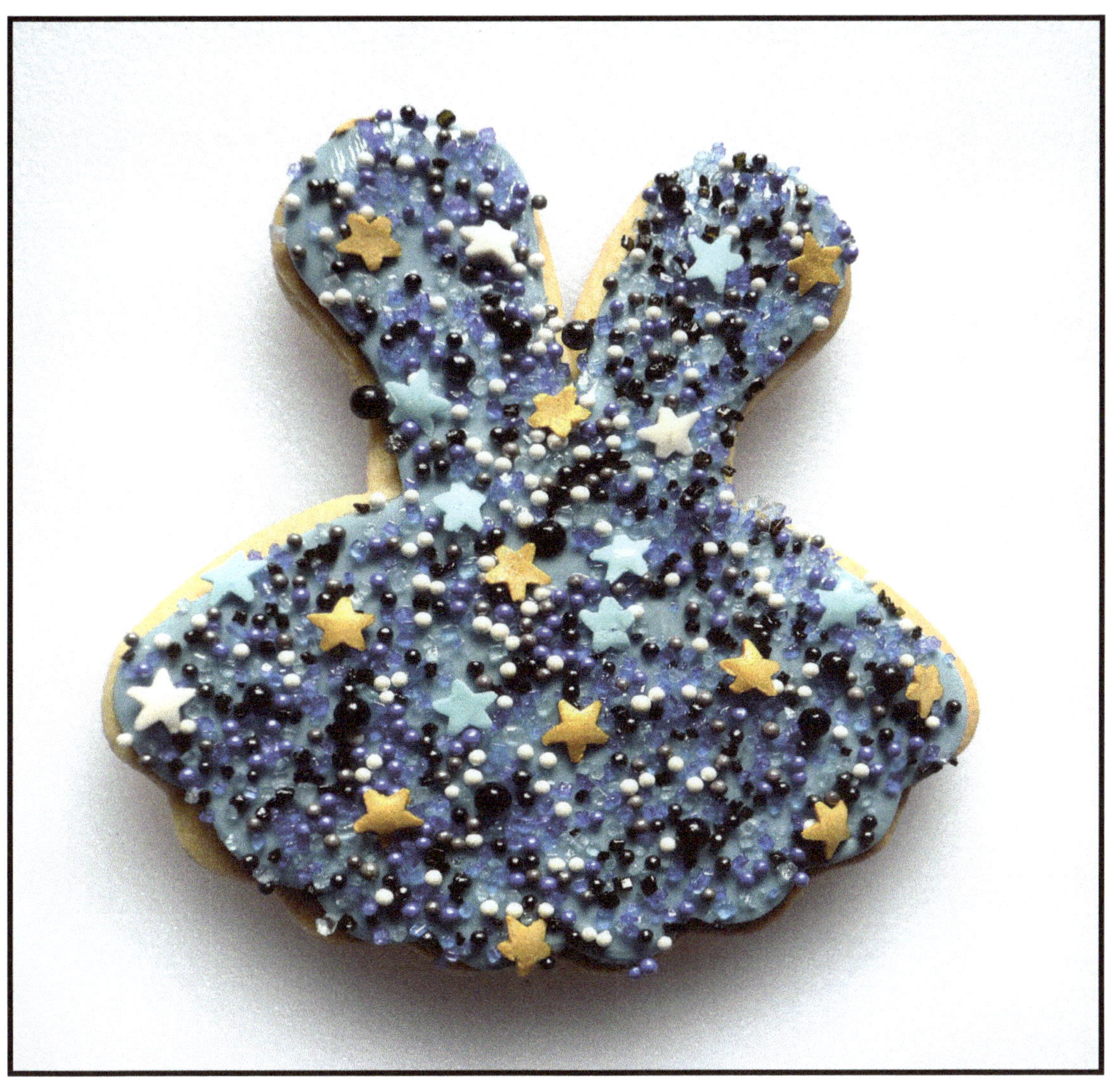

Materials:
- Dress cookie
- 0.7 oz. Fondarific Blue fondant
- Piping gel
- Food safe paint brush
- Xacto knife or pizza cutter

Tools:
- Party Dress Cookie Cutter (etsy.com, Sinful Cutters)
- Sweet Tooth Fairy Star Dust Sprinkle Mix

Suggested cellophane bag size is 4x6 inches to package this dress cookie.

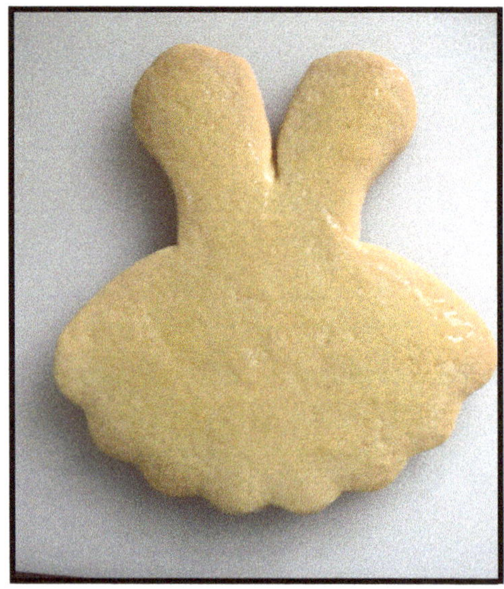

1. This cookie requires you to cut open the bodice before baking. Paint the dress cookie with piping gel.

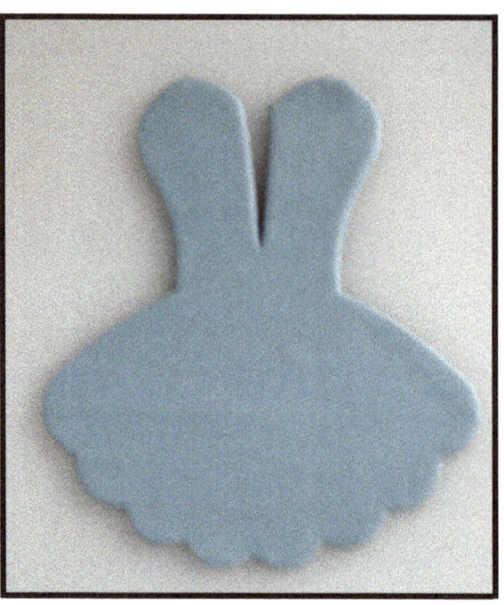

2. Roll out blue fondant. Use the dress cookie cutter to cut out the blue fondant dress. Use an Xacto knife or pizza cutter to cut open the bodice as shown.

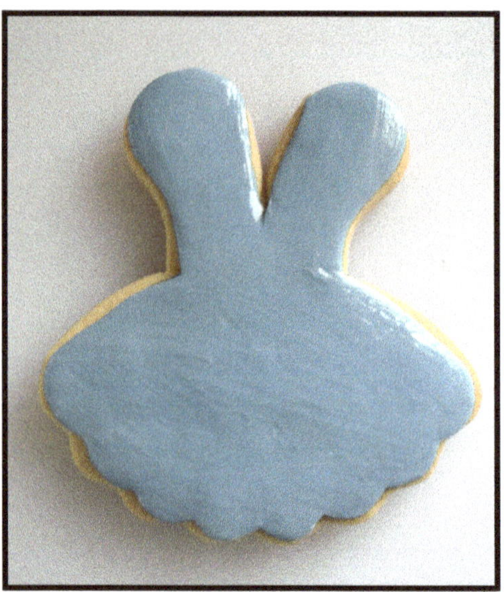

3. Attach the fondant cut-out to the top of the dress cookie. Paint the entire top of the blue fondant with piping gel.

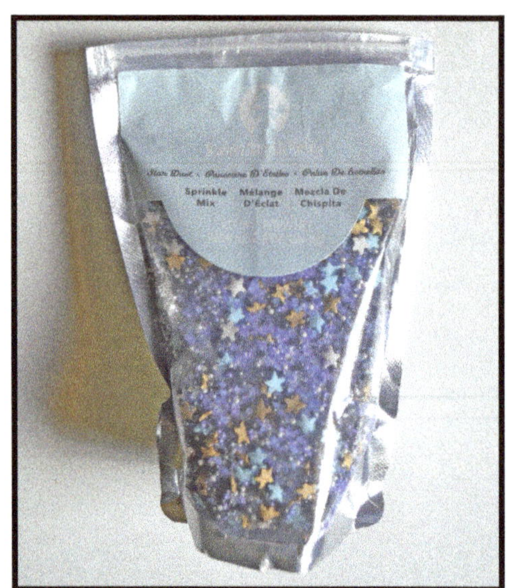

4. This is Sweet Tooth's Fairy Star Dust Sprinkle Mix.

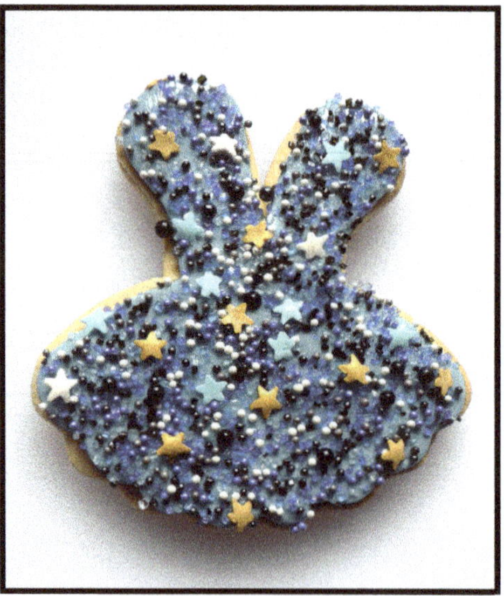

5. Use a bowl to hold the dress cookie with one hand, and use the other hand to sprinkle the entire surface of the fondant dress cut-out. Gently press sprinkles into fondant to secure.

Green Grass Dress Cookie

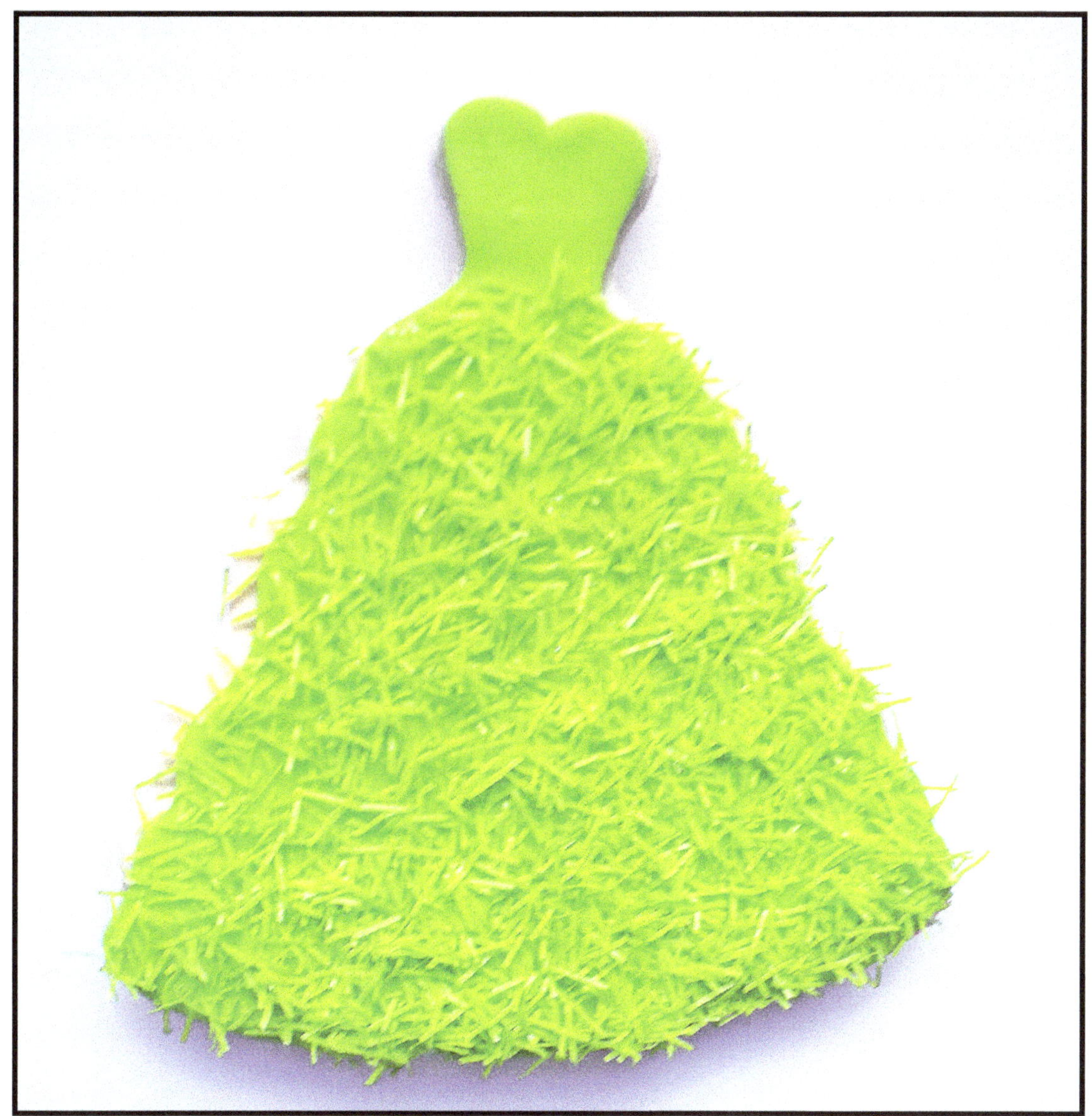

Materials:
- Dress cookie
- 1.0 oz. Fondarific Lime fondant
- Piping gel
- Food safe paint brush

Tools:
- Wedding Dress Outline #3
  (etsy.com, CookieCutterLady)
- Wilton Edible Accents Green
  Wafer Shreds

Suggested cellophane bag size is 6x8 inches to package this dress cookie.

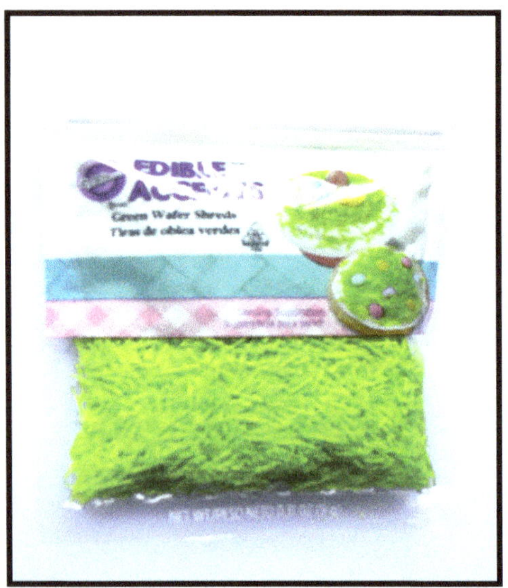 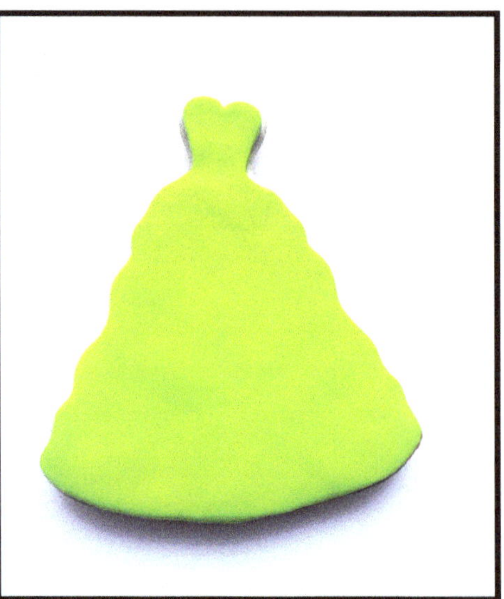 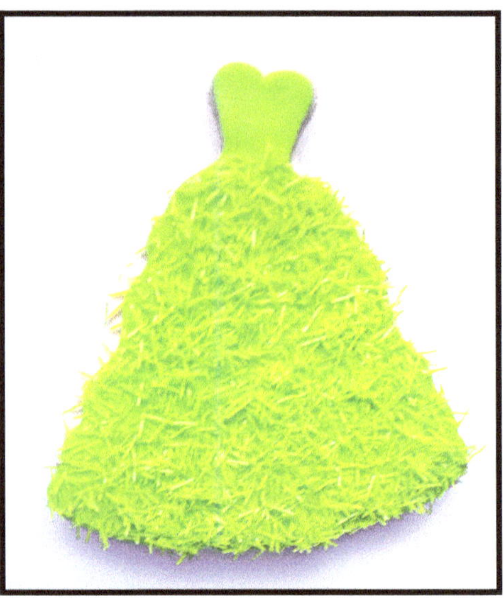

1. This is Wilton's Edible Accents Green Wafer Shreds.

2. Roll out lime fondant. Use the dress cookie cutter to cut out the lime fondant dress. Attach the fondant cut-out to the top of the dress cookie. Paint the entire bottom dress section of the lime fondant with piping gel.

3. Use a bowl to hold the dress cookie with one hand, and use the other hand to sprinkle the entire surface of the fondant dress cut-out. Gently press wafer shreds into fondant to secure. Remove excess.

Coral Rose Dress Cookies

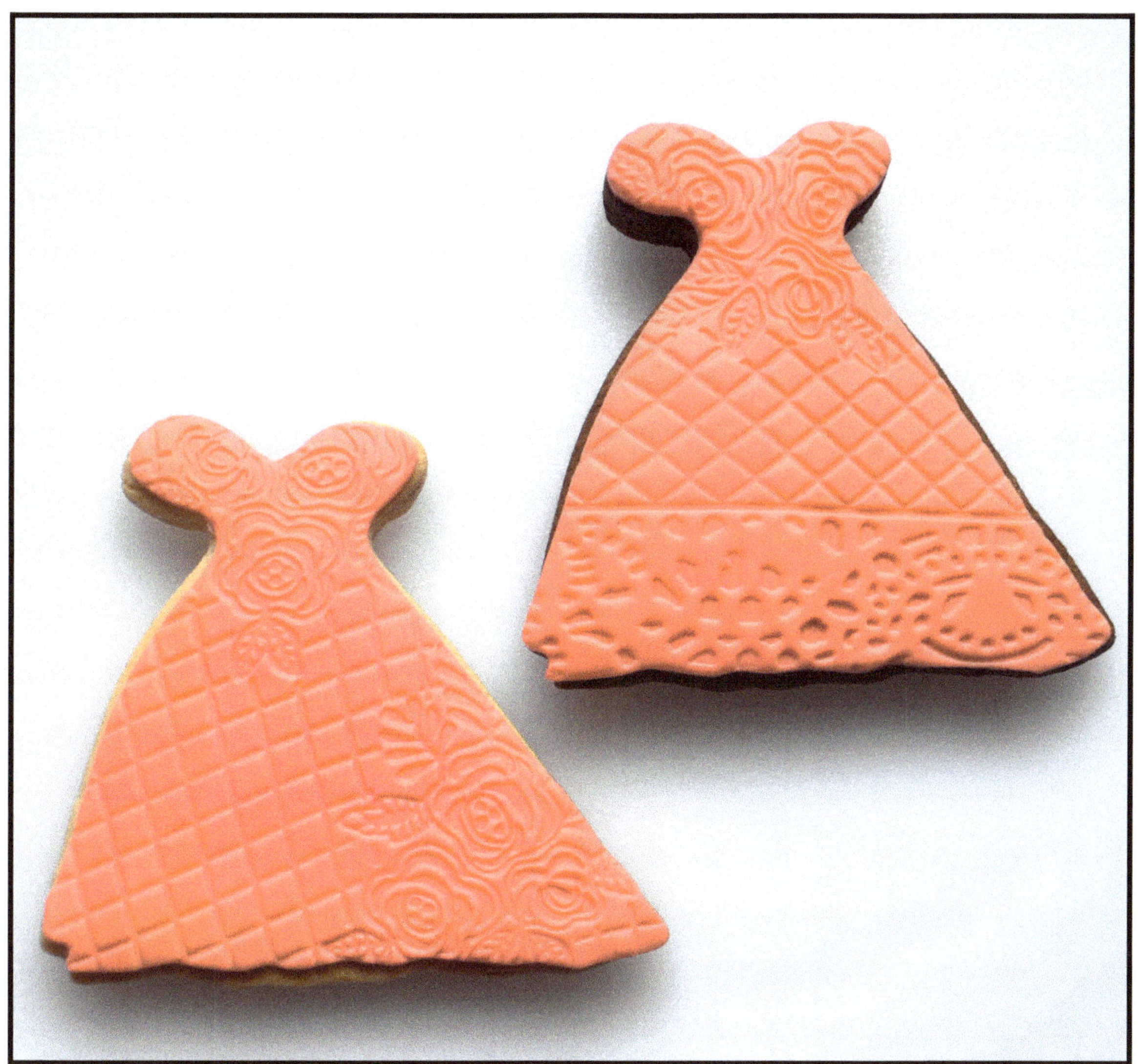

Materials:
- **Two dress cookies**
- **0.8 oz. Fondarific Coral fondant**
- **Piping gel**
- **Food safe paint brush**

Tools:
- **Princess cookie cutter**
- **Wilton Pattern Roller Lace**

Suggested cellophane bag size is 5x7 inches to package these dress cookies.

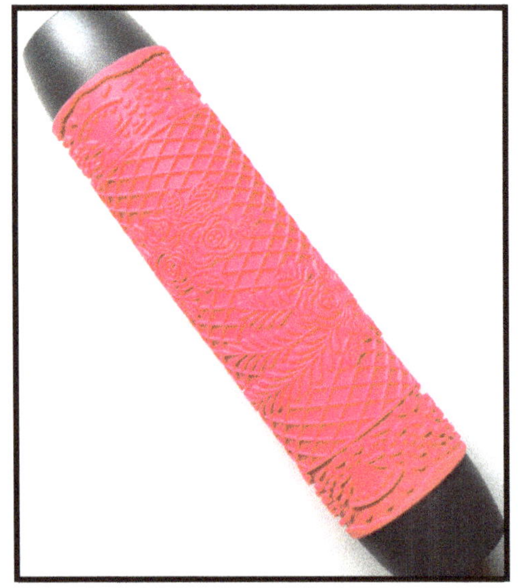

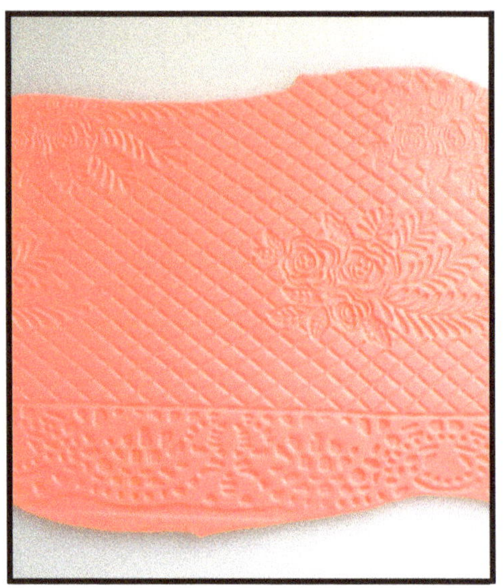

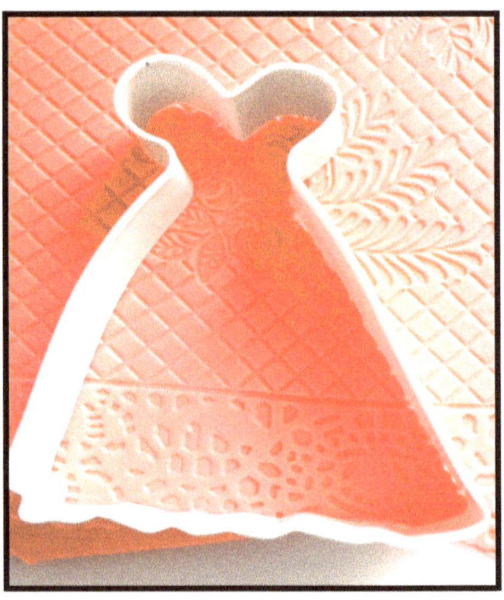

1. This is Wilton's Pattern Roller Lace.

2. Roll out coral fondant. Use the pattern roller to imprint the fondant.

3. Center the dress cookie cutter over the pattern as shown above. Press the dress cookie cutter firmly into the fondant, and then wiggle to release the fondant from the dress cookie cutter.

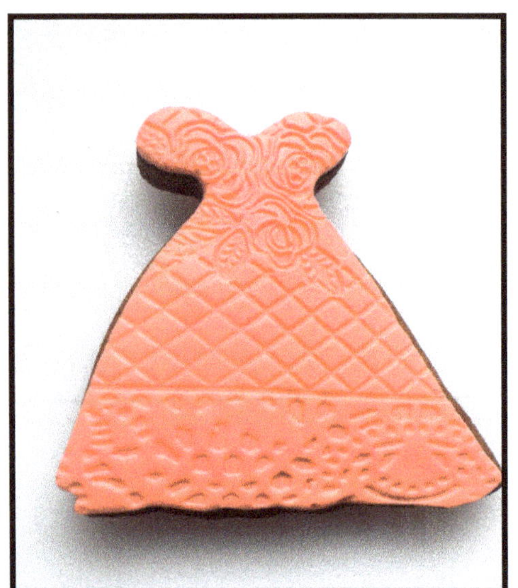

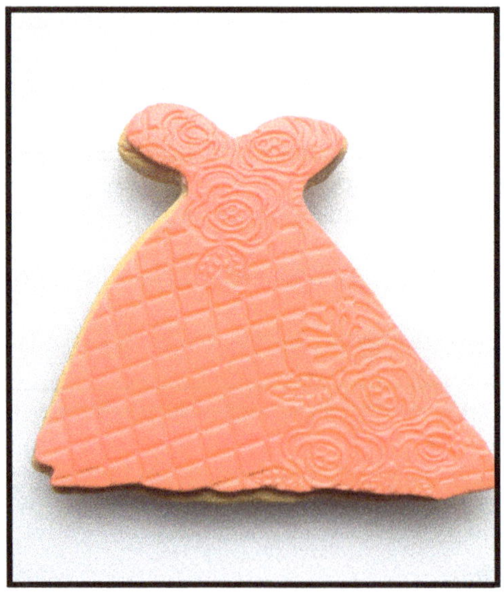

4. This is the first impression design cut-out. Use a paint brush to apply a thin layer of piping gel onto your dress cookie. Apply fondant cut-out to cookie, and gently smooth top.

5. This is the second impression design cut-out. Use a paint brush to apply a thin layer of piping gel onto your dress cookie. Apply fondant cut-out to cookie, and gently smooth top.

Pink Pattern Dress Cookie

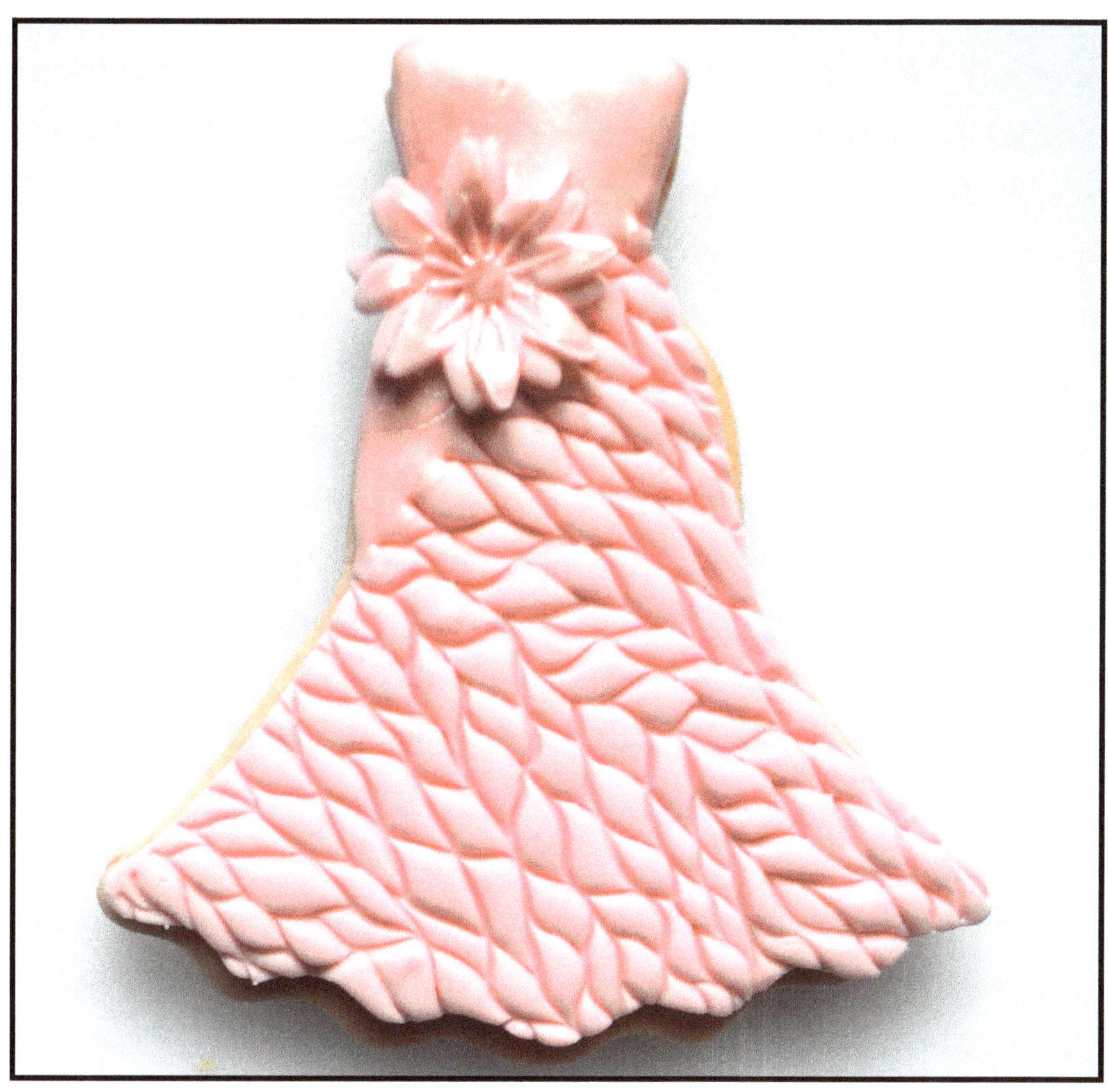

Materials:
- Dress cookie
- 0.7 oz. Fondarific Pink fondant
- Piping gel
- Food safe paint brush
- Lemon extract

Tools:
- LILIAO Wedding Dress Cookie Cutter (amazon.com)
- JOERSH Cake Fondant Embossing Mould 6 Pack Fondant Embosser Set (Waves) (amazon.com)
- Crystal Colors Fairy Pink Food Color
- Medium daisy plunger cutter
- Tip 1E

Suggested cellophane bag size is 5x7 inches to package this dress cookie.

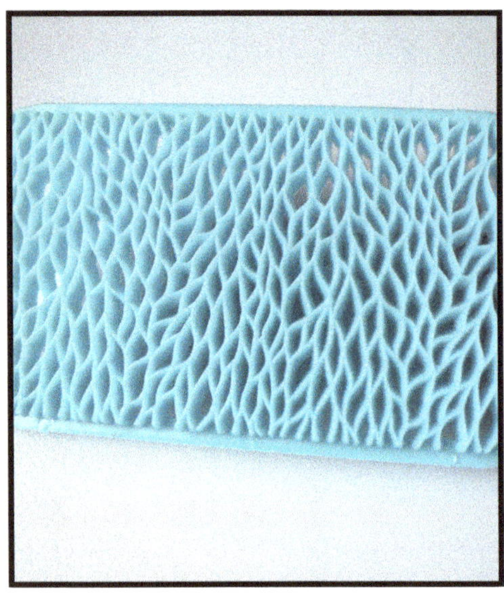 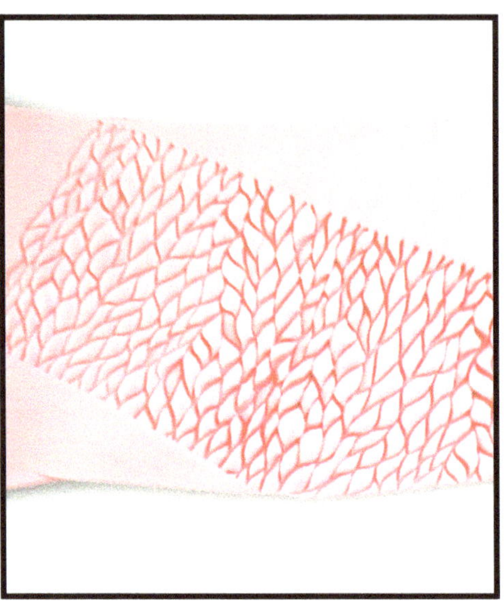 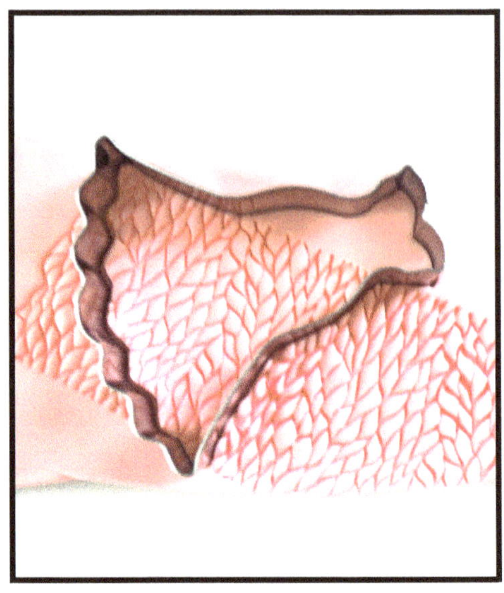

1. I call this tool the wave embosser.

2. Roll out pink fondant. Use the wave embosser to imprint the pink fondant.

3. Place the dress cookie cutter over the fondant design as shown above. Press the dress cookie cutter firmly into the fondant, and then wiggle to release the fondant from the dress cookie cutter. Use a paint brush to apply a thin layer of piping gel onto your dress cookie. Apply fondant cut-out to cookie, and gently smooth top.

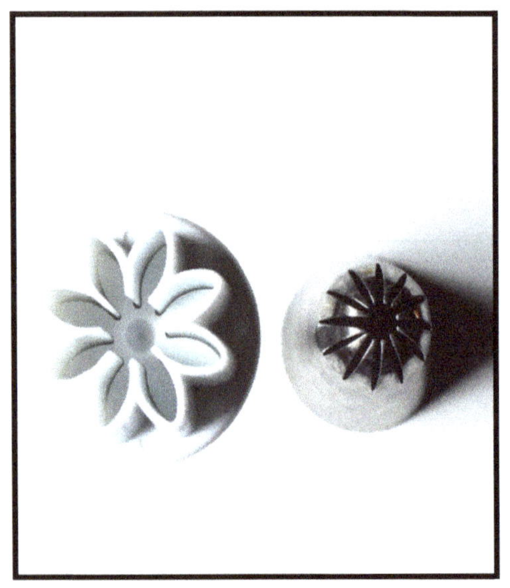 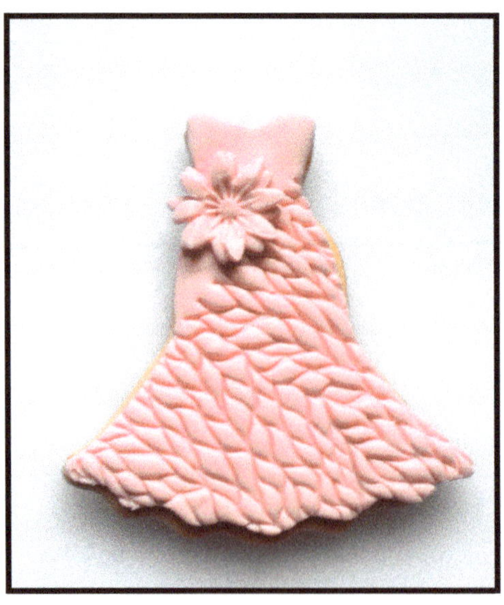 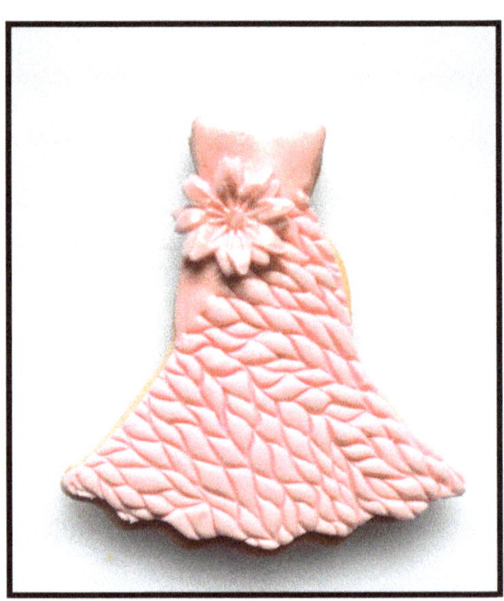

4. This is the large daisy plunger cutter and tip 1E. Cut out two daisy flowers.

5. Use a dab of piping gel on the back of the daisy flowers and attach to the waist as shown above. Gently press into the center of the daisy flower with icing Tip 1E. Remove the icing tip.

6. Make a paste of a little fairy pink food color dust and a drop of the lemon extract. Use a food safe paint brush and paint the bodice area and the daisy flowers with this paint. Let dry.

Hot Pink & Black Dress Cookie

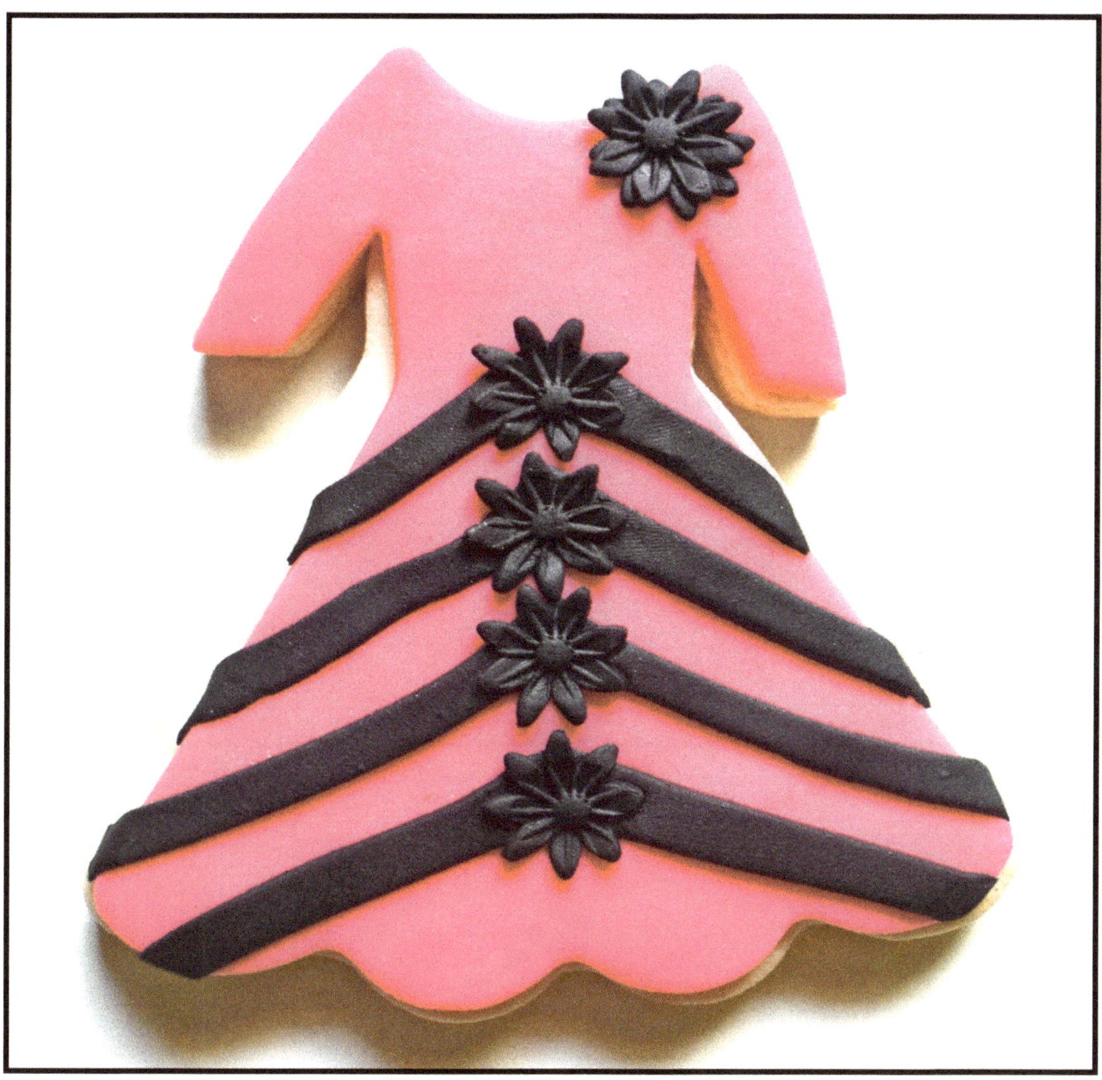

<table>
<tr><td>

Materials:
- Dress cookie
- 1.2 oz. Fondarific Hot Pink fondant
- 0.3 oz. Fondarific Black fondant
- Piping gel
- Food safe paint brush
- Pizza cutter or Xacto knife

</td><td>

Tools:
- The Diane Dress Cookie Cutter (etsy.com, Sinful Cutters)
- Medium daisy plunger cutter
- Tip 1E

</td></tr>
</table>

Suggested cellophane bag size is 5x7 inches to package this dress cookie.

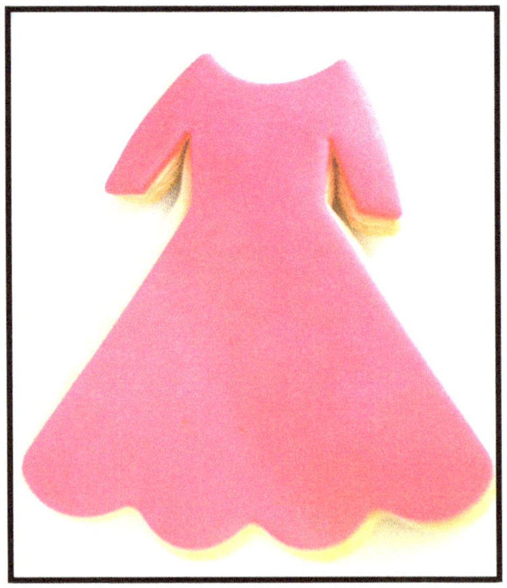 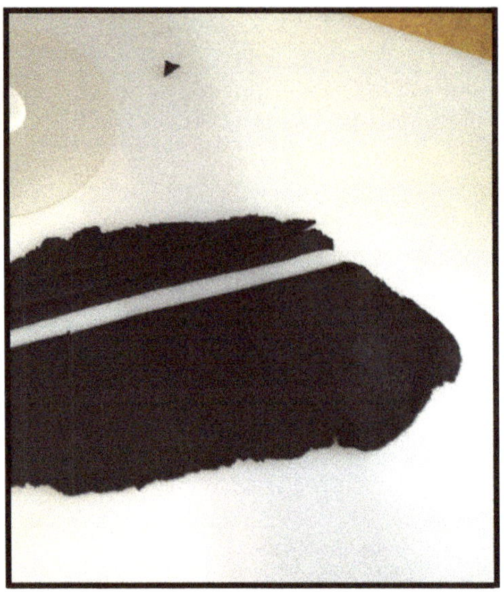 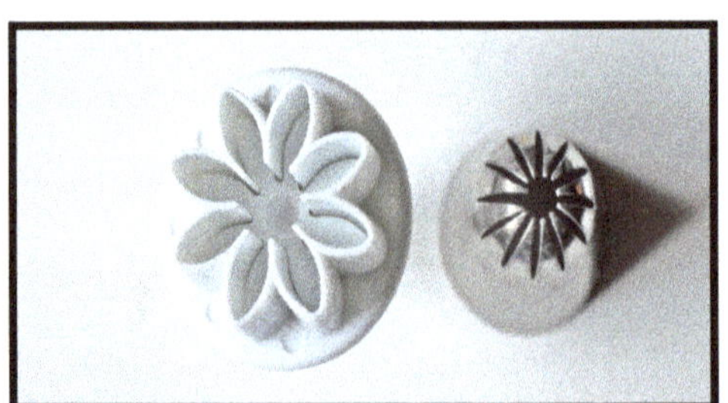 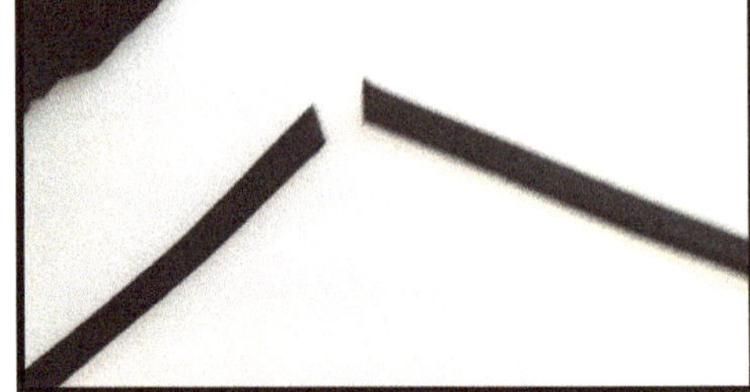

1. Roll out hot pink fondant. Use the dress cookie cutter to cut out the hot pink fondant dress. Use a paint brush to apply a thin layer of piping gel onto your dress cookie. Apply fondant cut-out to cookie, and gently smooth top. Set aside.

2. Roll out black fondant. Cut eight thin even strips.

3. The top picture shows the medium daisy plunger cutter and icing tip 1E. The bottom picture shows the thickness of the strips. Cut the ends as shown.

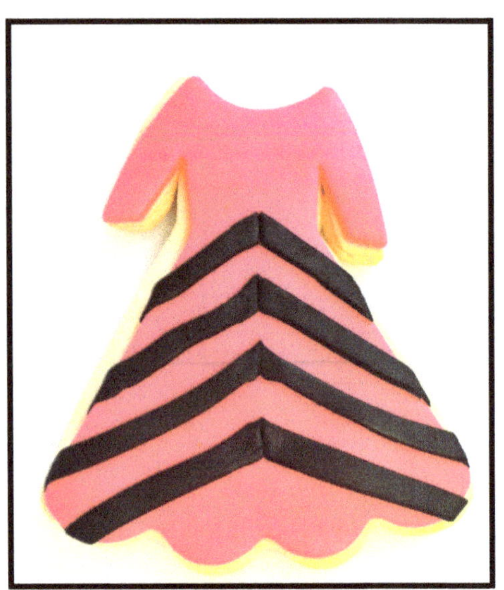 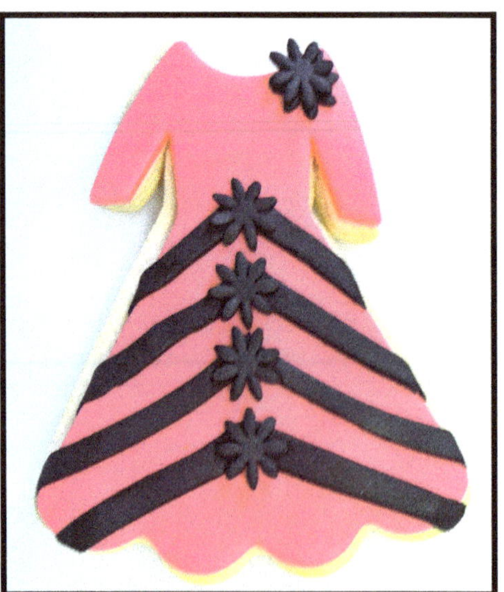 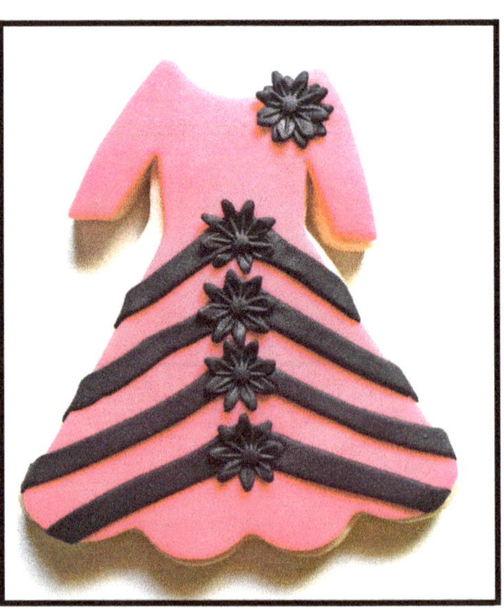

4. Apply the black fondant strips to the dress as shown, forming a point in the center of the dress.

5. Punch out six daisy fondant cut-outs. Attach at the seams of the strips, and then attach two daisy cut-outs to the top right side of the dress cookie as shown. Gently press in to secure to fondant.

6. Use icing tip 1E to imprint the centers of the black daisy fondant cut-outs.

Green Lace Dress Cookie

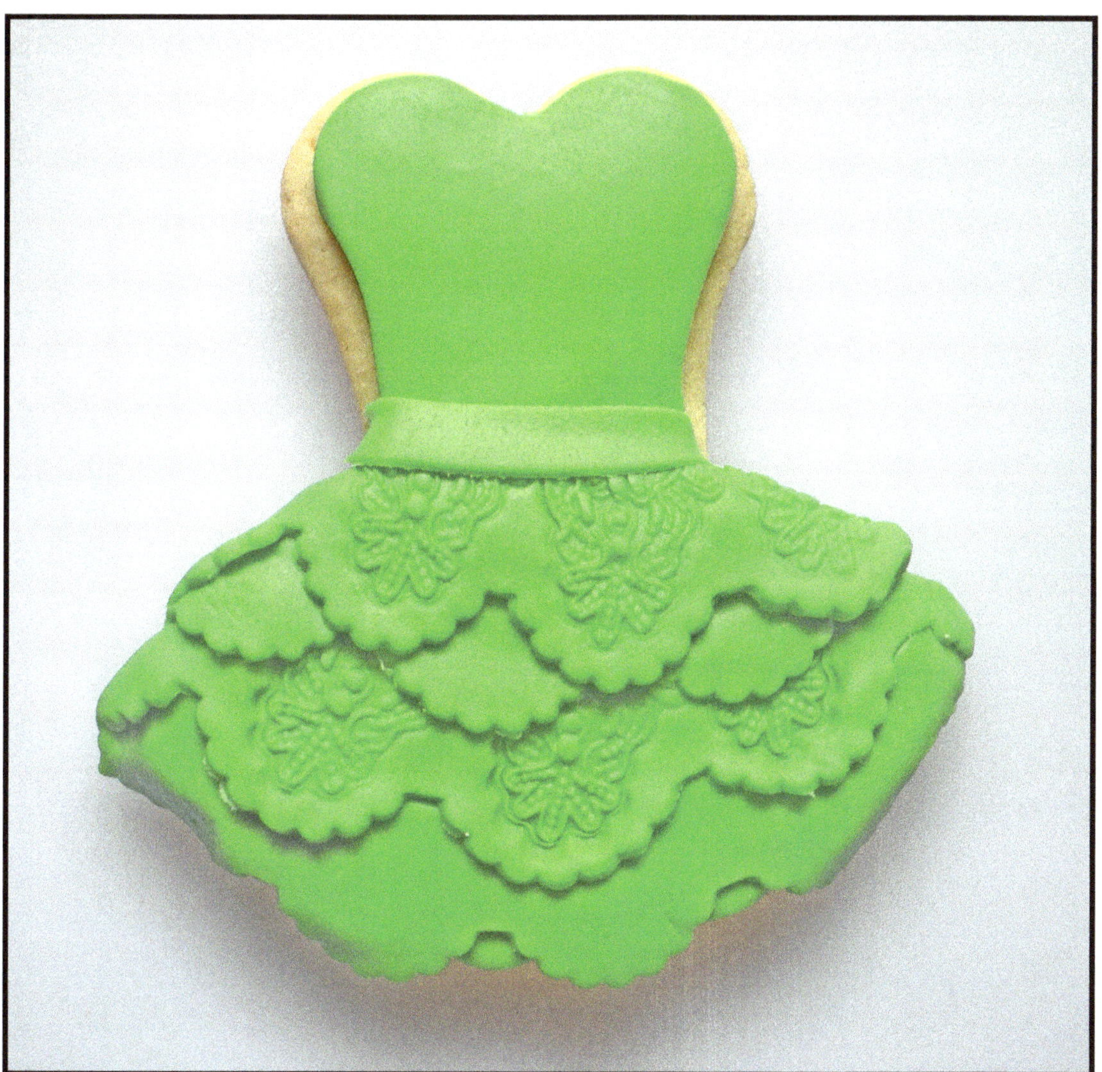

Materials:
- Dress cookie
- 1.2 oz. Fondarific Green fondant
- Piping gel
- Food safe paint brush
- Pizza cutter or Xacto knife

Tools:
- Party Dress Cookie Cutter (etsy.com, Sinful Cutters)
- Medium lace plunger cutter (hobbylobby.com)
- Wilton-Easy-Blooms-Flower-Cut-Outs

Suggested cellophane bag size is 4x6 inches to package this dress cookie.

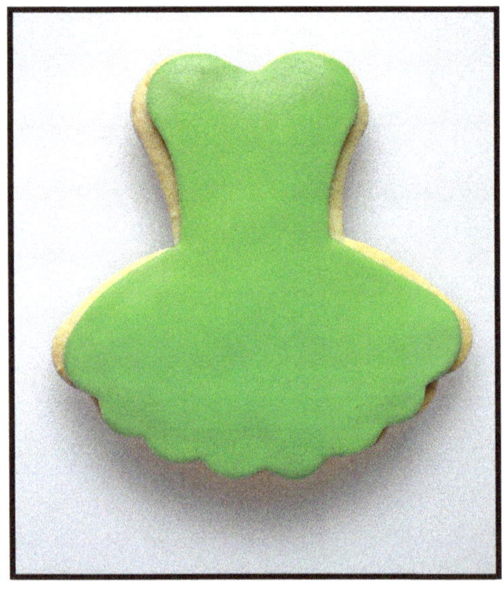

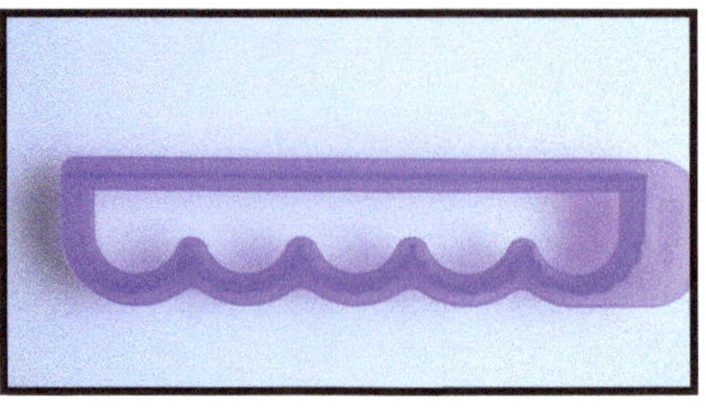

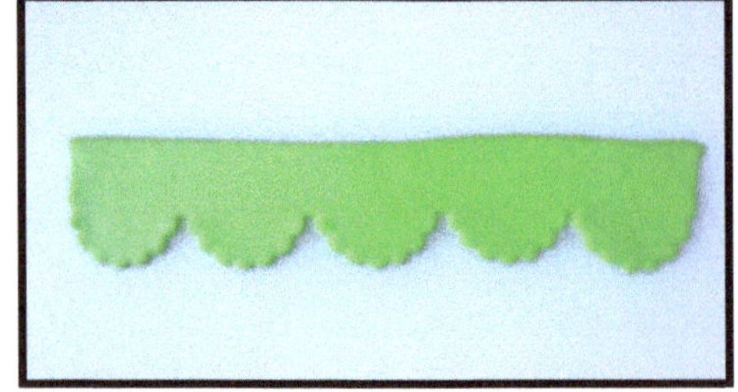

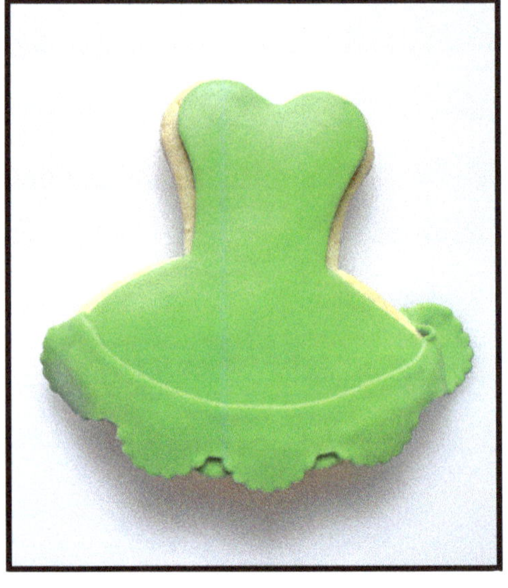

1. Roll out green fondant. Use the dress cookie cutter to cut out the green fondant dress. Use a paint brush to apply a thin layer of piping gel onto your dress cookie. Apply fondant cut-out to cookie, and gently smooth top. Set aside.

2. The top tool is Wilton's Easy Blooms Flower Cut-Outs. The bottom is the fondant cut-out. Cut out three green fondant cut-outs.

3. Attach the fondant cut-out to the bottom of the dress as shown.

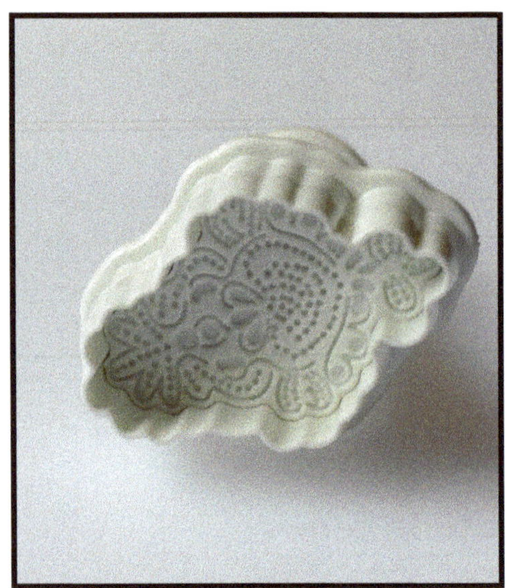

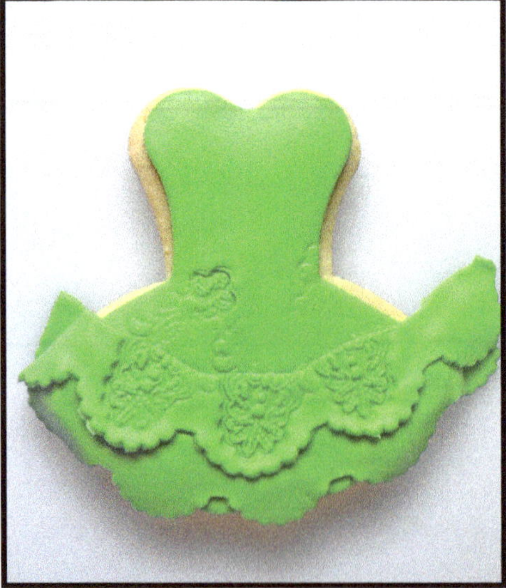

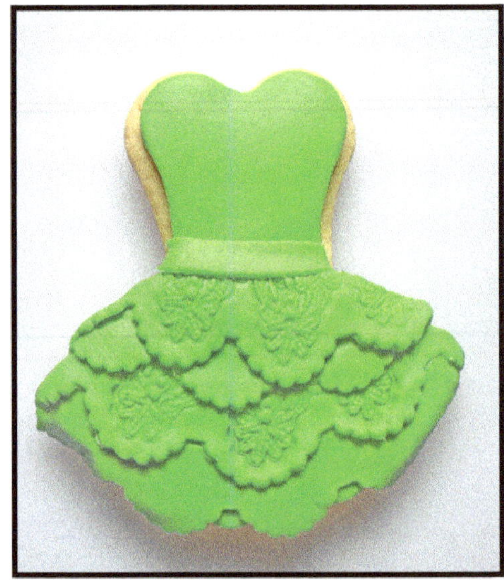

4. This is the medium lace plunger cutter. When you depress the plunger and hold it, you can imprint the fondant without cutting it. Imprint the fondant on two of the green fondant cut-outs as shown.

5. Apply the green lace fondant cut-out as shown. Repeat with a plain green lace fondant cut-out, and then another lace fondant cut-out. Trim the excess fondant from the left and right sides with an Xacto knife following the edge of the fondant dress skirt.

6. Cut a strip of fondant to place at the waist, and trim excess fondant with an Xacto knife.

Navy Peach Dress Cookie

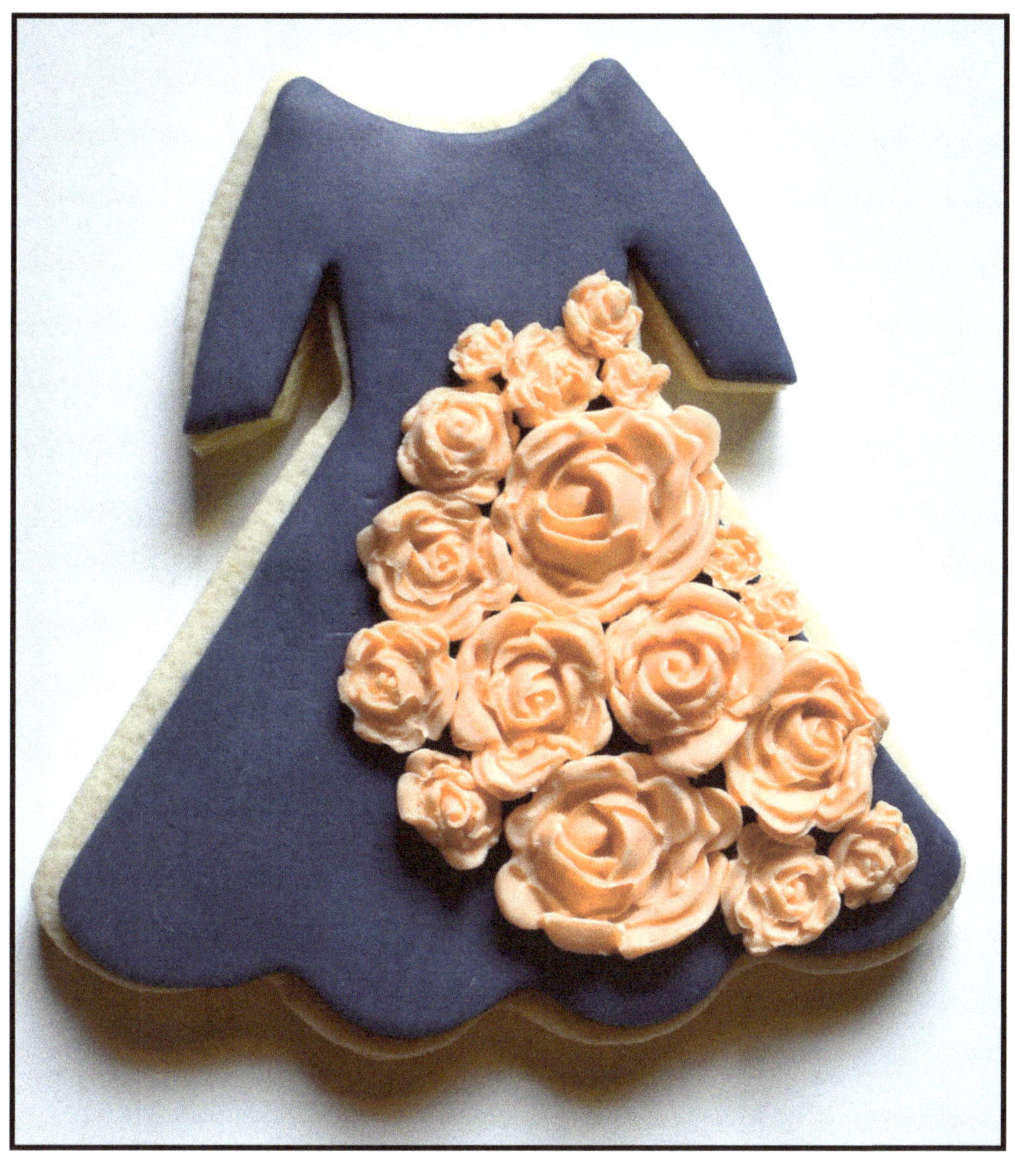

Materials:
- **Dress cookie**
- **1.1 oz. Fondarific Navy fondant**
- **0.3 oz. peach fondant**
- **Piping gel**
- **Food safe paint brush**

Tools:
- **The Diane Dress Cookie Cutter (etsy.com, Sinful Cutters)**
- **Rose silicone molds**

Suggested cellophane bag size is 5x7 inches to package this dress cookie.

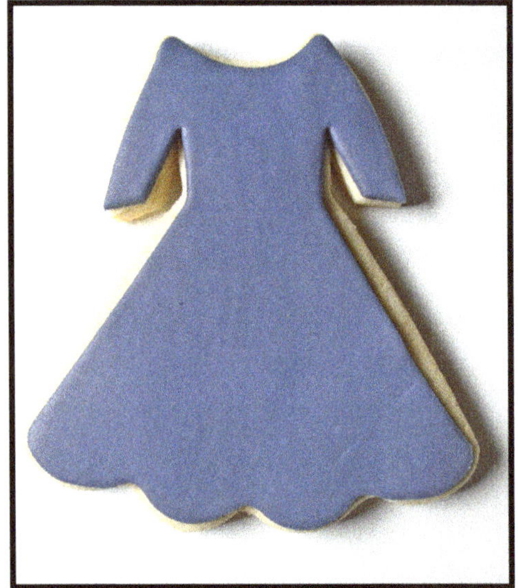

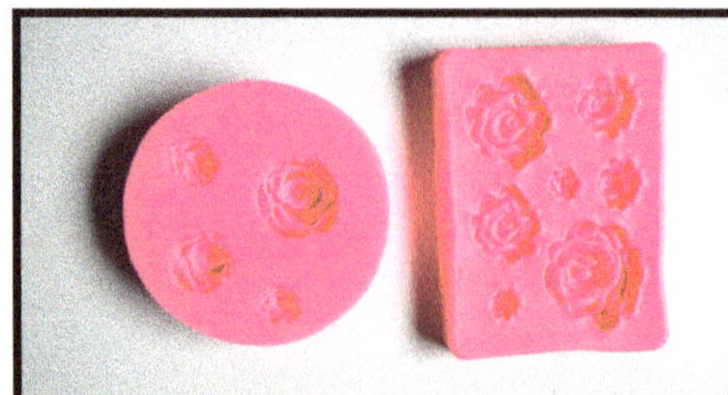

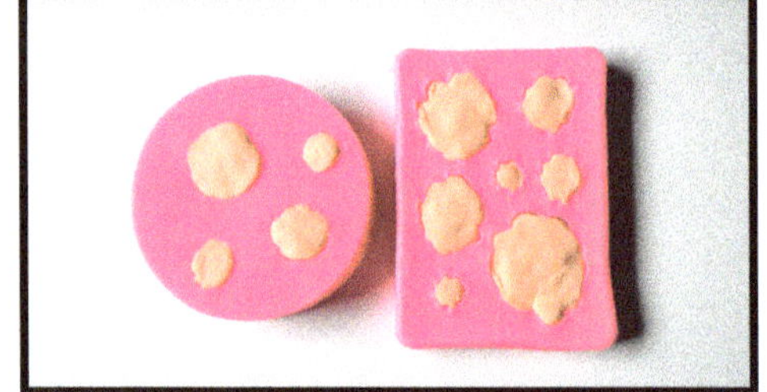

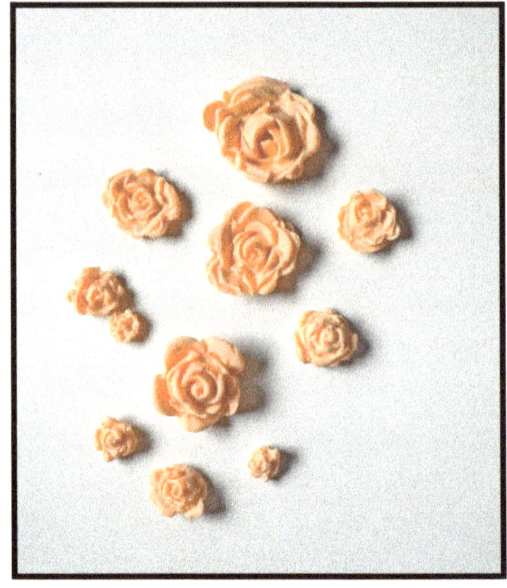

1. Roll out navy fondant. Use the dress cookie cutter to cut out the navy fondant dress. Use a paint brush to apply a thin layer of piping gel onto your dress cookie. Apply fondant cut-out to cookie, and gently smooth top. Set aside.

2. Press peach fondant into the cavities of the rose silicone molds as shown. Refrigerate until firm. Remove roses from the silicone molds.

3. These are some of the fondant roses. Make two sets of roses from the second rose silicone mold to complete this dress cookie design.

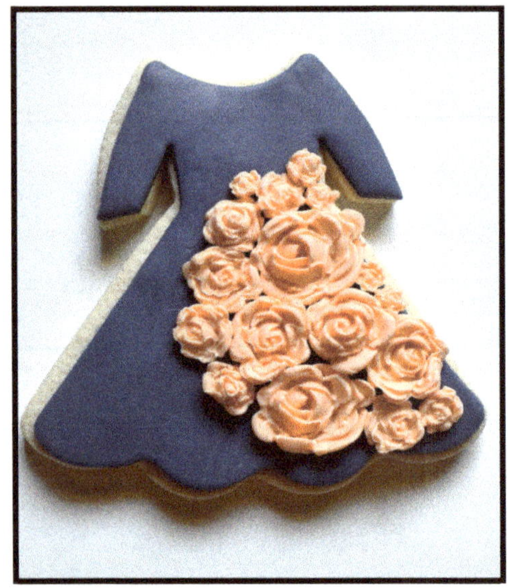

4. Use a dab of piping gel on the back of the fondant roses and attach the fondant roses to the dress cookie as shown.

Black Lace Dress Cookie

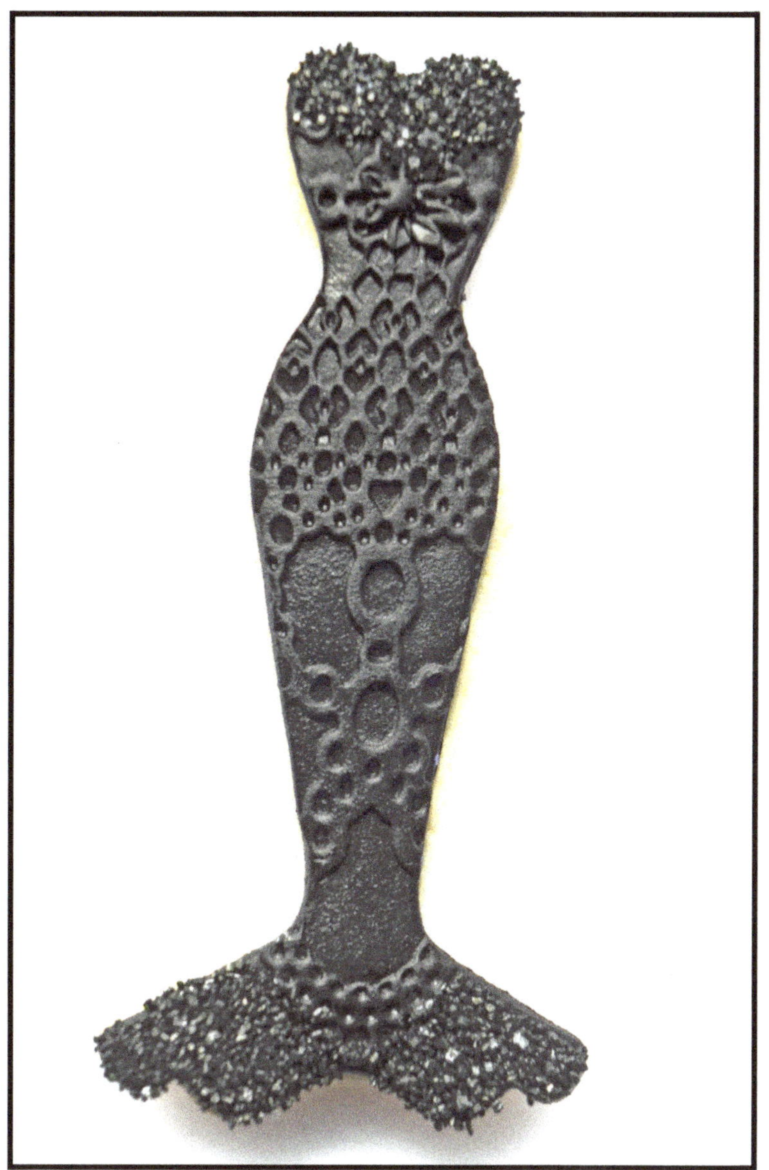

Materials:
- Dress cookie
- 0.31 oz. Fondarific Black fondant
- Piping gel
- Food safe paint brush

Tools:
- Wedding Dress Cookie Cutter (etsy.com, BakersToolsStore)
- Sunny Side Up Bakery Chantilly Lace Silicone Mold
- Black sanding sugar

Suggested cellophane bag size is 3x8 inches to package this dress cookie.

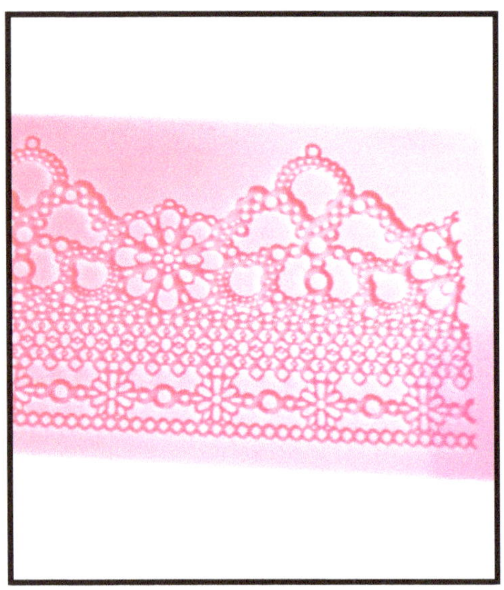

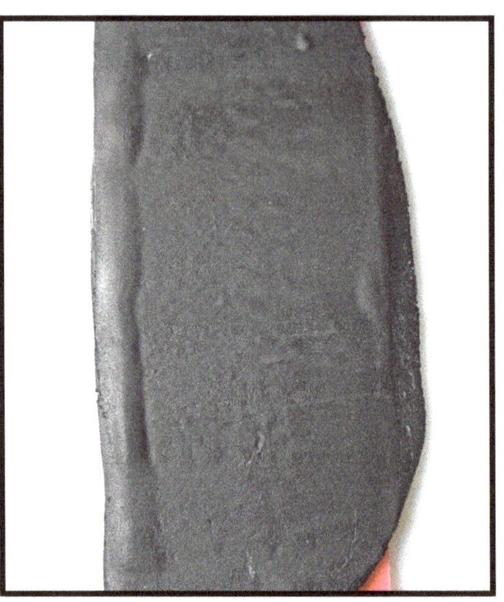

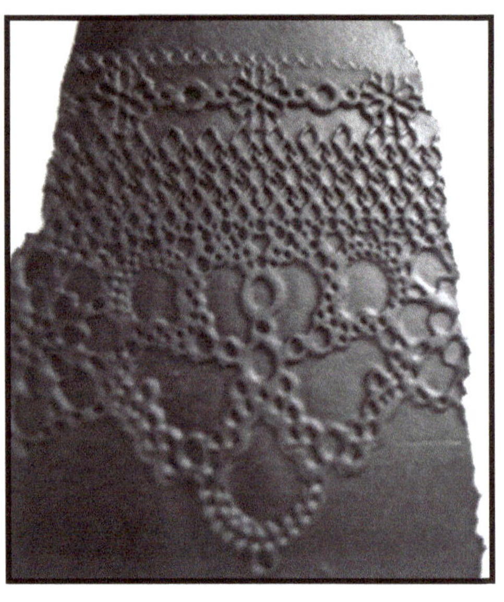

1. This is the Chantilly lace silicone mold.

2. Roll out black fondant. Lay black fondant on top of Chantilly Lace silicone mold. Use a rolling pin to roll over the black fondant using even pressure. Turn fondant over.

3. This is what the imprinted fondant looks like.

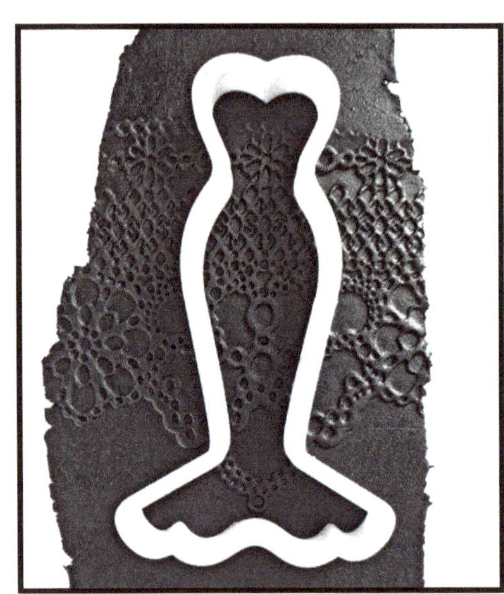

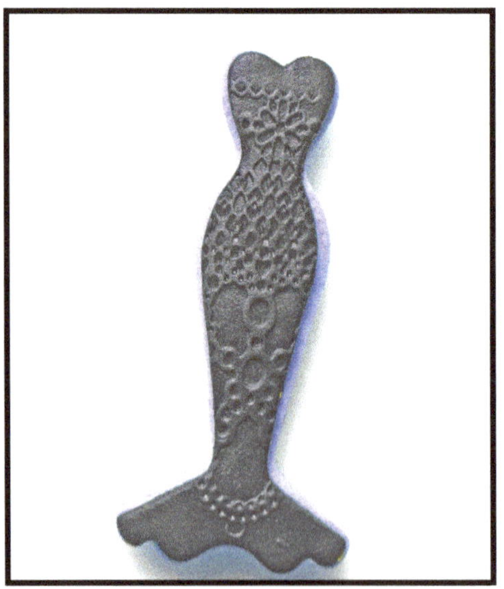

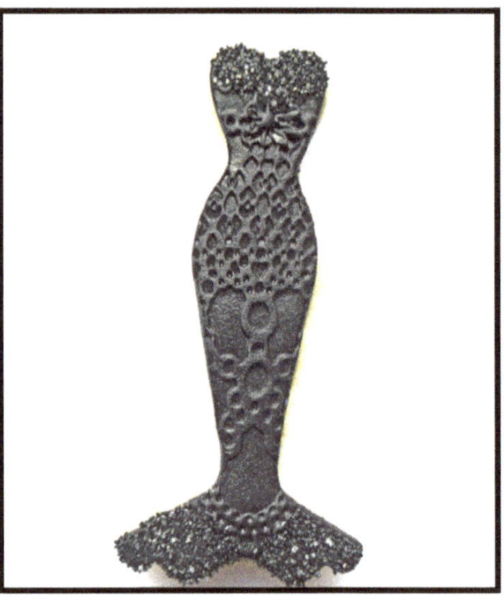

4. Center the dress cookie cutter over the design area as shown making sure that the bottom area is centered. Press the dress cookie cutter firmly into the fondant, and then wiggle to release the fondant from the dress cookie cutter.

5. Use a paint brush to apply a thin layer of piping gel onto your dress cookie. Apply fondant cut-out to cookie, and gently smooth top.

6. Paint the top and the bottom plain black fondant sections with piping gel, and then sprinkle black sanding sugar over both sections. Remove excess sugar.

Blue Hearts Dress Cookie

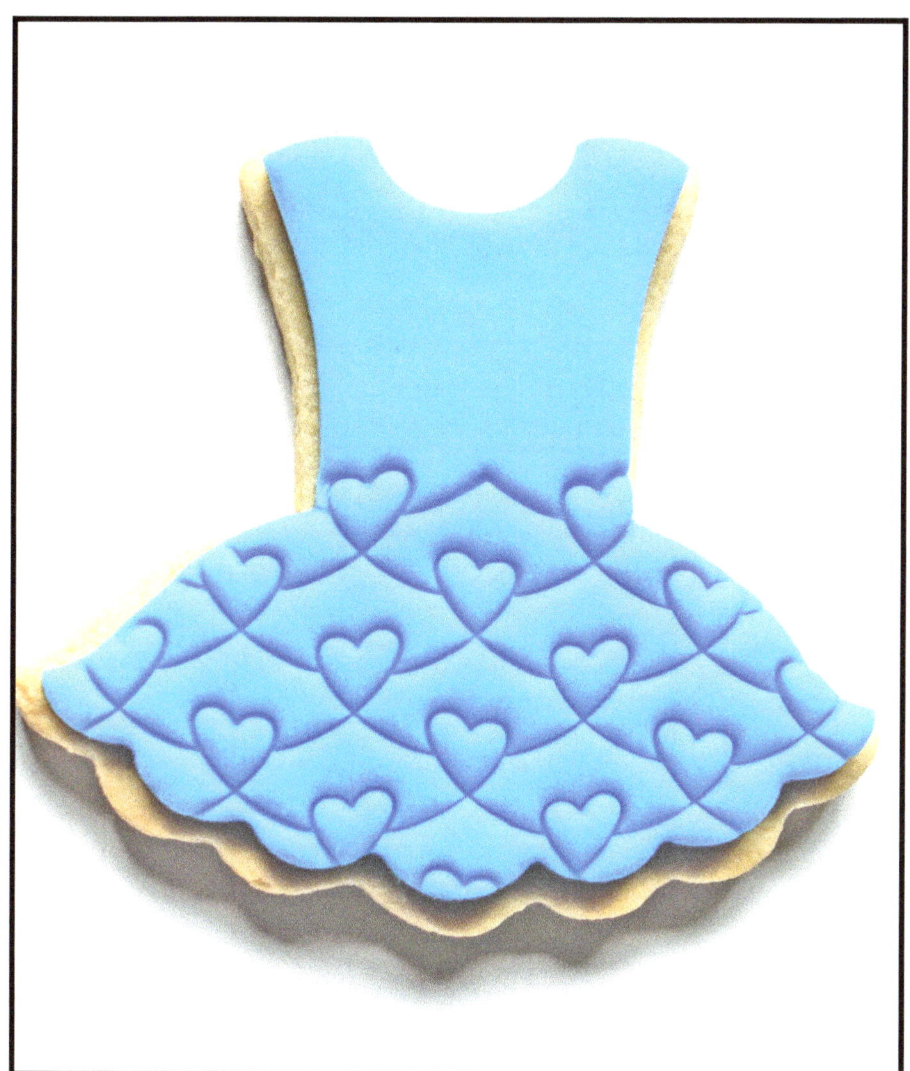

Materials:
- Dress cookie
- 0.6 oz. Fondarific Blue fondant
- Piping gel
- Food safe paint brush

Tools:
- Tutu and Dress Cookie Cutter (etsy.com, WhiskedAwayCutters)
- JOERSH Cake Fondant Embossing Mould 6 Pack Fondant Embosser Set (Hearts) (amazon.com)

Suggested cellophane bag size is 4x6 inches to package this dress cookie.

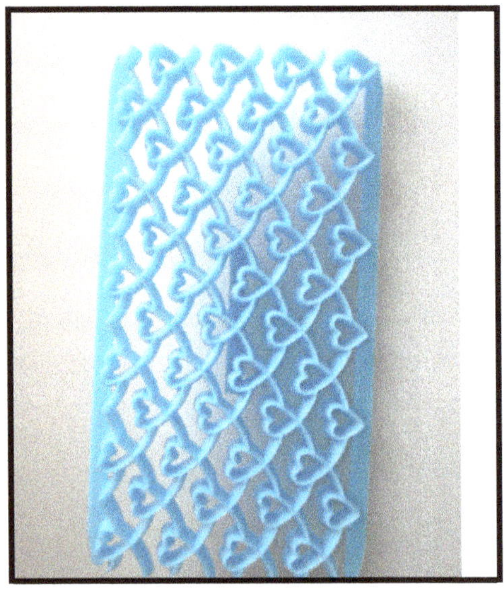

1. This is the heart embosser.

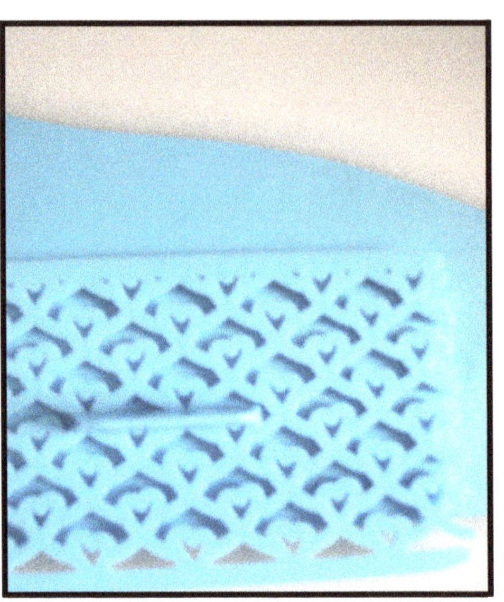

2. Roll out blue fondant. Use the heart embosser to imprint the blue fondant leaving a plain fondant area above.

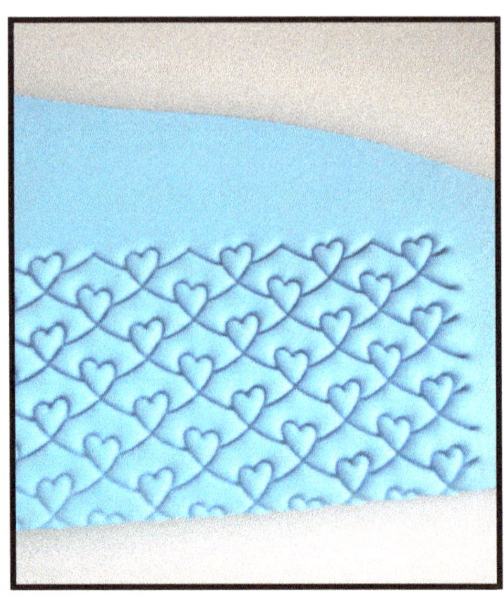

3. This is what the embossed fondant looks like.

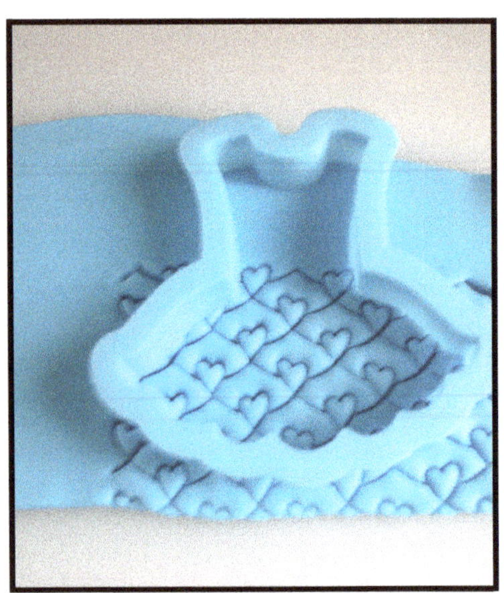

4. Place the dress cookie cutter over the fondant design as shown above. Press the dress cookie cutter firmly into the fondant, and then wiggle to release the fondant from the dress cookie cutter.

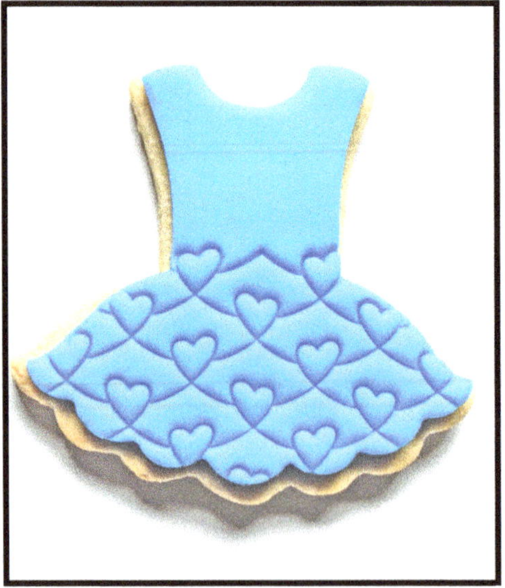

5. Use a paint brush to apply a thin layer of piping gel onto your dress cookie. Apply fondant cut-out to cookie, and gently smooth top.

Lavender Pattern Dress Cookie

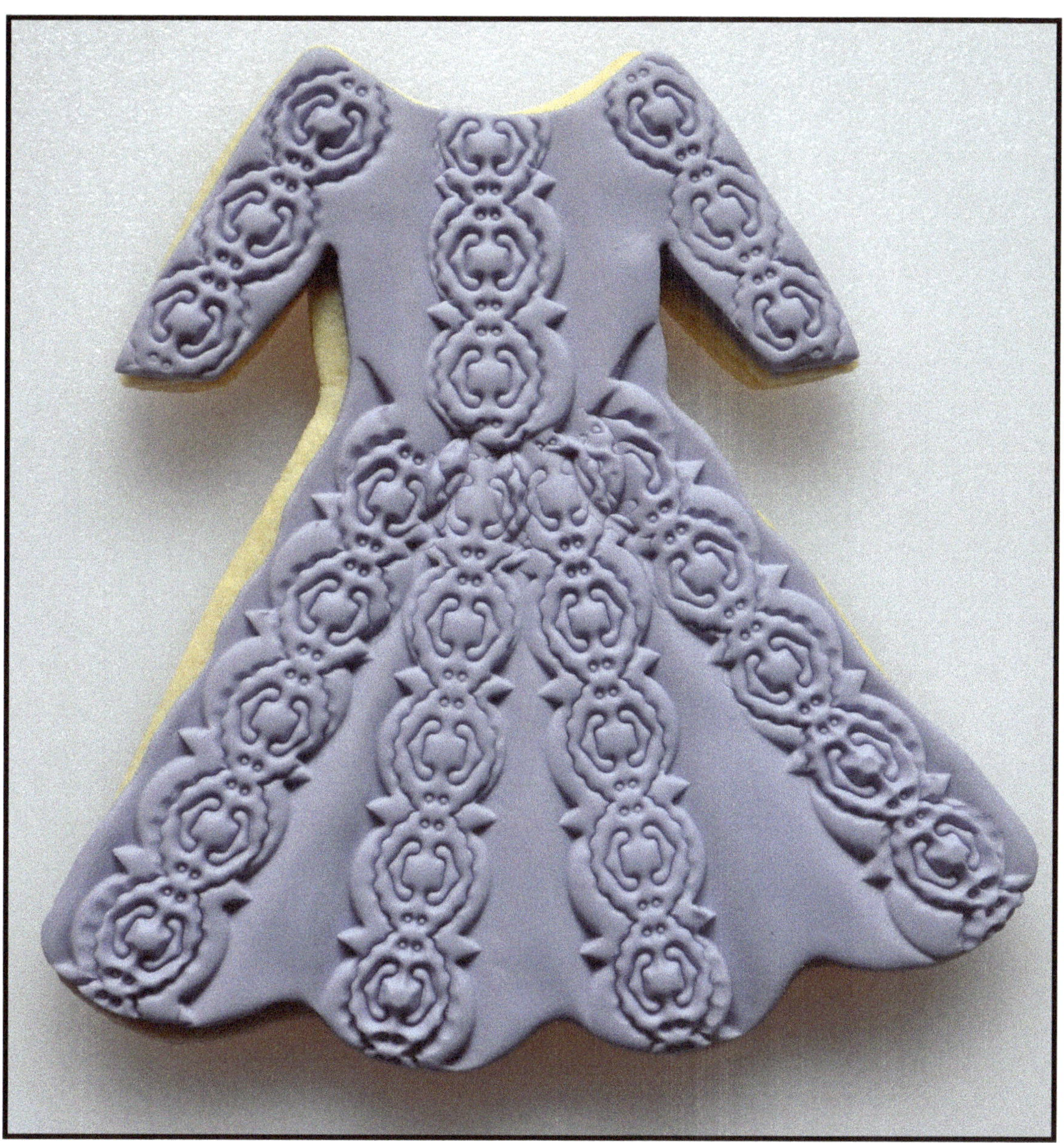

Materials:
- Dress cookie
- 1.2 oz. lavender fondant
- Piping gel
- Food safe paint brush

Tools:
- The Diane Dress Cookie Cutter (etsy.com, Sinful Cutters)
- Lace Strip Patchwork Cutter
- Cake comb

Suggested cellophane bag size is 5x7 inches to package this dress cookie.

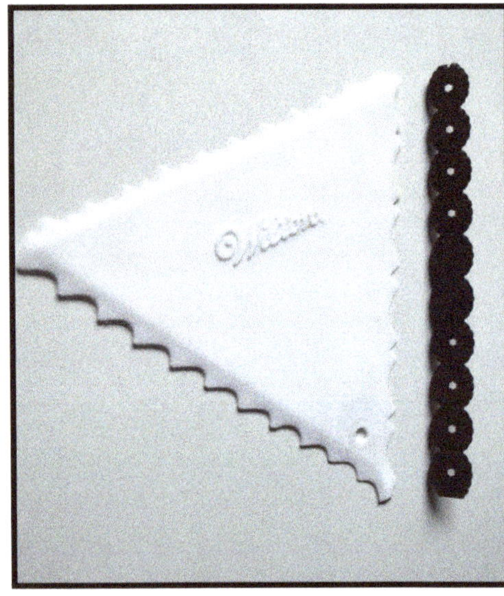 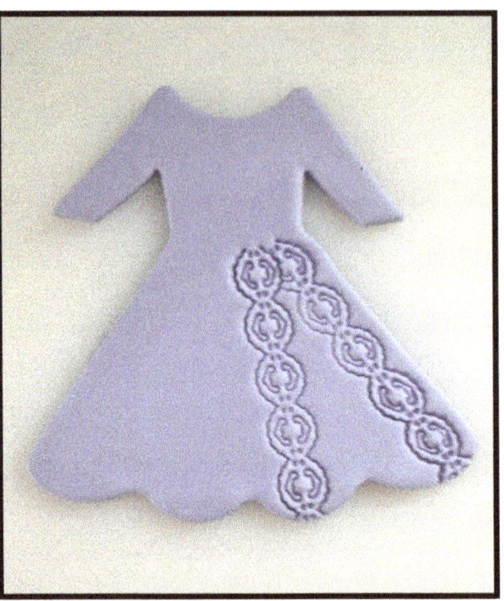 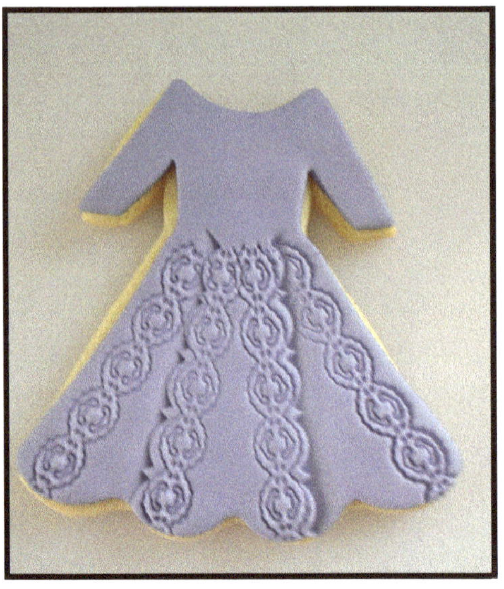

1. This is a picture of the lace strip tool and cake comb. The cake comb edge next to the lace strip tool is the side used on this dress cookie. Practice imprinting fondant with both tools before designing your dress cookie.

2. Roll out lavender fondant. Use the dress cookie cutter to cut out the lavender fondant dress. Use the lace strip to imprint the fondant as shown above. Use a bench scraper to lift the fondant cut-out. Set aside.

3. Use a paint brush to apply a thin layer of piping gel onto your dress cookie. Apply fondant cut-out to cookie, and gently smooth top. Continue to imprint the fondant with the lace strip as shown. Tilt the cake comb to the side, and then imprint the fondant as shown.

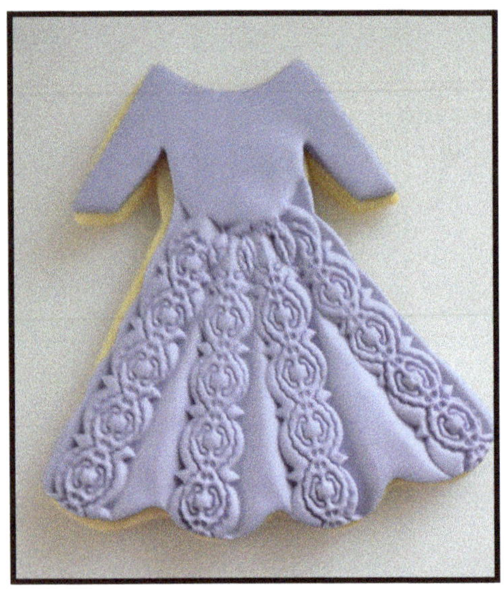 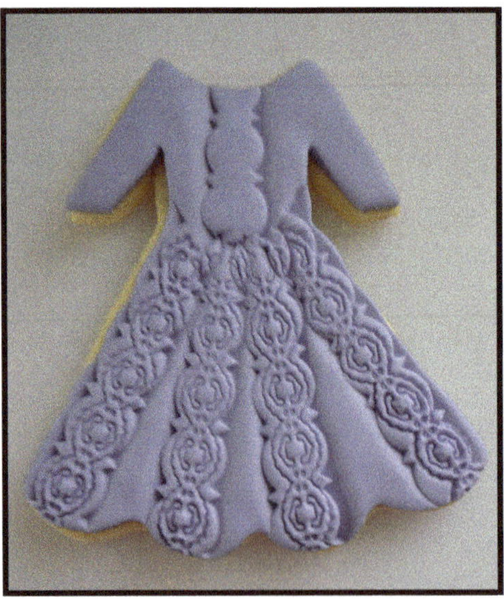 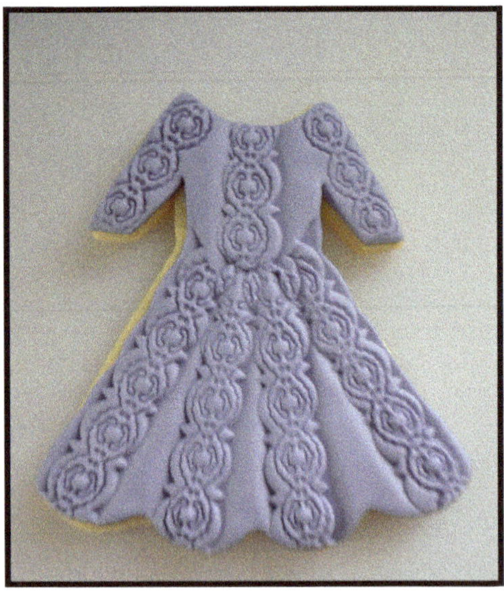

4. Continue to imprint the dress section with the cake comb as shown above.

5. Use the cake comb to make two impressions into the bodice top as shown above.

6. Press the lace tool into the center of the bodice design and the sleeves as shown above.

Peach Smock Dress Cookie

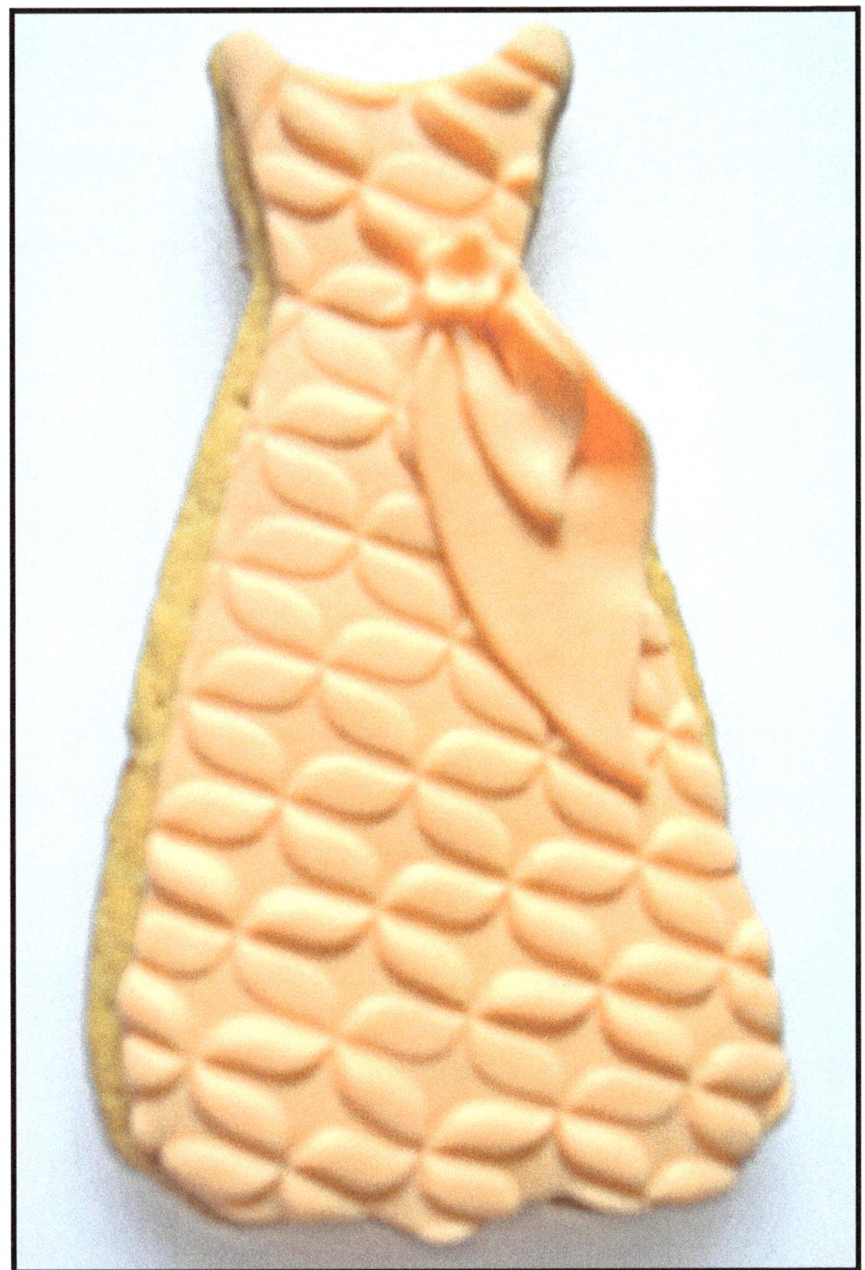

<table>
<tr><td>

Materials:
- Dress cookie
- 0.6 oz. peach fondant
- Piping gel
- Food safe paint brush
- Knife

</td><td>

Tools:
- Dress Cookie Cutter (flourbox.com)
- Patchwork Cutters Smocking Embosser
- Small and large leaf cutter
- Small blossom plunger cutter

</td></tr>
</table>

Suggested cellophane bag size is 4x6 inches to package this dress cookie.

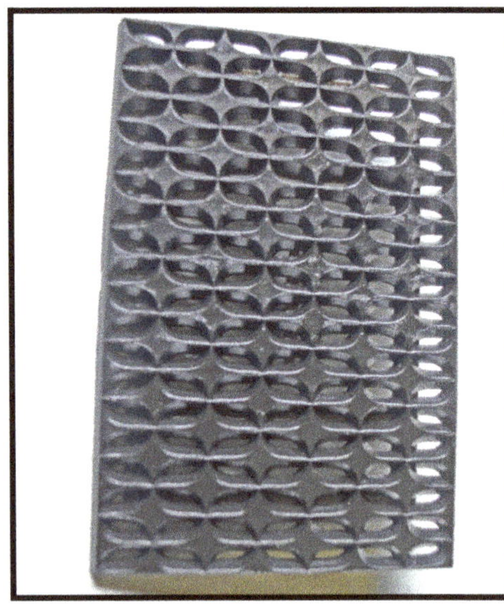

1. This is the smocking embosser.

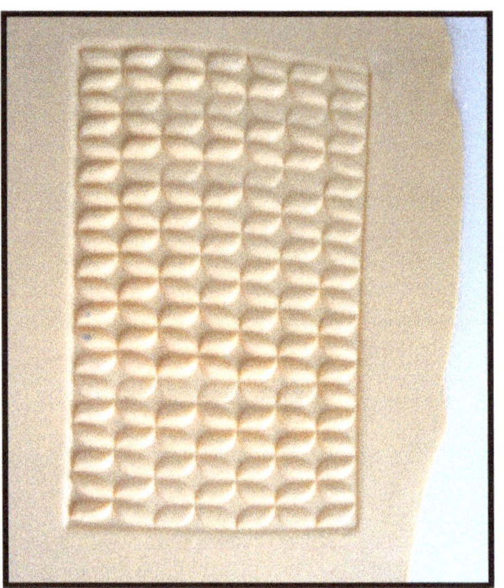

2. Roll out the peach fondant, and then use the smocking embosser to imprint the fondant.

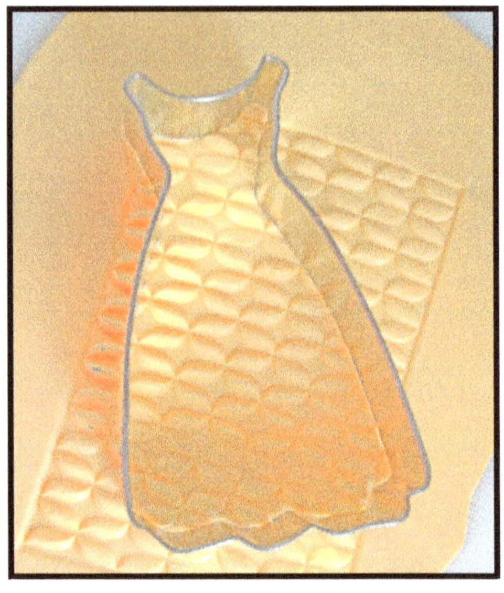

3. Place the dress cookie cutter over the fondant design as shown above. Press the dress cookie cutter firmly into the fondant, and then wiggle to release the fondant from the dress cookie cutter.

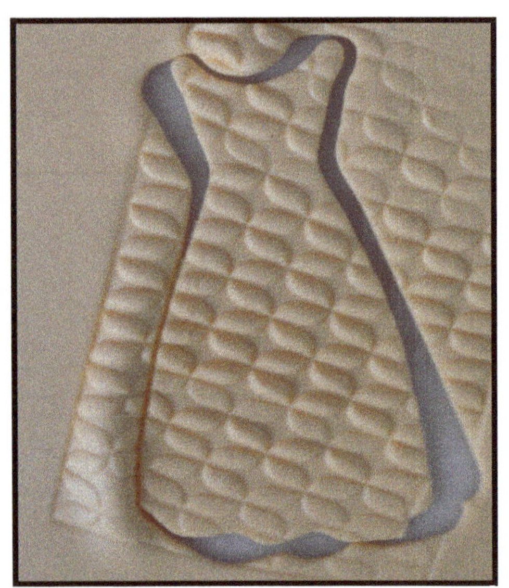

4. This is what the fondant cut-out looks like.

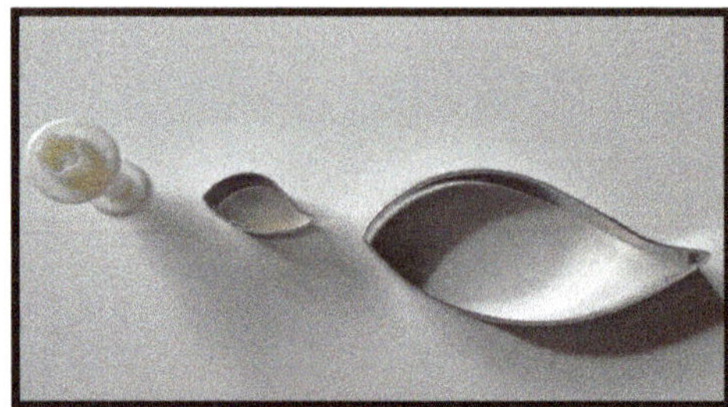

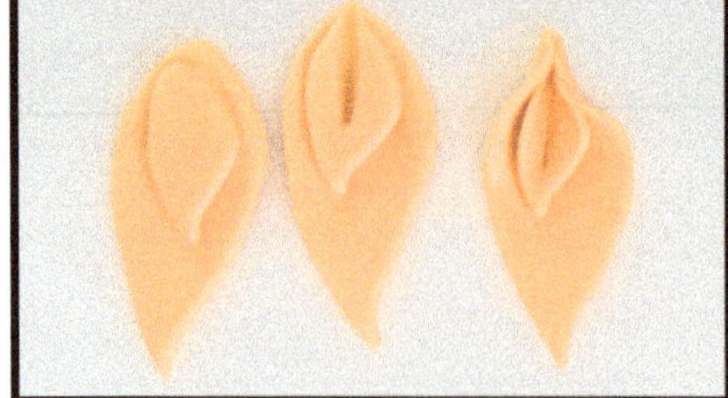

5. The top picture shows the small blossom plunger cutter and the leaf cutters used to cut out the fondant. The bottom picture shows the instructions. Cut out one large and one small fondant leaf. Use the back of a knife to imprint the small leaf. Pinch that edge together and press down.

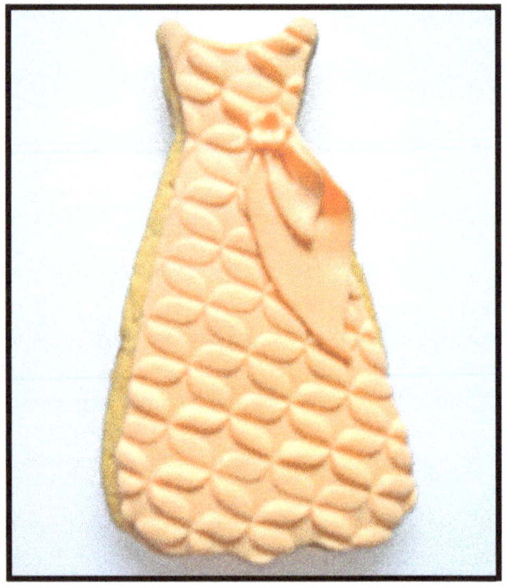

6. Use a paint brush to apply a thin layer of piping gel onto your dress cookie. Apply fondant cut-out to cookie, and gently smooth top. Attach leaves to dress cookie as shown. Cut one small fondant blossom and attach to top of leaf.

Purple Roses Dress Cookie

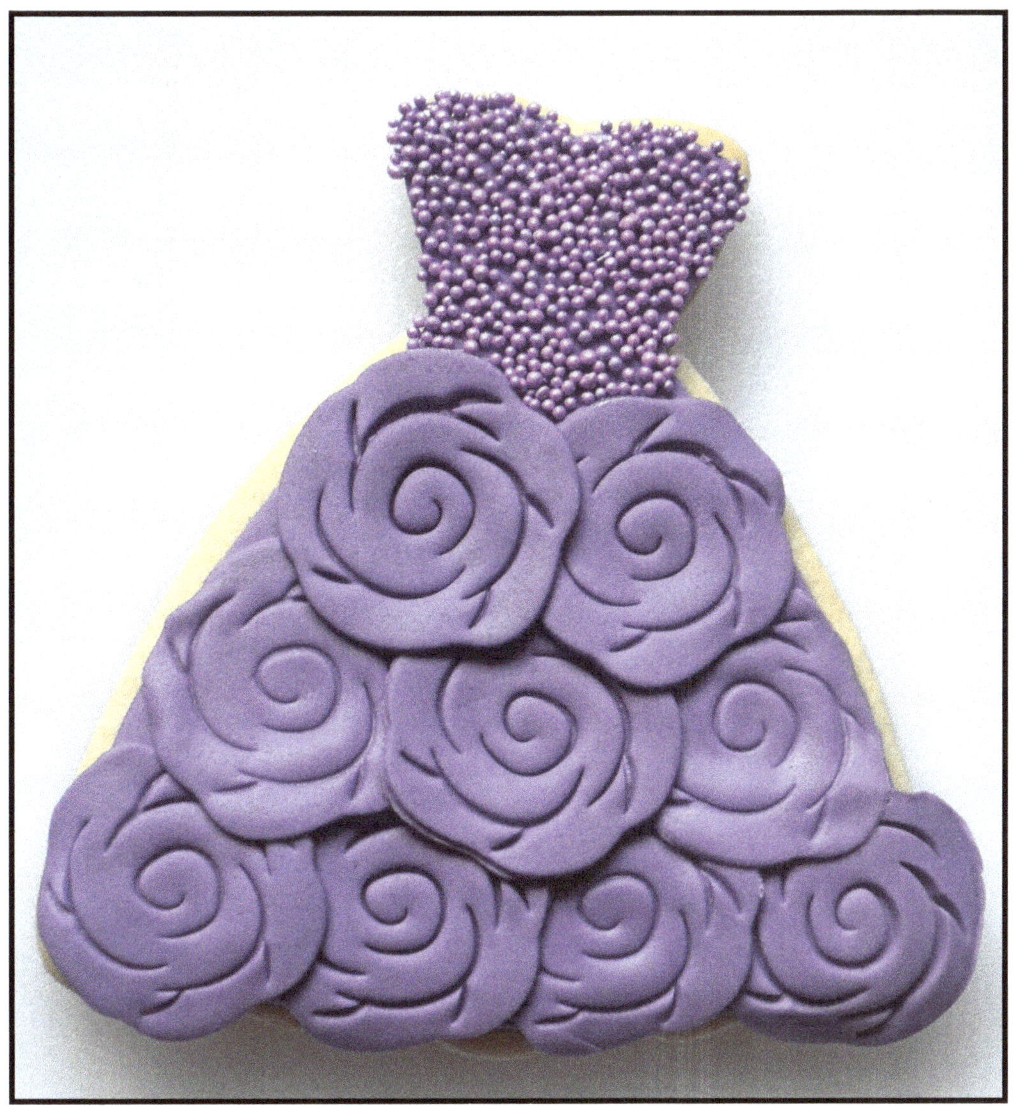

Materials:
- Dress cookie
- 1.1 oz. Fondarific Purple fondant
- Piping gel
- Food safe paint brush

Tools:
- Susan's Wedding Dress Cookie Cutter (etsy.com, WhiskedAwayCutters)
- Ateco Rose Plunger Cutter Set (medium)
- ChocoMaker Glamour Mix, Purple Shimmer Beads

Suggested cellophane bag size is 5x7 inches to package this dress cookie.

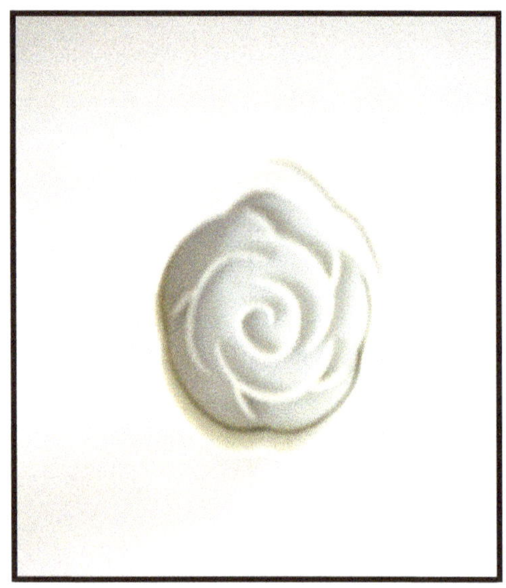

1. This is the medium rose plunger cutter.

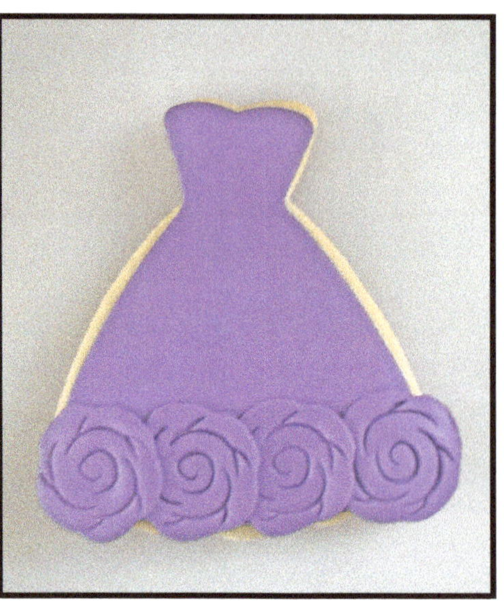

2. Roll out purple fondant. Use the dress cookie cutter to cut out purple fondant dress. Use a paint brush to apply a thin layer of piping gel onto your dress cookie. Apply fondant cut-out to cookie, and gently smooth top. Cut out nine roses. Apply four to the bottom of the dress cookie.

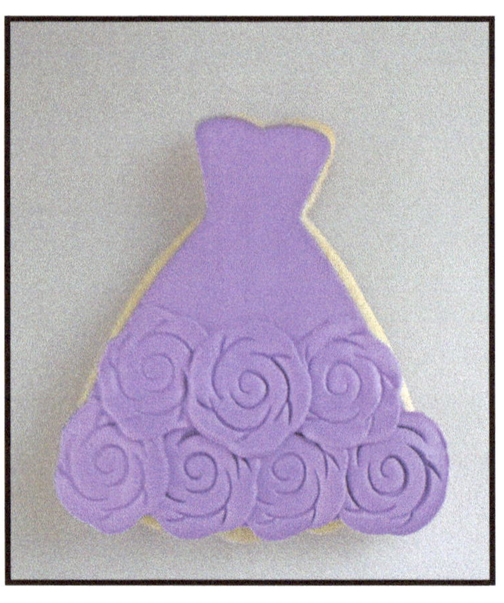

3. Apply three roses to the dress cookie as shown above. The two ends were placed on first, and then the center rose was added.

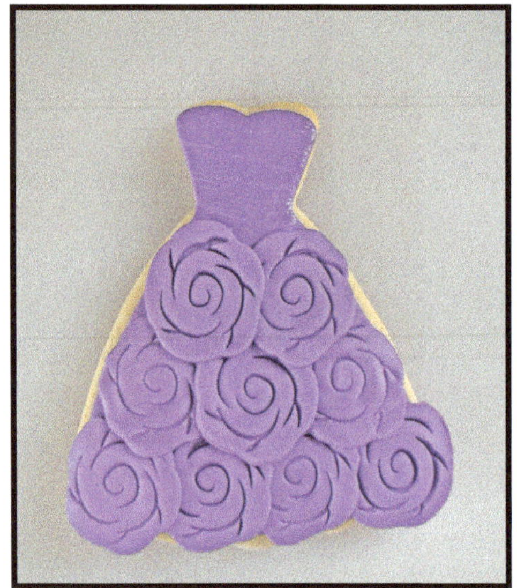

4. Add the top right rose first, and then the left rose. Paint the bodice top with piping gel.

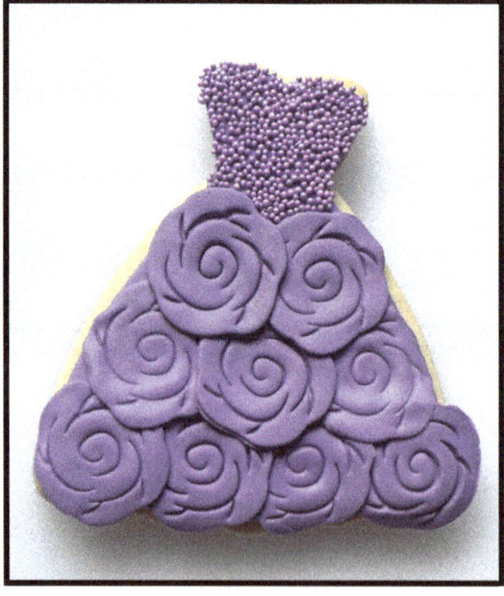

5. Sprinkle purple shimmer beads over piping gel covered bodice. Remove excess beads.

White Lace Gown Dress Cookie

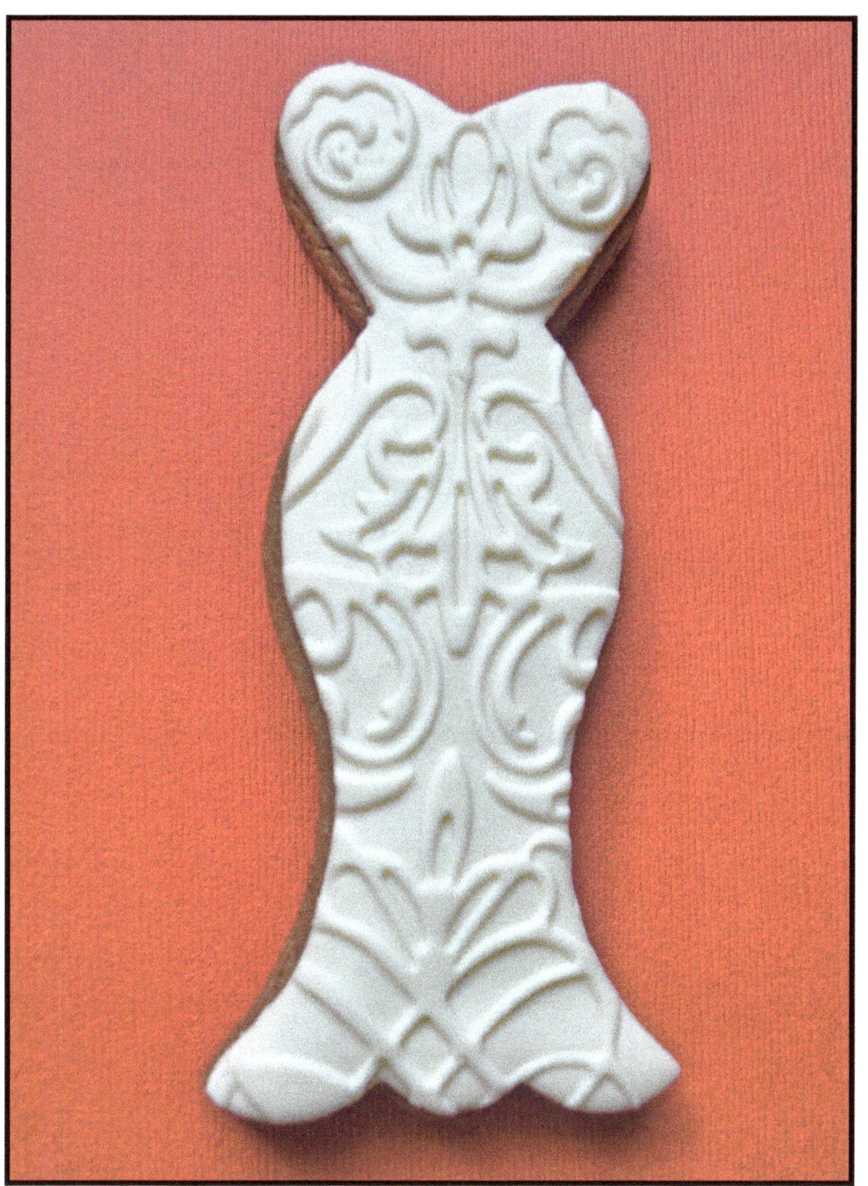

Materials:
- Dress cookie
- 0.5 oz. white fondant
- Piping gel
- Food safe paint brush

Tools:
- The Marilyn Gown Cookie Cutter (etsy.com, Sinful Cutters)
- Sunny Side Up Bakery Flourish Lace Silicone Mold (hobbylobby.com)

Suggested cellophane bag size is 3x8 inches to package this dress cookie.

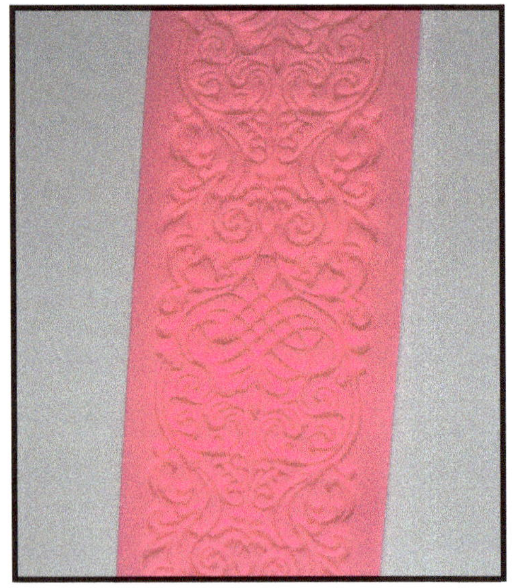

1. This is the flourish lace silicone mold.

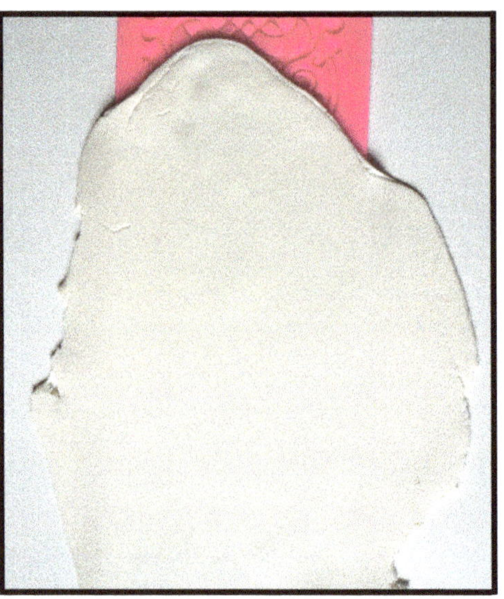

2. Roll out white fondant. Lay white fondant on top of flourish lace silicone mold. Use a rolling pin to roll over fondant using even pressure. Turn fondant over.

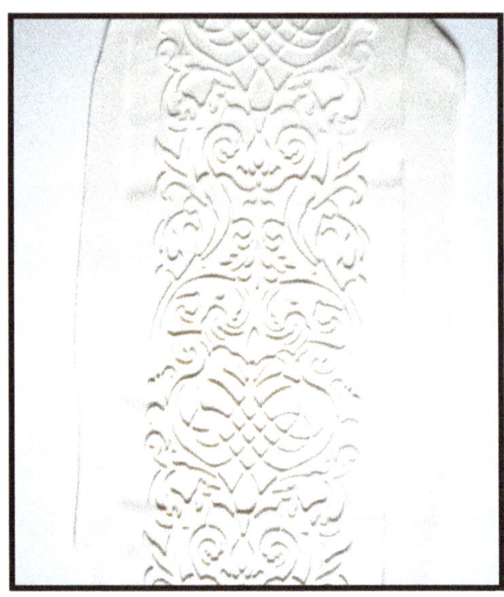

3. This is what the imprinted fondant looks like.

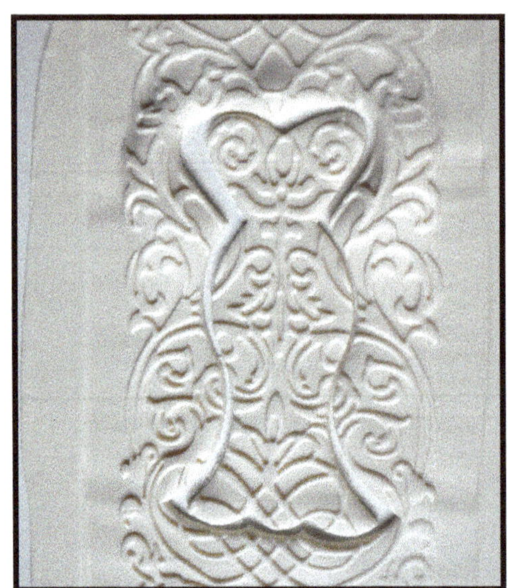

4. Center the dress cookie cutter over the design area as shown making sure that the bottom area is centered. Press the dress cookie cutter firmly into the fondant, and then wiggle to release the fondant from the dress cookie cutter.

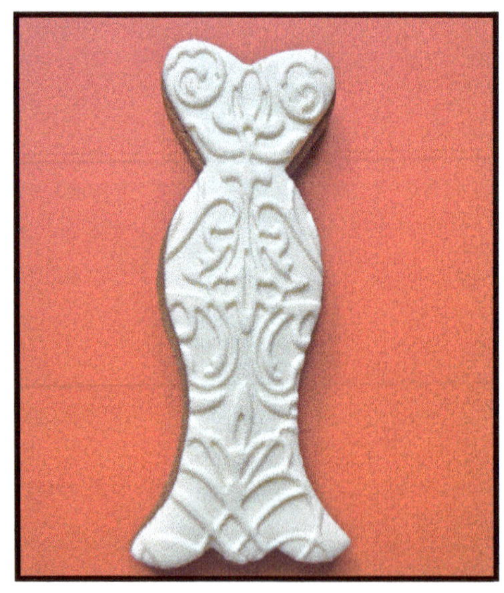

5. Use a paint brush to apply a thin layer of piping gel onto your dress cookie. Apply fondant cut-out to cookie, and gently smooth top.

Tan Flowers Dress Cookie

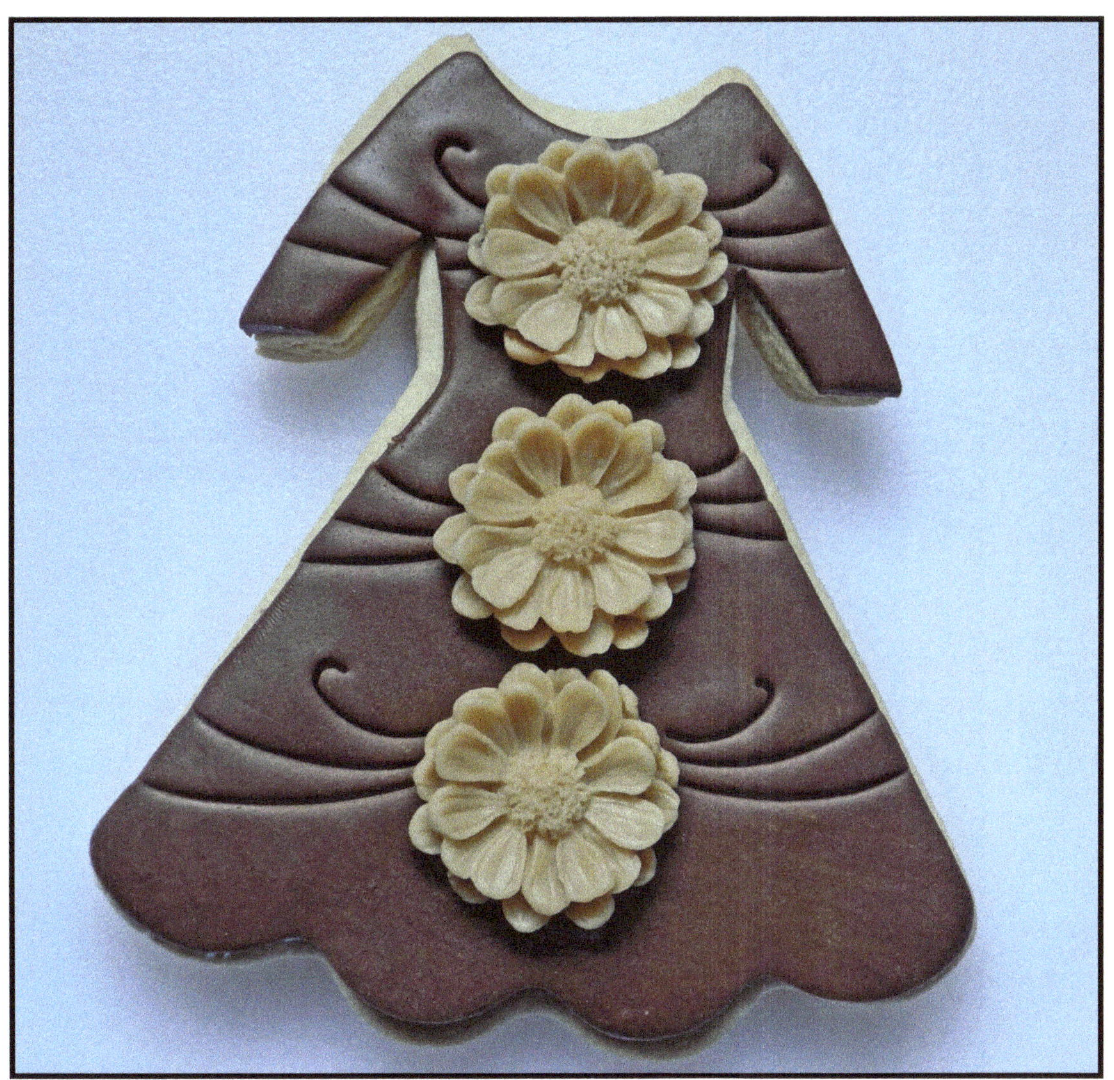

Materials:

- Dress cookie
- 1.2 oz. Fondarific Chocolate fondant
- 0.3 oz. Fondarific Coffee Mocha fondant
- Piping gel
- Food safe paint brush

Tools:

- The Diane Dress Cookie Cutter (etsy.com, Sinful Cutters)
- Patchwork Cutters Quilting Embosser
- Wilton's Designer Pattern Press Set, Flower Press
- 4-cavity fondant flower silicone mold

Suggested cellophane bag size is 5x7 inches to package this dress cookie.

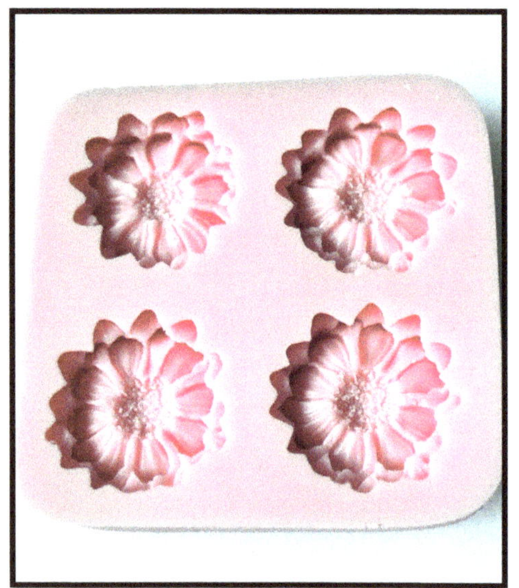

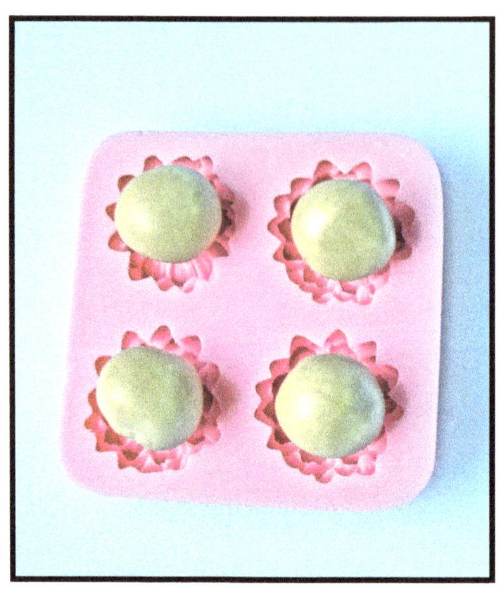

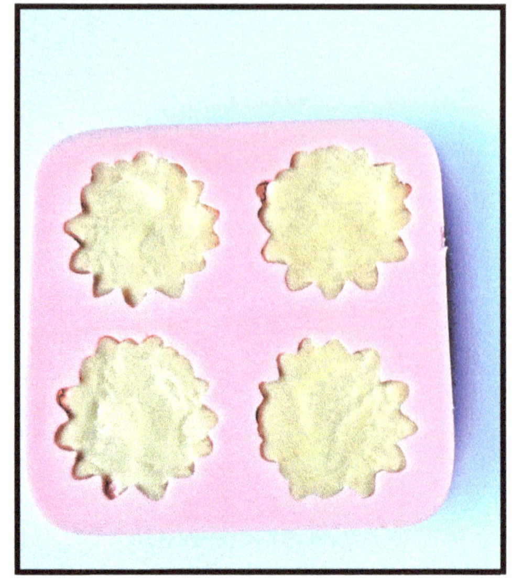

1. This is the four cavity blossom silicone mold.

2. Roll equal-sized balls of coffee mocha fondant and place into the blossom silicone mold cavities. You only need three blossoms for this dress cookie design.

3. Remove excess fondant. Refrigerate until firm. Remove from cavities. Set aside.

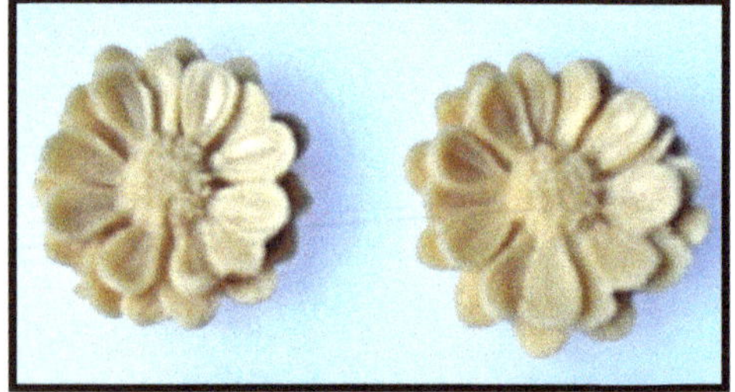

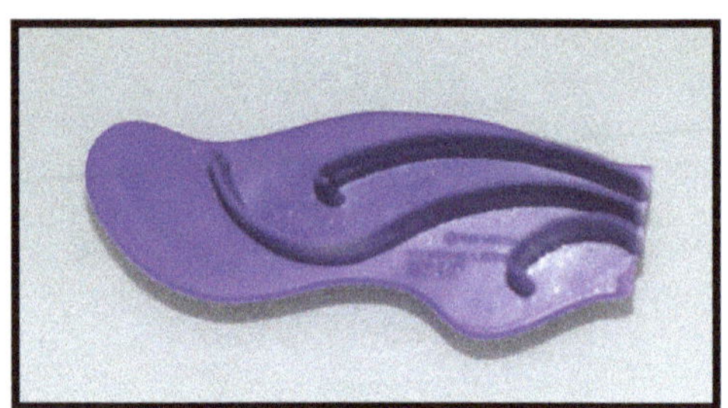

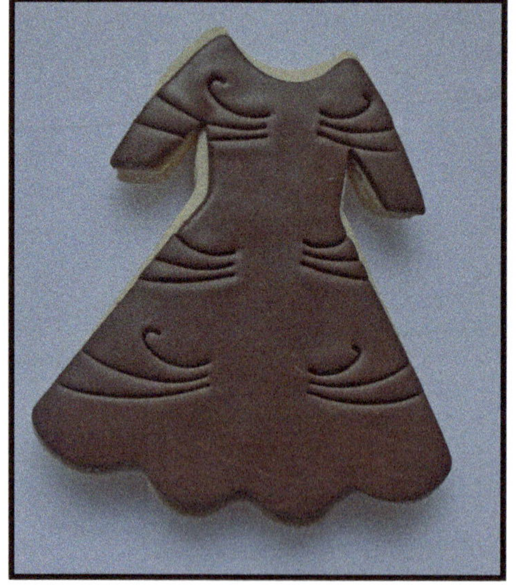

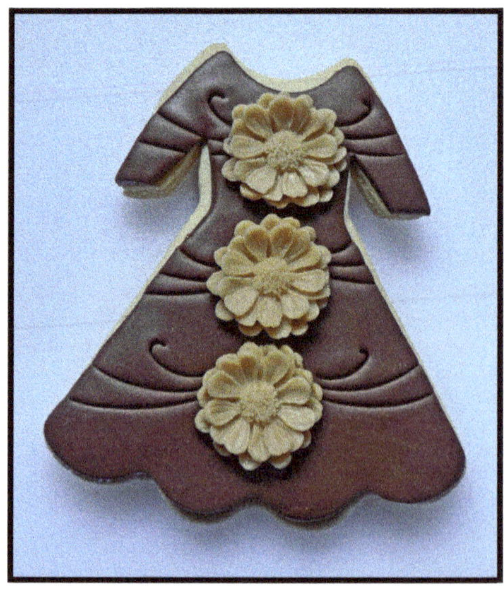

4. These are two of the fondant blossoms. You will use three of the fondant blossoms for this dress. The bottom picture shows the flower press. It has been broken in half. Use the large side for this cookie design.

5. Roll out chocolate fondant. Use the dress cookie cutter to cut out the chocolate fondant dress. Use a paint brush to apply a thin layer of piping gel onto your dress cookie. Apply fondant cut-out to cookie, and gently smooth top. Use flower press to make imprints into fondant dress as shown.

6. Put a dab of piping gel on the back of the fondant blossoms, and attach to the center of the fondant dress cookie design as shown.

Marbled Swirl Dress Cookie

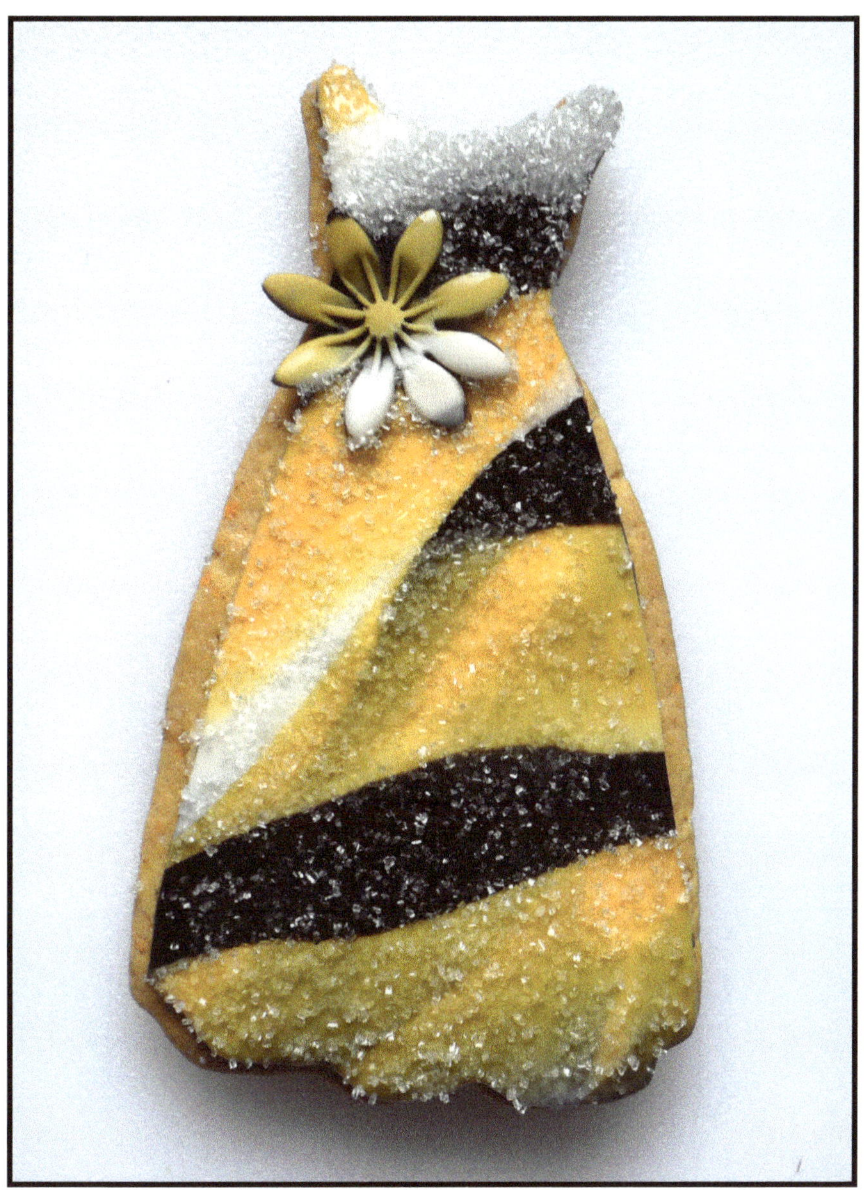

Suggested cellophane bag size is 4x6 inches to package this dress cookie.

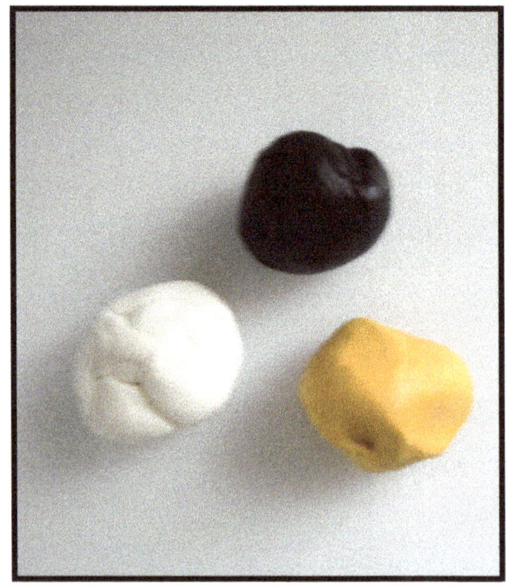

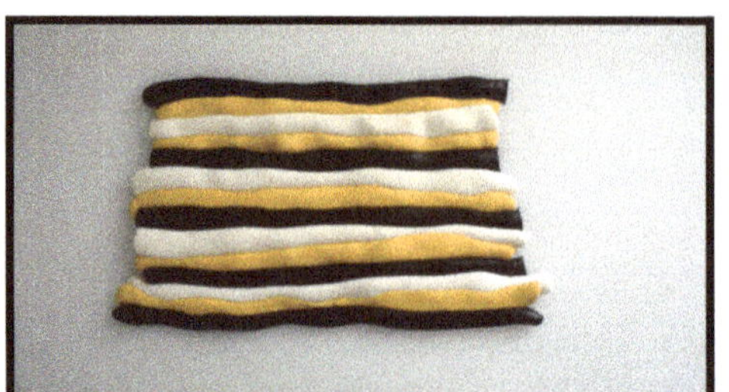

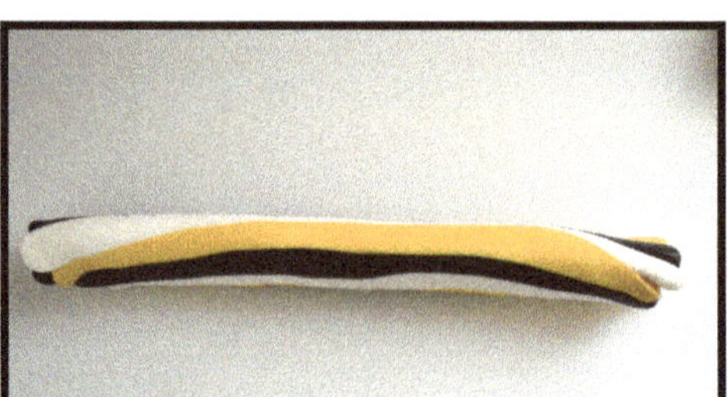

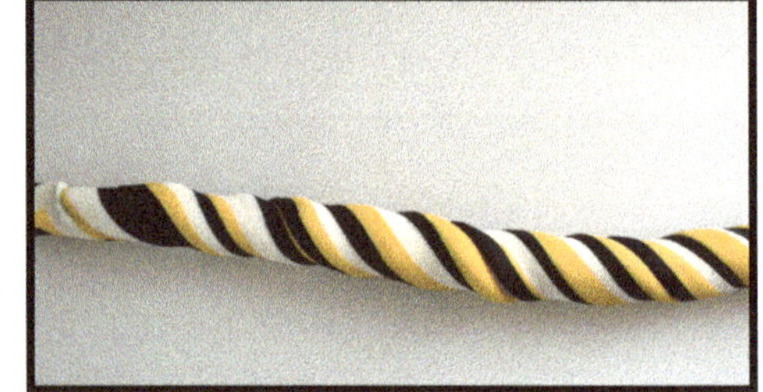

1. Here are the balls of black, white, and yellow fondant.

2. Make ropes of fondant from the fondant balls as shown above in the first picture. Use a rolling pin to flatten the ropes and make them even.

3. Lift the fondant and roll over into a log as shown in the first picture above. Using both hands, twist the fondant log until it is evenly twisted.

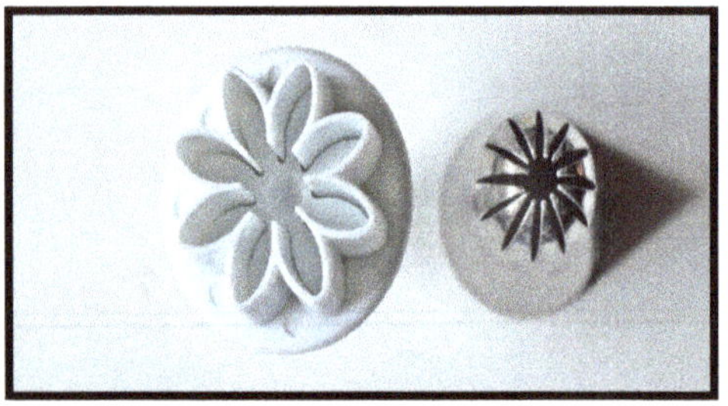

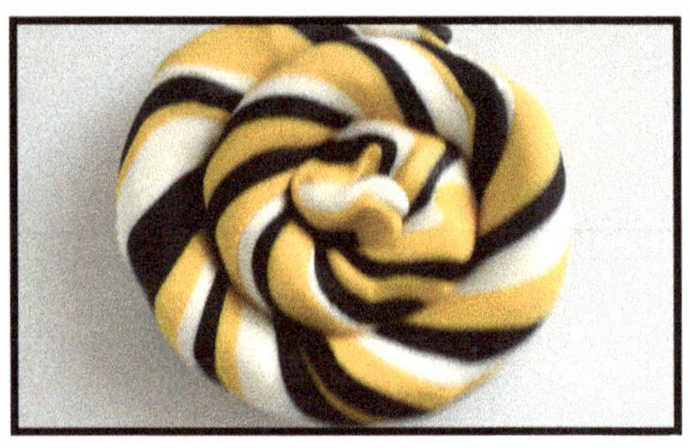

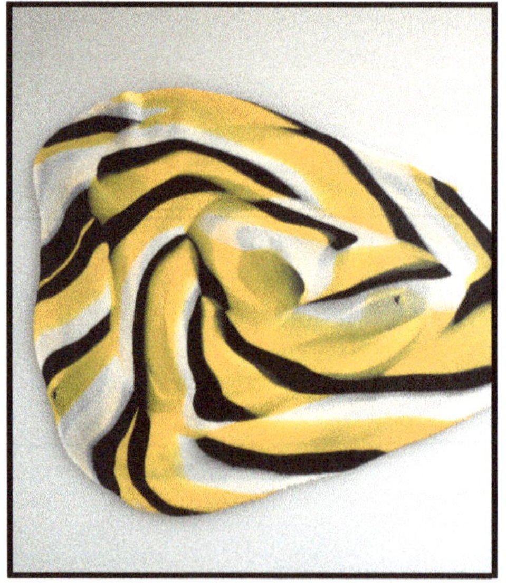

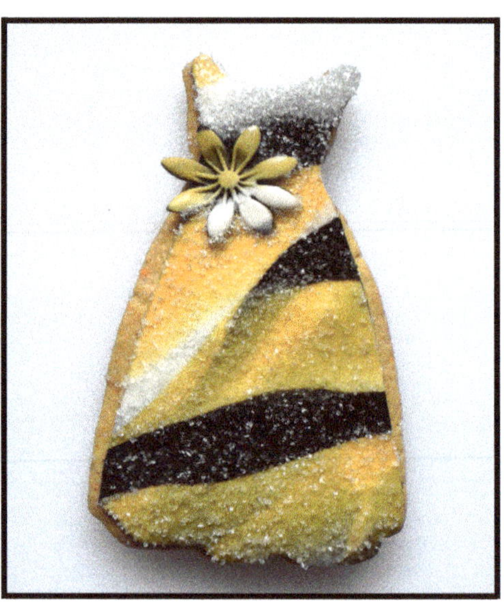

4. The top photo shows the daisy cutter and icing tip 1E. The bottom photo shows how you twist the fondant into a circle.

5. Use a rolling pin to roll out the marbled fondant. Now you can use your dress cutter to cut out dress. Press the dress cookie cutter firmly into the fondant, and then wiggle to release the fondant from the dress cookie cutter.

6. Use a paint brush to apply a thin layer of piping gel onto your dress cookie. Apply fondant cut-out to cookie, and gently smooth top. Paint the entire top of the marbled fondant with piping gel. Cover dress cookie with white sanding sugar. Remove excess. Cut out one fondant daisy and attach to bodice with a dab of piping gel. Press center with icing tip 1E.

Black Mini Dress Cookie

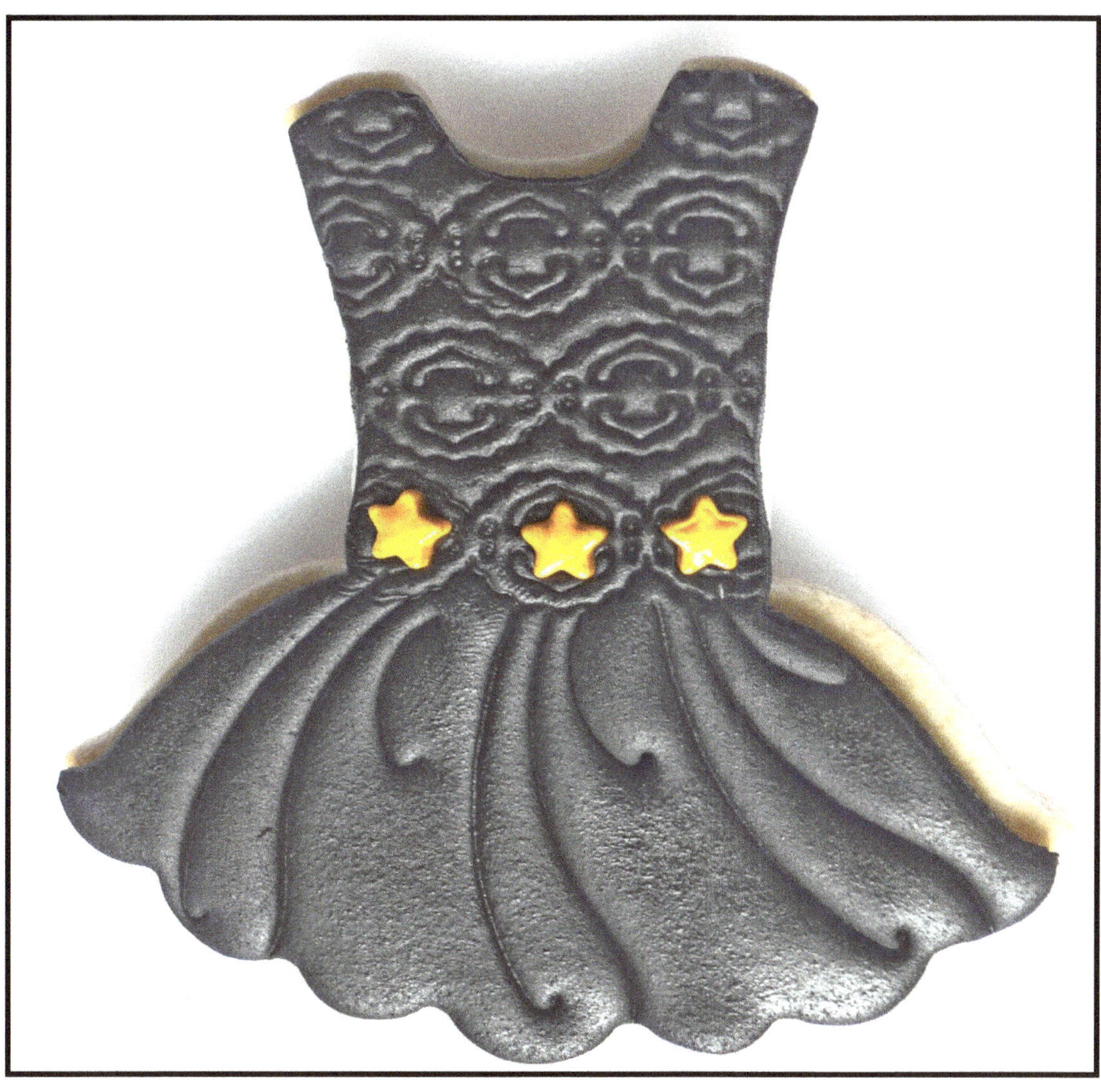

Suggested cellophane bag size is 4x6 inches to package this dress cookie.

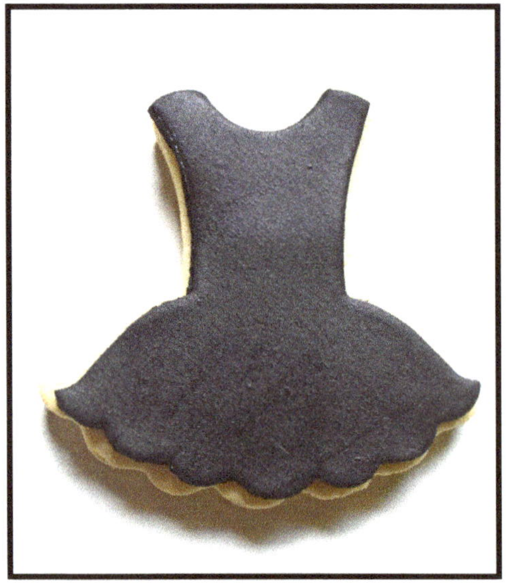 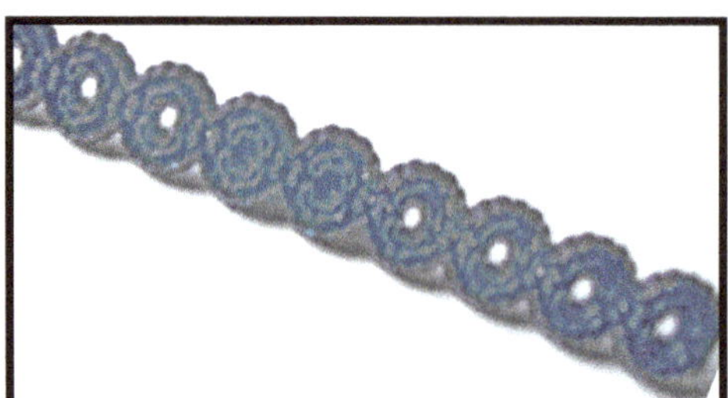 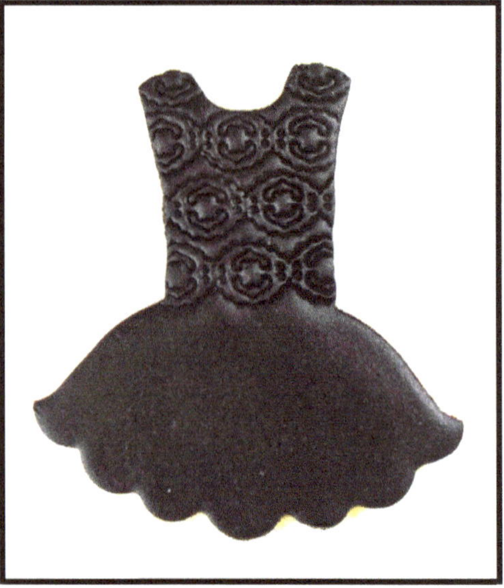

1. Roll out black fondant. Use the dress cookie cutter to cut out the black fondant dress. Use a paint brush to apply a thin layer of piping gel onto your dress cookie. Apply fondant cut-out to dress cookie, and gently smooth top.

2. This is the lace strip tool and the flower press. The flower press tool has been broken in half. Use the long side.

3. Use the lace strip tool to make three impressions into the bodice top as shown above.

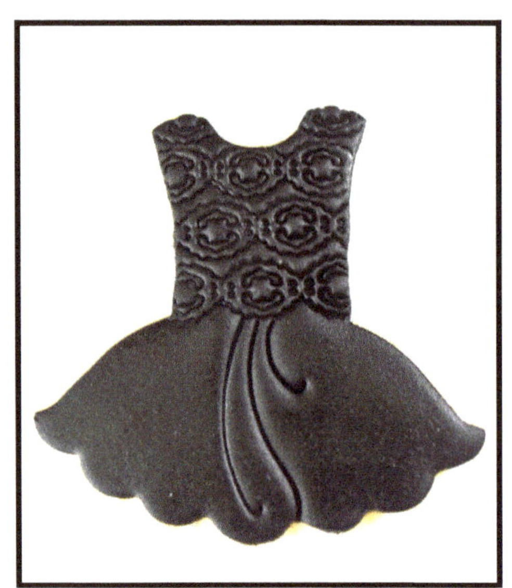 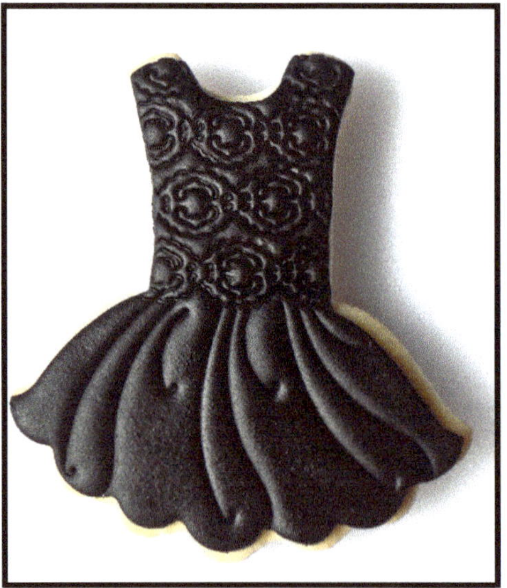 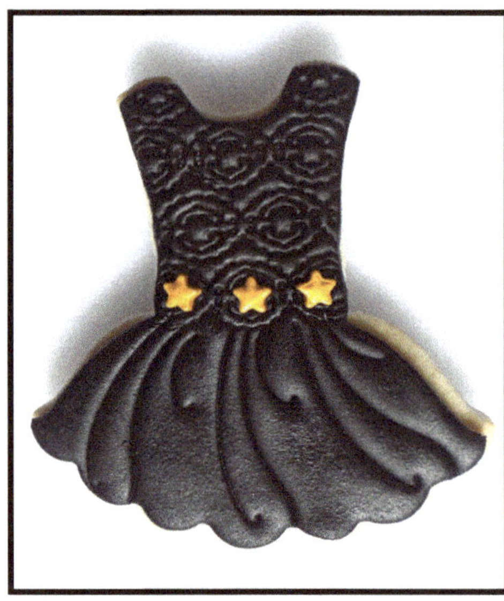

4. Use the flower press tool (large side) to make an impression in the center of the dress cookie skirt.

5. Make an impression into the left side and right side of the dress cookie skirt as shown above.

6. Press three gold stars into the center of the lace strip on the bottom part of the bodice as shown above

Blue Pattern Press Dress Cookie

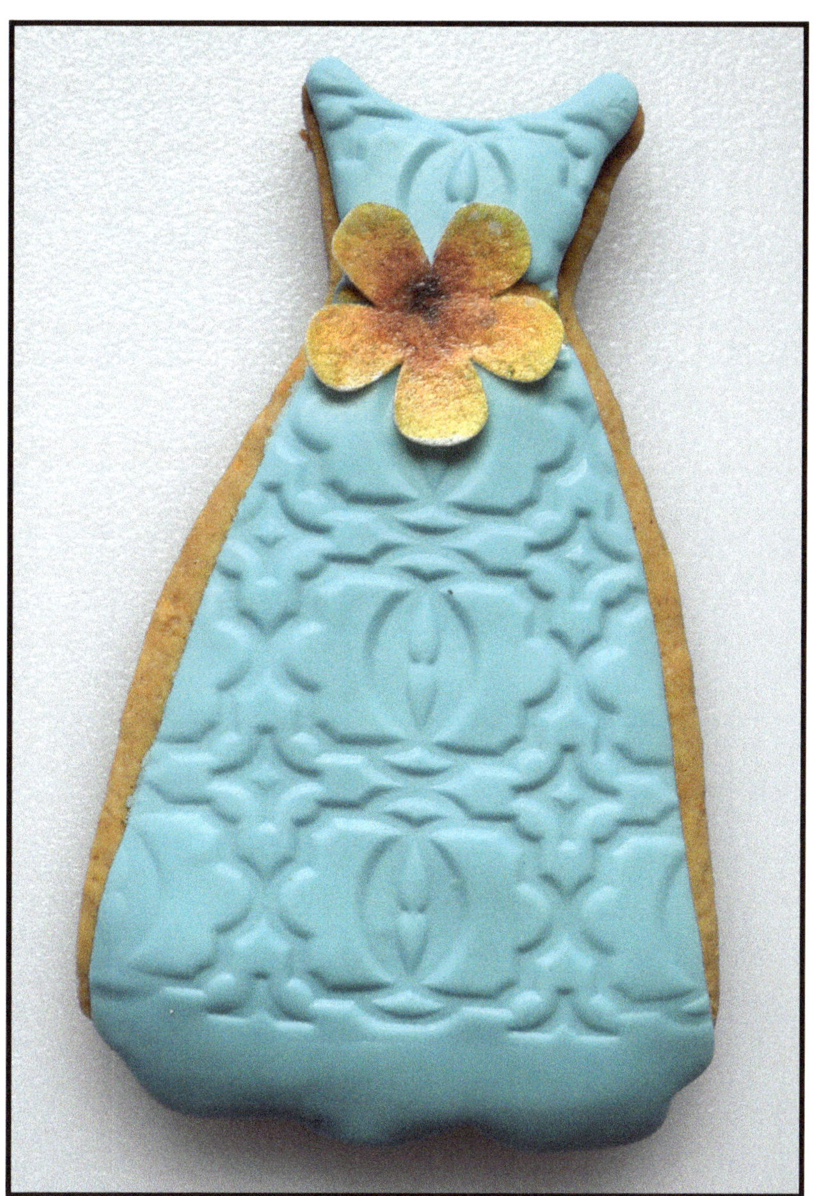

Materials:
- Dress cookie
- o.6 oz. Fondarific Blue fondant
- Piping gel
- Food safe paint brush

Tools:
- Dress Cookie Cutter (flourbox.com)
- Wilton Pattern Roller, Geometric Roller
- Wafer paper flowers (amazon.com)

Suggested cellophane bag size is 4x6 inches to package this dress cookie.

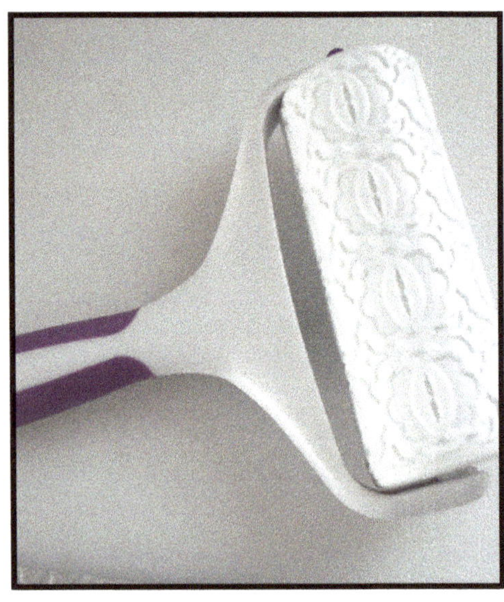

1. This is Wilton's Pattern Roller, Geometric print.

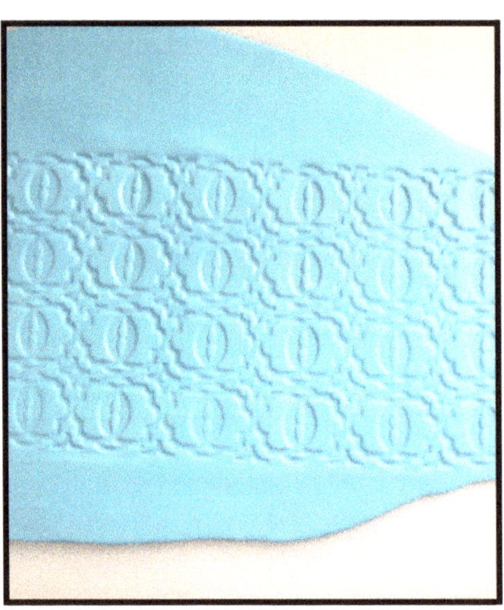

2. Roll out blue fondant. Using firm and even pressure, roll over the fondant with Wilton's Pattern Roller, Geometric print.

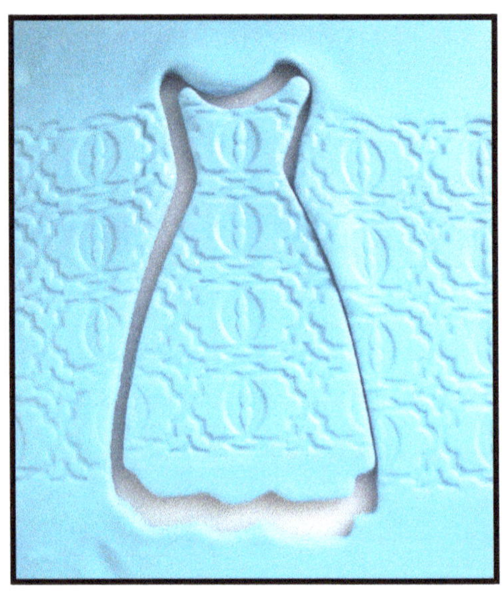

3. Center the dress cookie cutter over the design area as shown making sure that the dress design area is centered as shown. Press the dress cookie cutter firmly into the fondant, and then wiggle to release the fondant from the dress cookie cutter.

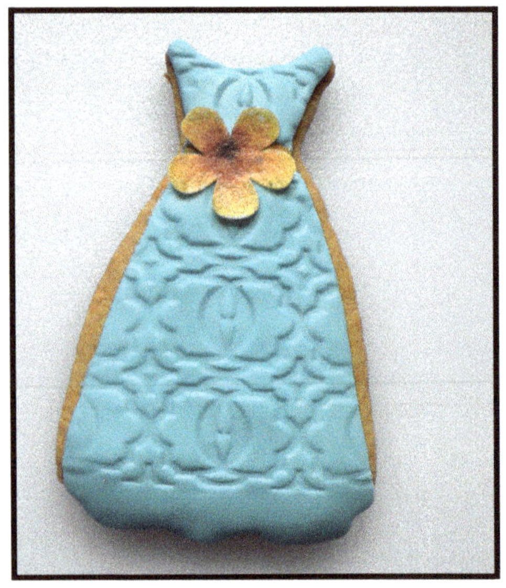

4. Use a paint brush to apply a thin layer of piping gel onto your dress cookie. Apply fondant cut-out to cookie, and gently smooth top. Attach wafer flower to waist with a dab of piping gel.

Purple Pattern Dress Cookie

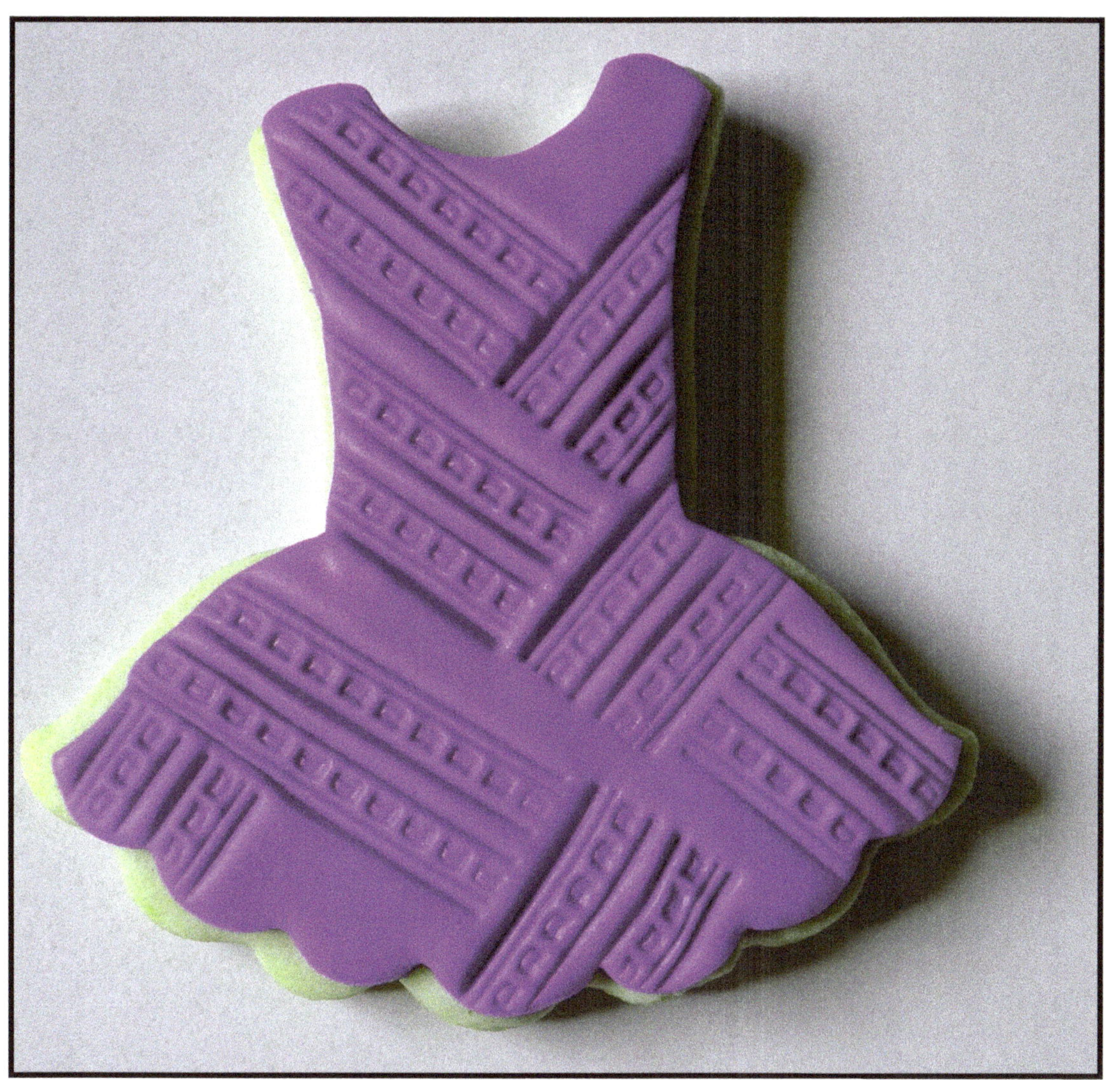

Materials:
- Dress cookie
- 0.6 oz. Fondarific Purple fondant
- Piping gel
- Food safe paint brush

Tools:
- Tutu and Dress Cookie Cutter (etsy.com, WhiskedAwayCutters)
- CK Products Ribbon Fondant Cutter Set (Barley and Eyelet)

Suggested cellophane bag size is 4x6 inches to package this dress cookie.

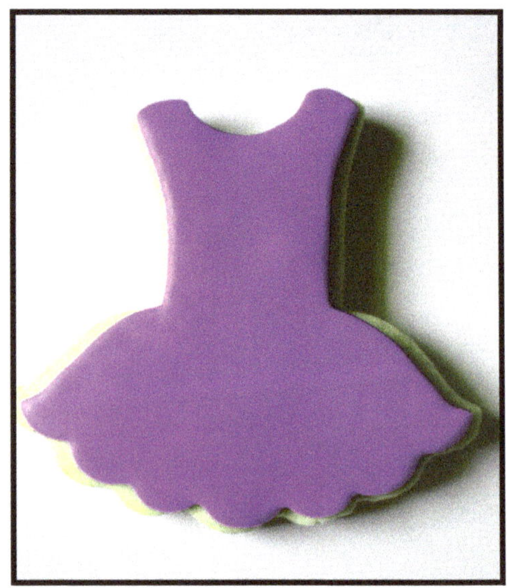

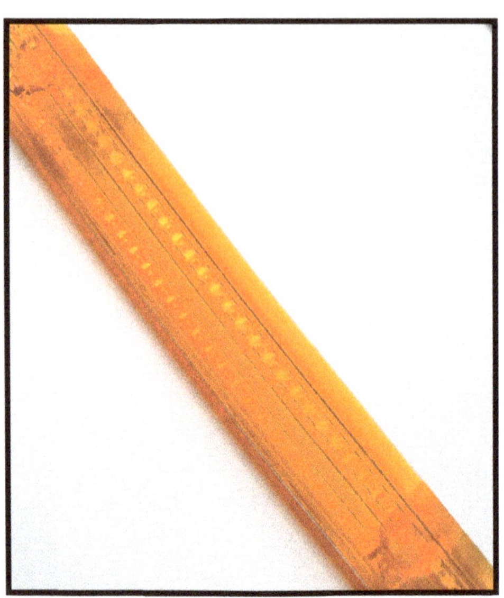

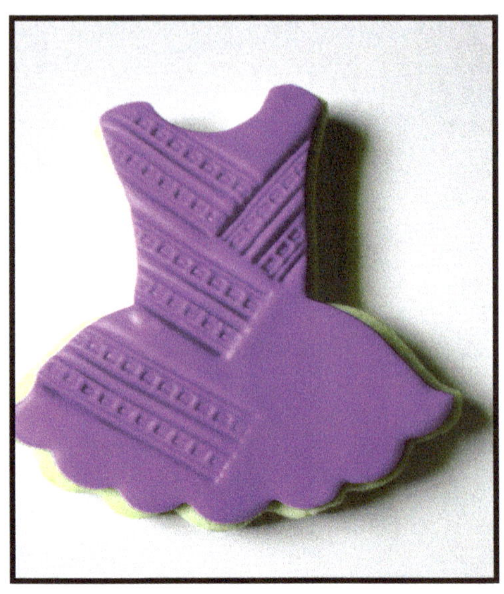

1. Roll out purple fondant. Use the dress cookie cutter to cut out the purple fondant dress. Use a paint brush to apply a thin layer of piping gel onto your dress cookie. Apply fondant cut-out to cookie, and gently smooth top.

2. This is the ribbon fondant cutter.

3. Use the ribbon fondant cutter to imprint the fondant as shown above. Start with the left side impressions, and then start with the right side. Use even pressure to imprint the fondant.

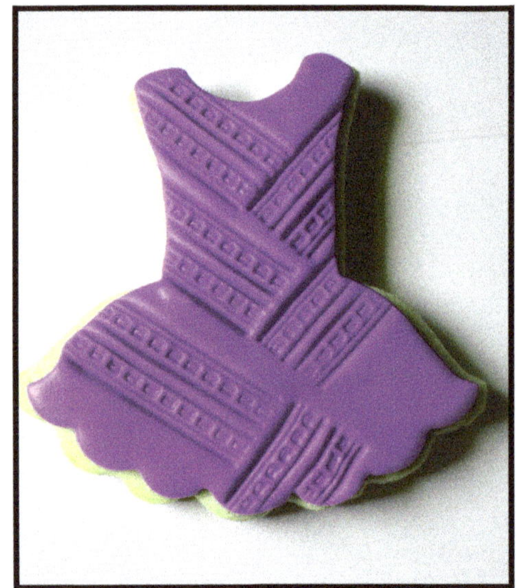

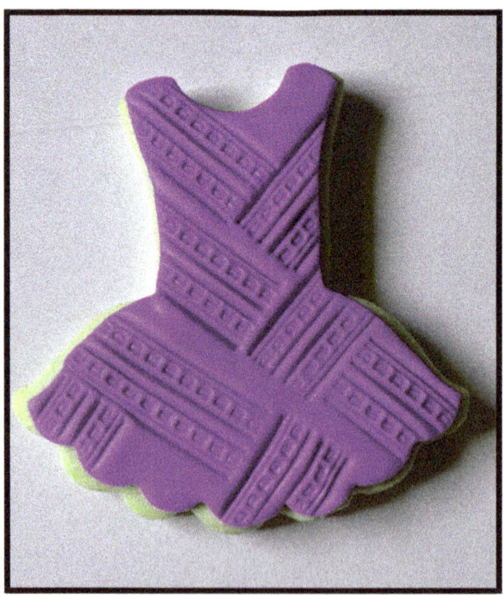

4. Continue imprinting the fondant with the ribbon fondant cutter on the right side. Make the impression on the bottom right.

5. Make the last two impressions on the left side bottom and right side bottom.

White Flowers Dress Cookie

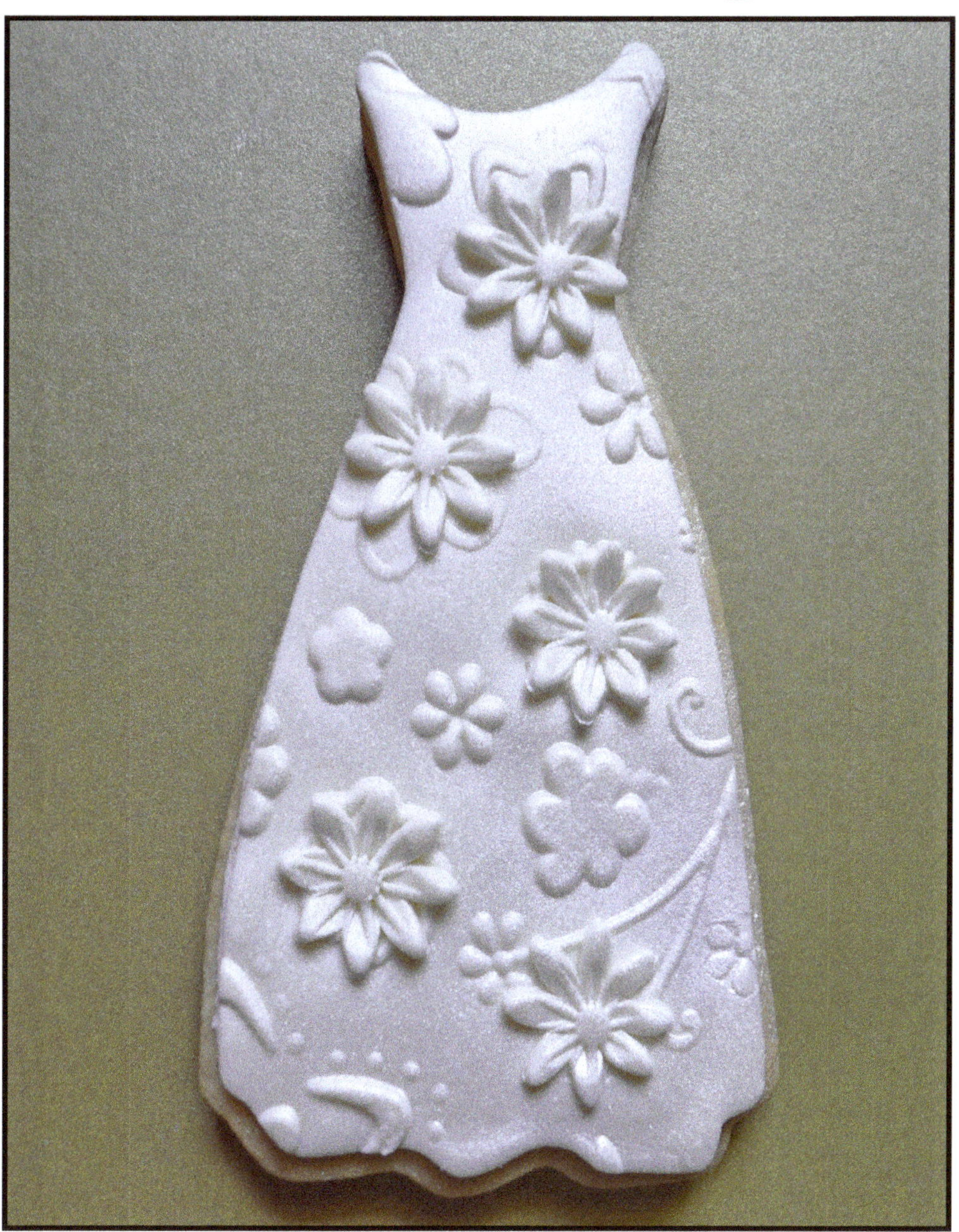

Suggested cellophane bag size is 4x6 inches to package this dress cookie.

 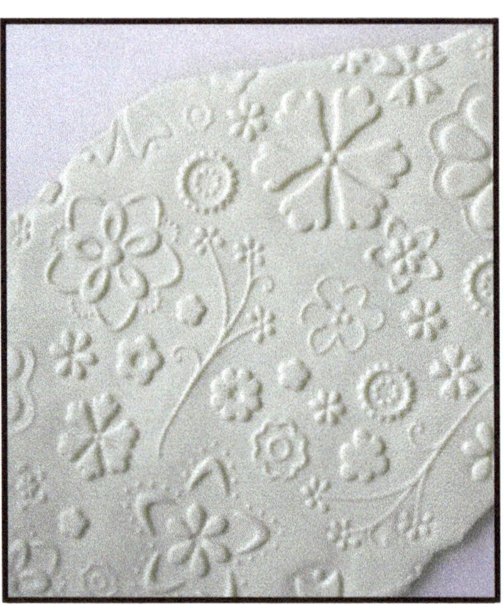 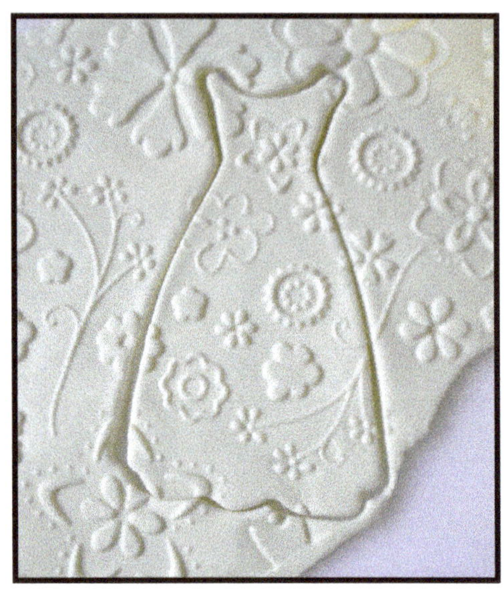

1. Roll out white fondant. Use the Flower Fun County Kitchen Texture Sheet (raised side up as shown). Evenly roll over the texture sheet.

2. Remove the texture sheet.

3. Center the dress cookie cutter over the design area you choose. Press the dress cookie cutter firmly into the fondant, and then wiggle to release the fondant from the dress cookie cutter.

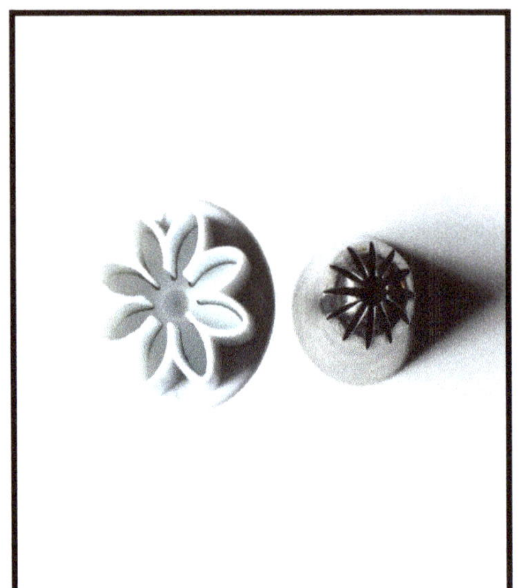 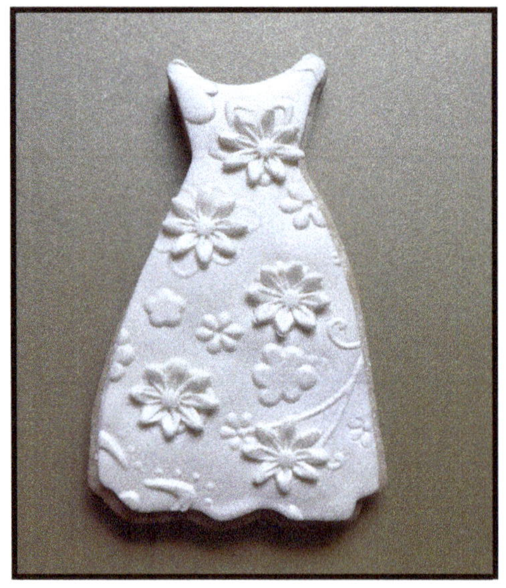

4. This is the medium daisy plunger cutter and icing tip 1E.

5. Use a paint brush to apply a thin layer of piping gel onto your dress cookie. Apply fondant cut-out to cookie, and gently smooth top. Roll out white fondant and cut out five daisies with the plunger cutter, and attach to dress as shown. Use picture as example. Press center of daisies with icing tip 1E.

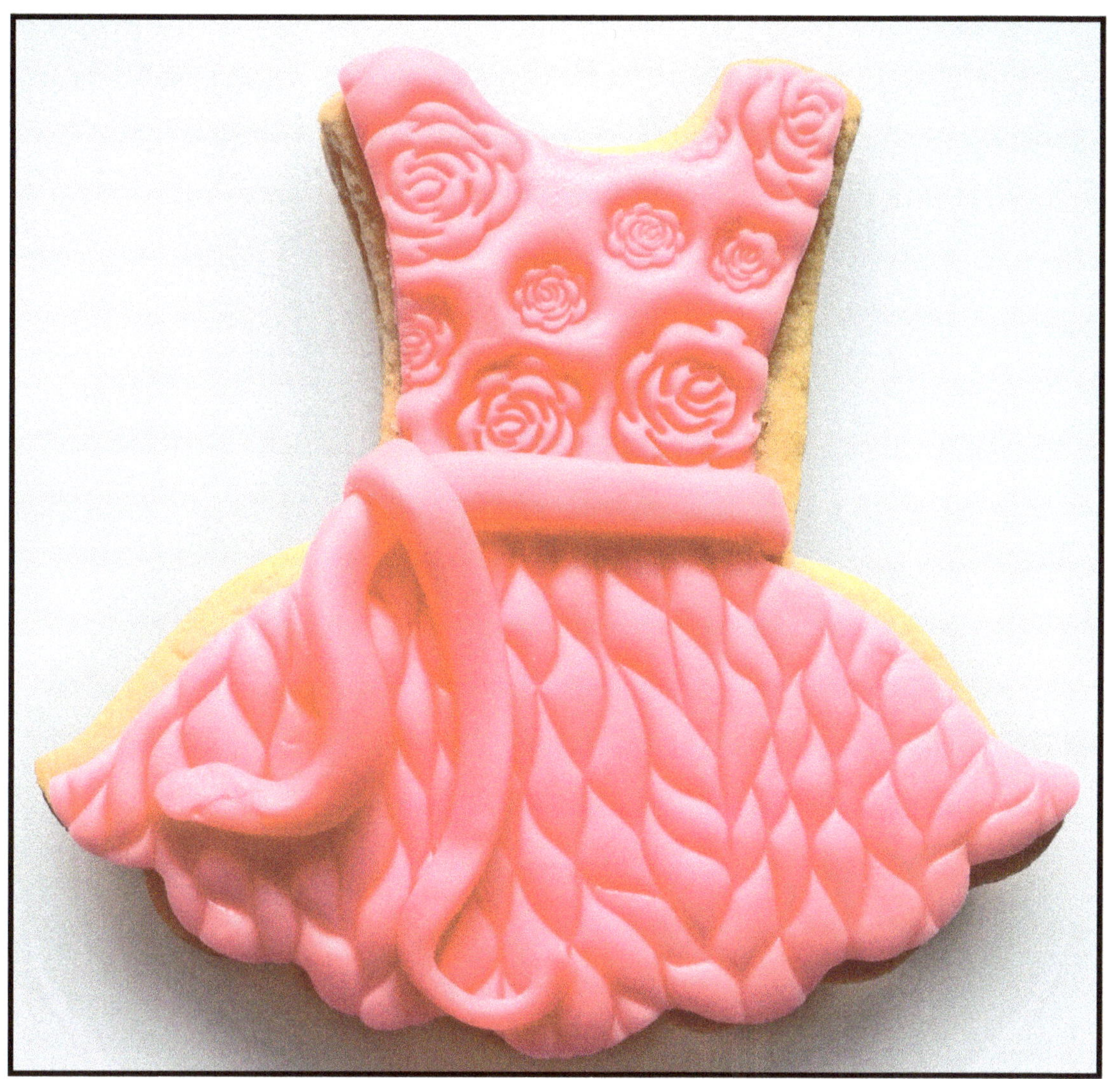

<table>
<tr><td>

Materials:
- **Dress cookie**
- **0.6 oz. Fondarific Pink fondant**
- **Piping gel**
- **Food safe paint brush**
- **Pizza cutter or Xacto knife**

</td><td>

Tools:
- **Tutu and Dress Cookie Cutter (etsy.com, WhiskedAwayCutters)**
- **JOERSH Cake Fondant Embossing Mould 6 Pack Fondant Embosser Set (Roses & Waves) (amazon.com)**

</td></tr>
</table>

Suggested cellophane bag size is 4x6 inches to package this dress cookie.

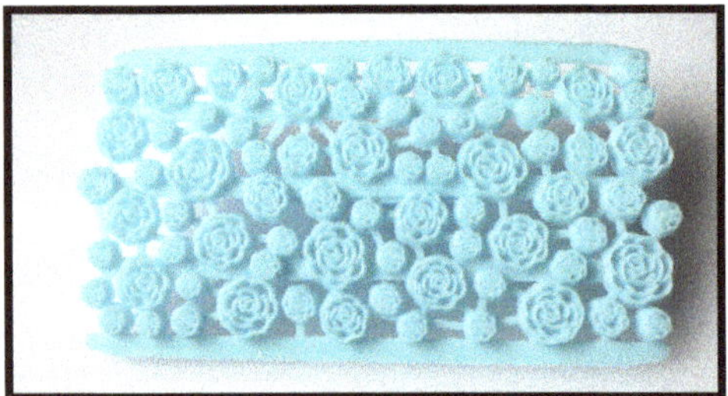

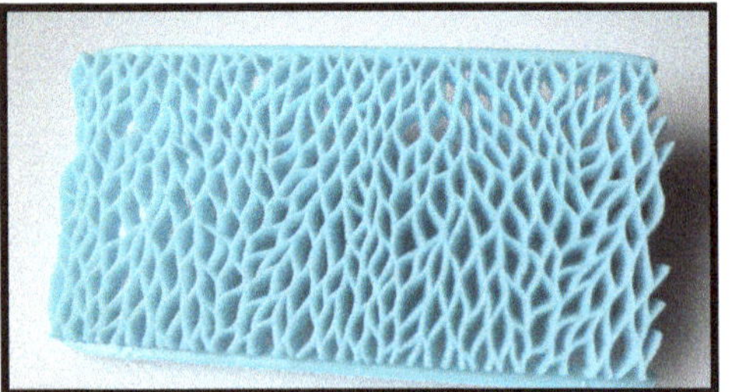

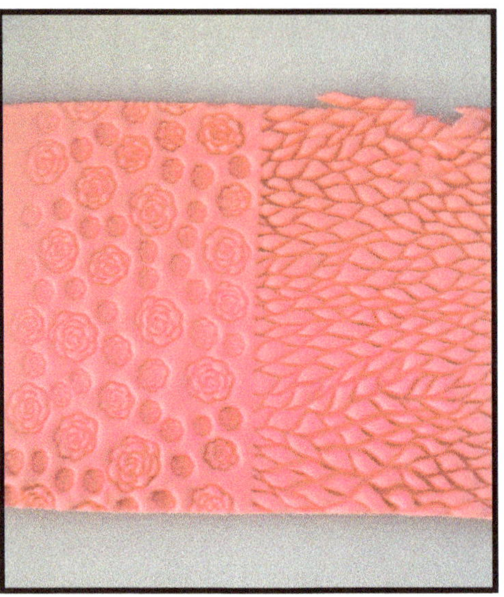

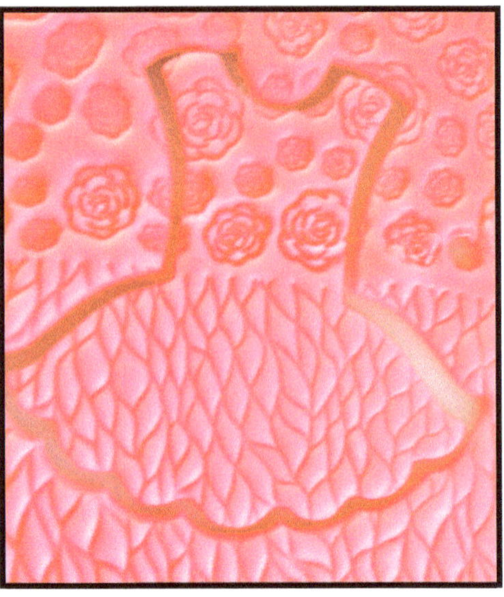

1. Pictured above are the rose embossing mold and the wave embossing mold.

2. Roll out the pink fondant. Use even pressure to imprint half of the fondant with the rose embossing mold, and the other half with the wave embossing mold. Use a bench scraper to lift the fondant up, and then place it back on the surface.

3. Center the dress cookie cutter over the design area as shown. Press the dress cookie cutter firmly into the pink fondant, and then wiggle to release the fondant from the dress cookie cutter.

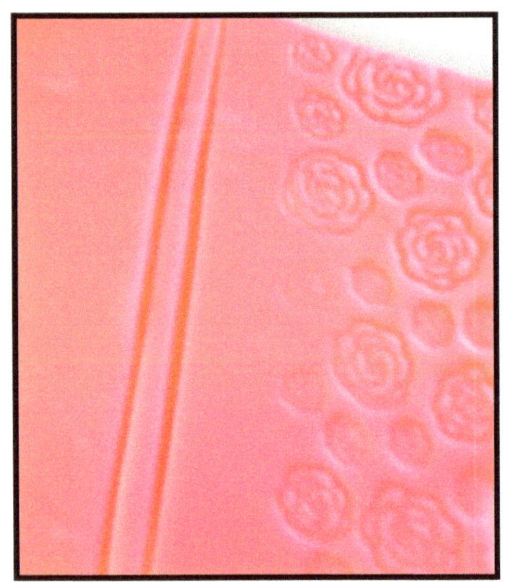

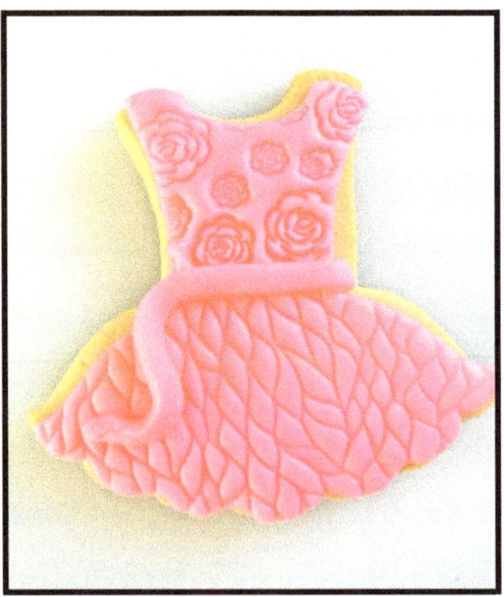

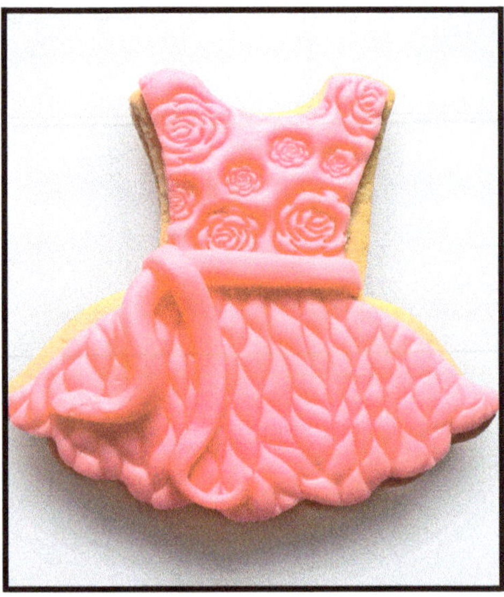

4. Use a pizza cutter or knife to cut a pink strip of fondant as shown.

5. Use a paint brush to apply a thin layer of piping gel onto your dress cookie. Apply fondant cut-out to cookie, and gently smooth top. Cut the fondant strip in half and attach to the waist as shown above, curving the end.

6. Add the second part of the pink fondant trim to the waist as shown. Gently press into fondant dress to secure.

Red Gown Dress Cookie

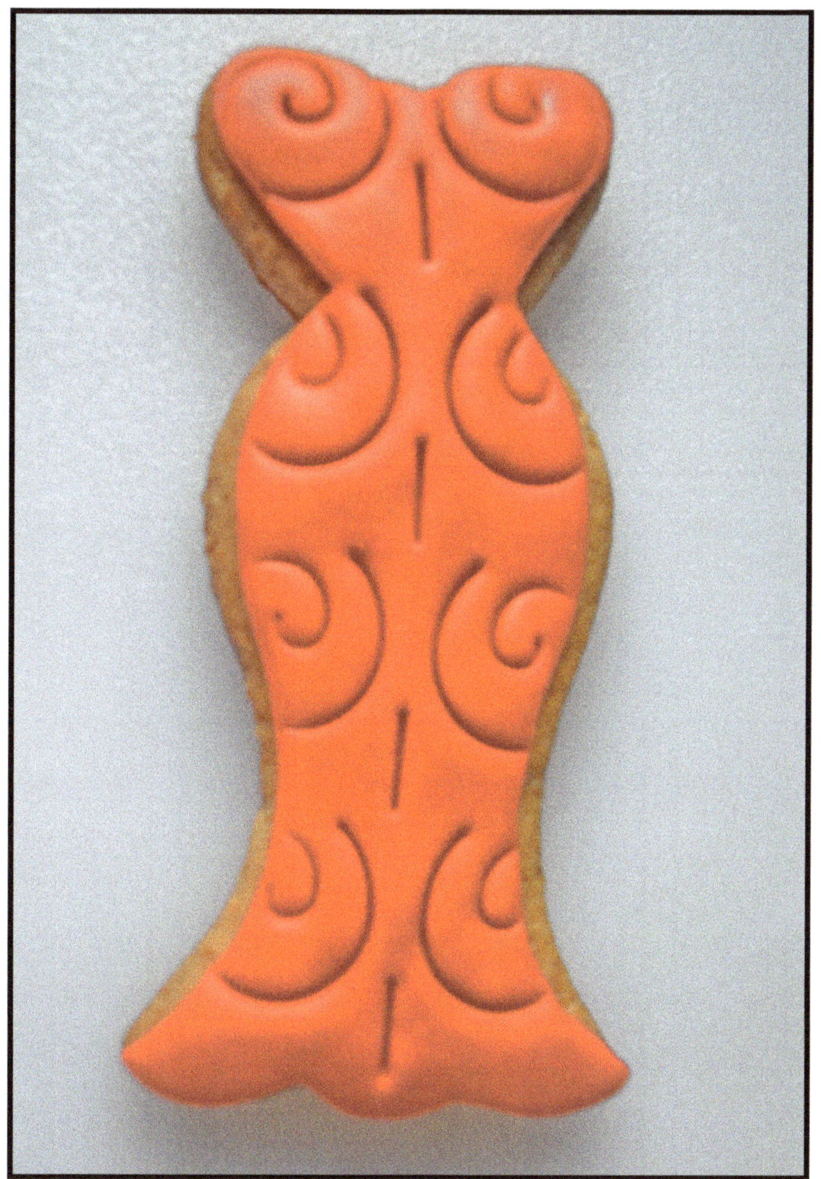

Materials:
- Dress cookie
- 0.6 oz. Fondarific Red fondant
- Piping gel
- Food safe paint brush

Tools:
- The Marilyn Gown Cookie Cutter (etsy.com, Sinful Cutters)
- Wilton's Designer Pattern Press Set, Curlicues Press

Suggested cellophane bag size is 3x8 inches to package this dress cookie.

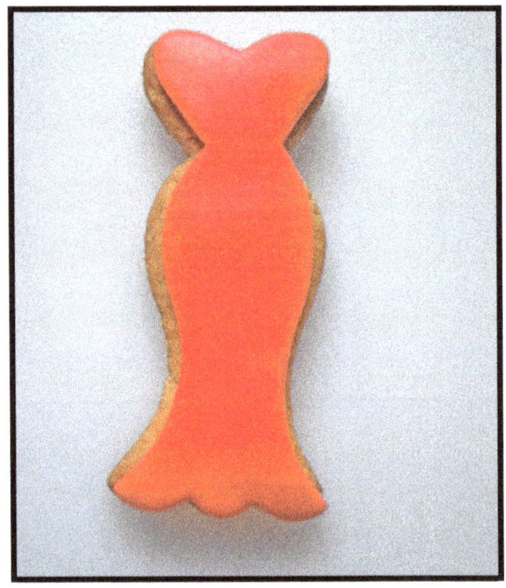

1. Roll out red fondant. Use the dress cookie cutter to cut out the red fondant dress. Use a paint brush to apply a thin layer of piping gel onto your dress cookie. Apply fondant cut-out to cookie, and gently smooth top.

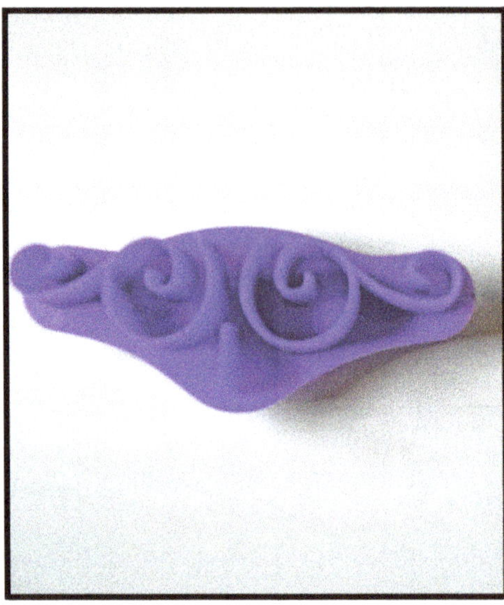

2. This is the curlicues press.

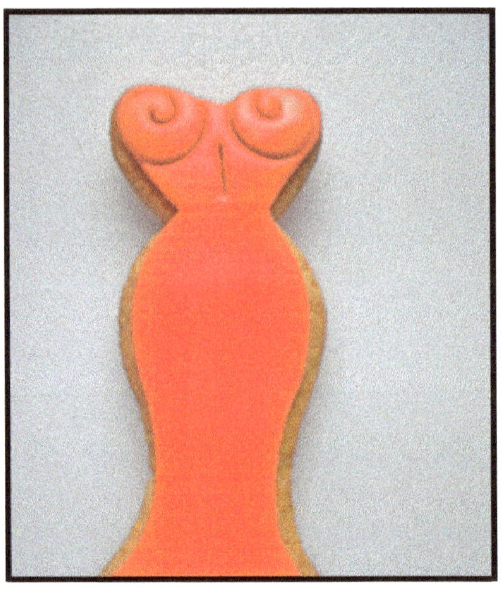

3. Gently press the curlicues press into the top part of the fondant dress as shown above. Remove.

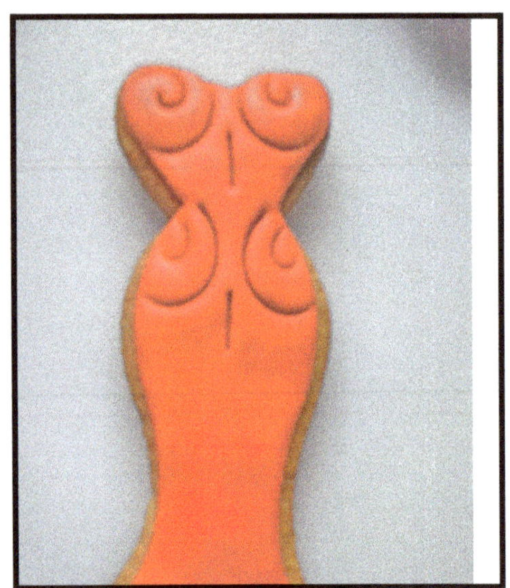

4. Gently press the curlicues press into the waist part of the fondant dress as shown above. Remove.

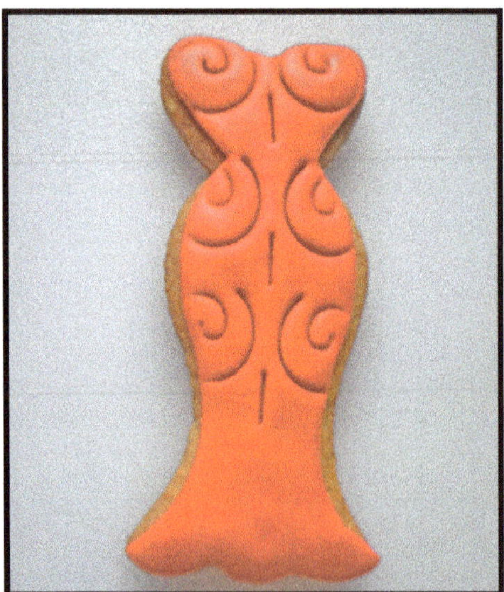

5. Gently press the curlicues press into the bottom dress part of the fondant dress as shown above. Remove.

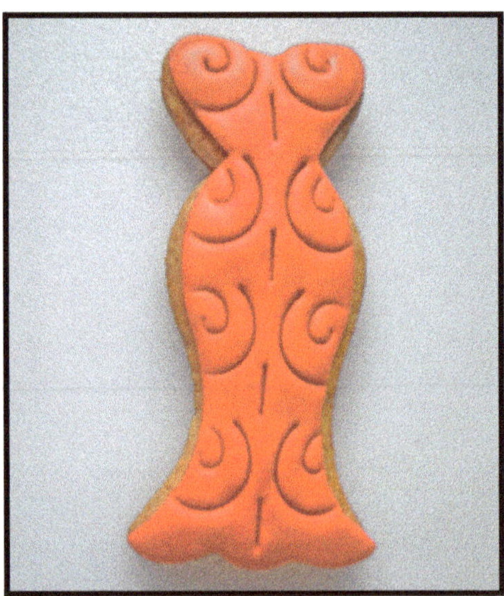

6. Gently press the curlicues press into the bottom dress part of the fondant dress as shown above. Remove.

Lavender Lace Dress Cookie

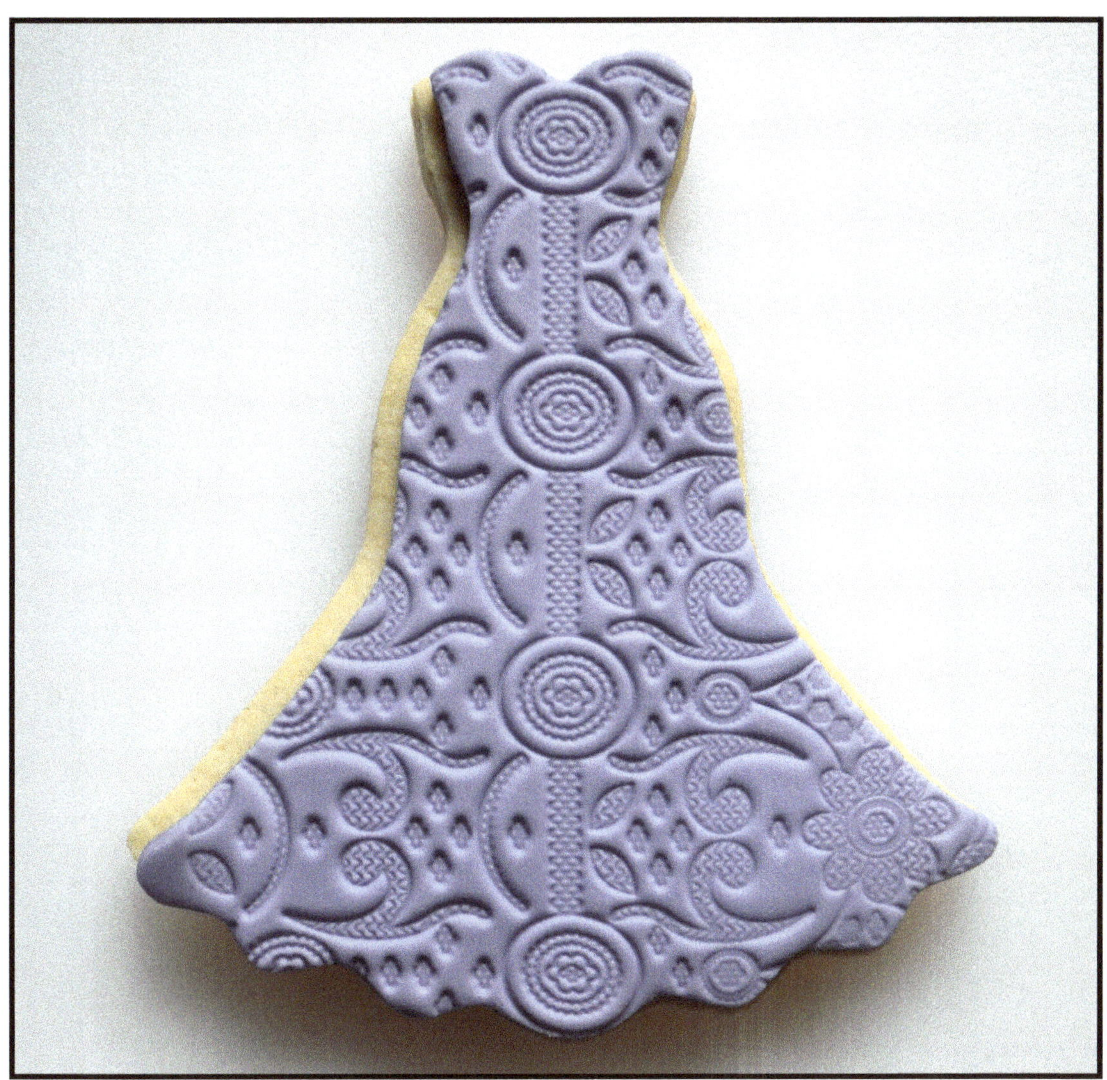

Materials:
- Dress cookie
- o.6 oz. lavender fondant
- Piping gel
- Food safe paint brush

Tools:
- LILIAO Wedding Dress Cookie Cutter (amazon.com)
- Sculpey Texture Makers Chantilly Lace Pattern Press

Suggested cellophane bag size is 5x7 inches to package this dress cookie.

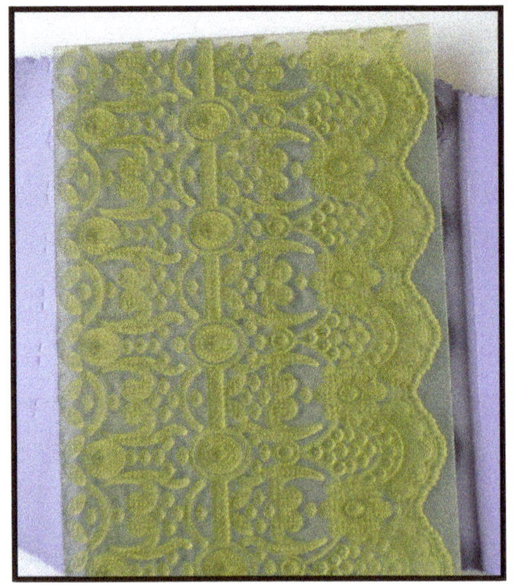

1. This is the green Chantilly Lace pattern press.

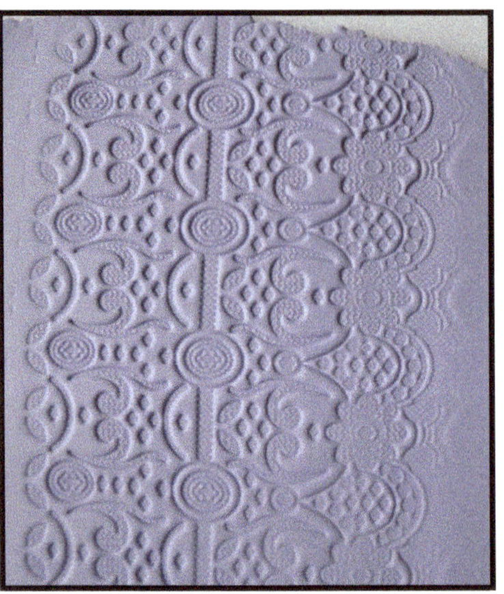

2. Roll out lavender fondant. With even pressure, place the Chantilly Lace pattern press on top and use a rolling pin to roll over it. Remove pattern press. Use bench scraper to lift fondant pattern up and then place back onto surface.

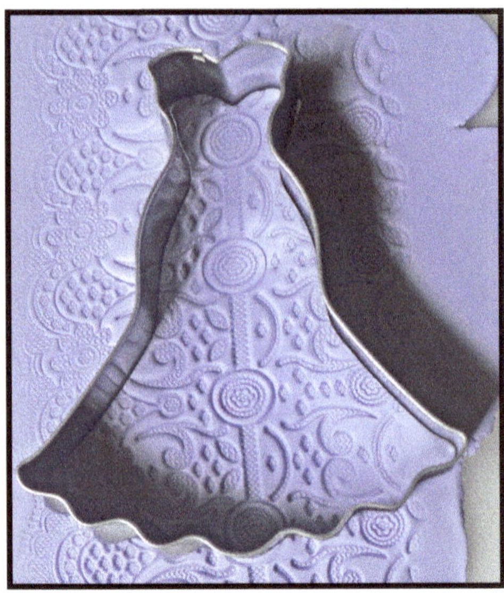

3. Center the dress cookie cutter over the design area as shown. Press the dress cookie cutter firmly into the lavender fondant, and then wiggle to release the fondant from the dress cookie cutter.

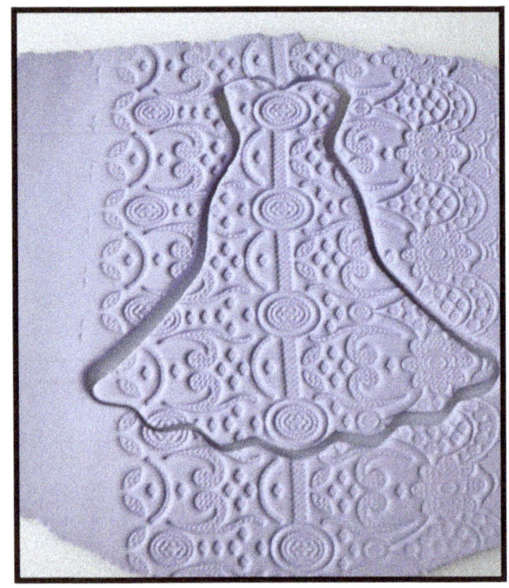

4. This is what the fondant cut-out looks like.

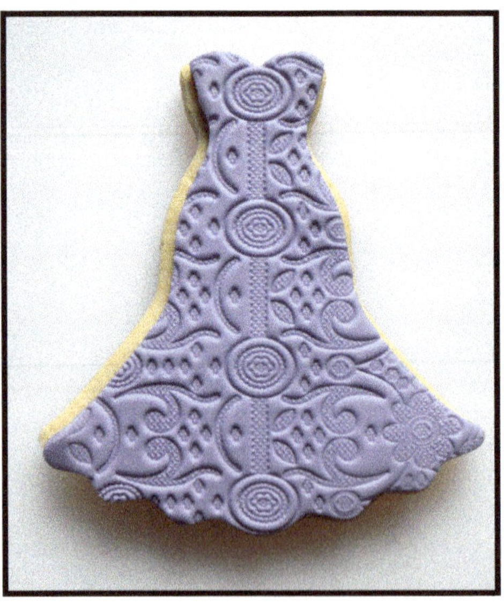

5. Use a paint brush to apply a thin layer of piping gel onto your dress cookie. Apply fondant cut-out to cookie, and gently smooth top.

Cream Mini Dress Cookies

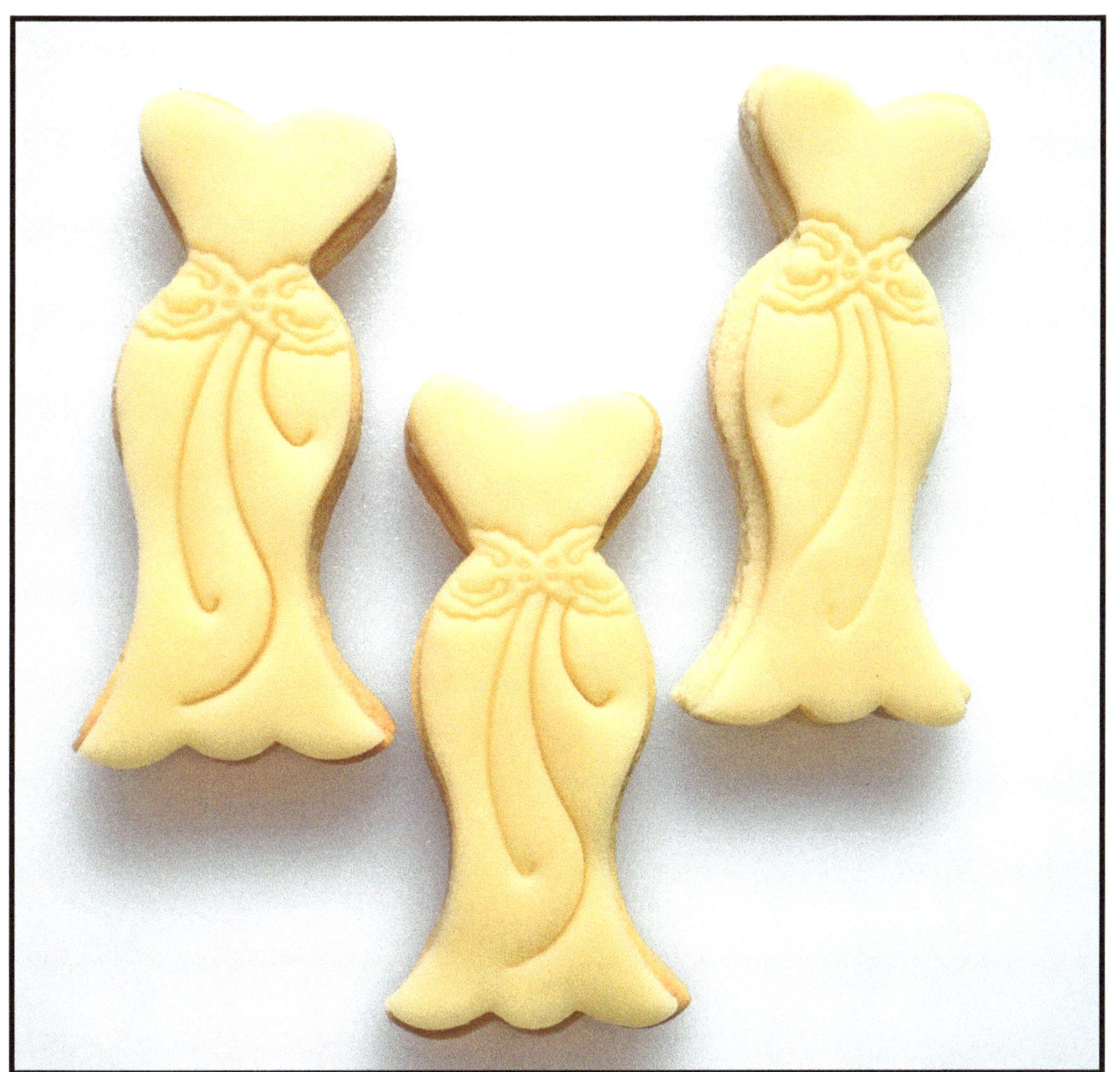

Materials:
- Three small dress cookies
- 0.6 oz. Fondarific Cinnamon Bun fondant
- Piping gel
- Food safe paint brush

Tools:
- The Marilyn Gown Cookie Cutter (smallest size) (etsy.com, Sinful Cutters)
- Wilton's Designer Pattern Press Set, Flower Press
- Lace Strip Patchwork Cutter

Suggested cellophane bag size is 2x6 inches to package these dress cookies.

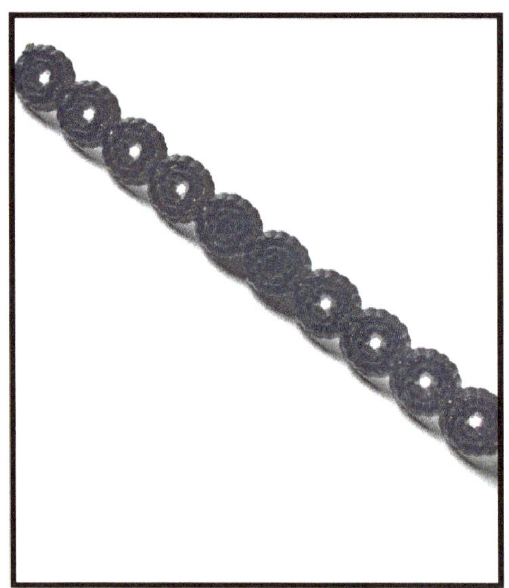

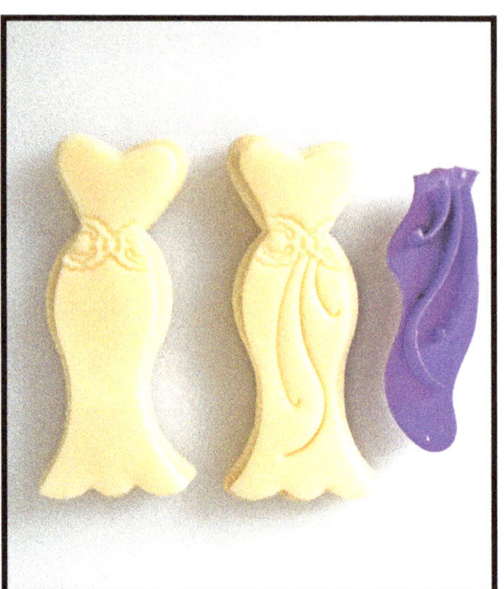

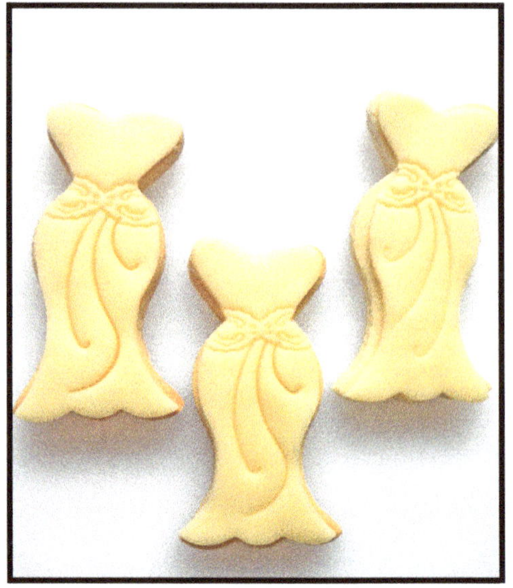

1. This is the lace strip tool.

2. Roll out cinnamon bun fondant. Use the small dress cookie cutter to cut out three cinnamon bun fondant dresses. Use a paint brush to apply a thin layer of piping gel onto your dress cookies. Apply fondant cut-outs to cookie, and gently smooth top.

3. Use the lace strip tool to make the waist impressions in the fondant on the dress cookies as shown above. Use the flower press (small side) to make the drape designs on the dress cookies as shown. The third cookie was done with the other section of the blue flower press cutter for a different look.

Silver Tulip Dress Cookie

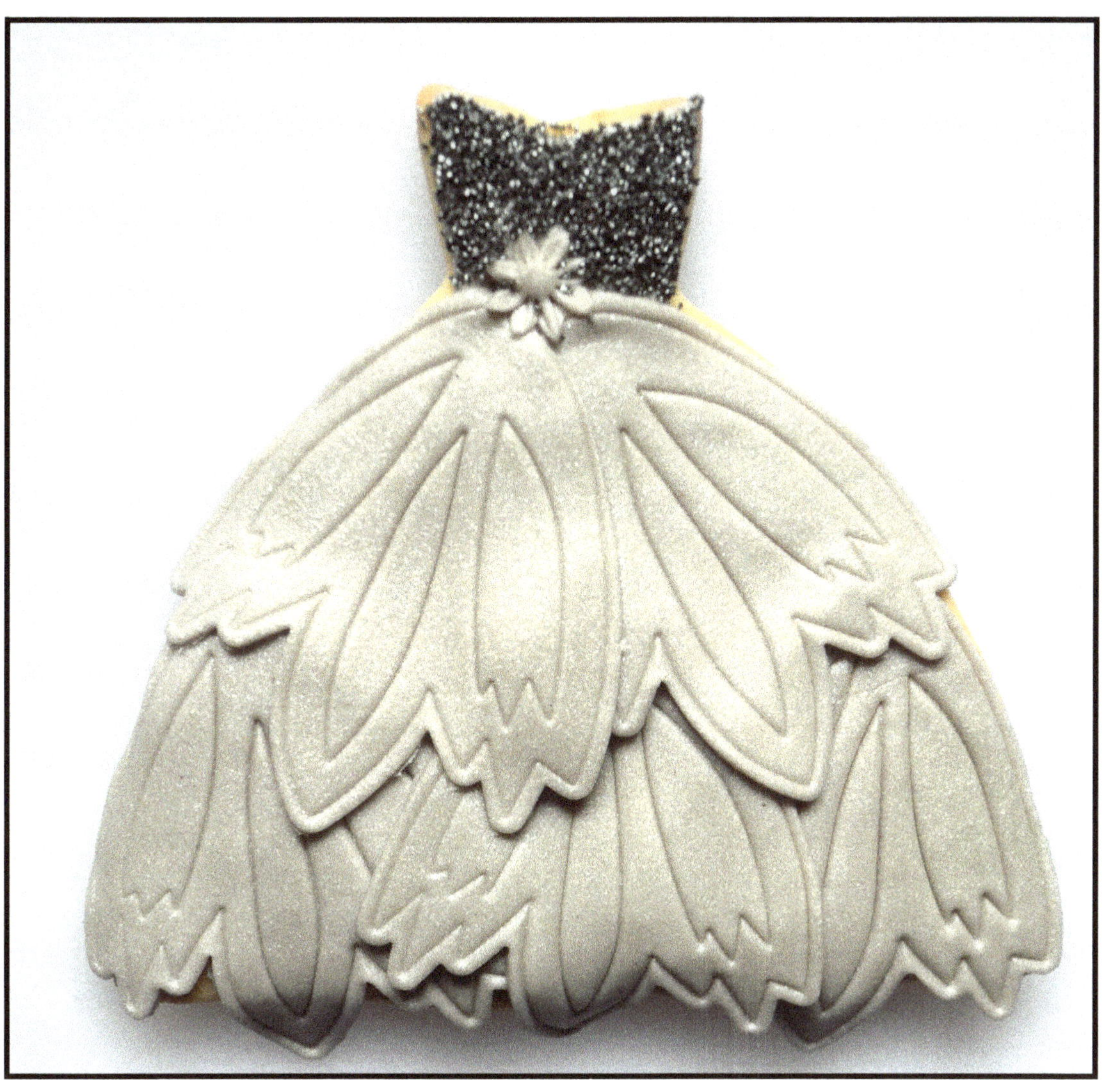

<table>
<tr><td valign="top">

Materials:
- **Dress cookie**
- **1.2 oz. Satin Ice Silver Shimmer fondant**
- **Piping gel**
- **Food safe paint brush**
- **Pizza cutter or Xacto knife**

</td><td valign="top">

Tools:
- **Ann Clark Gown Cookie Cutter (amazon.com)**
- **Large tulip plunger cutter**
- **Silver sanding sugar**
- **Small daisy plunger cutter**
- **Tip 1E**

</td></tr>
</table>

Suggested cellophane bag size is 6x8 inches to package this dress cookie.

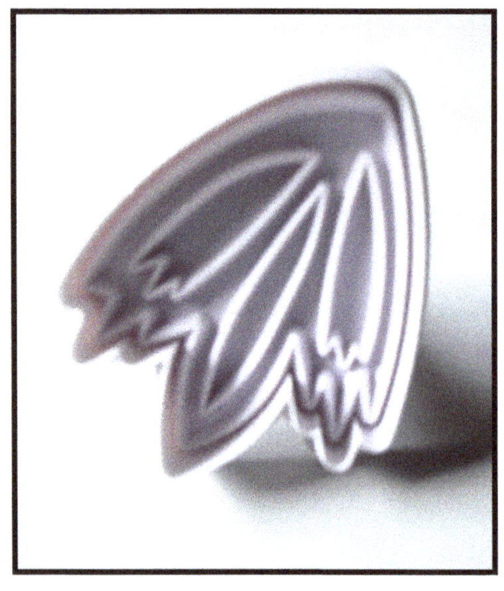

1. This is the large tulip plunger cutter.

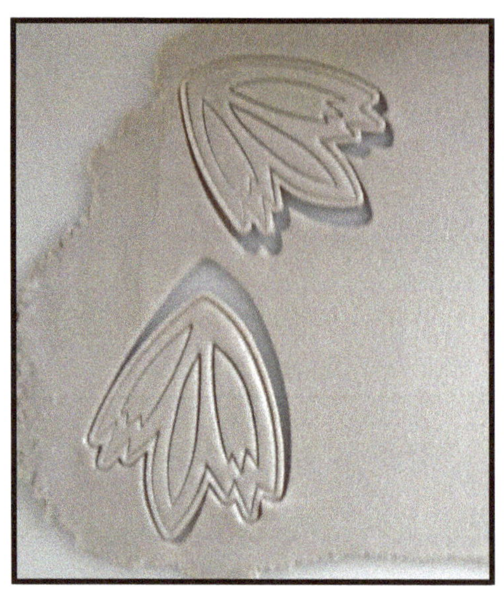

2. Roll out silver fondant. Use large tulip plunger cutter to cut out five fondant tulip cut-outs. Use the dress cookie cutter to cut out just the bodice part of the dress cookie.

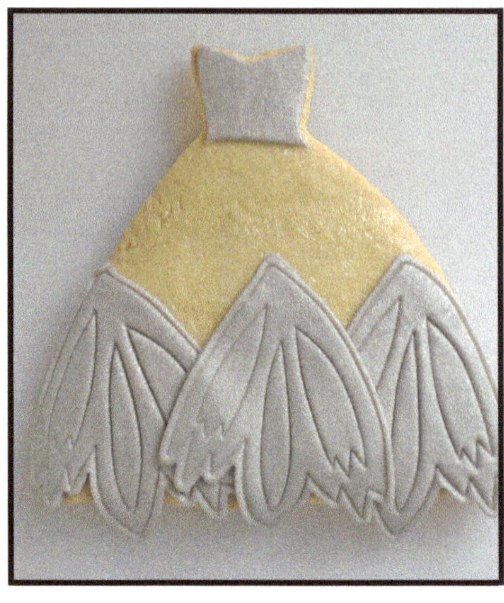

3. Apply piping gel to the dress cookie. Attach the fondant bodice cut-out to the top of the dress cookie. Attach the fondant tulip cut-out to the bottom left, and then bottom right as shown above. Center the fondant tulip cut-out in the bottom center.

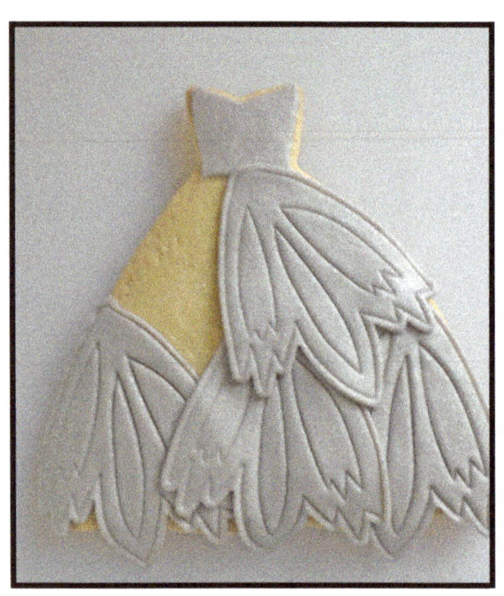

4. Attach the fondant tulip cut-out to the right side of the dress cookie, tilting it as shown above.

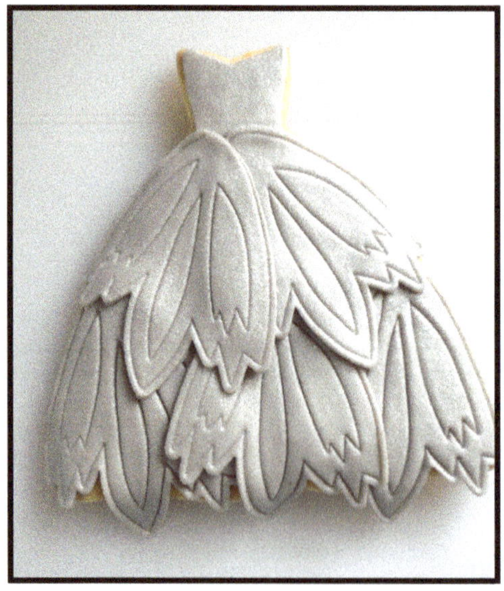

5. Attach the left side fondant tulip cut-out as shown above overlapping the right side.

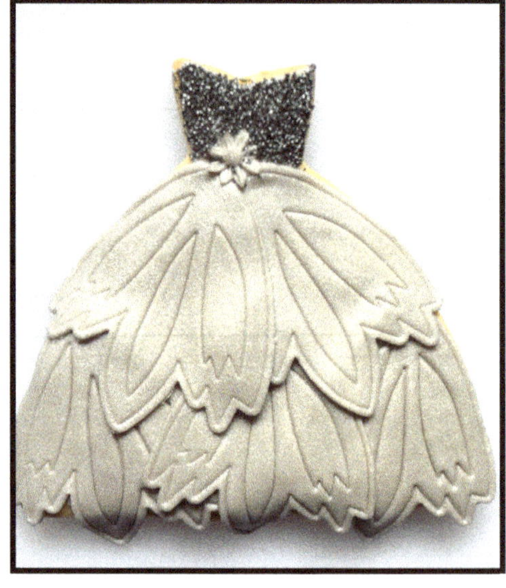

6. Paint the bodice portion with piping gel, and then apply silver sanding sugar to cover. Remove excess. Cut out one small fondant daisy flower with the plunger cutter. Apply to waist section as shown above. Use icing tip 1E to imprint center.

Orange Lace Dress Cookie

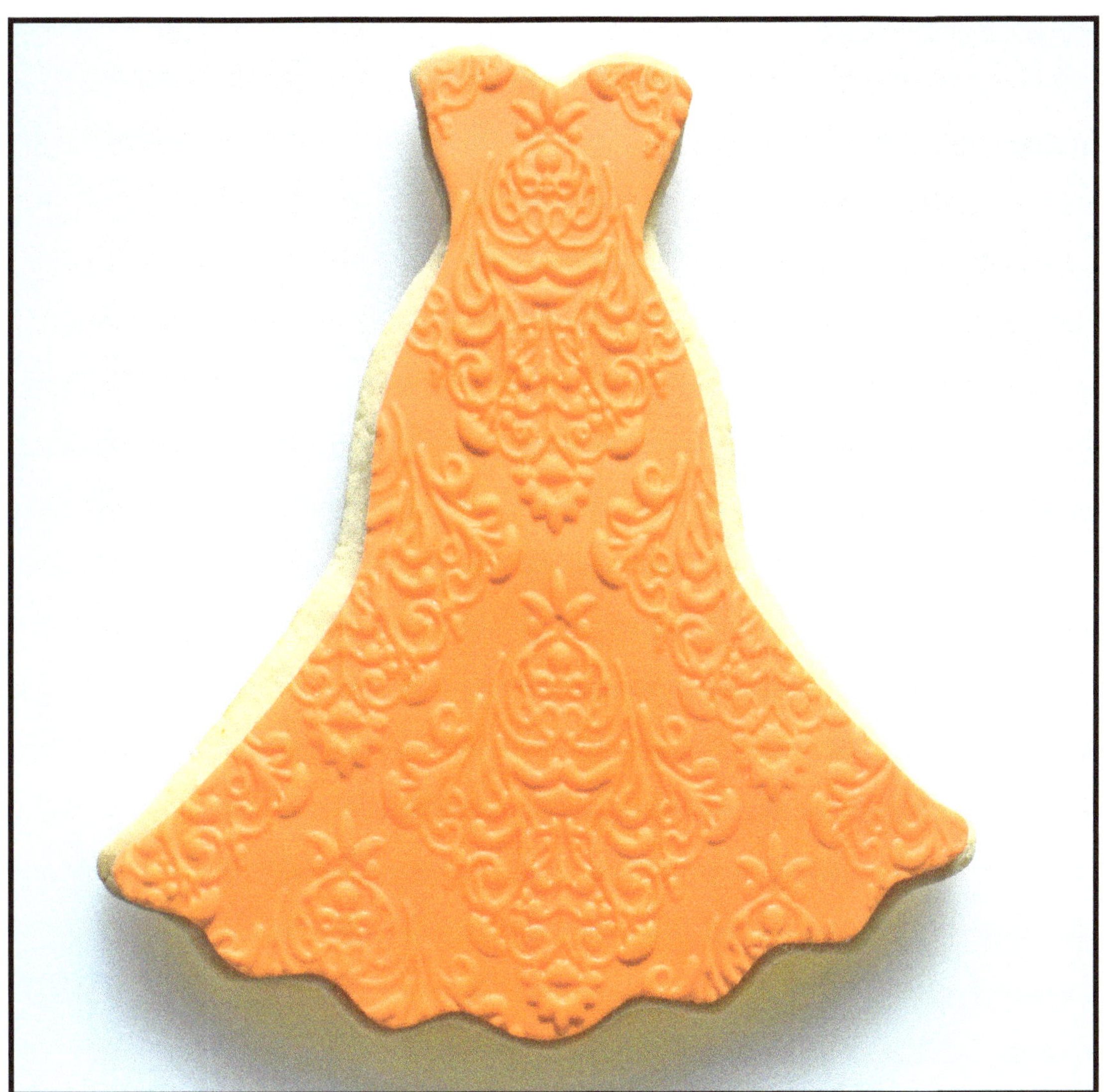

Materials:
- Dress cookie
- 0.6 oz. orange fondant
- Piping gel
- Food safe paint brush

Tools:
- LILIAO Wedding Dress Cookie Cutter (amazon.com)
- CK Damask Impression Mat

Suggested cellophane bag size is 5x7 inches to package this dress cookie.

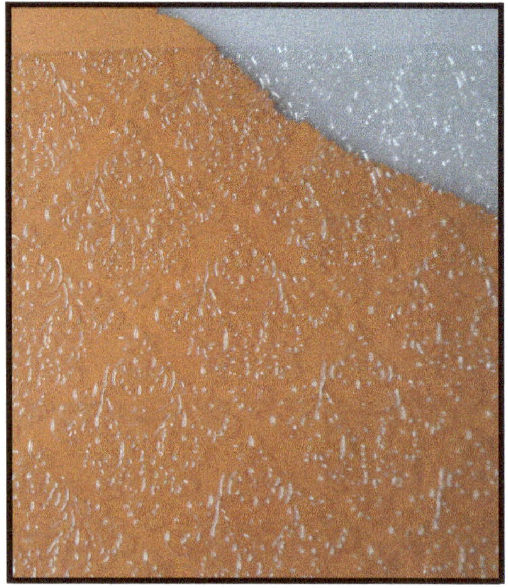 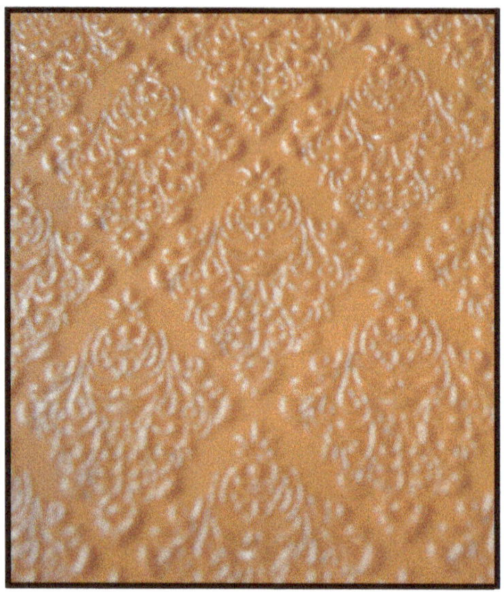 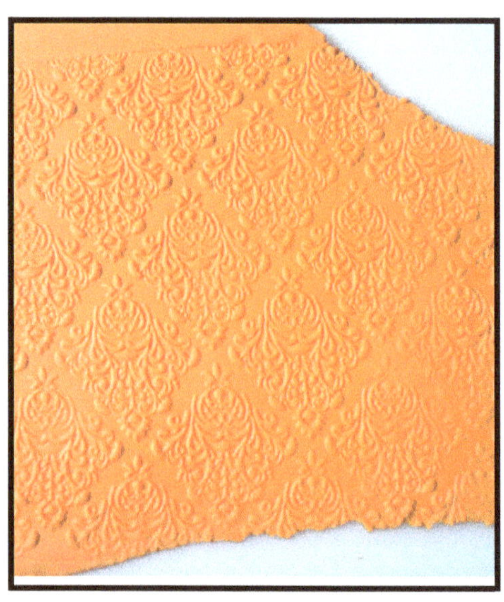

1. Roll out orange fondant. With even pressure, place the damask impression mat on top (raised side up as shown) and use a rolling pin to roll over it.

2. Use your fingers to rub over the impression mat to make sure it is secure. Remove.

3. Use bench scraper to lift fondant pattern up, and then place it back onto the surface.

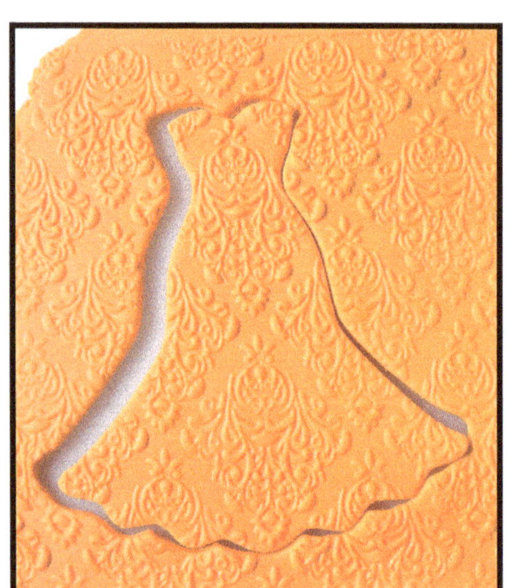 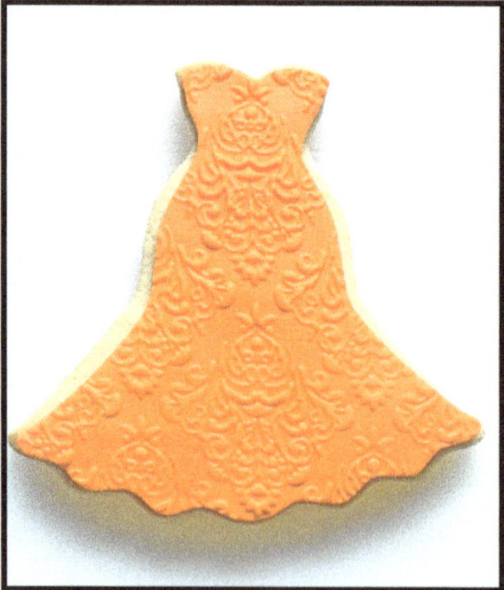

4. Center the dress cookie cutter over the fondant design area as shown. Press the dress cookie cutter firmly into the orange fondant, and then wiggle to release the fondant from the dress cookie cutter.

5. Use a paint brush to apply a thin layer of piping gel onto your dress cookie. Apply fondant cut-out to cookie, and gently smooth top.

Metallic Gold Dress Cookie

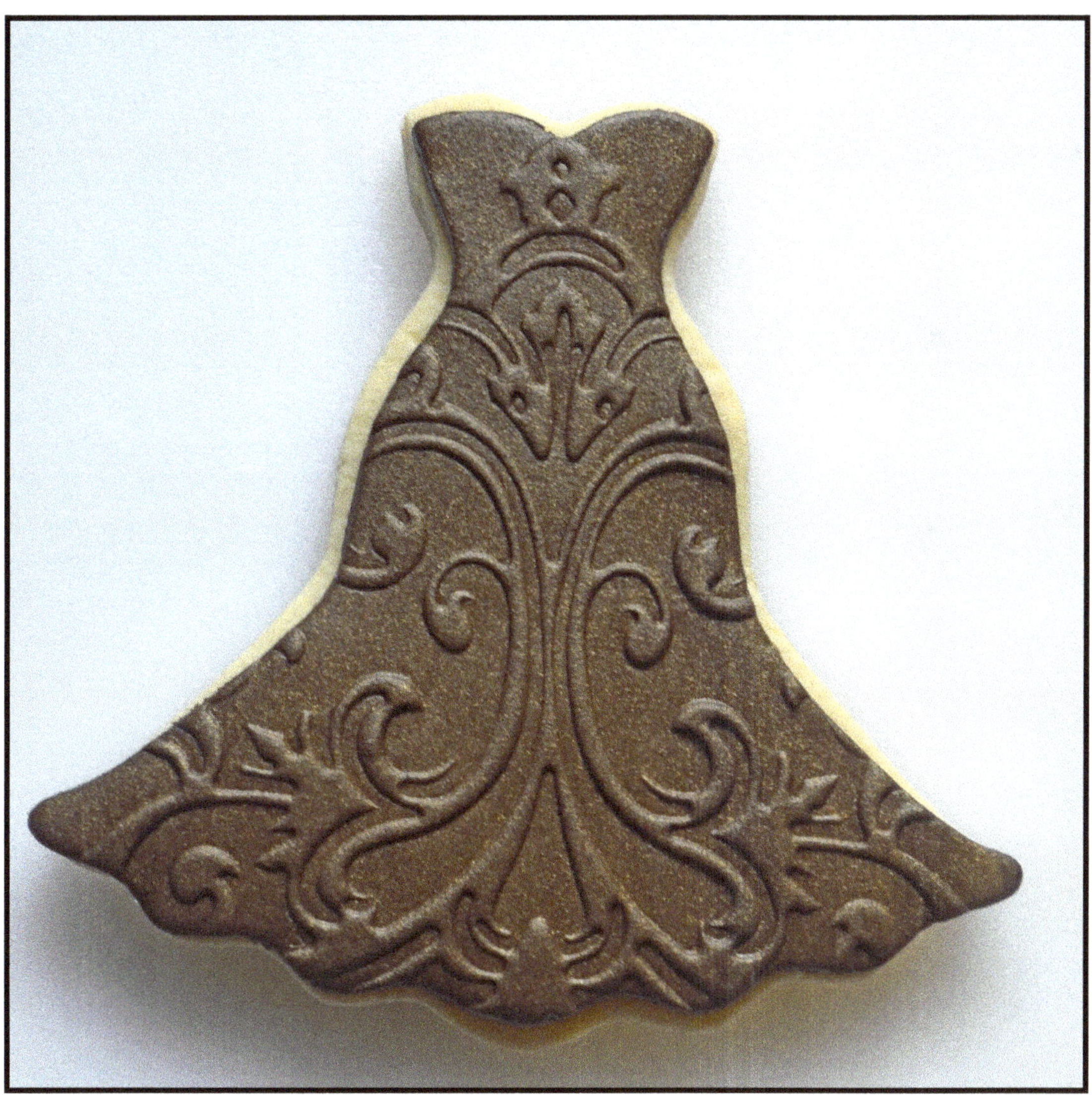

Materials:
- Dress cookie
- 0.4 oz. Sunny Side Up Bakery Gold Vanilla fondant
- 0.2 oz. Fondarific Black fondant
- Piping gel
- Food safe paint brush

Tools:
- LILIAO Wedding Dress Cookie Cutter (amazon.com)
- Sunny Side Up Bakery Filigree Lace Silicone Mold (hobbylobby.com)

Suggested cellophane bag size is 5x7 inches to package this dress cookie.

1. This is the Filigree Lace Silicone Mold.

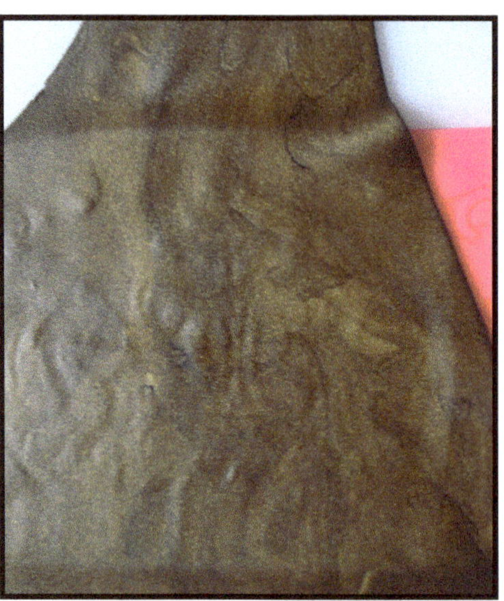

2. Completely blend the gold and black fondant together. Roll out. Lay metallic fondant on top of filigree lace silicone mold. Use a rolling pin to roll over fondant using even pressure. Turn fondant over.

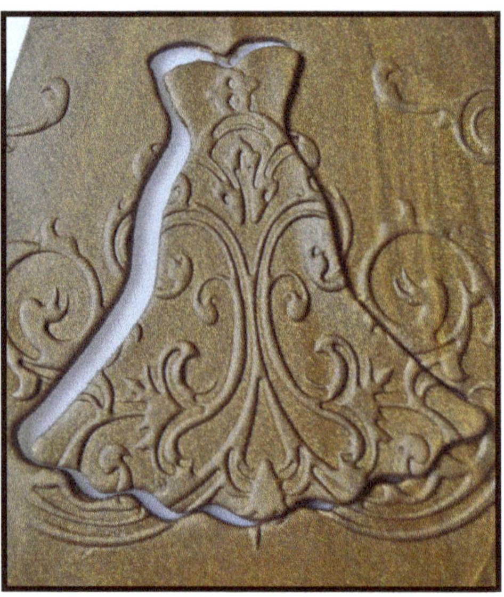

3. Center the dress cookie cutter over the design area as shown. Press the dress cookie cutter firmly into the metallic fondant, and then wiggle to release the fondant from the dress cookie cutter.

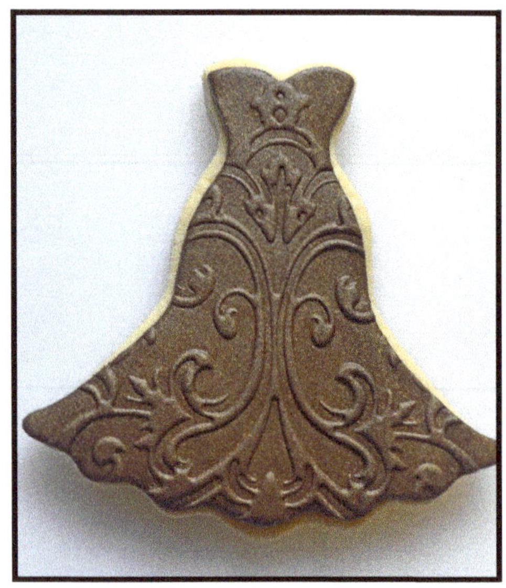

4. Use a paint brush to apply a thin layer of piping gel onto your dress cookie. Apply fondant cut-out to cookie, and gently smooth top.

Gold Pressed Dress Cookie

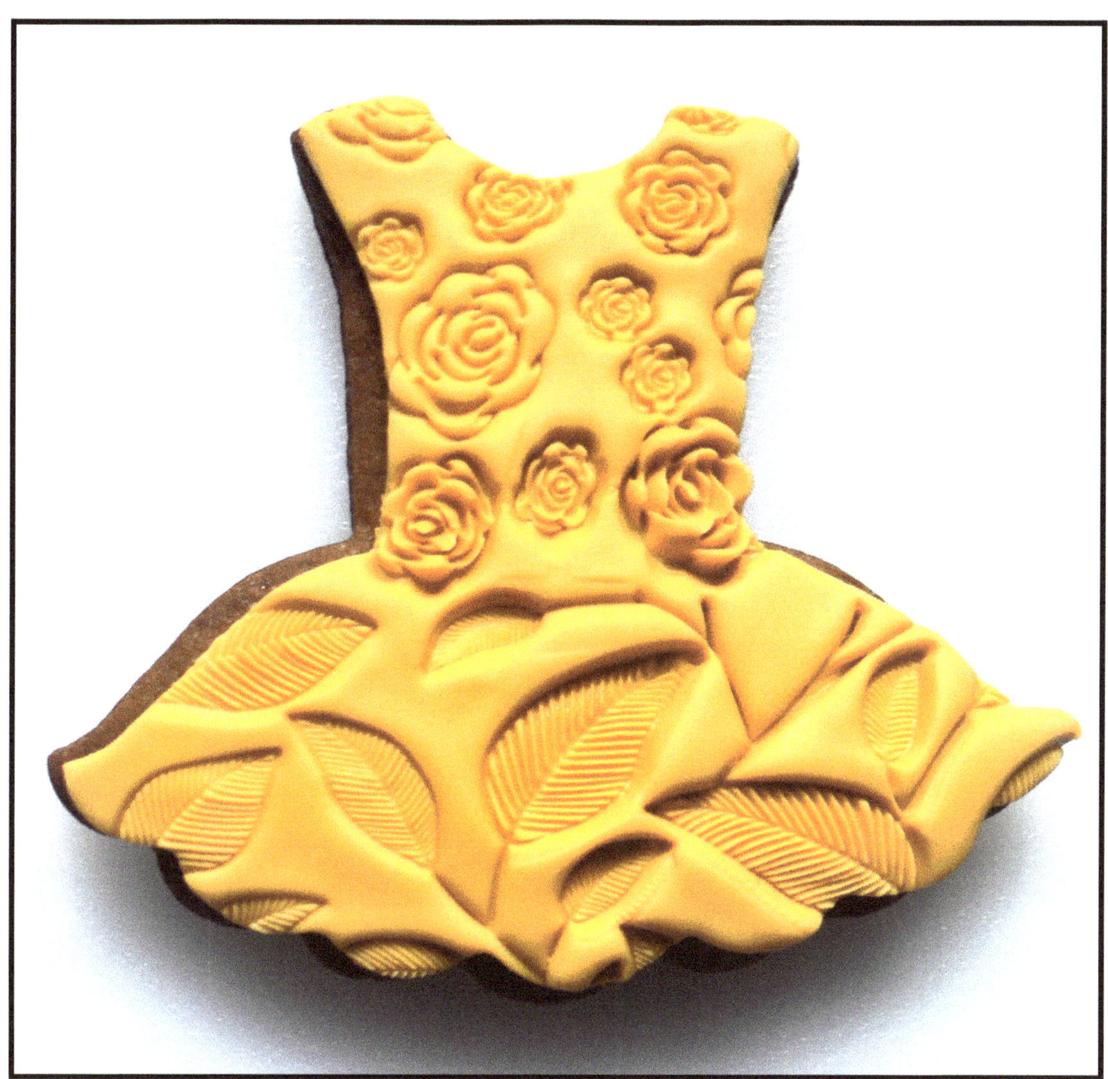

Materials:
- Dress cookie
- 0.8 oz. gold fondant
- Piping gel
- Food safe paint brush

Tools:
- Tutu and Dress Cookie Cutter (etsy.com, WhiskedAwayCutters)
- JOERSH Cake Fondant Embossing Mould 6 Pack Fondant Embosser Set (Roses & Leaves) (amazon.com)

Suggested cellophane bag size is 4x6 inches to package this dress cookie.

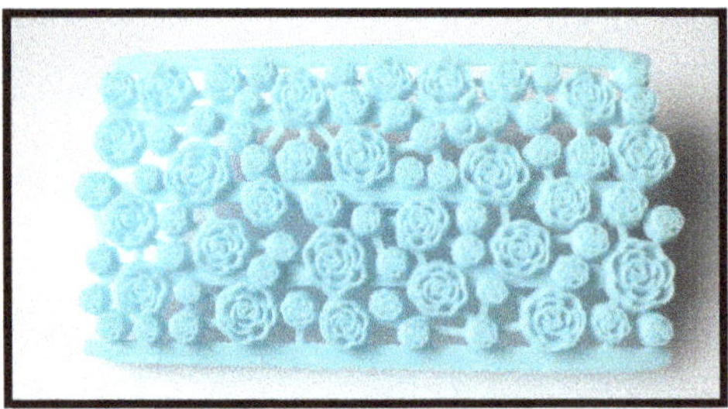

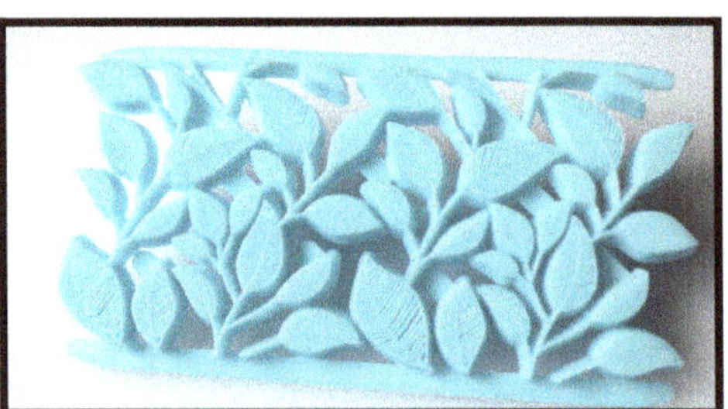

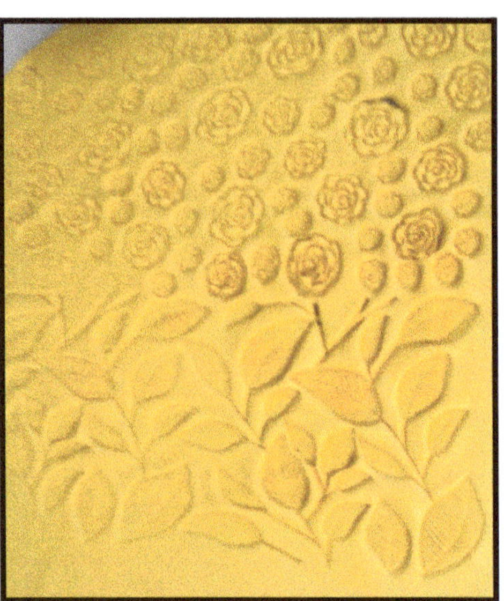

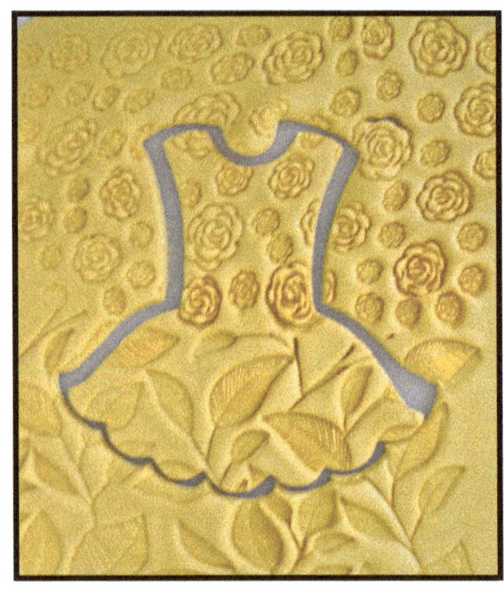

1. Pictured above are the rose embossing mold and the leaves embossing mold.

2. Roll out the gold fondant. Use even pressure to imprint half of the fondant with the rose embossing mold, and the other half with the leaves embossing mold. Use a bench scraper to lift the fondant up, and then place it back on the surface.

3. Center the dress cookie cutter over the design area as shown. Press the dress cookie cutter firmly into the gold fondant, and then wiggle to release the fondant from the dress cookie cutter.

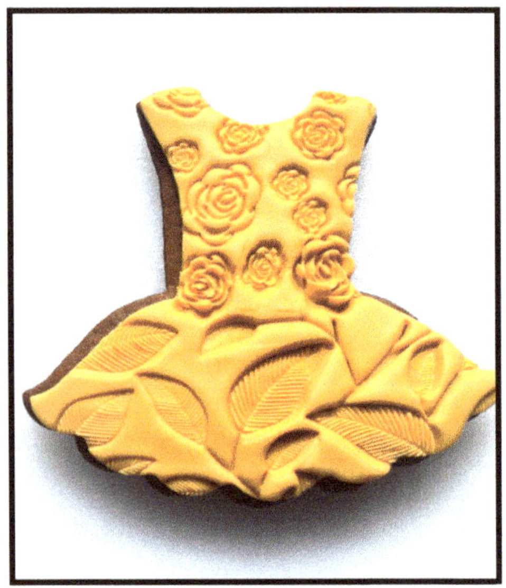

4. Use a paint brush to apply a thin layer of piping gel onto your dress cookie. Apply fondant cut-out to cookie, and gently smooth top.

Purple Lace Dress Cookie

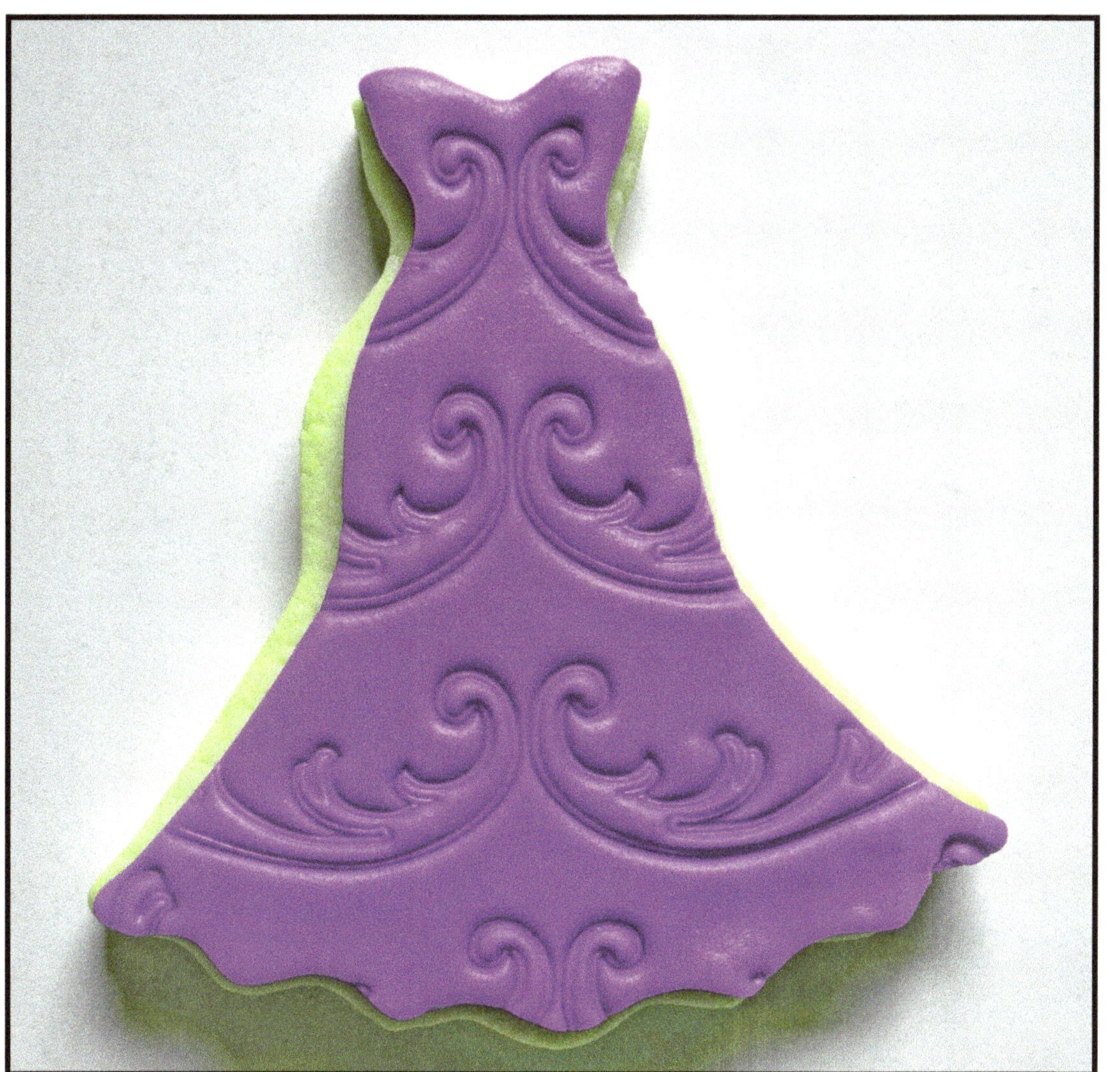

Materials:
- Dress cookie
- 0.6 oz. Fondarific Purple fondant
- Piping gel
- Food safe paint brush

Tools:
- LILIAO Wedding Dress Cookie Cutter (amazon.com)
- JEM Scrolls & Pansy Fondant Cutters

Suggested cellophane bag size is 5x7 inches to package this dress cookie.

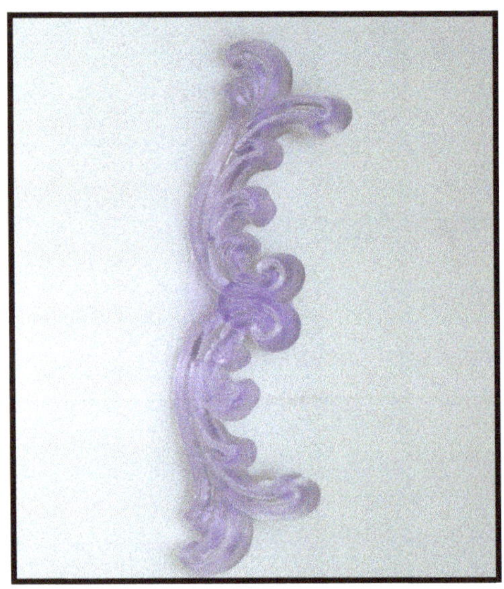

1. This is the JEM scroll tool to use for this design.

2. Roll out purple fondant. Use JEM scroll to imprint the fondant four times as shown above. Use a bench scraper to lift the fondant up and place it back on the surface.

3. Center the dress cookie cutter over the design area as shown. Press the dress cookie cutter firmly into the purple fondant, and then wiggle to release the fondant from the dress cookie cutter.

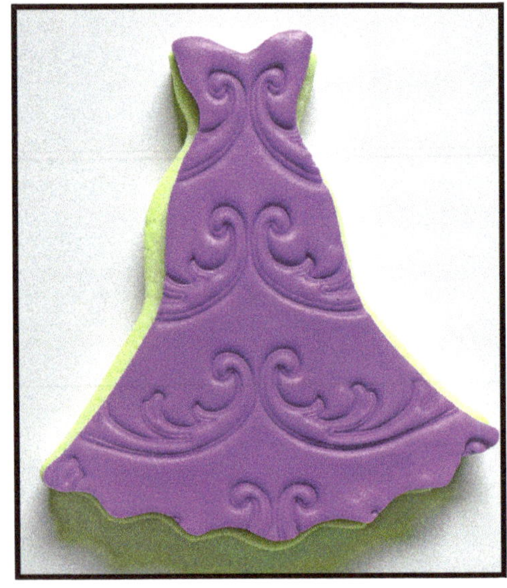

4. Use a paint brush to apply a thin layer of piping gel onto your dress cookie. Apply fondant cut-out to cookie, and gently smooth top.

Blue Imprint Dress Cookie

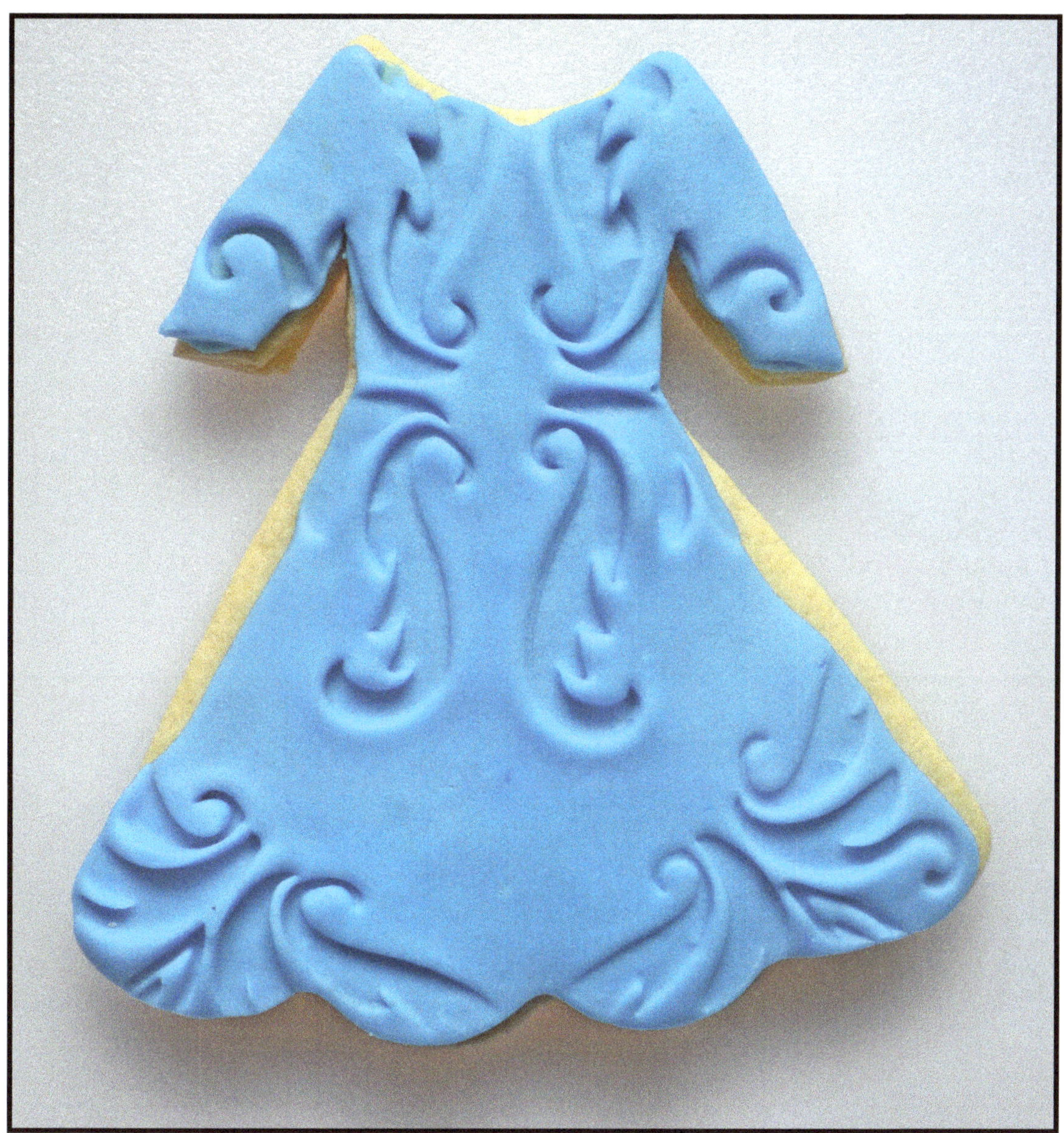

Suggested cellophane bag size is 5x7 inches to package this dress cookie.

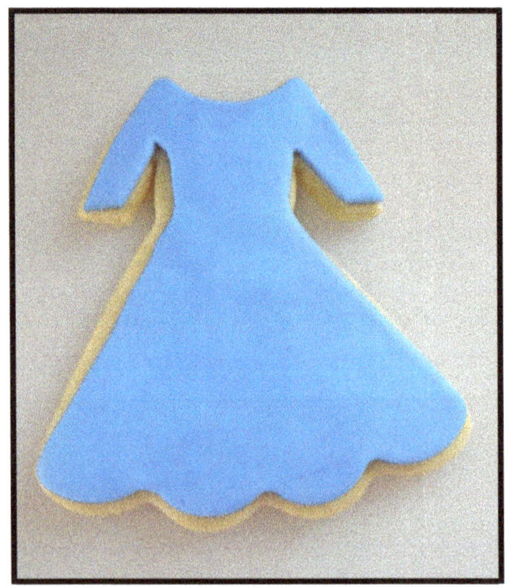 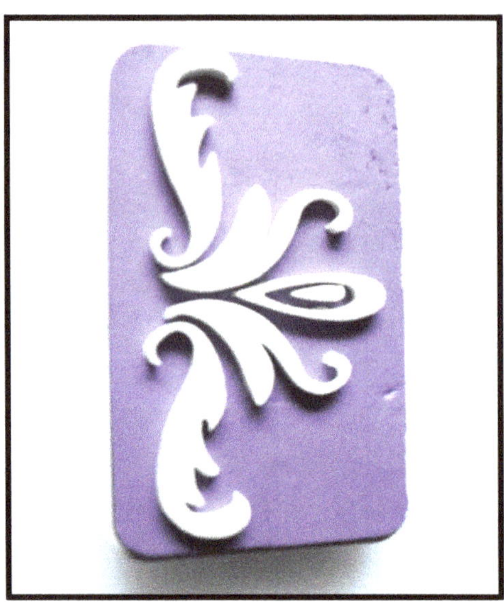 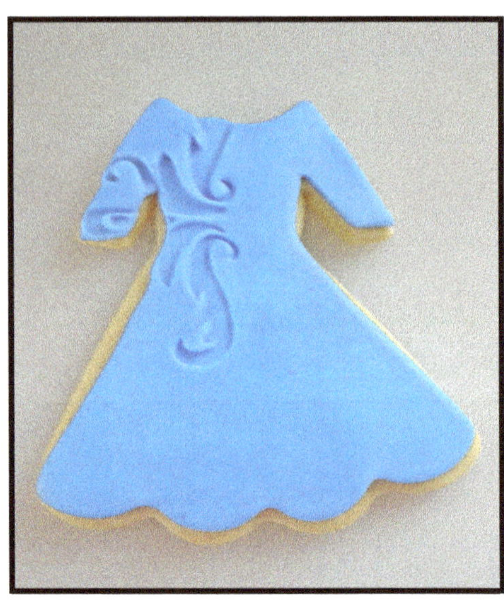

1. Roll out blue fondant. Use the dress cookie cutter to cut out the blue fondant dress. Use a paint brush to apply a thin layer of piping gel onto your dress cookie. Apply fondant cut-out to cookie, and gently smooth top.

2. This is the flourish cake stamp to use for this dress cookie design.

3. Use the flourish cake stamp as shown above to imprint left side of bodice dress cookie.

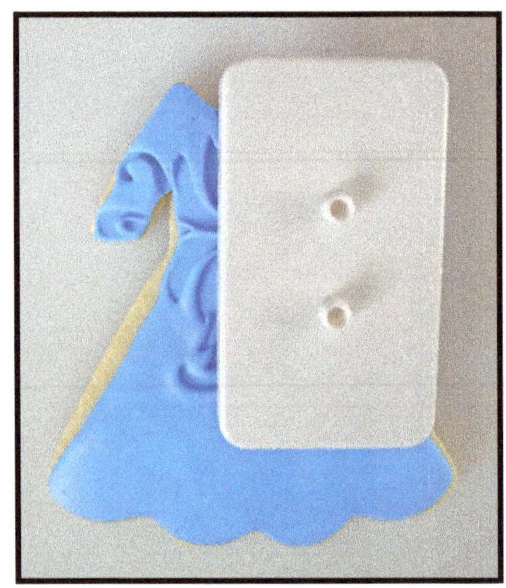 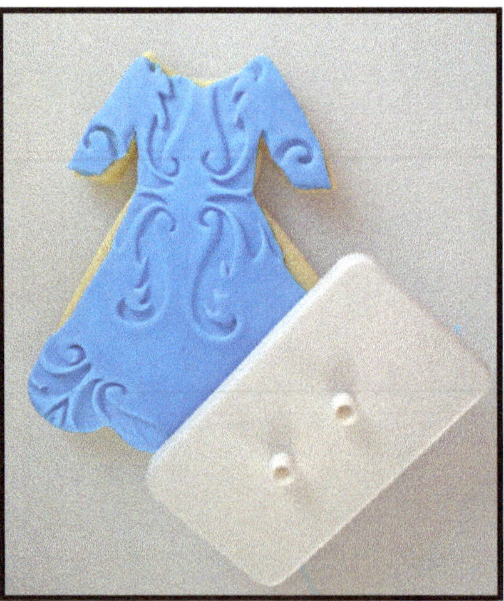 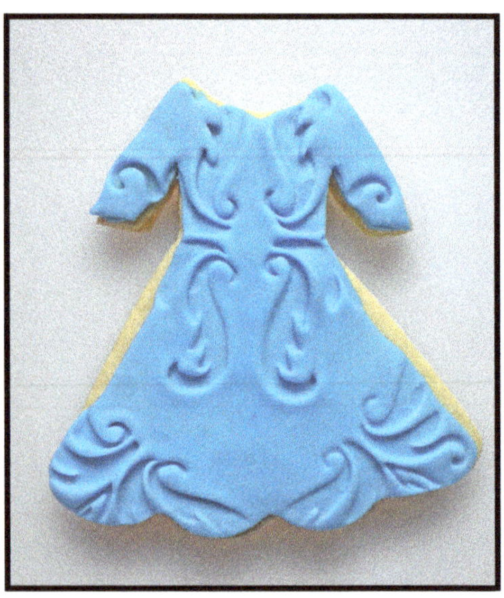

4. Use the flourish cake stamp as shown above to imprint right side of bodice dress cookie. Lean over to look at the white sponge and match it to the left-sided impression. Press firmly and remove.

5. Use the flourish cake stamp as shown above to imprint left bottom side of dress cookie. Use the flourish cake stamp as shown above to imprint left right bottom side of dress cookie.

6. This is the final dress cookie design.

Burgundy Butterfly Dress Cookies

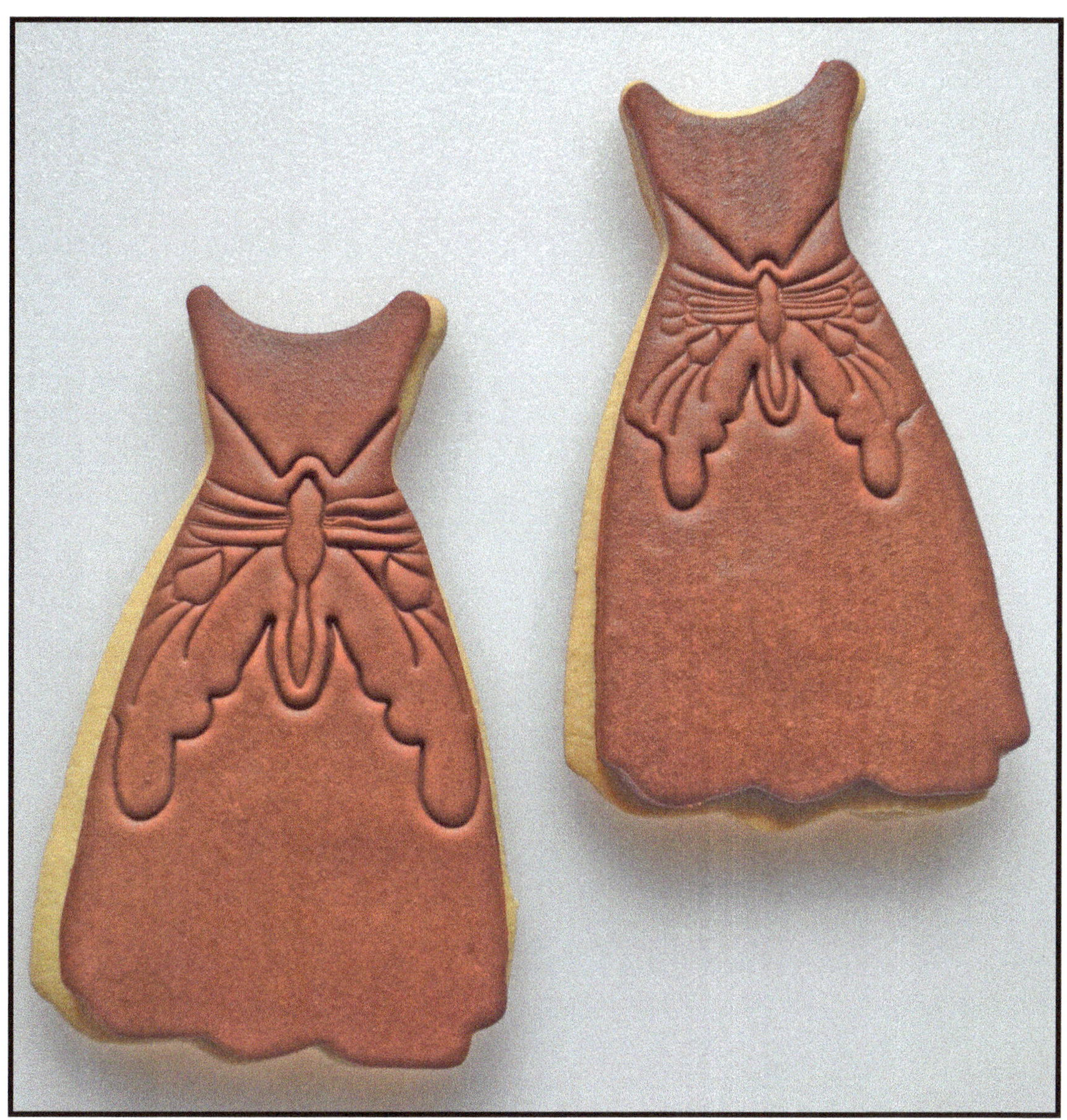

Materials:
- Two dress cookies
- 1.3 oz. Fondarific Burgundy fondant
- Piping gel
- Food safe paint brush

Tools:
- Dress Cookie Cutter (flourbox.com)
- 2-piece Butterfly Fondant Cake Embossing Mold

Suggested cellophane bag size is 4x6 inches to package these dress cookies.

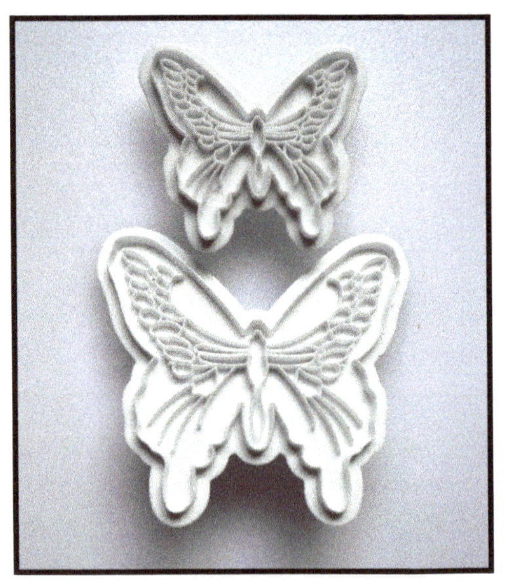

1. Here are the small and large butterfly embossing molds.

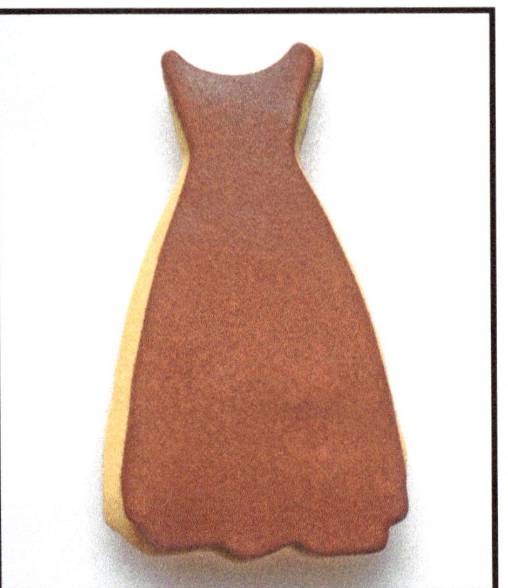

2. Roll out burgundy fondant. Use the dress cookie cutter to cut out the burgundy fondant dresses. Use a paint brush to apply a thin layer of piping gel onto your dress cookies. Apply fondant cut-out to cookies and gently smooth top.

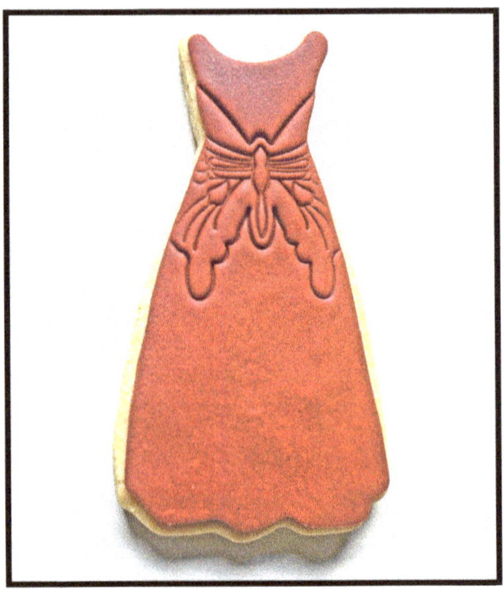

3. Center small butterfly embossing mold over dress cookie, and gently press into fondant to emboss the design. Remove.

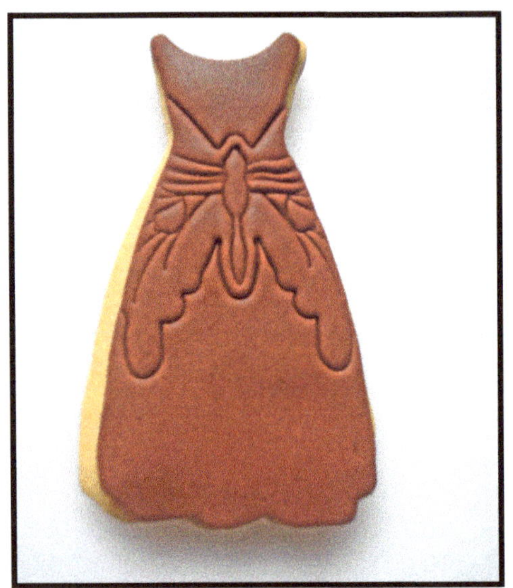

4. Center large butterfly embossing mold over dress cookie, and gently press into fondant to emboss the design. Remove.

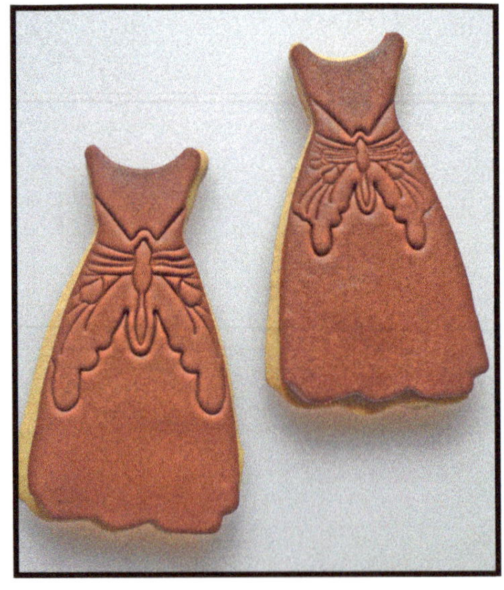

5. These are the final dress cookie designs.

Gold Strip Dress Cookie

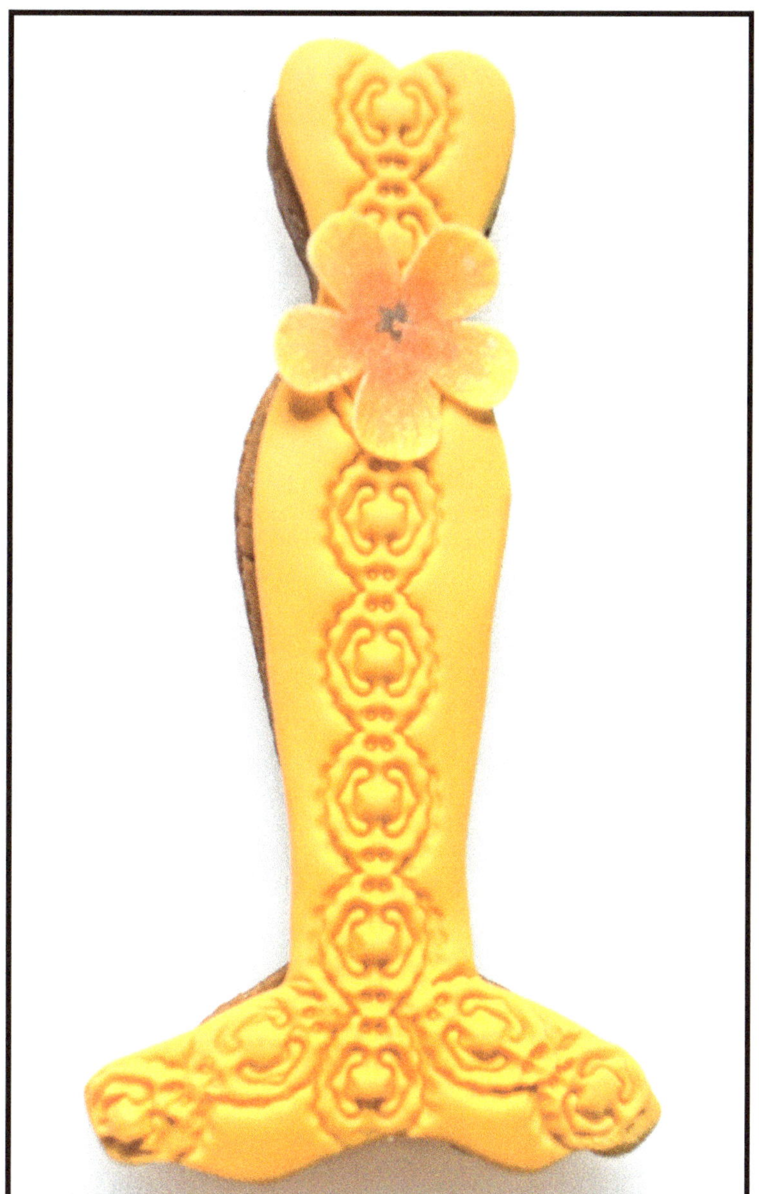

Materials:
- Dress cookie
- 0.5 oz. gold fondant
- Piping gel
- Food safe paint brush

Tools:
- Wedding Dress Cookie Cutter (etsy.com, BakersToolsStore)
- Lace Strip Patchwork Cutter
- Wafer paper flowers (amazon.com)

Suggested cellophane bag size is 3x8 inches to package this dress cookie.

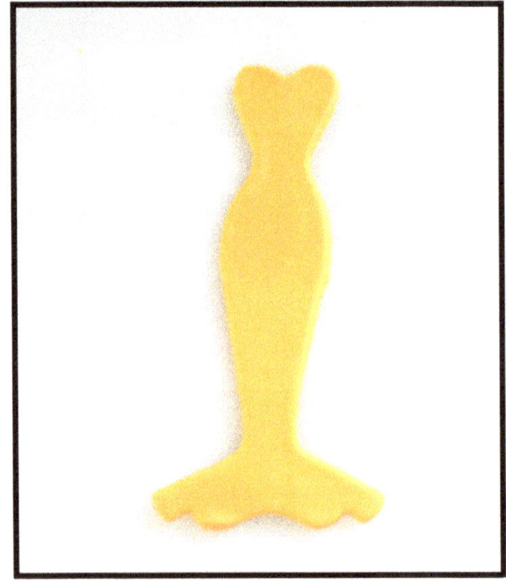

1. Roll out gold fondant. Use the dress cookie cutter to cut out the gold fondant dress.

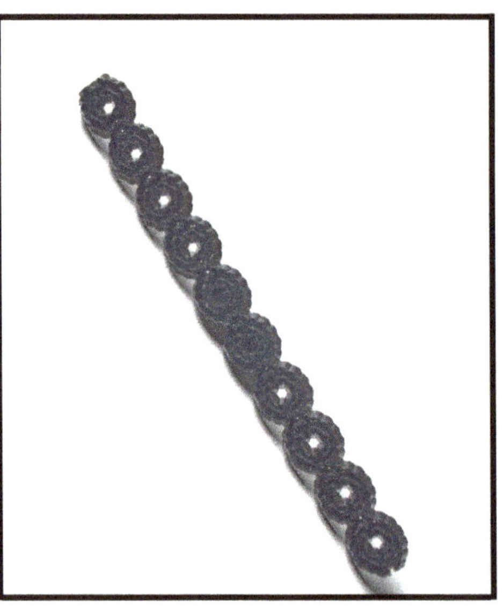

2. This is the lace strip tool.

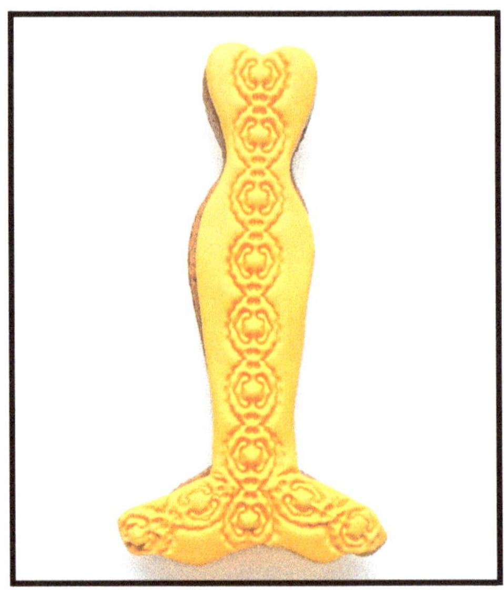

3. Use a paint brush to apply a thin layer of piping gel onto your dress cookie. Apply fondant cut-out to cookie, and gently smooth top. Center the lace strip tool in the center of the dress cookie and imprint the design. Repeat for the bottom left and right as shown.

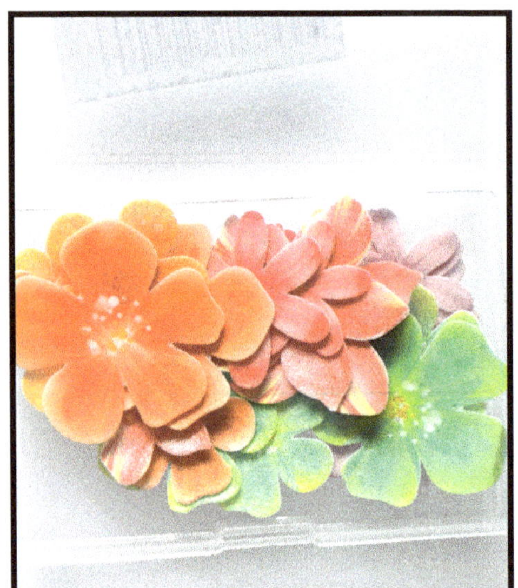

4. These are the wafer flowers.

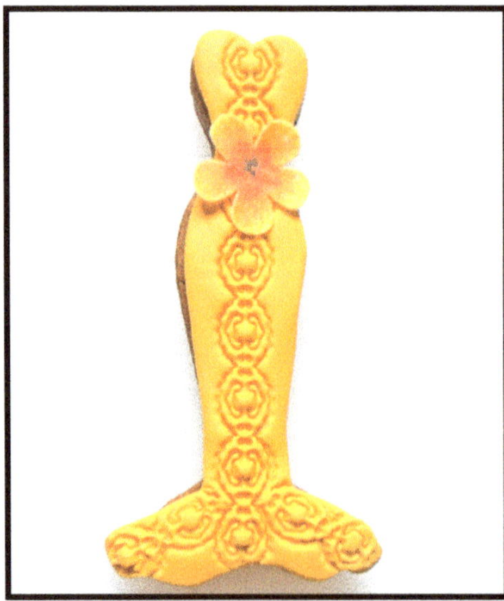

5. Dab a little piping gel on the back of the wafer flower and attach to the center of the waist on the dress cookie.

Peach Bridesmaid Dress Cookies

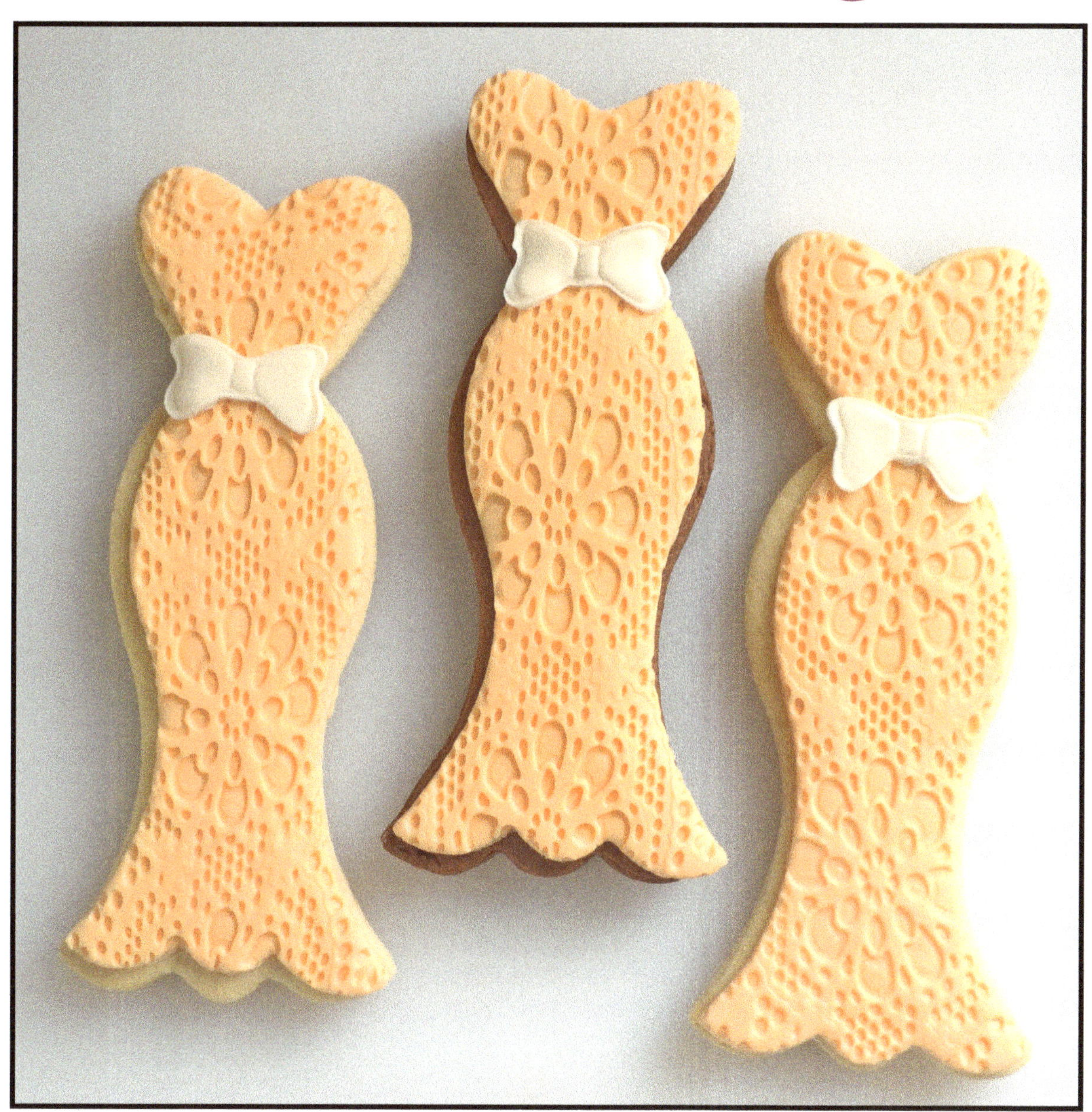

Materials:
- Three dress cookies
- 1.5 oz. peach fondant
- Piping gel
- Food safe paint brush

Tools:
- The Marilyn Gown Cookie Cutter (etsy.com, Sinful Cutters)
- Sunny Side Up Bakery Floral Lace Silicone Mold (hobbylobby.com)
- Medium bow plunger cutter

Suggested cellophane bag size is 3x8 inches to package these dress cookies.

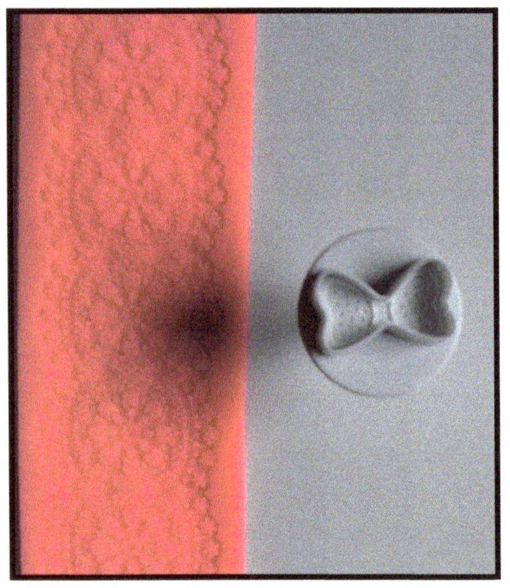

1. This is the Floral Lace Silicone Mold and the medium bow plunger cutter.

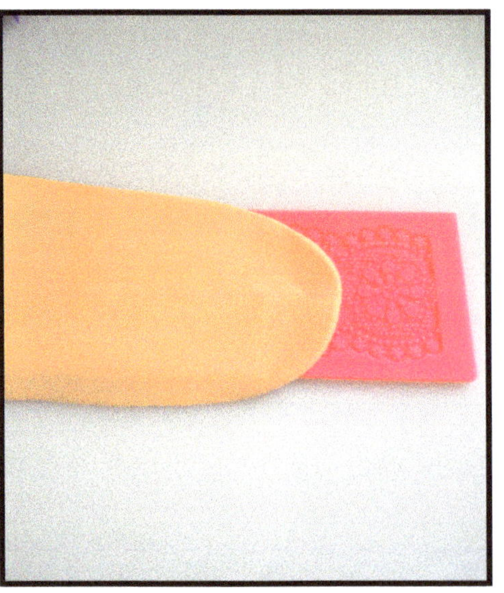

2. Roll out peach fondant. Lay peach fondant on top of floral lace silicone mold. Use a rolling pin to roll over fondant using even pressure. Turn fondant over.

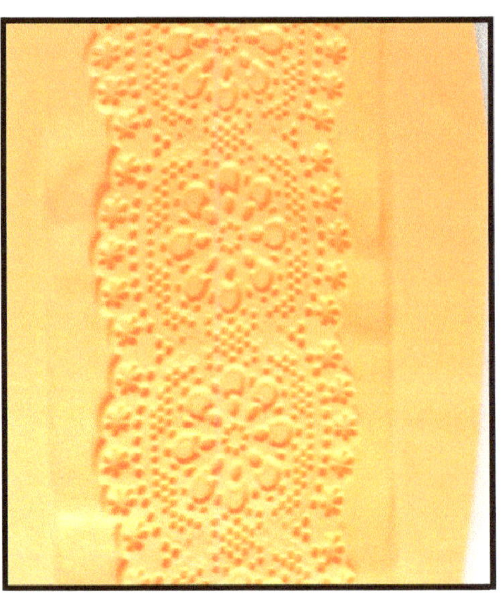

3. This is what the imprinted fondant looks like.

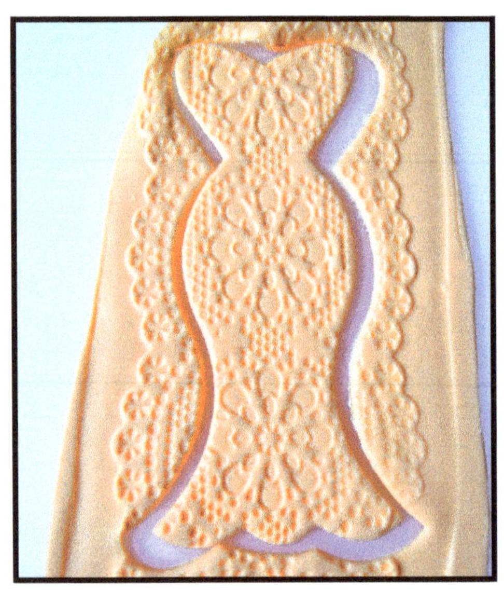

4. Center the dress cookie cutter over the design area as shown. Press the dress cookie cutter firmly into the peach fondant, and then wiggle to release the fondant from the dress cookie cutter.

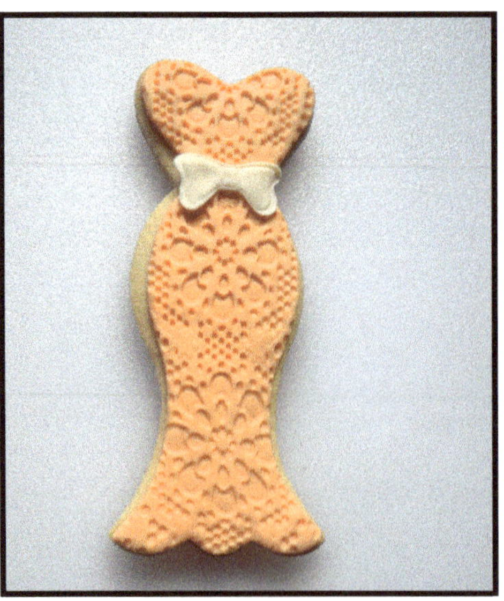

5. Use a paint brush to apply a thin layer of piping gel onto your dress cookie. Apply fondant cut-out to cookie, and gently smooth top. Repeat for other dress cookies. Roll out white fondant and use bow plunger cutter to cut out three bows. Attach to dress cookie waist as shown.

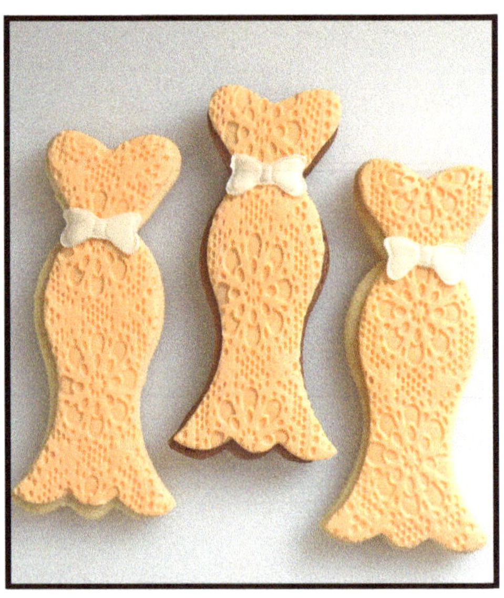

6. These are the final dress cookies. I used a chocolate cookie for the middle one to make it stand out.

Pink Swirl Dress Cookie

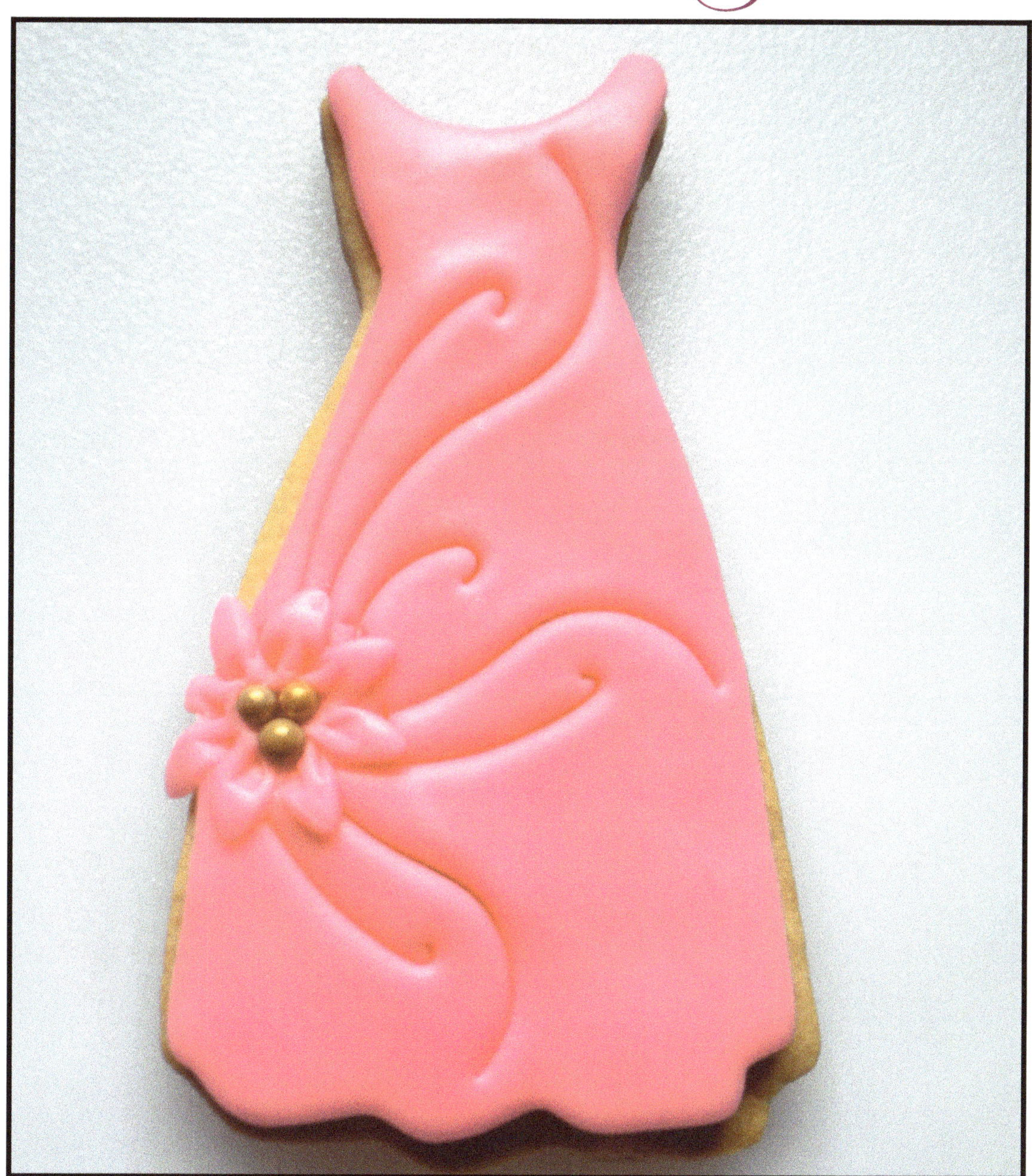

Materials:
- Dress cookie
- 0.7 oz. Fondarific Pink fondant
- Piping gel
- Food safe paint brush

Tools:
- Dress Cookie Cutter (flourbox.com)
- Wilton's Designer Pattern Press Set, Flower Press
- Large daisy plunger cutter
- Tip 1E
- Wilton Gold Sugar Pearls
- Ball tool

Suggested cellophane bag size is 4x6 inches to package this dress cookie.

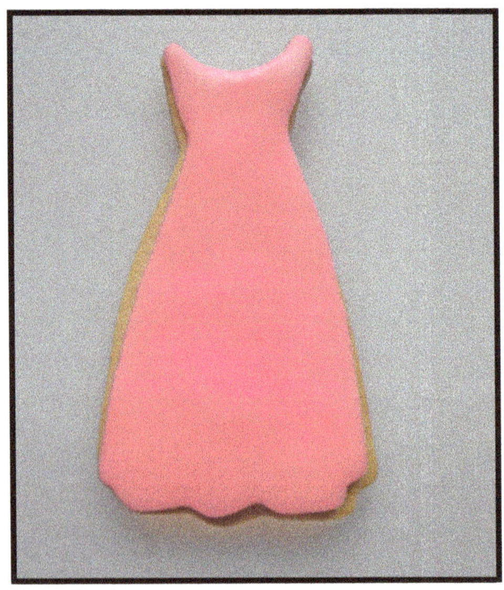

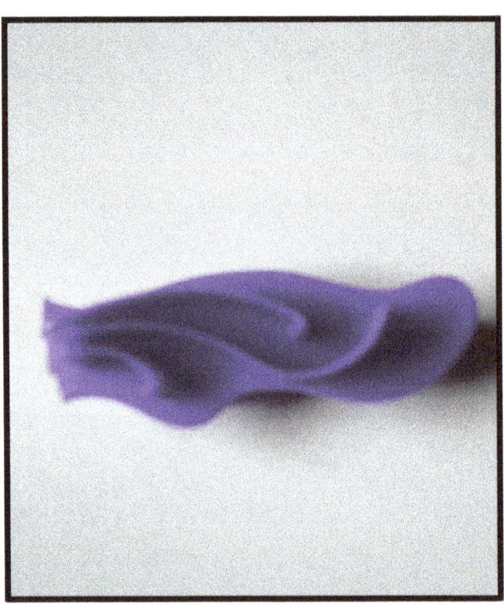

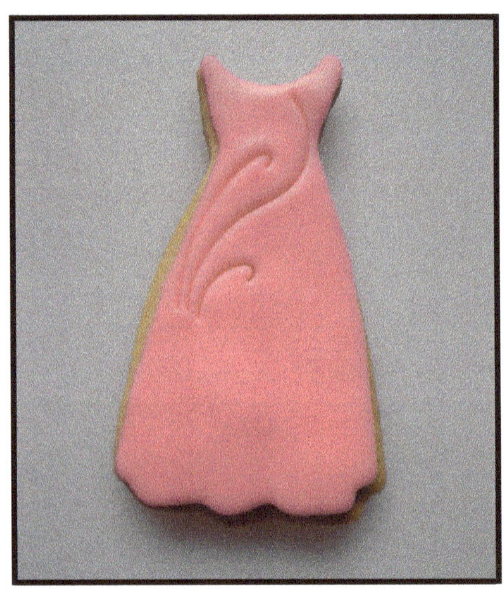

1. Roll out pink fondant. Use the dress cookie cutter to cut out the pink fondant dress. Use a paint brush to apply a thin layer of piping gel onto your dress cookie. Apply fondant cut-out to cookie, and gently smooth top.

2. This is the flower press. It has been broken in half. Use the large side for this cookie design.

3. Use the flower press tool to imprint the dress cookie as shown.

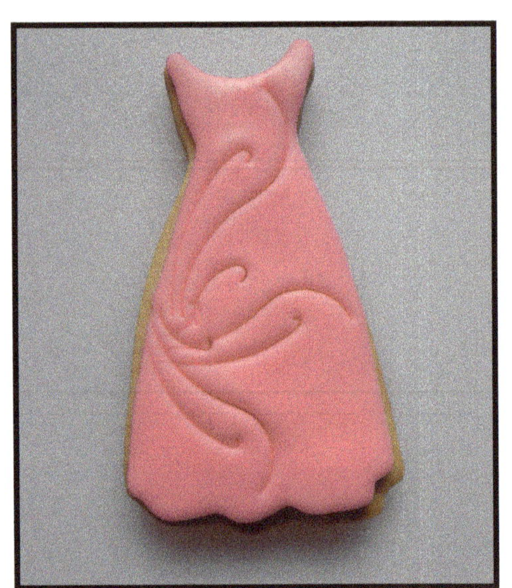

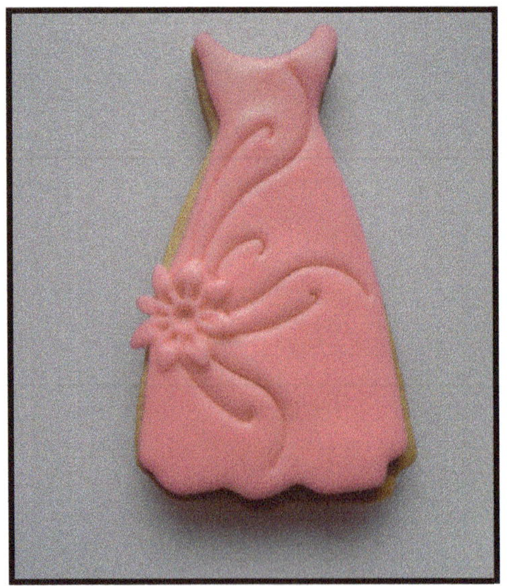

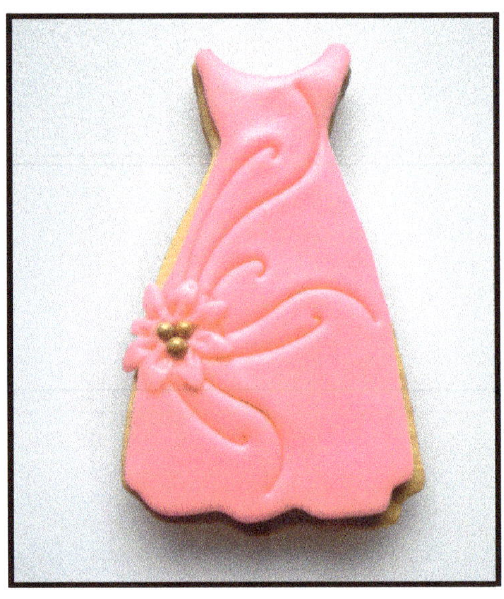

4. Use the flower press tool to imprint the dress cookie center, and then imprint lower dress area.

5. Use the medium daisy plunger to cut out one fondant flower. Attach to dress cookie as shown. Imprint the fondant daisy cut-out with icing tip 1E. Use a ball tool to imprint the center of the fondant daisy cut-out. Add a dab of piping gel to the center.

6. Place three gold beads in the center of the fondant daisy as shown. Press down to secure.

Silver Dots Dress Cookie

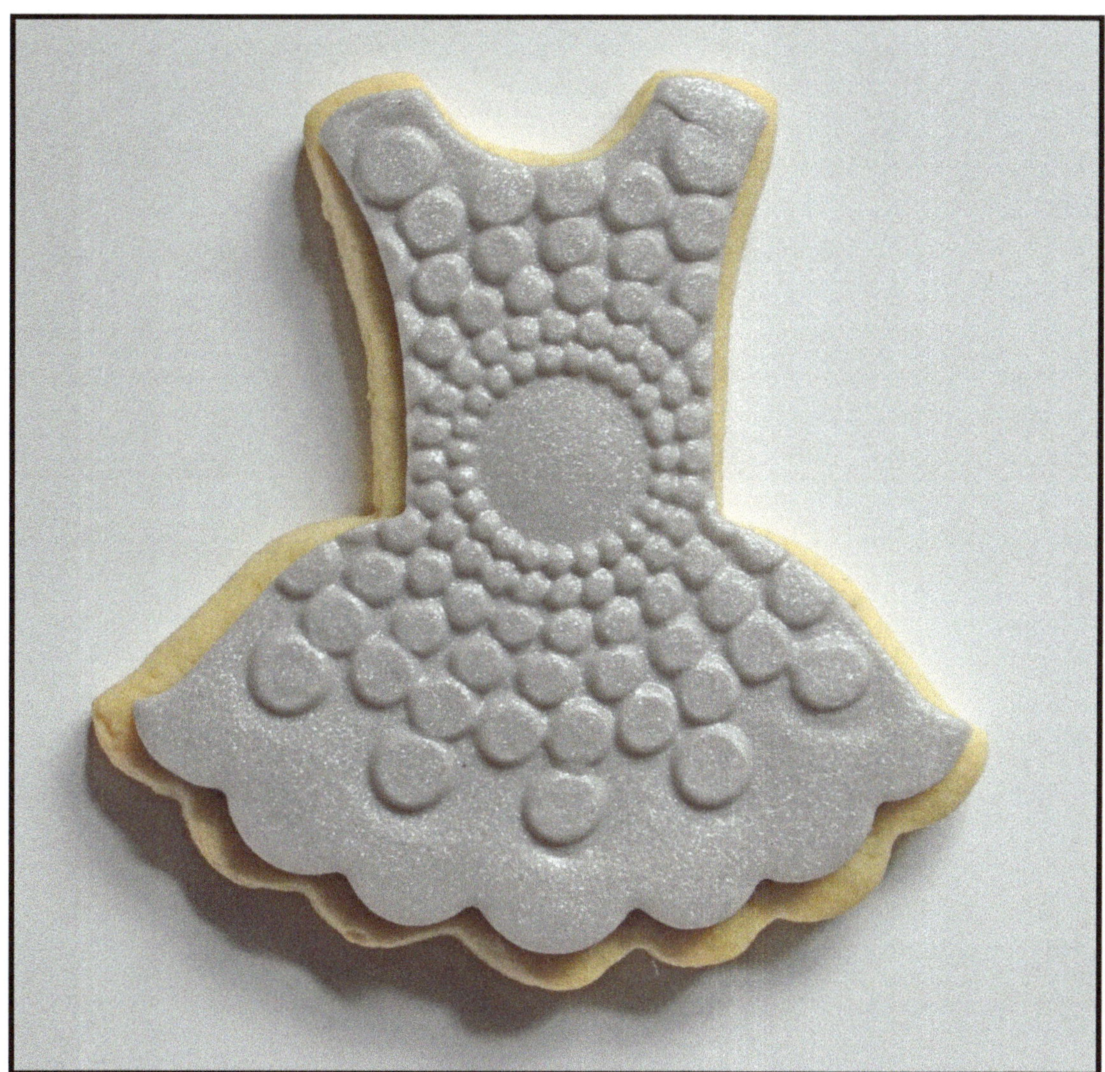

<table>
<tr><td>

Materials:
- **Dress cookie**
- **0.6 oz. Satin Ice Silver Shimmer fondant**
- **Piping gel**
- **Food safe paint brush**

</td><td>

Tools:
- **Tutu and Dress Cookie Cutter (etsy.com, WhiskedAwayCutters)**
- **Geometric Cupcake and Cookie Texture Tops**

</td></tr>
</table>

Suggested cellophane bag size is 4x6 inches to package this dress cookie.

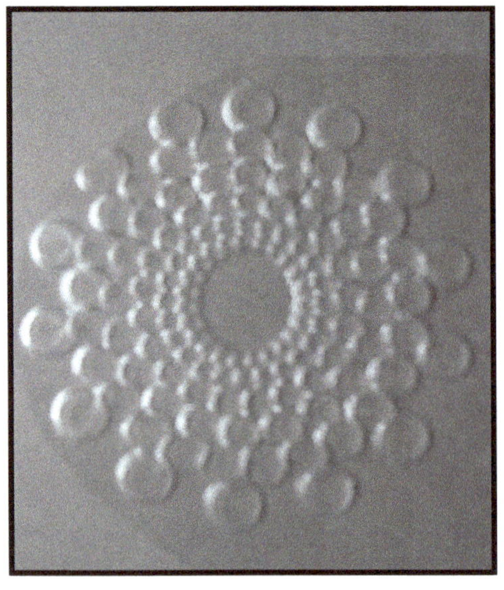

1. Roll out silver fondant. Place Geometric dots mat on top of fondant. Use rolling pin to roll over texture mat. Remove.

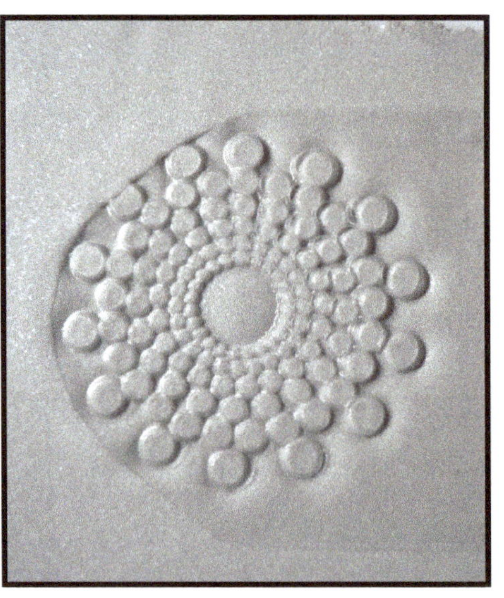

2. This is what the imprinted fondant looks like.

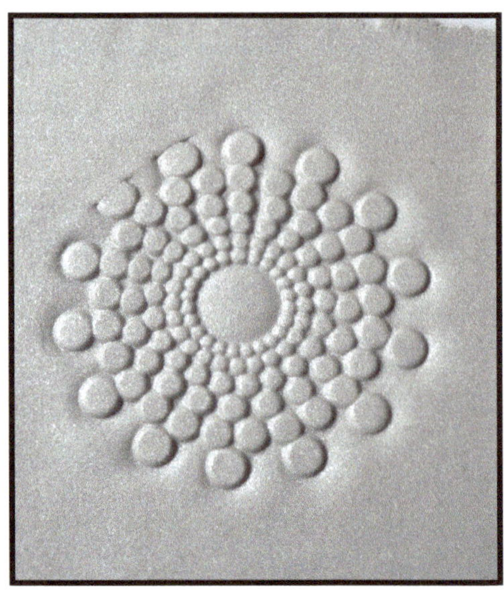

3. Use your finger to smooth the edge area around the design to remove the line.

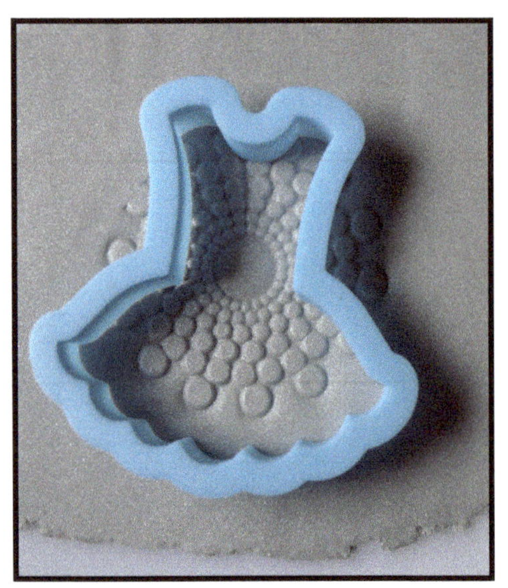

4. Center the dress cookie cutter over the fondant impression area as shown. Press the dress cookie cutter firmly into the silver fondant, and then wiggle to release the fondant from the dress cookie cutter.

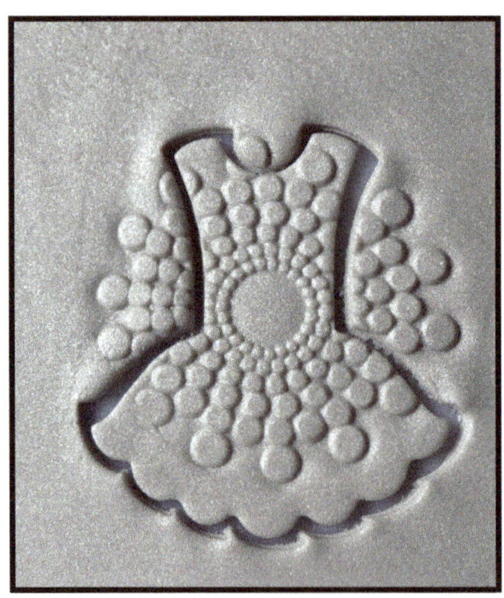

5. This is what the fondant cut-out looks like.

6. Use a paint brush to apply a thin layer of piping gel onto your dress cookie. Apply fondant cut-out to cookie, and gently smooth top.

White Lace Dress Cookie

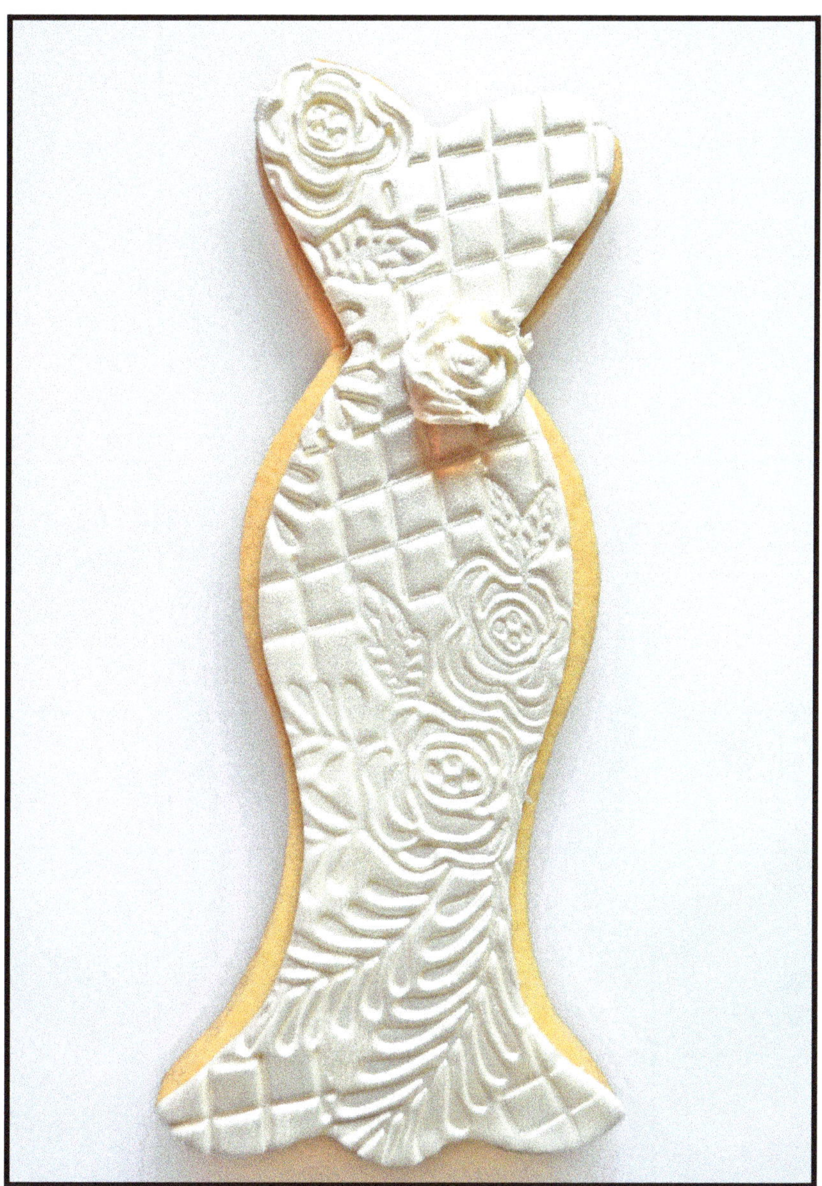

Materials:
- **Dress cookie**
- **0.5 oz. white fondant**
- **Piping gel**
- **Food safe paint brush**
- **Parchment paper**

Tools:
- **The Marilyn Gown Cookie Cutter (etsy.com, Sinful Cutters)**
- **Wilton's Pattern Roller Lace**
- **Wilton Pearl Edible Spray**
- **Small rose silicone mold**

Suggested cellophane bag size is 3x8 inches to package this dress cookie.

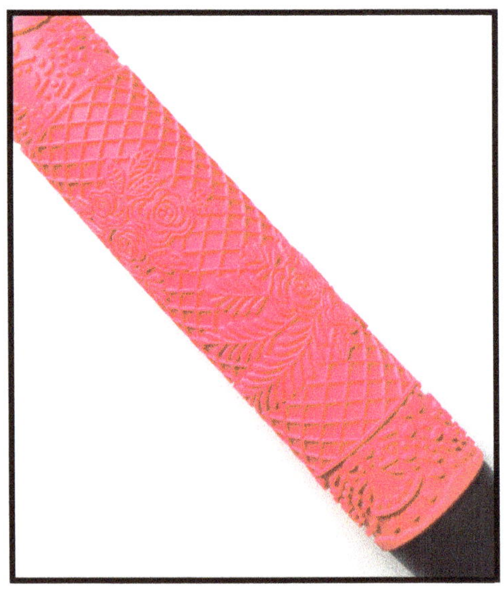

1. This is Wilton's Pattern Roller (Lace).

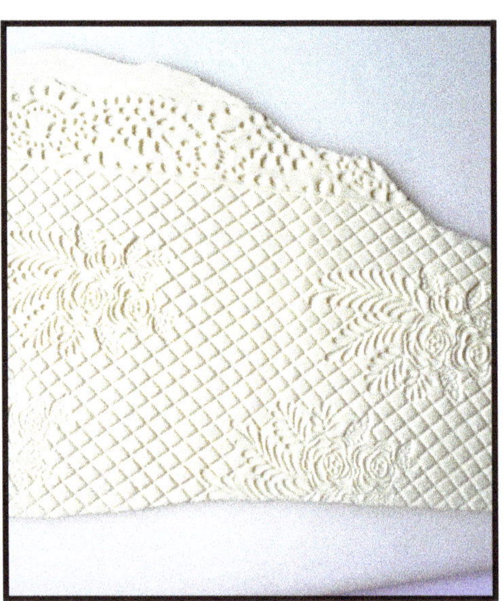

2. Roll out white fondant. Using firm pressure, roll Wilton's Pattern Roller (Lace) over the fondant evenly as shown above. Use bench scraper to lift fondant up and place it back on the surface.

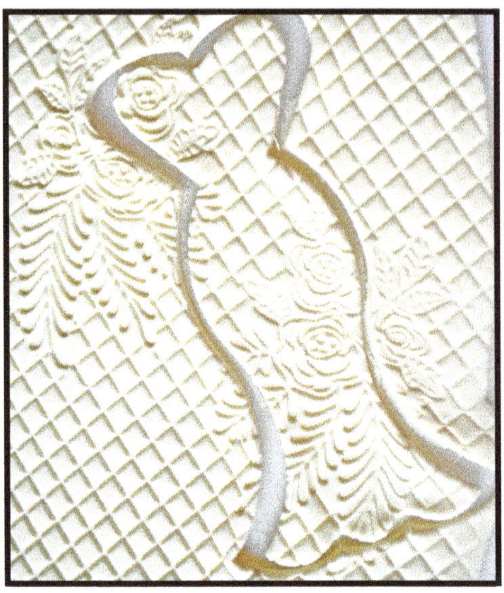

3. Center the dress cookie cutter over the design area. Press the dress cookie cutter firmly into the white fondant, and then wiggle to release the fondant from the dress cookie cutter.

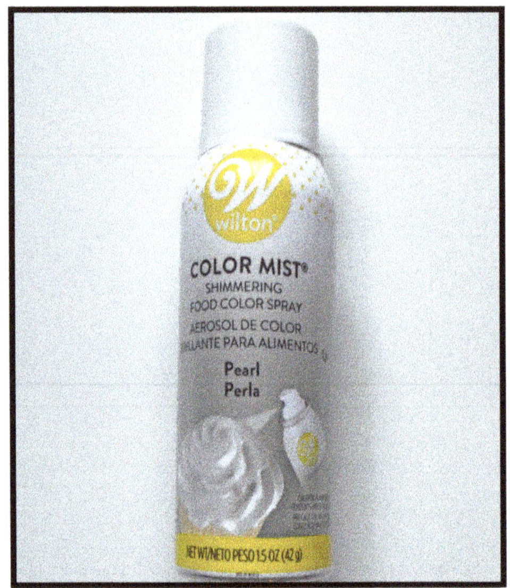

4. This is Wilton's Edible Spray in pearl. Use a parchment sheet to place your fondant cut-out on, and then spray the top with the edible pearl spray. Let the spray dry.

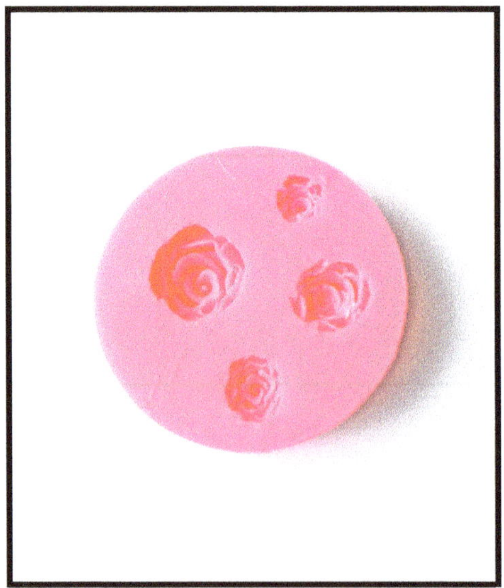

5. This is the rose silicone mold. Place white fondant into the smallest cavity and refrigerate until firm.

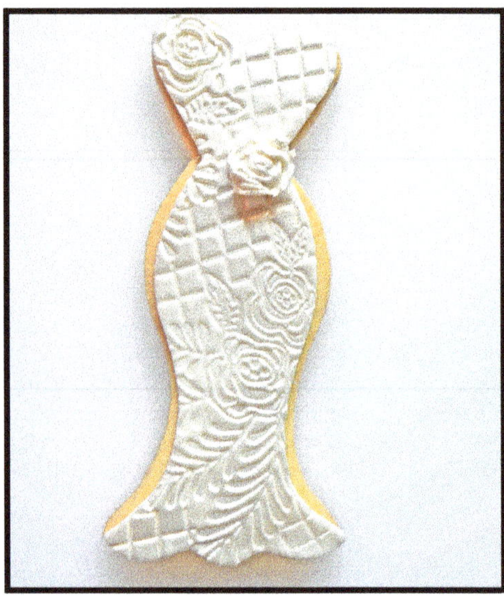

6. Use a paint brush to apply a thin layer of piping gel onto your dress cookie. Gently lift fondant cut-out from the parchment paper and apply it to cookie, and gently smooth top. Place a dab of piping gel on the back of the fondant rose, and attach it to waist as shown.

Yellow Sprinkles Dress Cookie

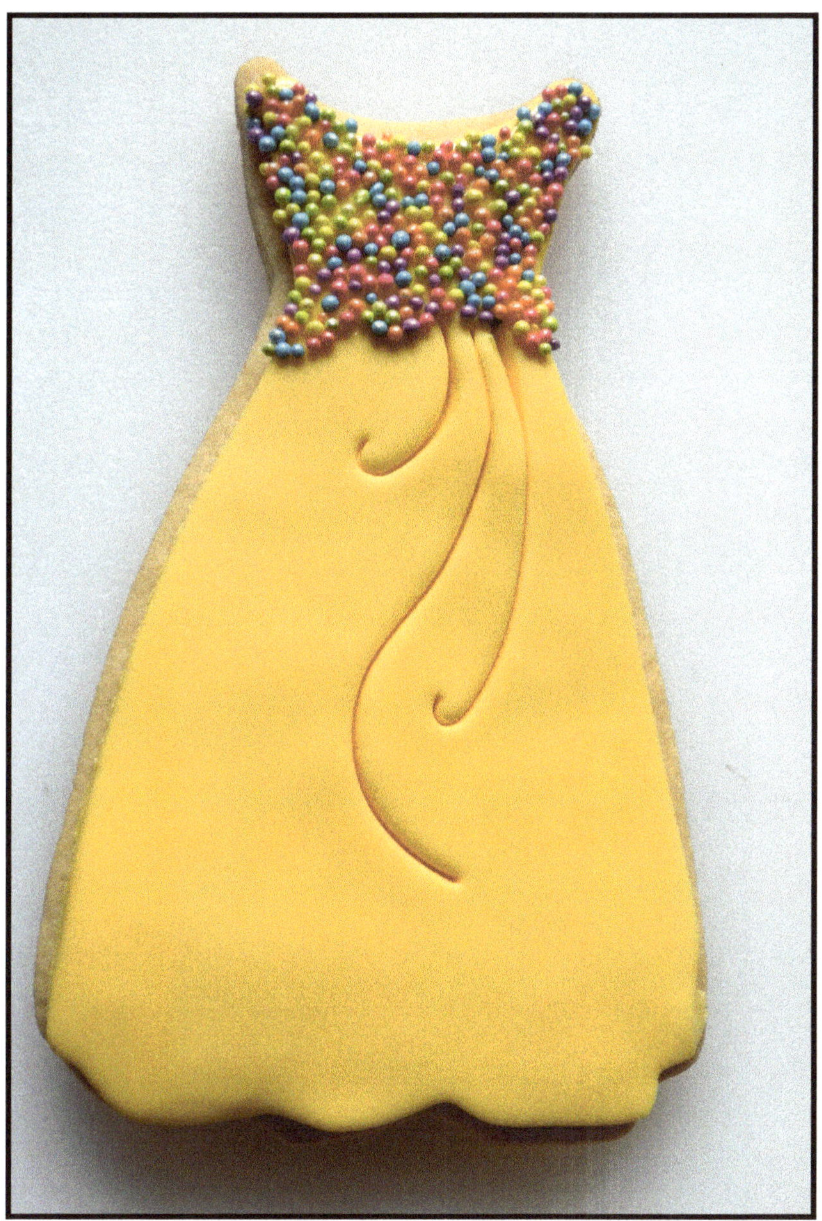

Materials:
- Dress cookie
- 0.7 oz. yellow fondant
- Piping gel
- Food safe paint brush

Tools:
- Dress Cookie Cutter (flourbox.com)
- Wilton's Designer Pattern Press Set, Flower Press
- ChocoMaker Shimmer Beads

Suggested cellophane bag size is 4x6 inches to package this dress cookie.

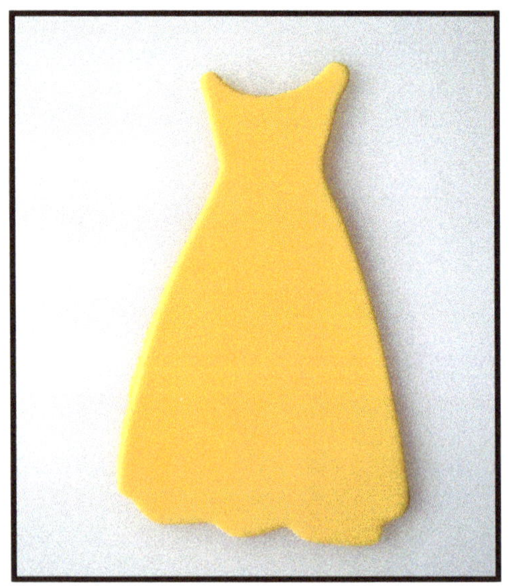 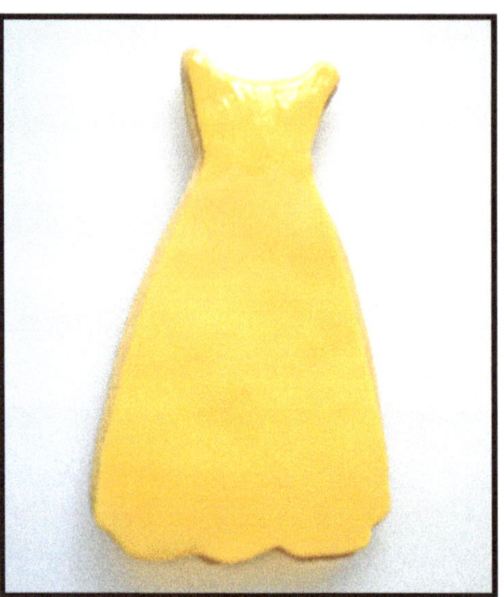 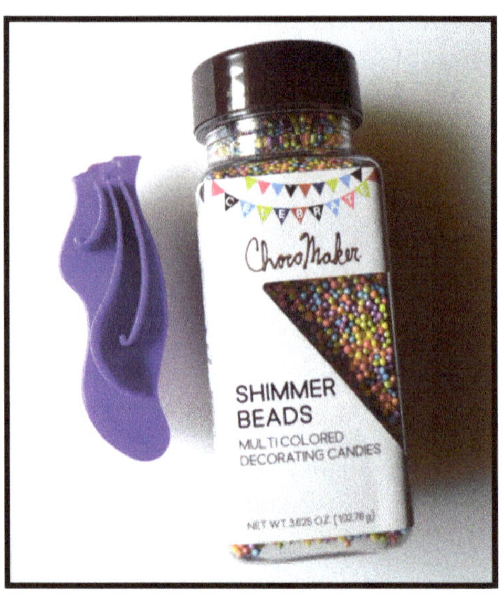

1. Roll out yellow fondant. Use the dress cookie cutter to cut out the yellow fondant dress.

2. Use a paint brush to apply a thin layer of piping gel onto your dress cookies. Apply fondant cut-out to cookie, and gently smooth top. Use a paint brush to apply a thin layer of piping gel to the bodice part of the cookie dress as shown above.

3. This is the flower press and the shimmer beads. The flower press was broken in half.

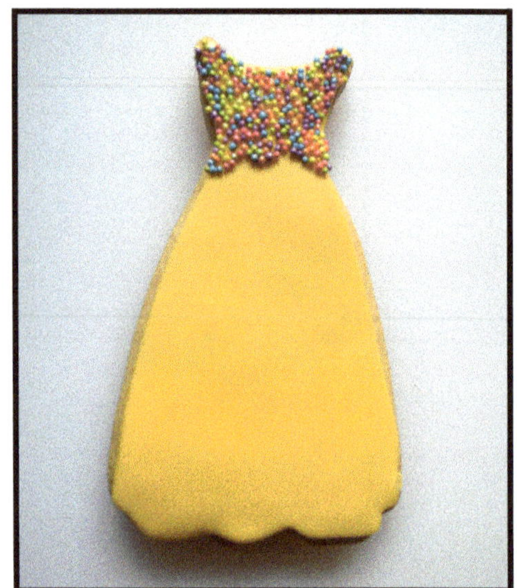 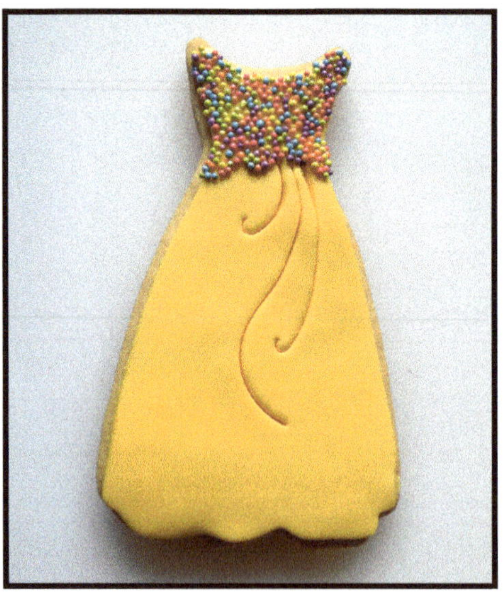

4. Use a bowl and hold the dress cookie with one hand, and use the other hand to sprinkle the shimmer beads over the entire bodice. Gently press sprinkles into fondant to secure. Remove excess.

5. Use the large side of the flower press to imprint fondant dress as shown.

Silver Pattern Dress Cookies

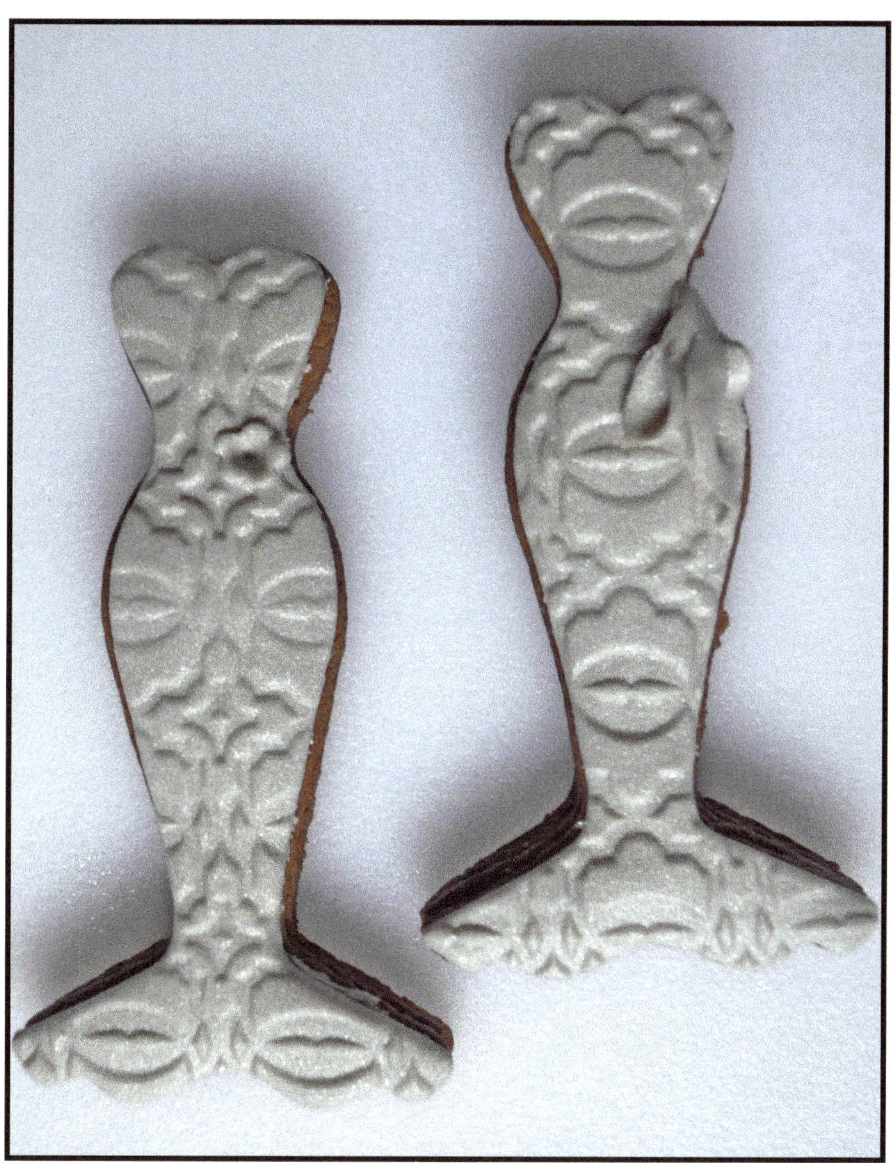

Materials:
- Two dress cookies
- 0.7 oz. Satin Ice Silver Shimmer fondant
- Piping gel
- Food safe paint brush

Tools:
- Wedding Dress Cookie Cutter (etsy.com, BakersToolsStore)
- Wilton Pattern Roller, Geometric Roller
- Large leaf cutter
- Small blossom cutter

Suggested cellophane bag size is 3x8 inches to package these dress cookies.

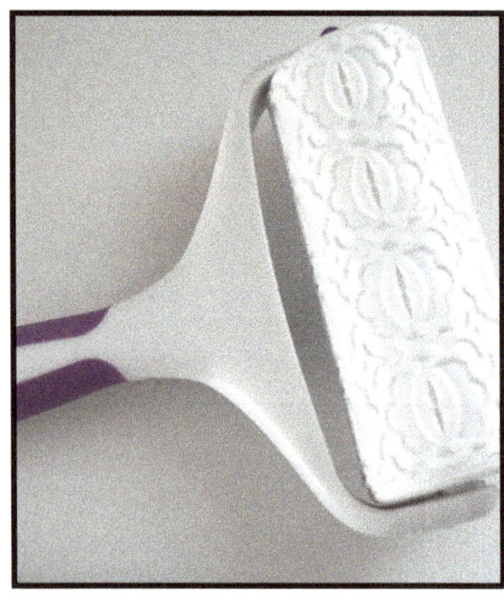 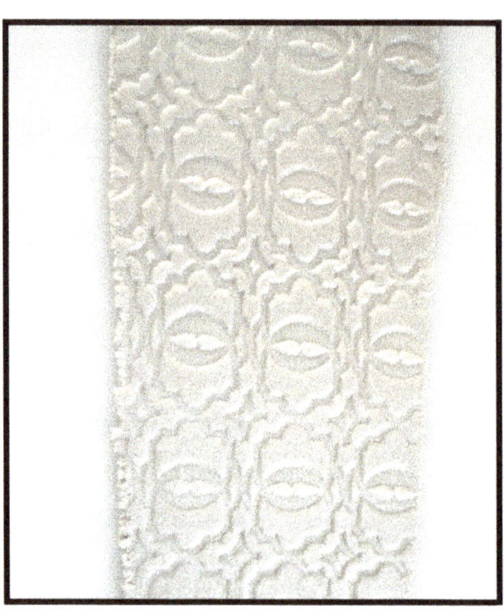 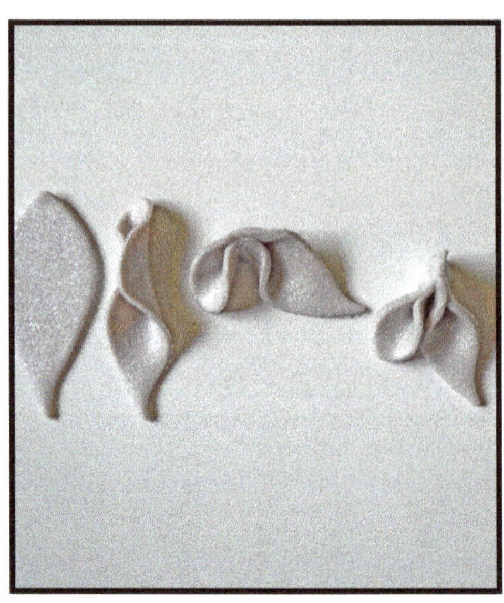

1. This is Wilton's Pattern Roller, Geometric print.

2. Roll out silver fondant. Using firm pressure, roll Wilton's Pattern Roller, Geometric print, over the fondant evenly. Center the dress cookie cutter over the design area. Press the dress cookie cutter firmly into the silver fondant, and then wiggle to release the fondant from the dress cookie cutter. Repeat for the second dress cookie.

3. Use a large leaf cutter to make the waist detail on the right dress cookie. Pinch the top part and then turn the top part to the left and squeeze the top part together. Gently press down to pinch edge. Set aside.

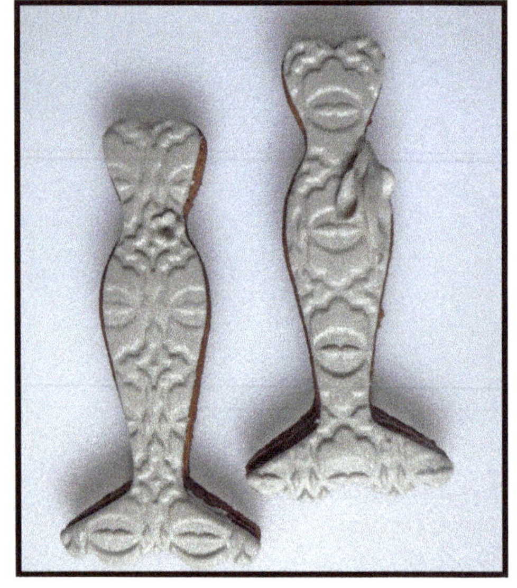

4. Use a paint brush to apply a thin layer of piping gel onto your dress cookies. Apply fondant cut-out to cookies, and then gently smooth top. Use blossom plunger cutter to cut out one flower, and attach to dress cookie at waist. Attach leaf fondant design cut-out to second dress cookie at waist as shown.

Gold Sprinkles Dress Cookie

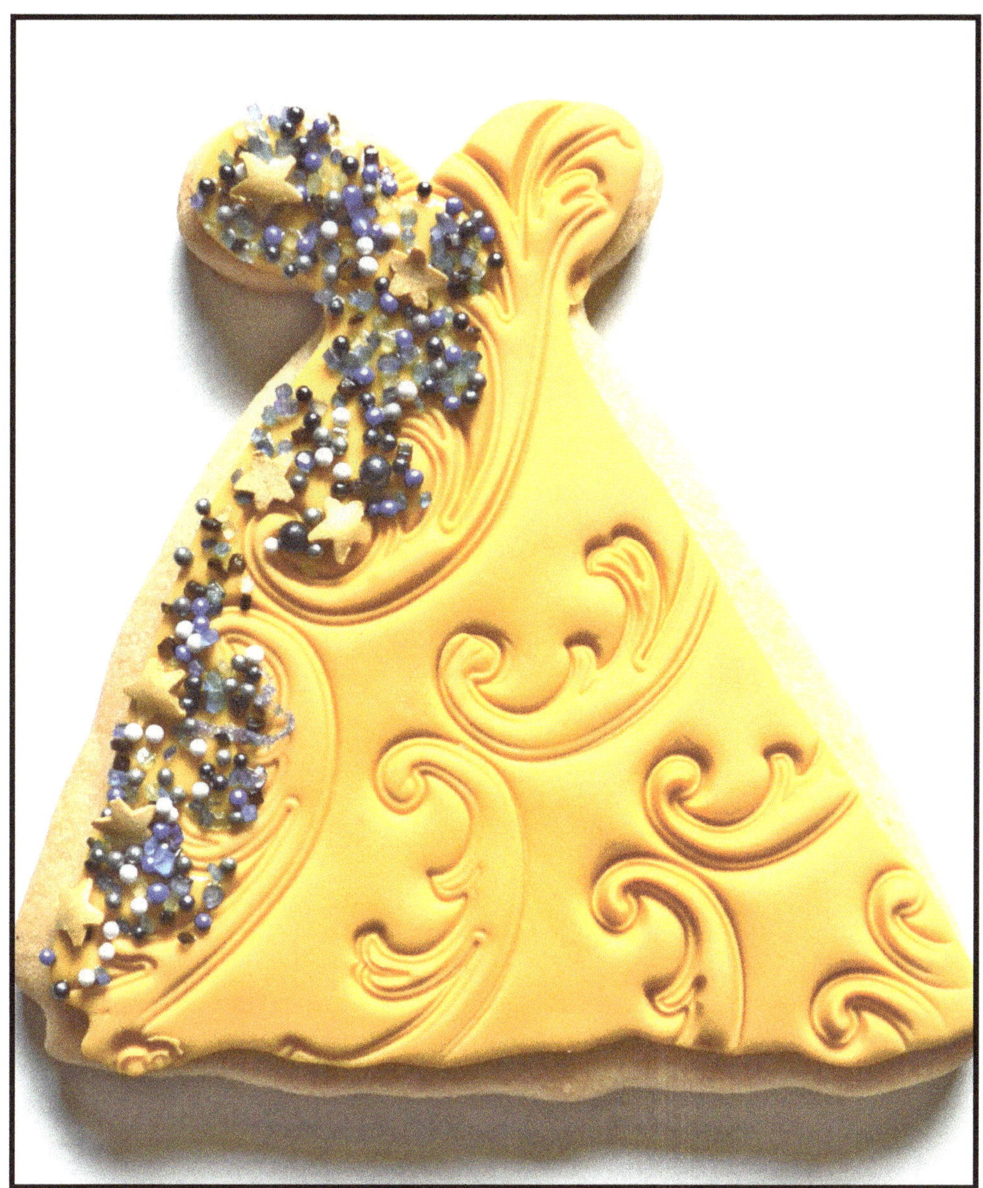

Materials:
- Dress cookie
- 0.7 oz. gold fondant
- Piping gel
- Food safe paint brush

Tools:
- Princess Cookie Cutter
- JEM Scrolls & Pansy Fondant Cutters
- Sweet Tooth Fairy Star Dust Sprinkle Mix

Suggested cellophane bag size is 5x7 inches to package this dress cookie.

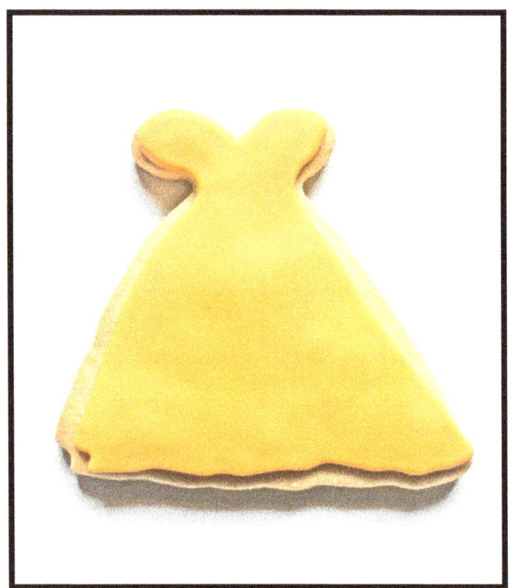

1. Roll out gold fondant. Use the dress cookie cutter to cut out the gold fondant dress. Use a paint brush to apply a thin layer of piping gel onto your dress cookie. Apply fondant cut-out to cookie, and gently smooth top.

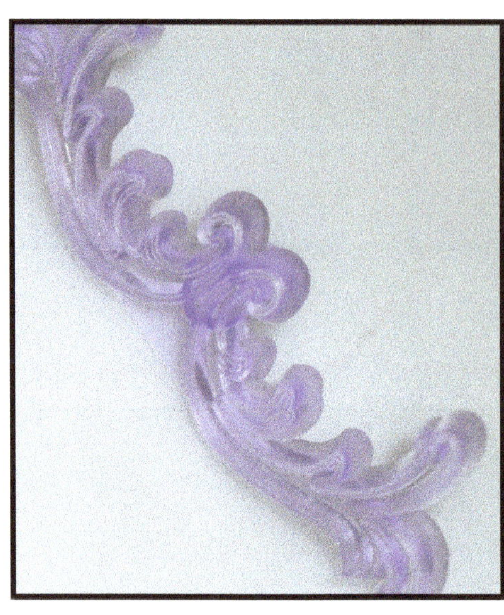

2. This is the JEM scroll tool.

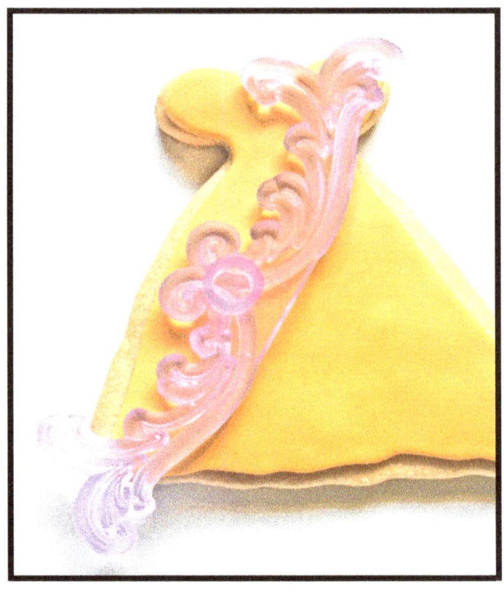

3. Use the JEM scroll tool to imprint the top of the dress cookie as shown above. Press gently and imprint the design. Remove tool.

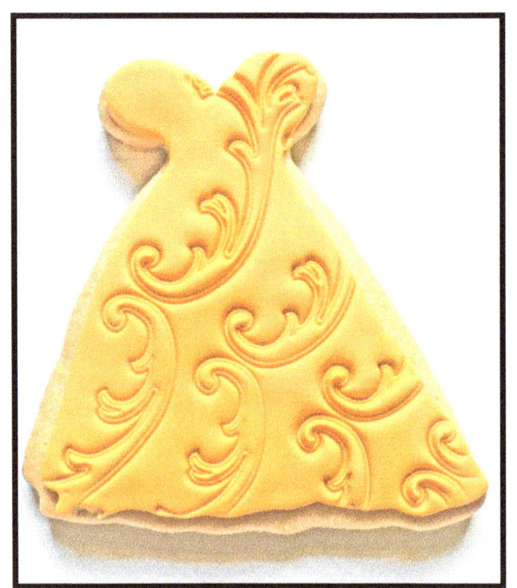

4. Repeat the impressions three more times as shown above. Remove tool.

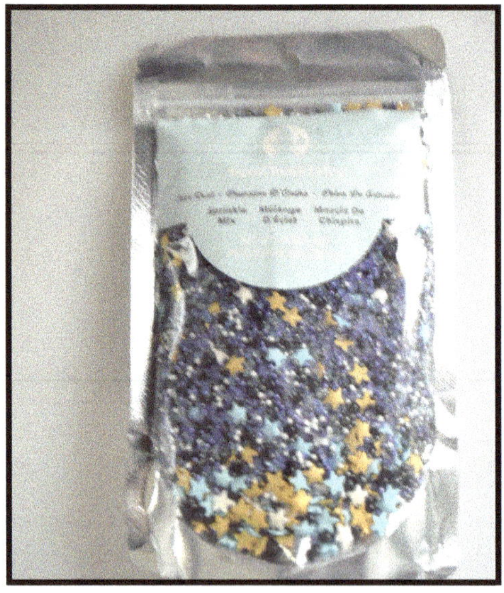

5. These are the sprinkles for the top side of this dress cookie.

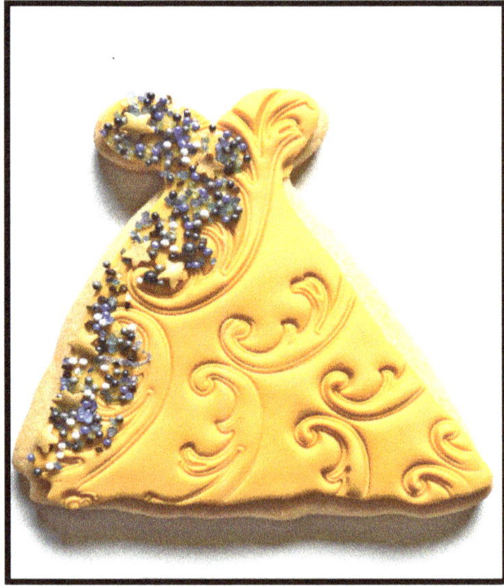

6. Paint the left area with piping gel, and then sprinkle the multi-colored sprinkles over the piping gel. Remove the blue stars and add more gold stars in this area. Remove excess sprinkles.

White Large Roses Dress Cookie

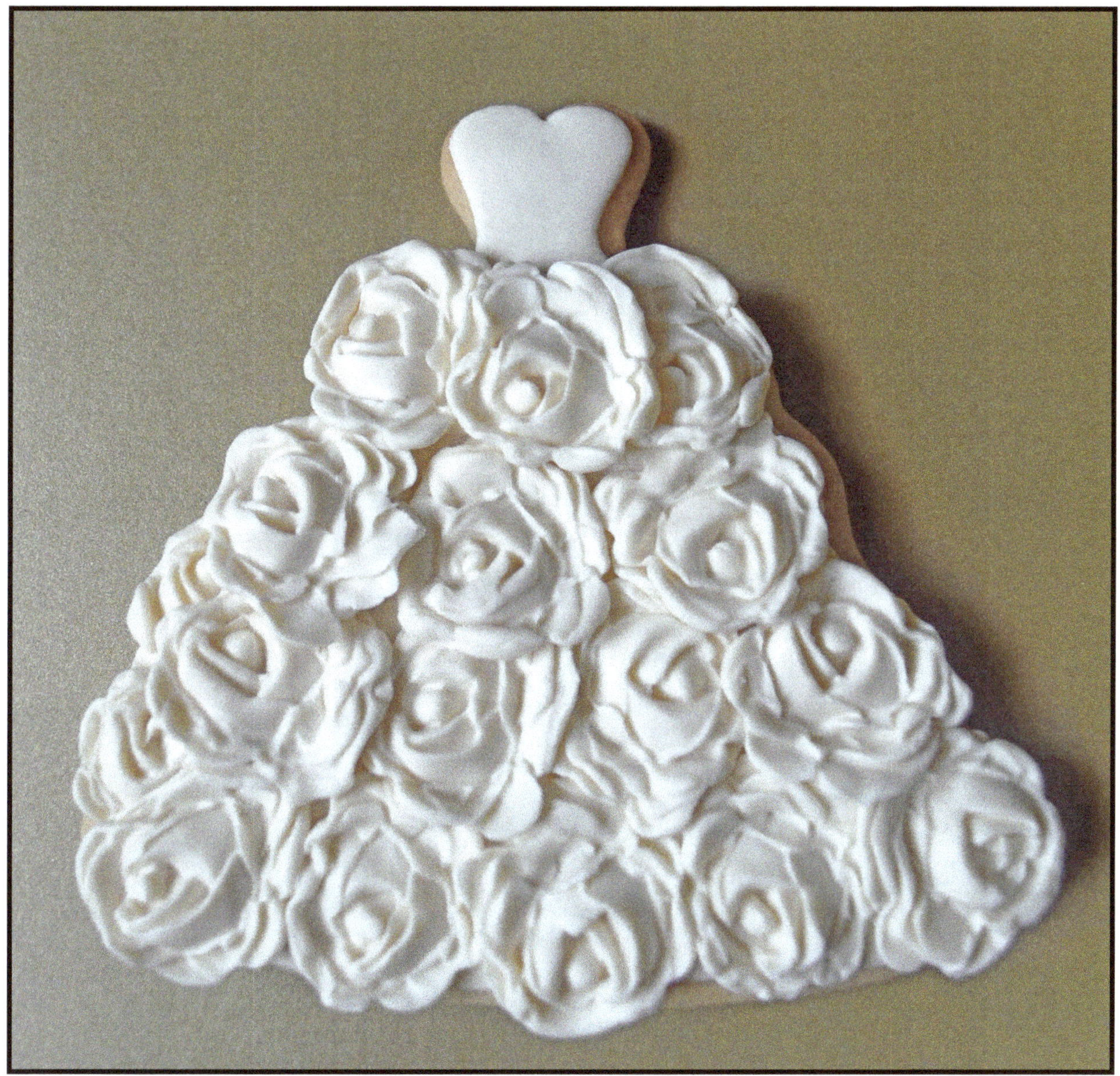

Materials:
- **Dress cookie**
- **3.4 oz. Fondarific Wedding White fondant**
- **Piping gel**
- **Food safe paint brush**
- **Pizza cutter or Xacto knife**

Tools:
- **Wedding Dress Outline #3 (etsy.com, CookieCutterLady)**
- **Large Rose Silicone Mold (hobbylobby.com)**

Suggested cellophane bag size is 6x8 inches to package this dress cookie.

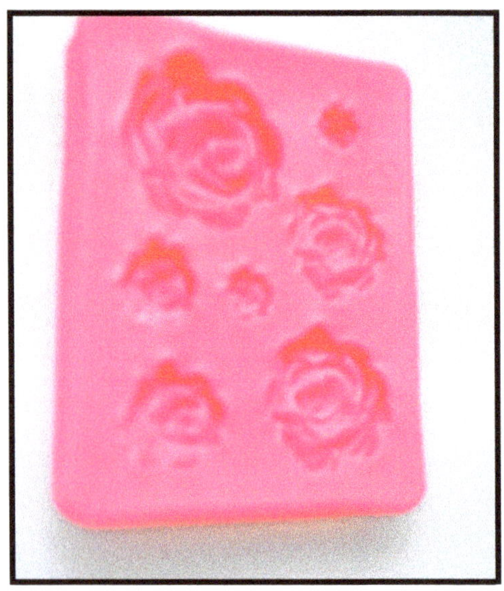

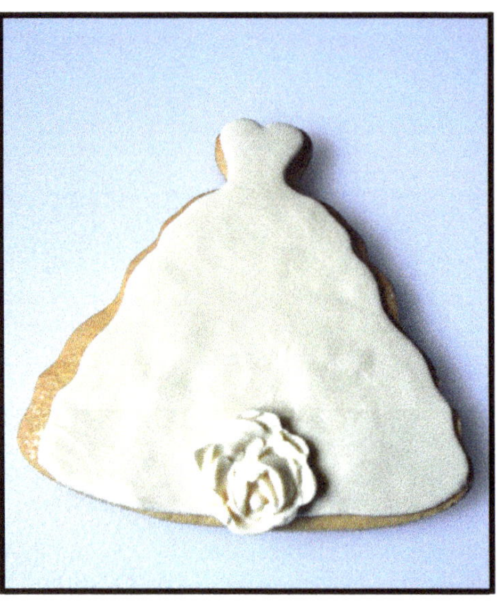

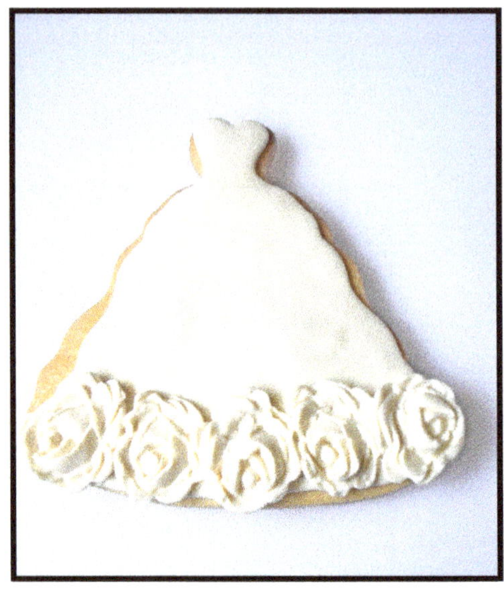

1. This is the large rose silicone mold. Refrigerate mold for a couple hours. Use white fondant to mold 16 large fondant roses. Set aside.

2. Roll out white fondant. Use the dress cookie cutter to cut out the white fondant dress. Use a paint brush to apply a thin layer of piping gel onto your dress cookie. Apply fondant cut-out to cookie, and gently smooth top. Center fondant rose on bottom middle section of dress cookie.

3. Add two more fondant roses to the left and right side of the bottom of the dress cookie. Gently press to secure.

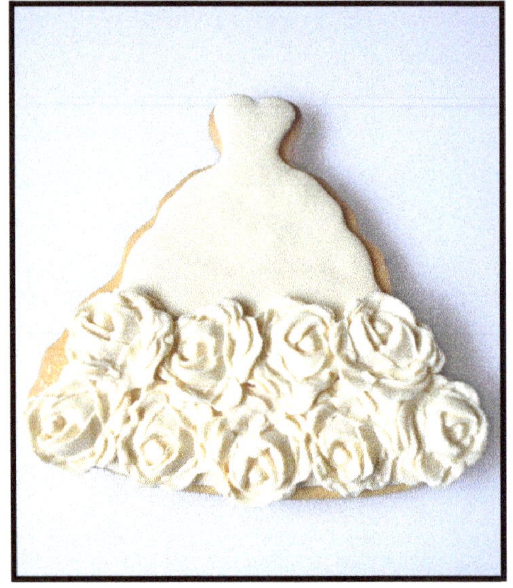

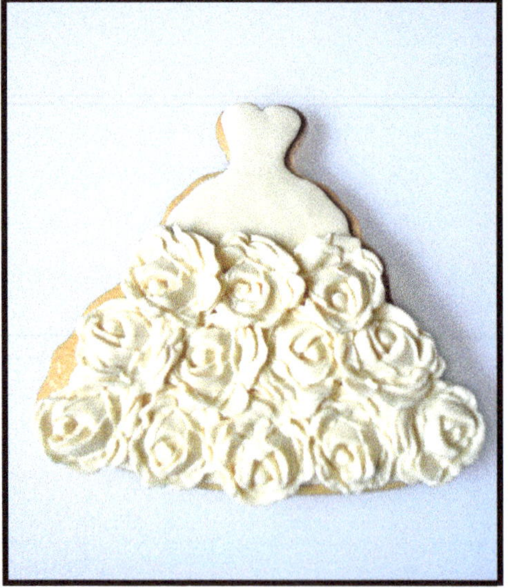

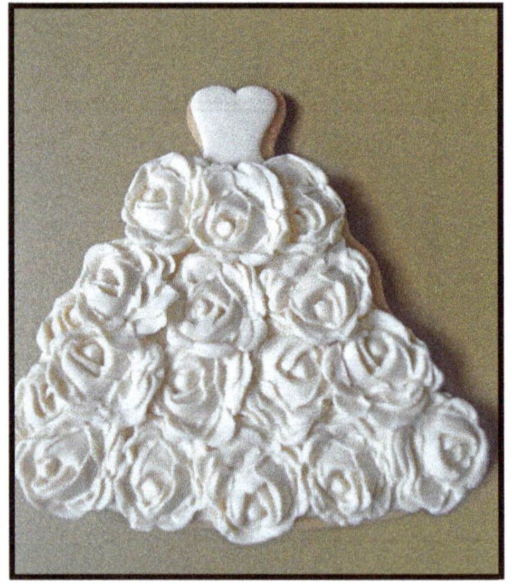

4. Add four fondant roses to the center of the last row of fondant roses as shown. Press to secure.

5. Add three fondant roses to the center of the second row of fondant roses as shown. Press to secure. If there is open space on the left side, cut one of the fondant roses and place it along the edge with the rose edge showing.

6. Add one fondant rose on the left side of the top of the dress cookie, and then one fondant rose on the right side of the top of the dress cookie. Place the last fondant rose in the center on the top of the dress cookie. Press to secure.

Silver Cake Comb Dress Cookie

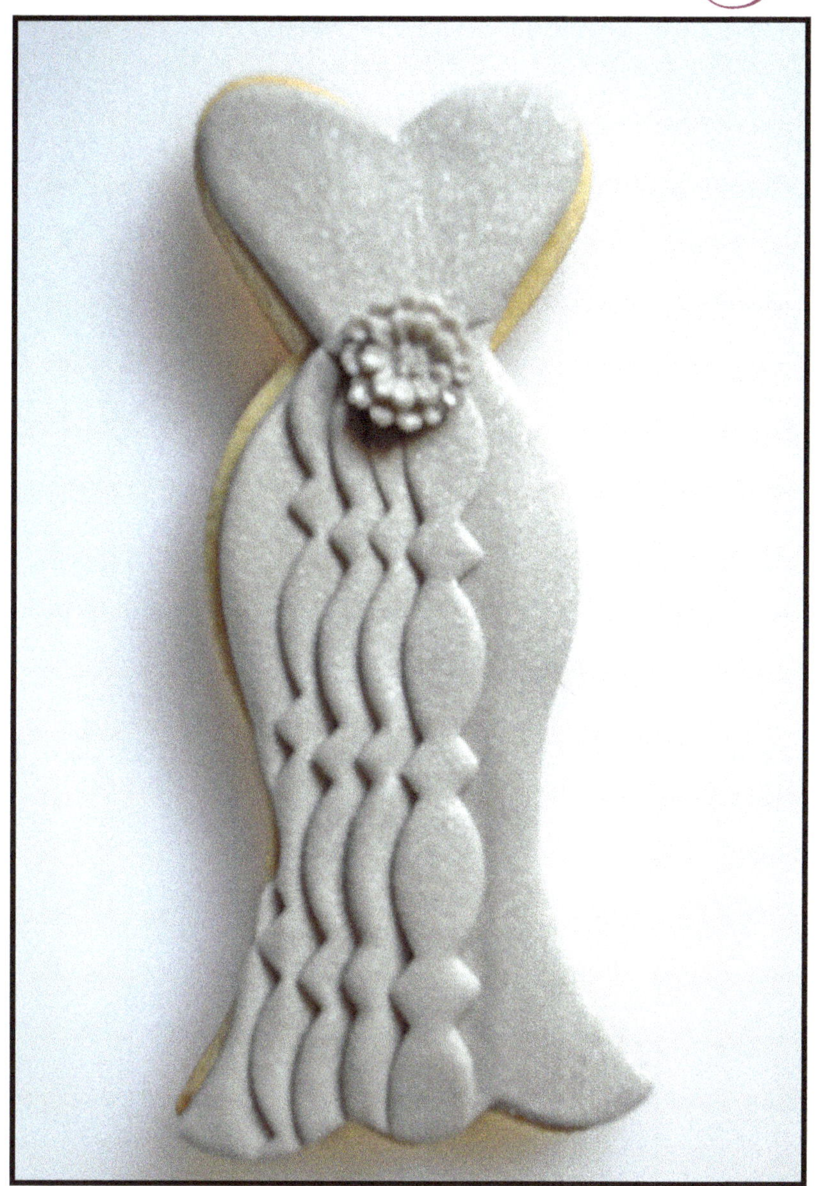

Suggested cellophane bag size is 3x8 inches to package this dress cookie.

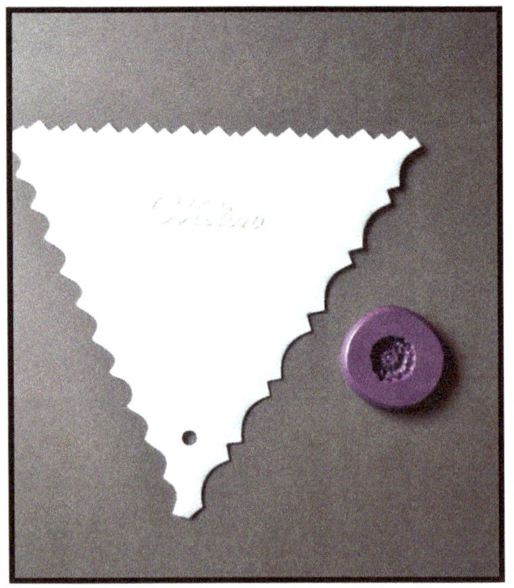

1. This is the cake comb and the chrysanthemum flower mold. The cake comb edge near the flower mold is the side used on this dress cookie design.

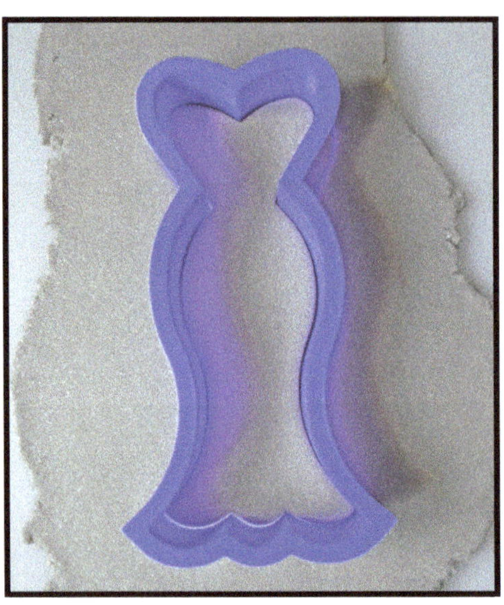

2. Roll out silver fondant. Use the dress cookie cutter to cut out the silver fondant dress.

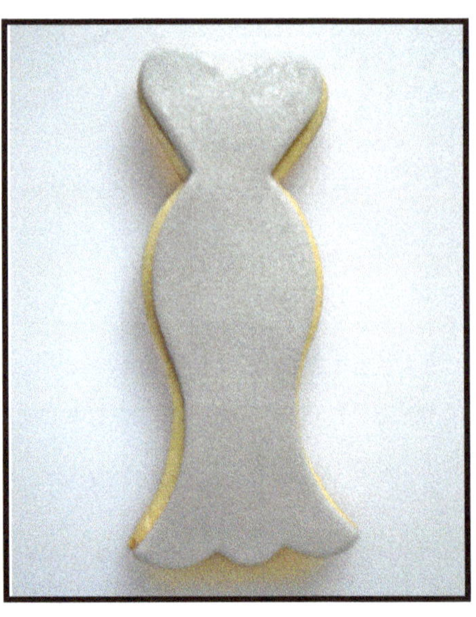

3. Use a paint brush to apply a thin layer of piping gel onto your dress cookie. Apply fondant cut-out to cookie, and gently smooth top.

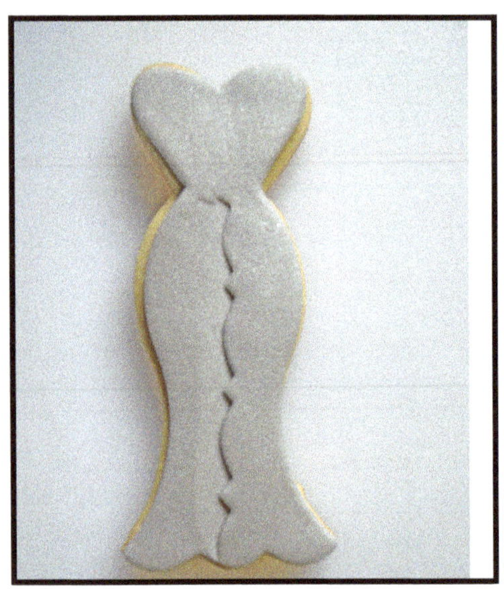

4. Use the cake comb turned at an angle to press into the fondant dress cookie as shown.

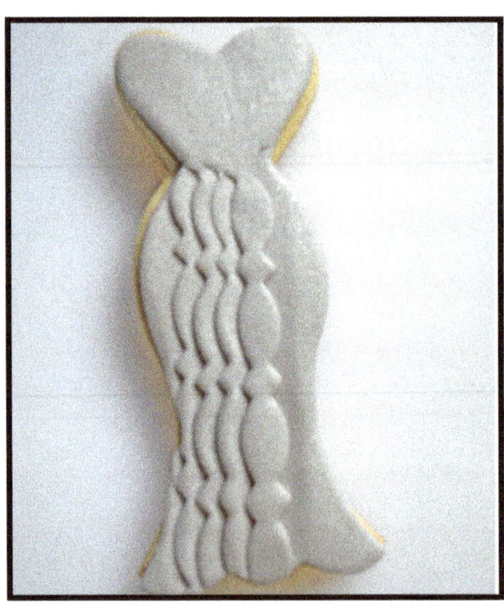

5. Continue to press the cake comb into the fondant dress cookie as show on the left side. Make one imprint on the right side of the dress cookie.

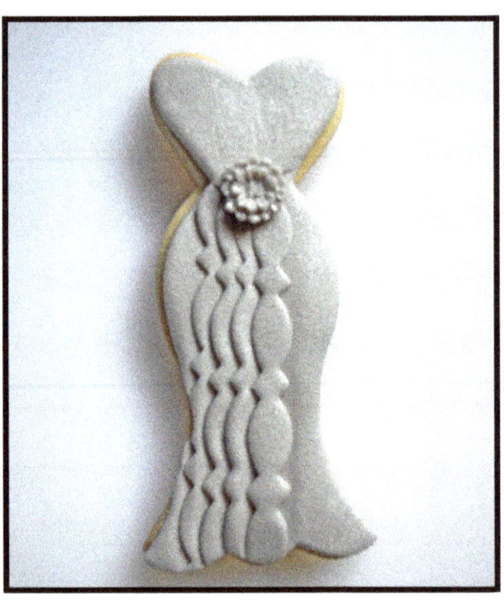

6. Press silver fondant into the chrysanthemum flower mold. Refrigerate until set. Add a dab of piping gel to the back of the flower mold, and attach it as shown.

Yellow Lattice Dress Cookie

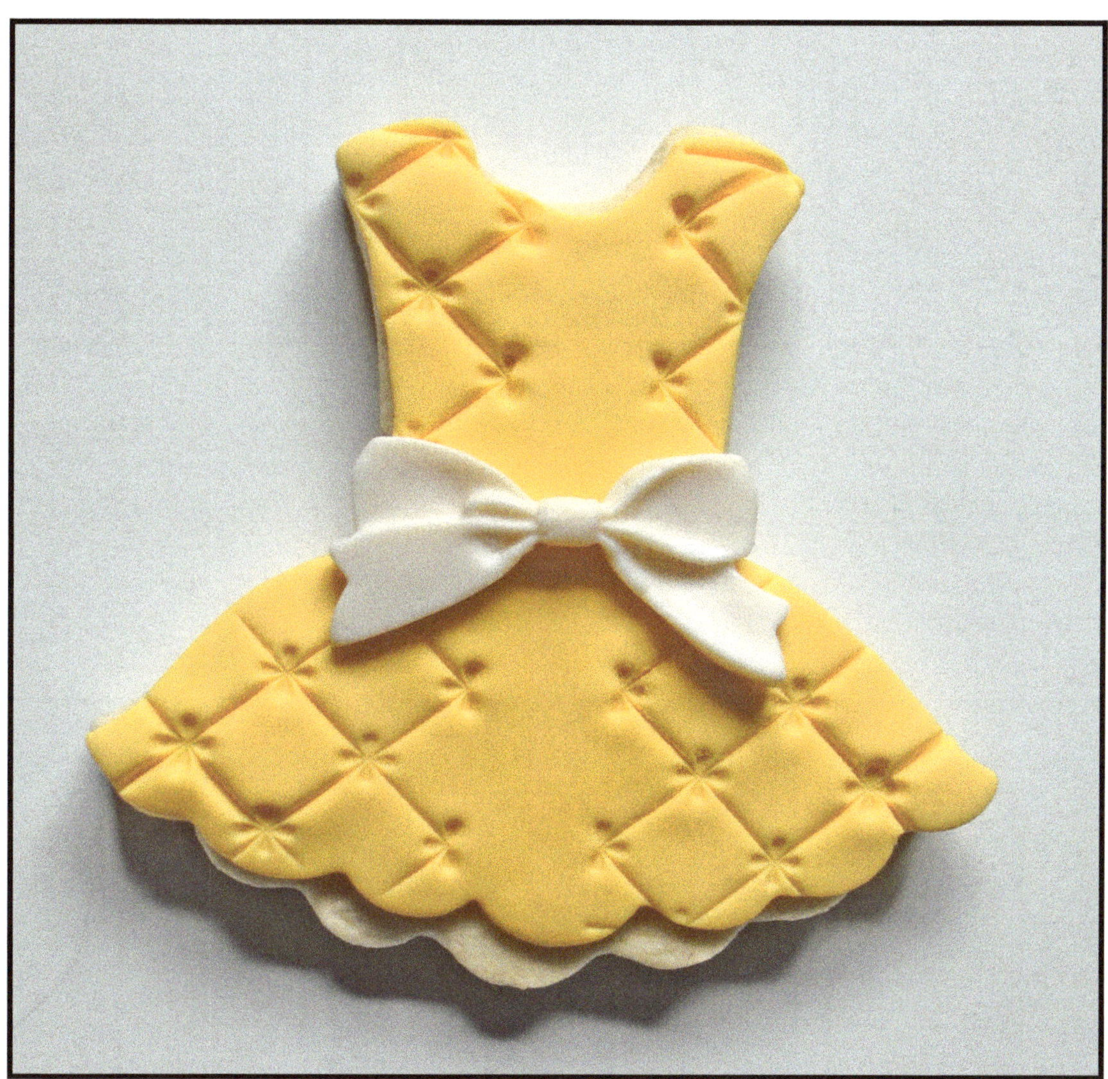

Materials:
- Dress cookie
- 0.5 oz. yellow fondant
- 0.1 oz. white fondant
- Piping gel
- Food safe paint brush

Tools:
- Tutu and Dress Cookie Cutter (etsy.com, WhiskedAwayCutters)
- Patchwork Cutters Quilting Embosser
- Bows silicone mold (hobbylobby.com)

Suggested cellophane bag size is 4x6 inches to package this dress cookie.

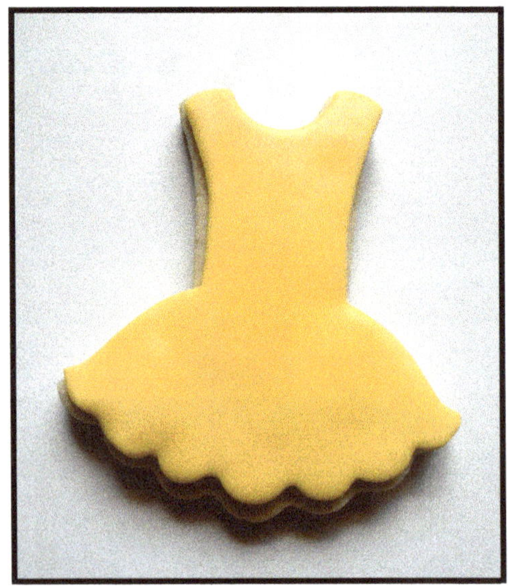

1. Roll out yellow fondant. Use the dress cookie cutter to cut out the yellow fondant dress. Use a paint brush to apply a thin layer of piping gel onto your dress cookie. Apply fondant cut-out to cookie, and gently smooth top.

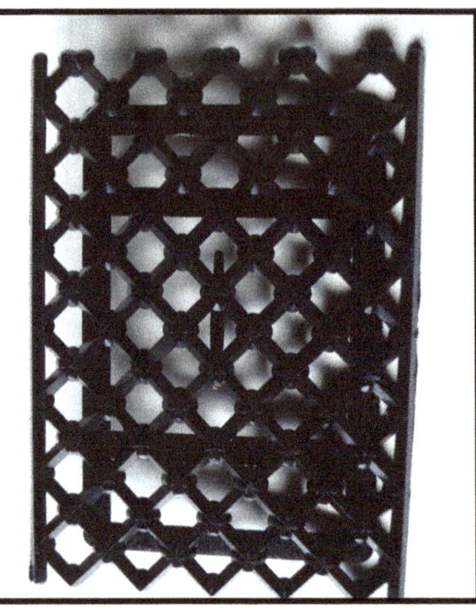

2. This is Patchwork Cutter's Quilting Embosser.

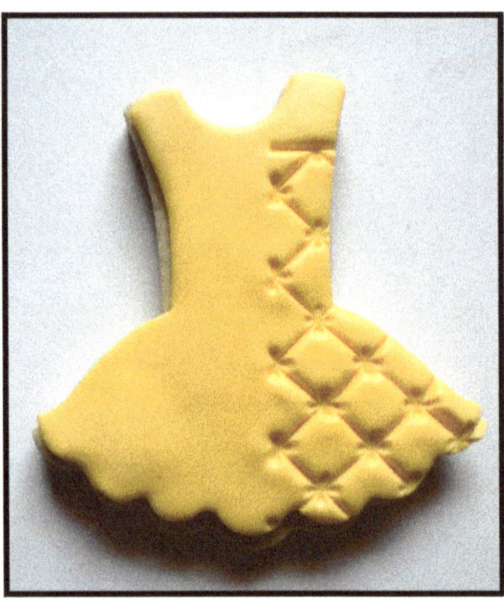

3. Turn the Quilting Embosser to the side with the bow side facing and imprint the right side of the dress cookie. Remove.

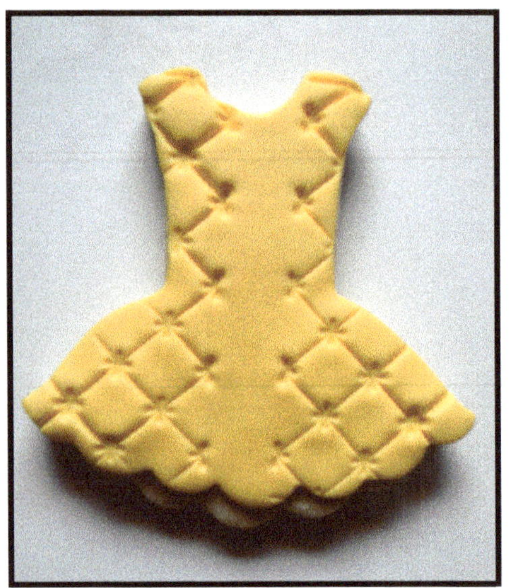

4. Line up the bows on the left side with the right side bows and imprint the dress cookie.

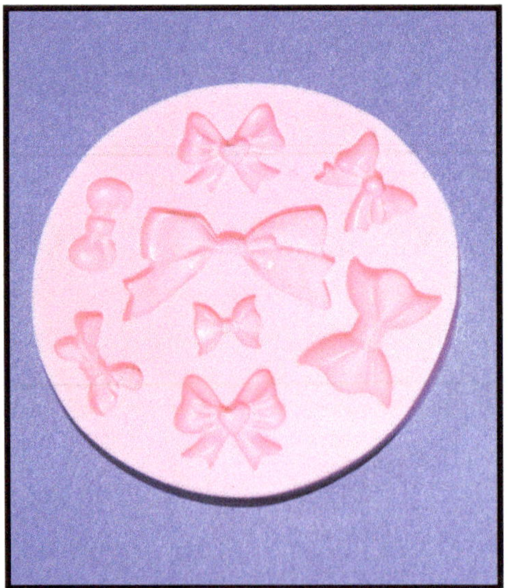

5. Use white fondant to fill the cavity of the large-sized bow silicone mold. Refrigerate until firm. Remove.

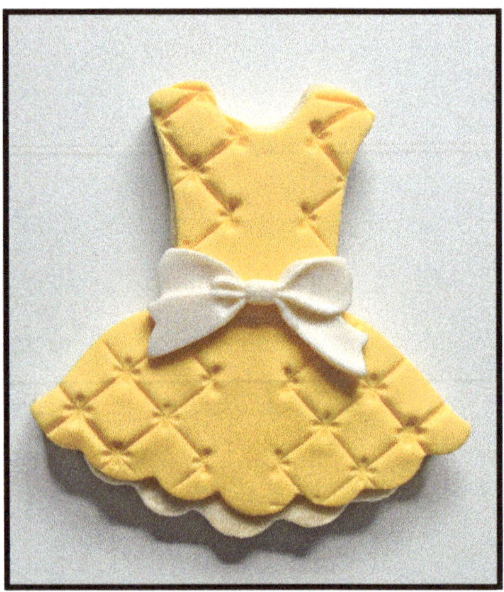

6. Dab a little piping gel on the back of the gold fondant bow, and attach it to dress cookie as shown.

Lavender Black Dress Cookie

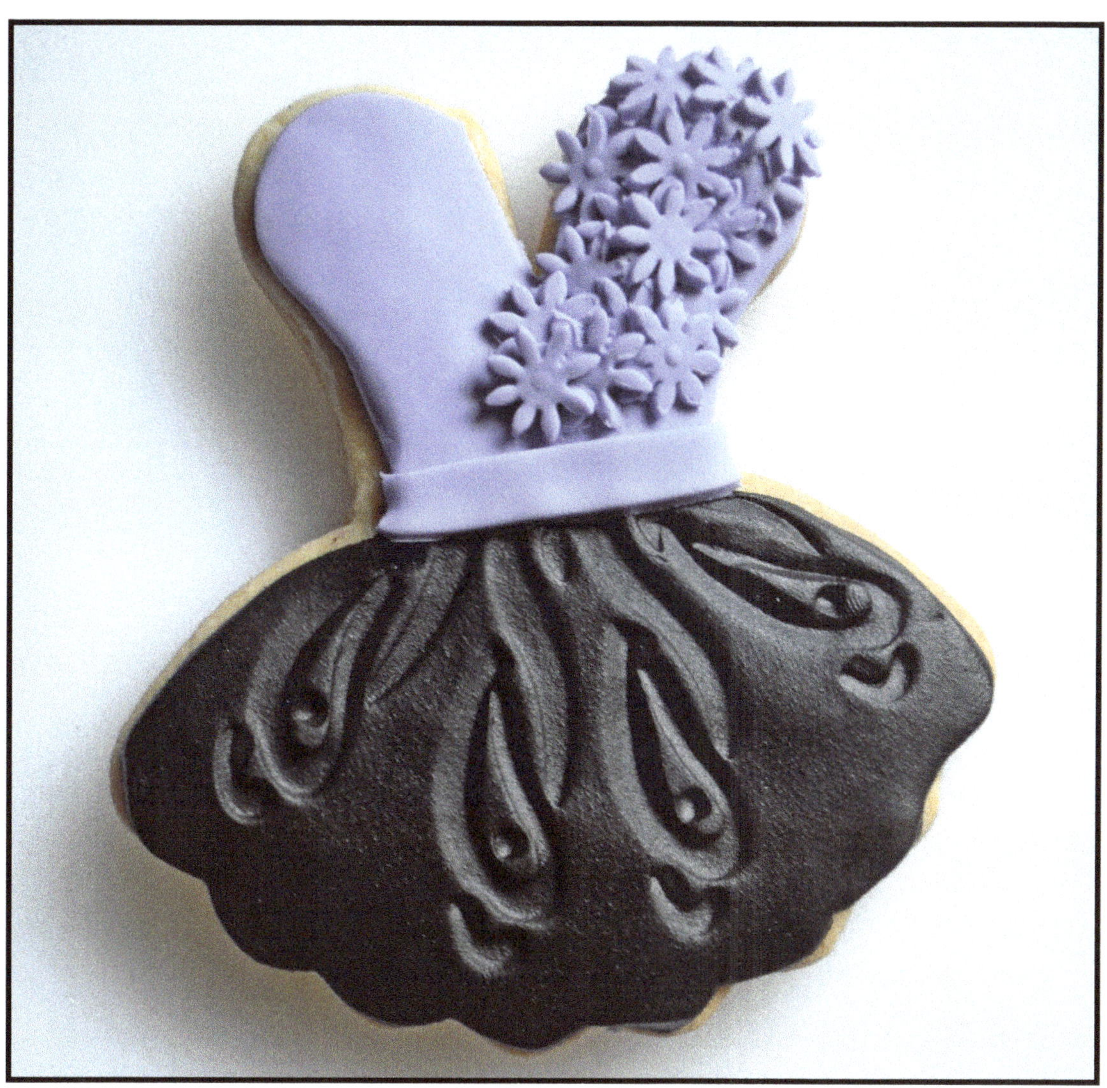

Materials:
- Dress cookie
- 0.4 oz. lavender fondant
- 0.4 oz. Fondarific Black fondant
- Piping gel
- Food safe paint brush
- Pizza cutter or Xacto knife

Tools:
- Party Dress Cookie Cutter (etsy.com, Sinful Cutters)
- Small daisy plunger cutter
- Wilton Cake Stamp Set (Flourishes)

Suggested cellophane bag size is 4x6 inches to package this dress cookie.

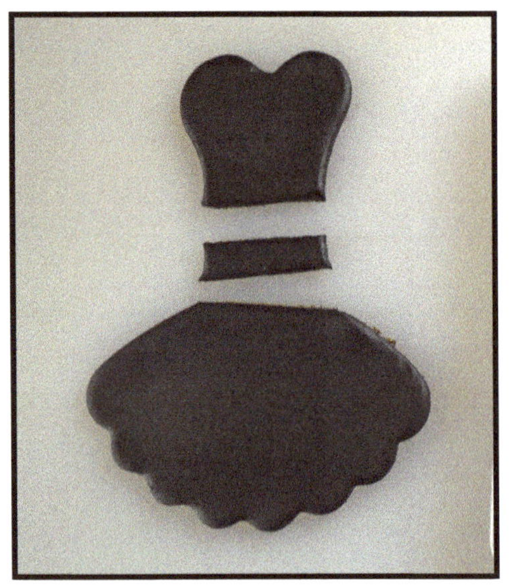

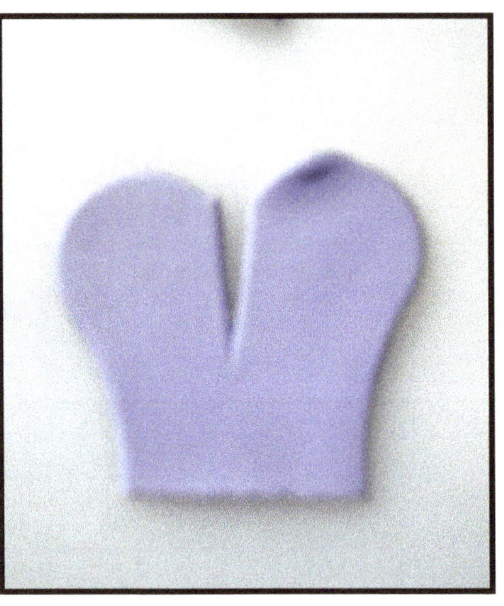

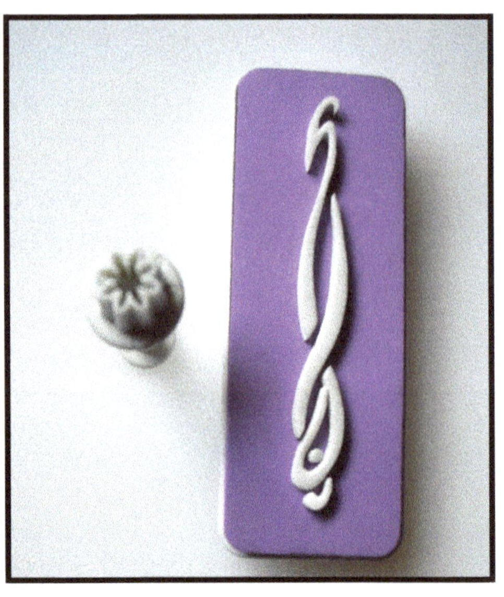

1. Roll out black fondant. Use the dress cookie cutter to cut out the black fondant dress. Cut the bottom part of the dress apart from the bodice area.

2. Roll out lavender fondant. Use the dress cookie cutter to cut out the lavender fondant dress. Cut the bodice apart from the dress skirt.

3. This is the small daisy plunger cutter and the cake stamp used in this dress cookie design.

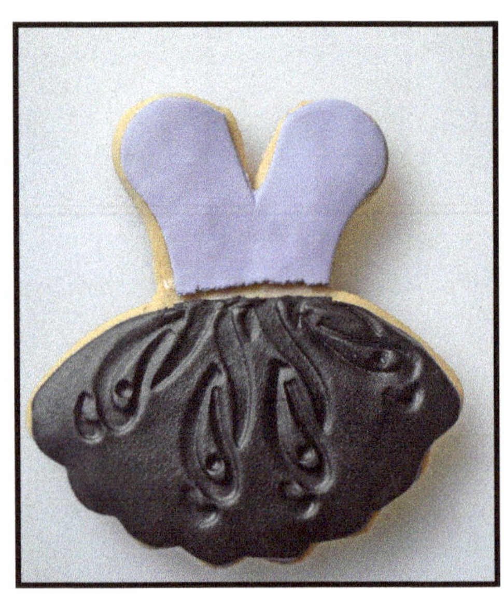

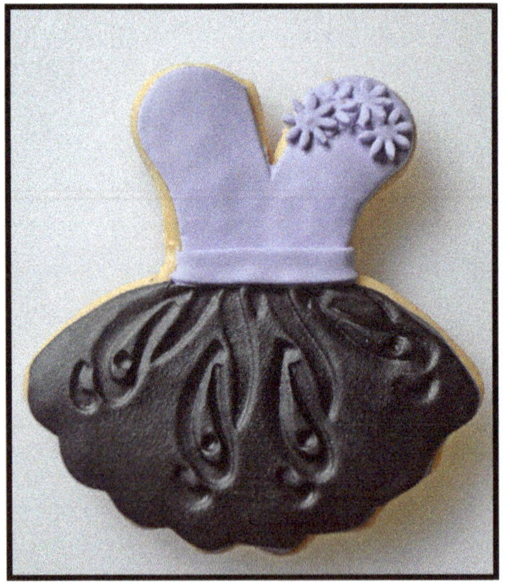

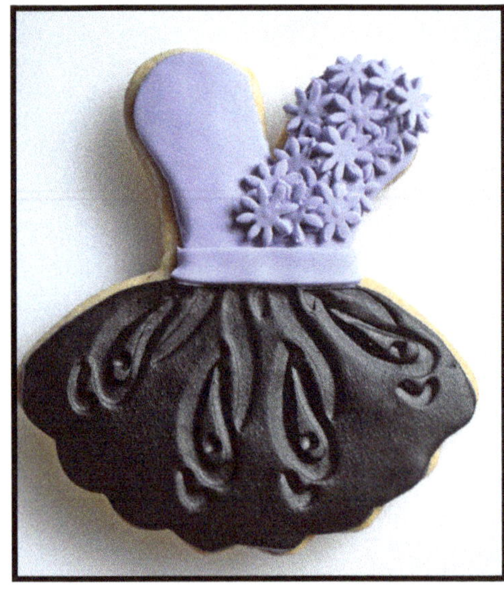

4. Use a paint brush to apply a thin layer of piping gel onto your dress cookie. Apply black fondant cut-out to dress cookie, and gently smooth top. Use the cake stamp to imprint the fondant four times as shown. Apply lavender fondant bodice to top of dress cookie, and gently smooth top.

5. Cut out a small strip of lavender fondant. and attach to the waist. Use the small daisy plunger cutter and start punching out small fondant daisies. Attach to top right of bodice top on the dress cookie. Overlap the fondant daisies as you go along. Press to secure to bodice.

6. Continue adding small fondant daisies to the right side of the bodice until you fill that side, and touch the waist.

Chocolate Daisy Dress Cookie

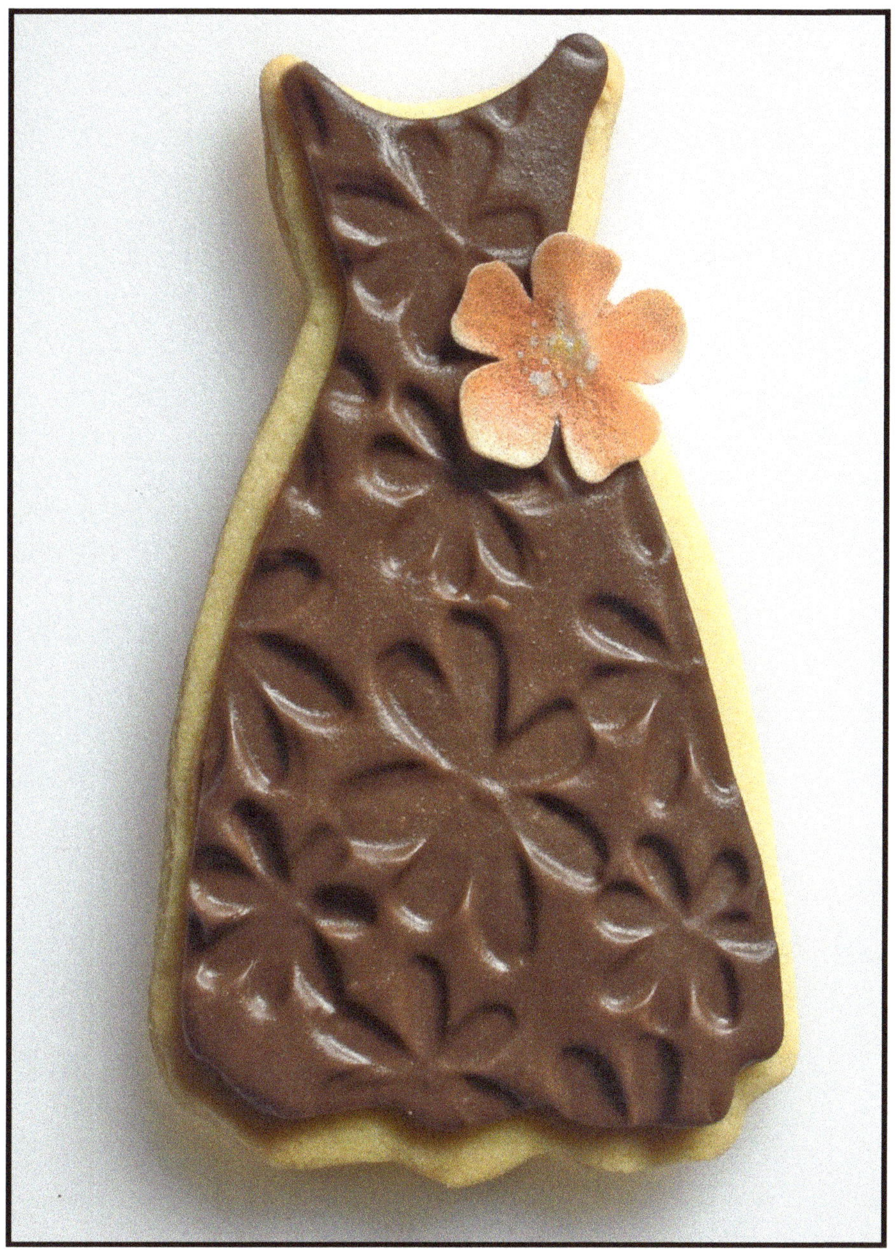

Materials:
- Dress cookie
- 0.6 oz. Fondarific Chocolate fondant
- Piping gel
- Food safe paint brush

Tools:
- Dress Cookie Cutter (flourbox.com)
- CK Floral Icing Impression Mat
- Wafer paper flowers (amazon.com)

Suggested cellophane bag size is 4x6 inches to package this dress cookie.

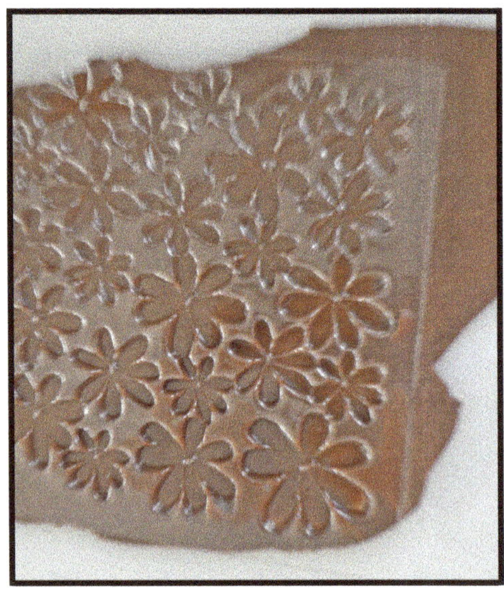 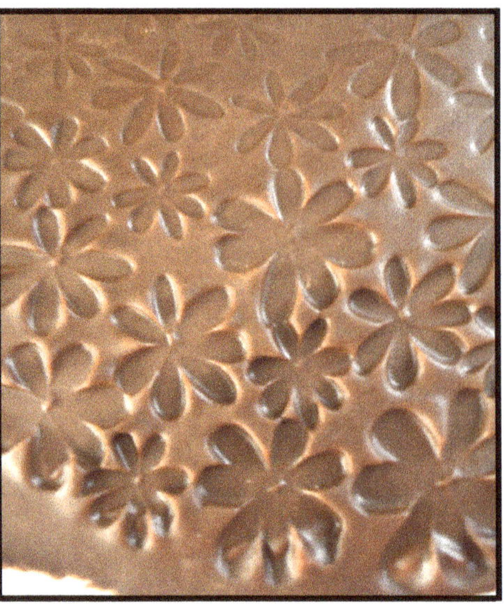 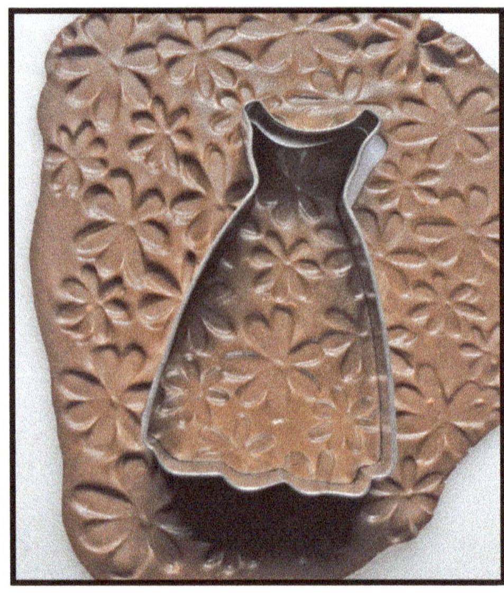

1. Roll out chocolate fondant. Use the floral icing impression mat (raised side down as shown). Use a rolling pin to evenly roll over the impression mat. Remove the mat.

2. This is what the embossed fondant looks like. Use a bench scraper to lift the chocolate fondant up, and then place it back on the surface.

3. Center the dress cookie cutter over the design area as shown. Press the dress cookie cutter firmly into the chocolate fondant, and then wiggle to release the fondant from the dress cookie cutter.

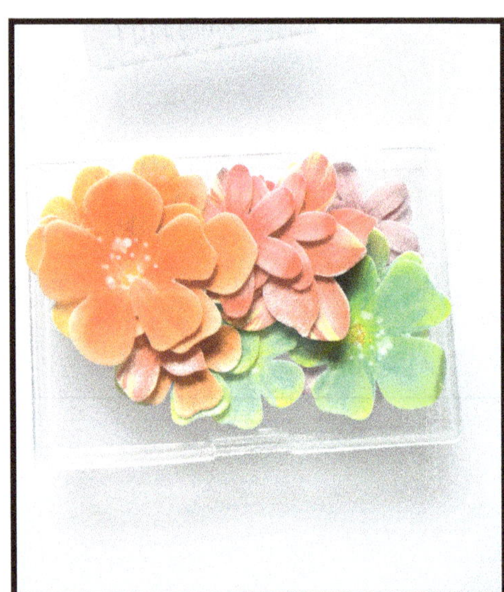 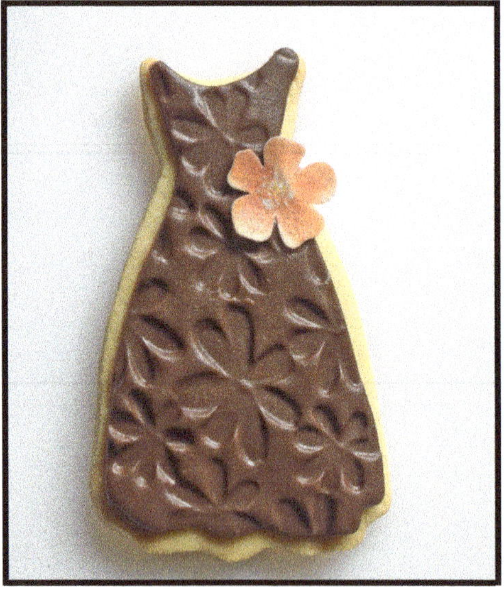

4. These are the wafer flowers.

5. Use a paint brush to apply a thin layer of piping gel onto your dress cookie. Apply fondant cut-out to cookie, and gently smooth top. Place a dab of piping gel on the back of the wafer flower, and attach to dress cookie as shown.

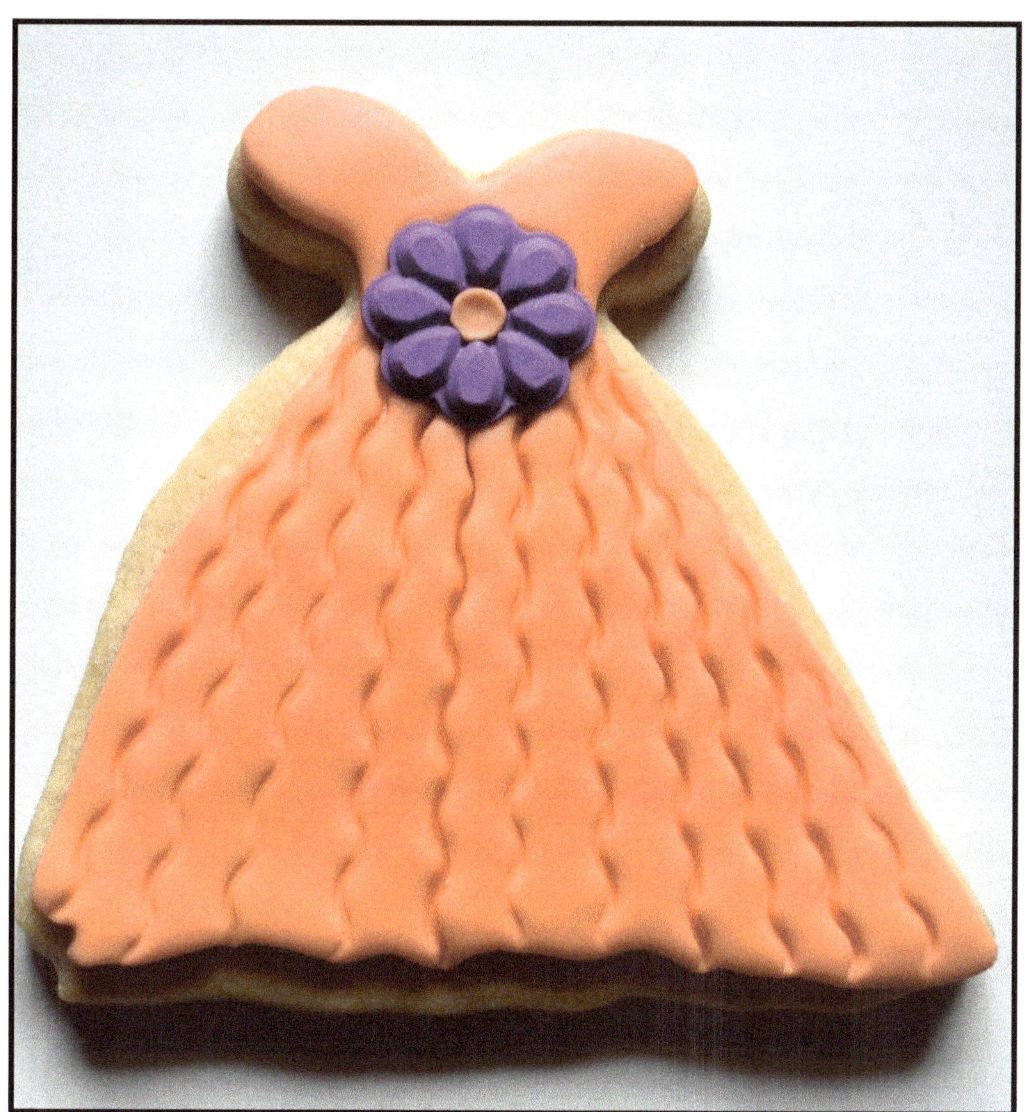

Materials:
- Dress cookie
- 0.7 oz. Fondarific Coral fondant
- 0.1 oz. purple fondant
- Piping gel
- Food safe paint brush

Tools:
- Princess Cookie Cutter
- Wilton Wedding Jewelry Fondant and Gum Paste Mold
- Wilton's Detail Embosser Set

Use cellophane bag size 5x7 inches to bag this dress cookie.

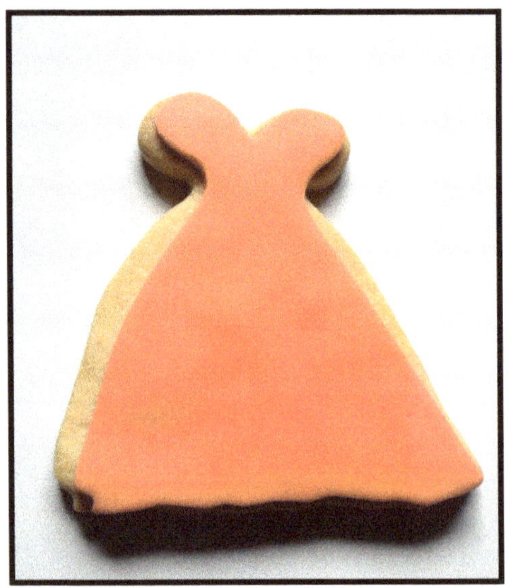

1. Roll out coral fondant. Use the dress cookie cutter to cut out the coral fondant dress. Use a paint brush to apply a thin layer of piping gel onto your dress cookie. Apply fondant cut-out to cookie, and gently smooth top.

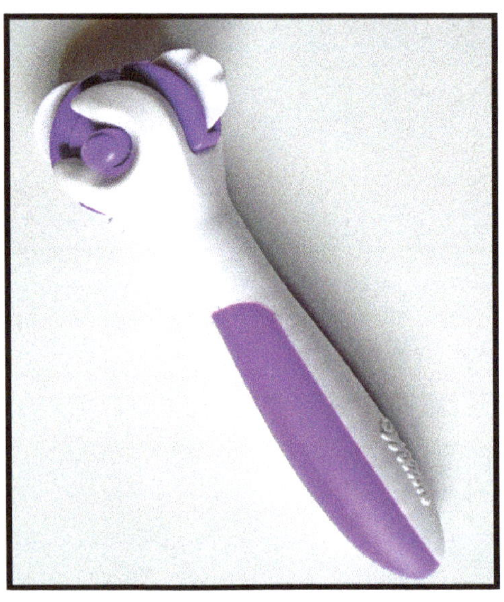

2. This is Wilton's Detail Embosser Set. It has three sides.

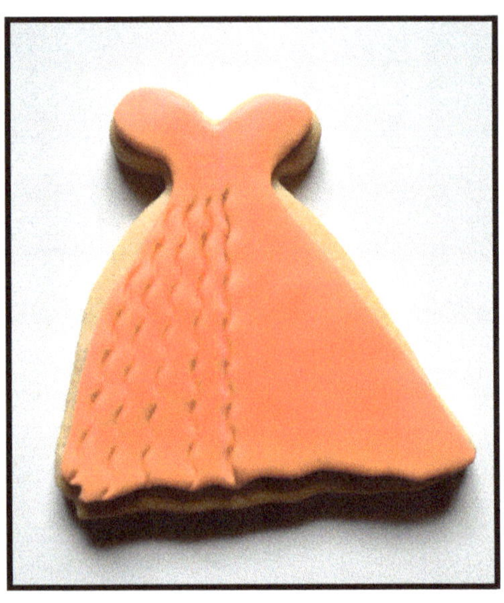

3. Use the wavy side to make the indentations in the fondant as shown above.

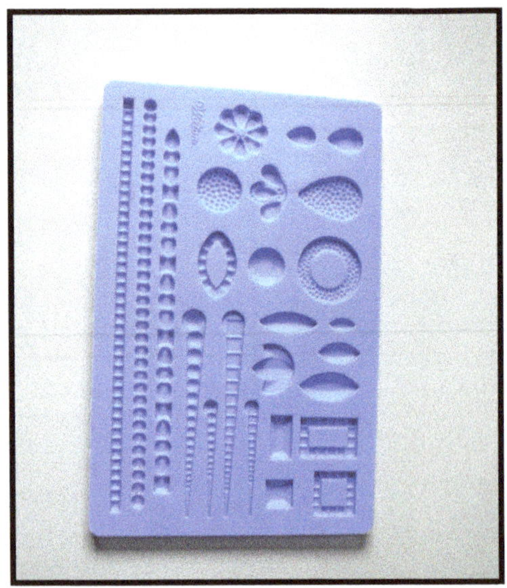

4. This is Wilton's Wedding Jewelry Fondant and Gum Paste Mold. Use purple fondant to mold the blossom flower. Refrigerate until firm. Remove.

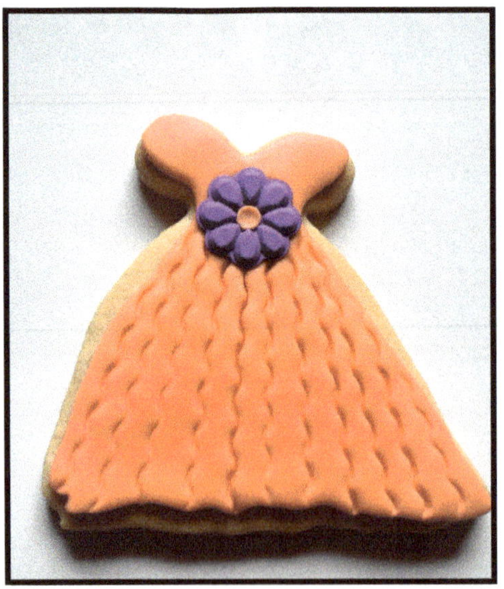

5. Use a dab of piping gel to place the blossom flower onto the dress cookie. Use a dab of piping gel to attach a small piece of coral fondant to the center of the blossom flower. Press the center down.

Lavender Tulip Dress Cookie

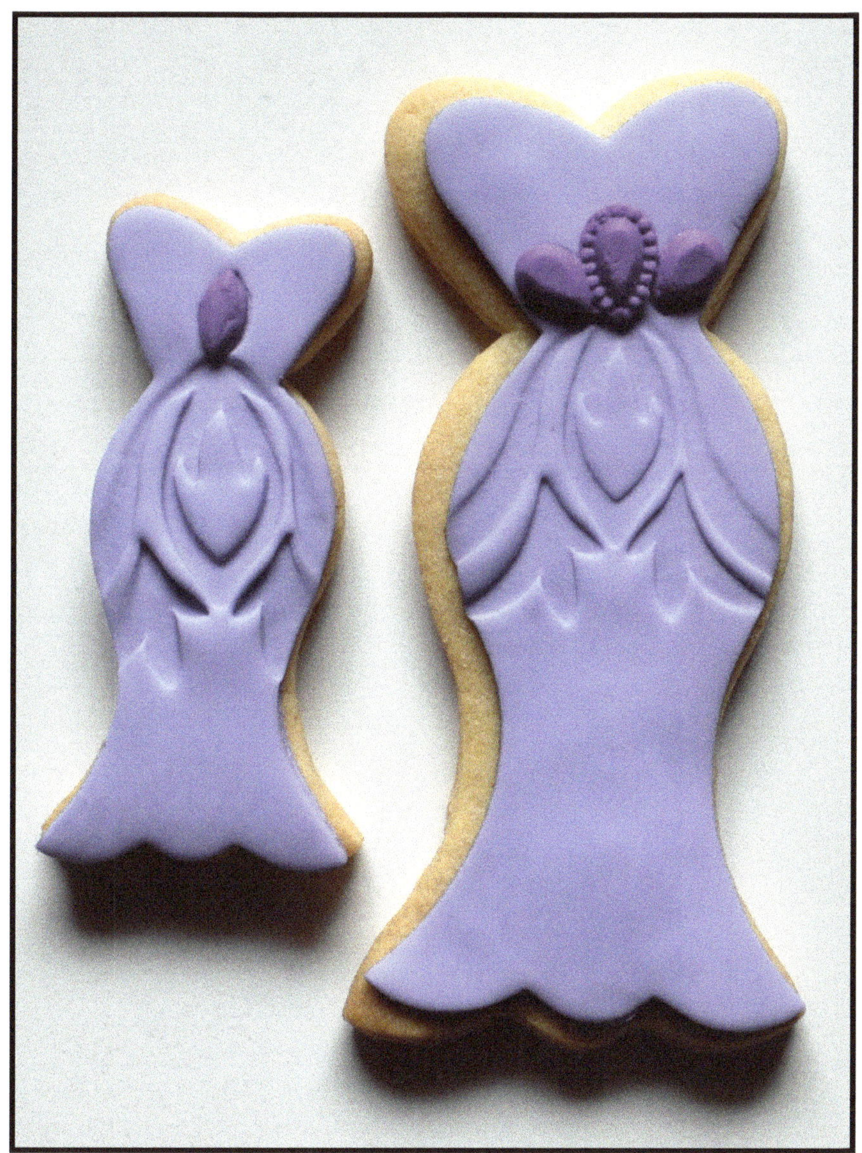

<table>
<tr><td>

Materials:
- One small and one large dress cookie
- 0.74 oz. lavender fondant
- 0.3 oz. Fondarific Purple fondant
- Piping gel
- Food safe paint brush

</td><td>

Tools:
- The Marilyn Gown Cookie Cutter (smallest and largest) (etsy.com, Sinful Cutters)
- Wilton Wedding Jewelry Fondant and Gum Paste Mold
- Wilton Cake Stamp Set (Flourishes)

</td></tr>
</table>

Use cellophane bag sizes 2x6 inches and 3x8 inches to bag these dress cookies.

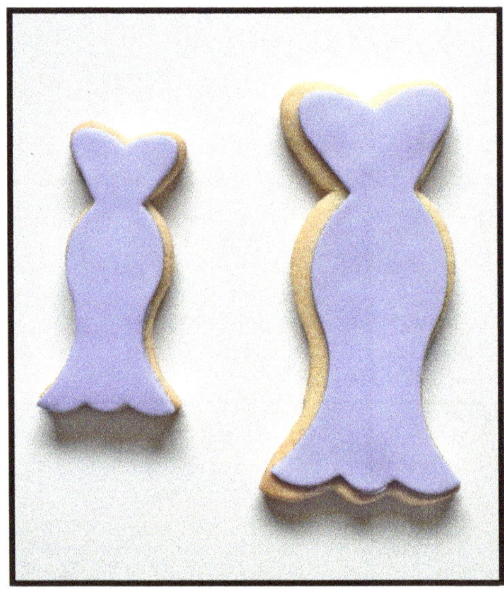

1. Roll out lavender fondant. Use the dress cookie cutters to cut out the lavender fondant dresses. Use a paint brush to apply a thin layer of piping gel onto your dress cookies. Apply fondant cut-outs to cookies, and gently smooth top.

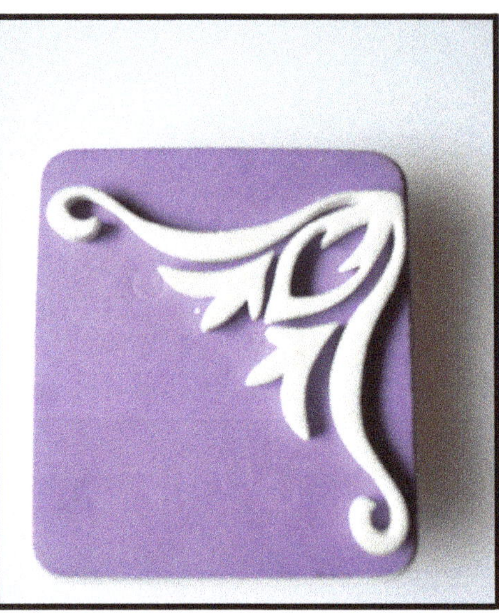

2. This is what I call the tulip tool. Turn it over and use it to imprint both of the dress cookies as shown.

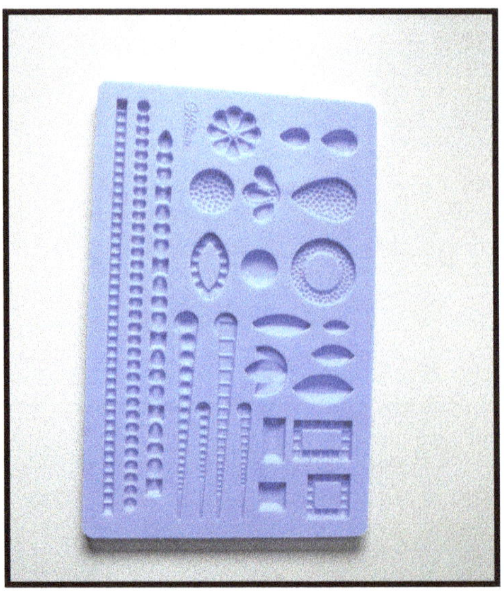

3. This is Wilton's Wedding Jewelry Fondant and Gum Paste Mold. Use it to mold a single small purple jewel and one three-part jewel. Refrigerate until firm. Remove.

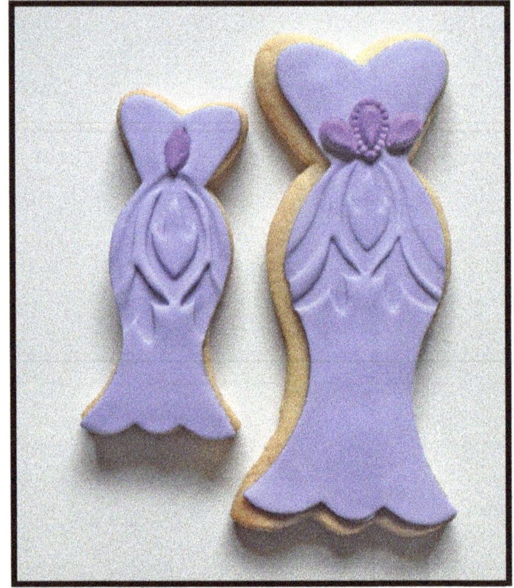

4. Apply the fondant jewels to the top of the upside down tulip design on the dress cookies as shown. Press in gently to secure.

Gray Ribbon Dress Cookie

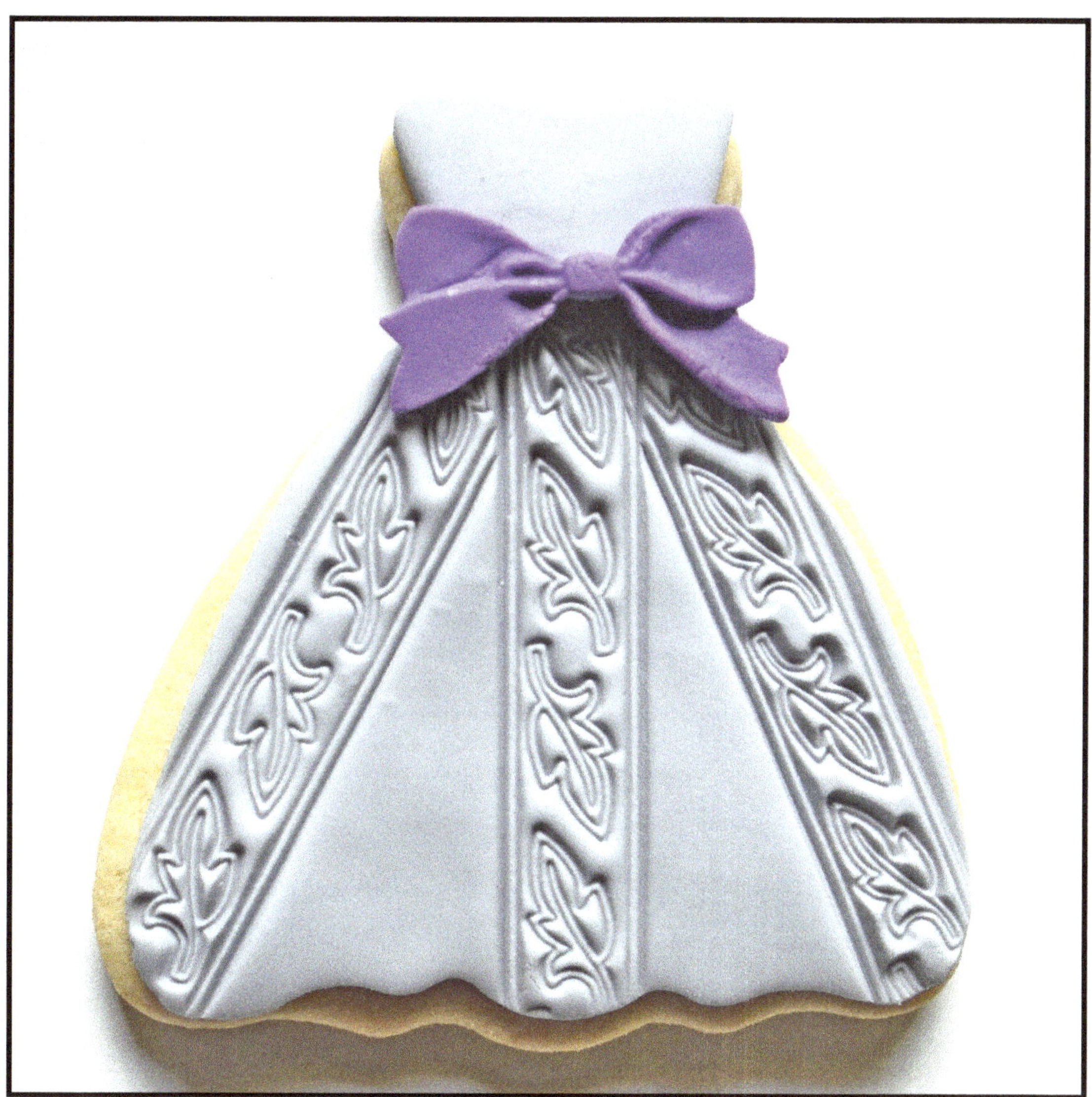

Materials:
- Dress cookie
- 0.56 oz. gray fondant
- 0.1 oz. purple fondant
- Piping gel
- Food safe paint brush

Tools:
- Susan's Wedding Dress Cookie Cutter (etsy.com, WhiskedAwayCutters)
- CK Products Ribbon Fondant Cutter Set (Barley and Eyelet)
- Bows silicone mold (hobbylobby.com)

Use cellophane bag size 5x7 inches to bag this dress cookie.

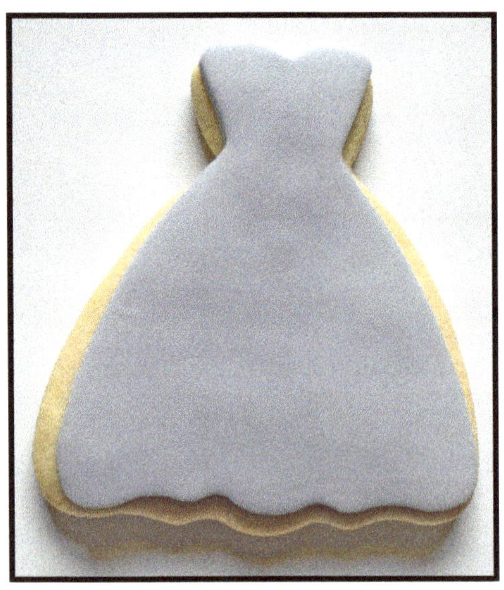

1. Roll out gray fondant. Use the dress cookie cutter to cut out the gray fondant dress. Use a paint brush to apply a thin layer of piping gel onto your dress cookie. Apply fondant cut-out to cookie, and gently smooth top.

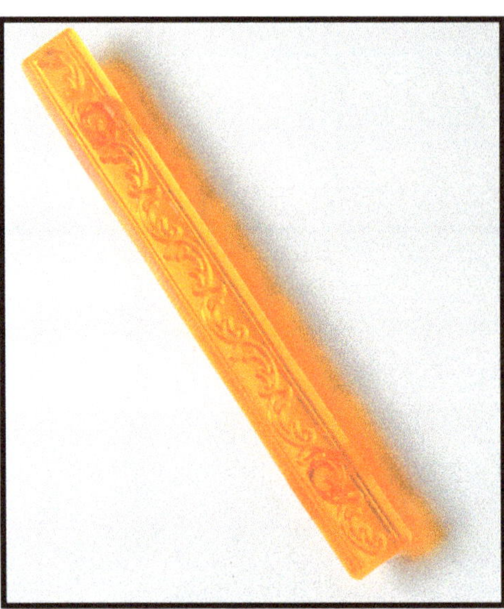

2. This is a ribbon fondant cutter tool that is used to imprint the fondant. It looks like cascading leaves with lines on the border.

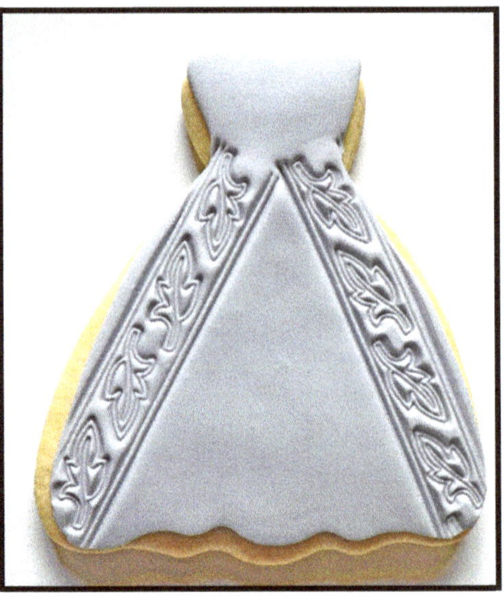

3. Use this ribbon fondant cutter tool to imprint the fondant dress skirt on both sides as shown.

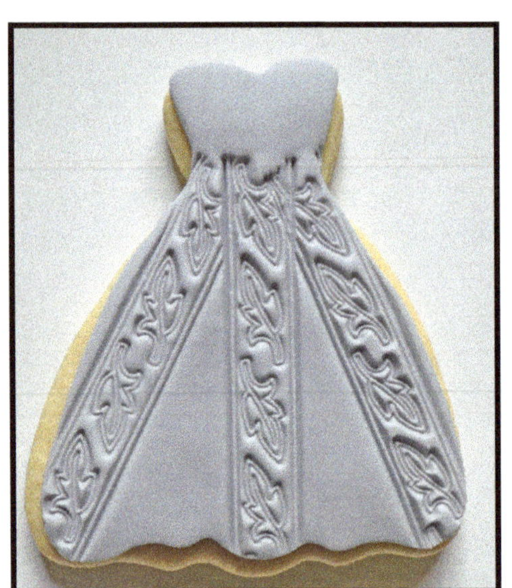

4. Imprint the center of the fondant dress skirt as shown.

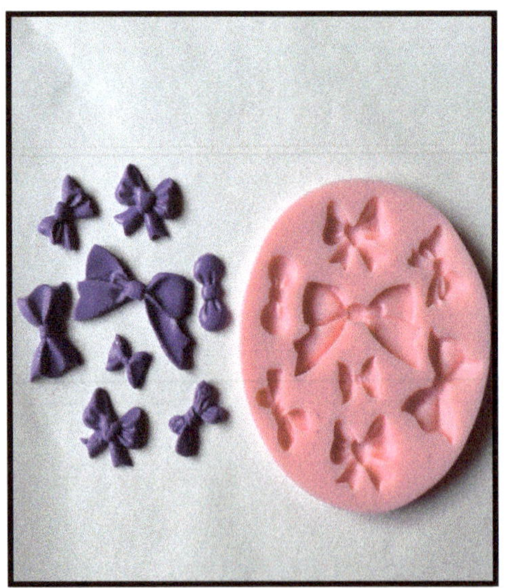

5. Use purple fondant to make a large fondant bow. Refrigerate until firm. Remove. I tested all of the fondant bows on this dress and liked the large fondant bow the best.

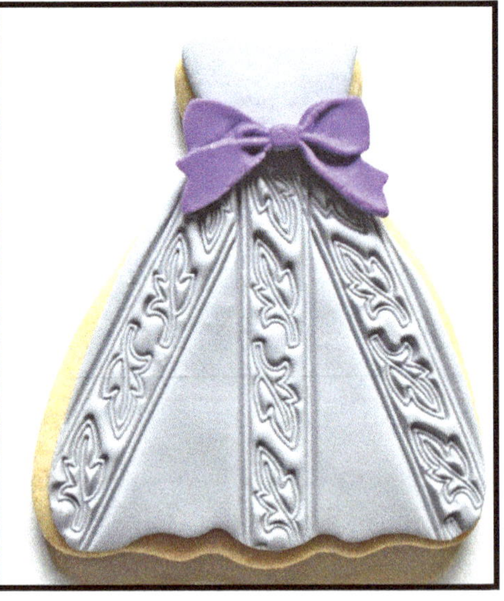

6. Use a dab of piping gel to attach the fondant bow to the waist of the dress cookie.

Black Ruffle Dress Cookie

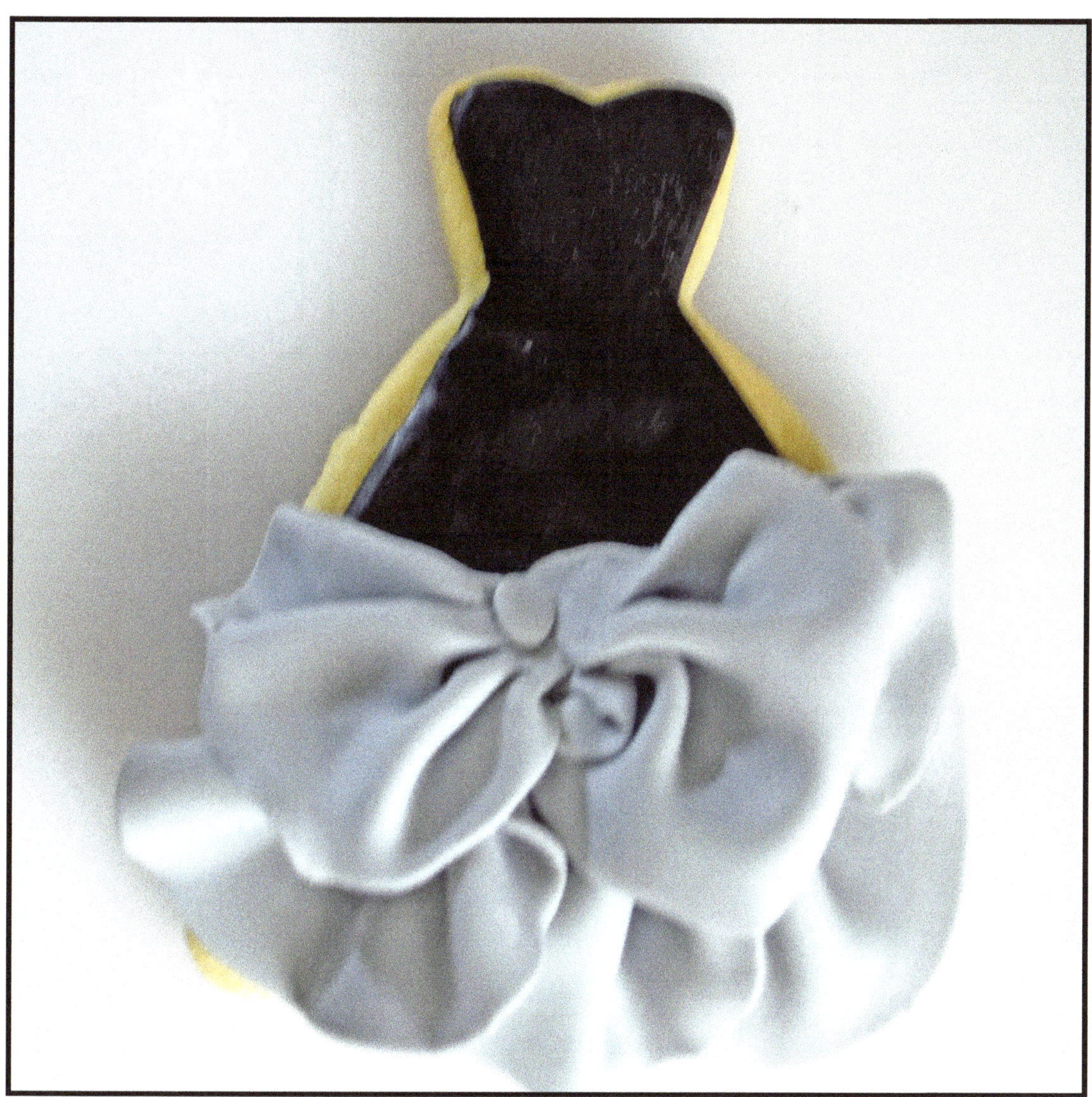

Use cellophane bag size 5x7 inches to bag this dress cookie.

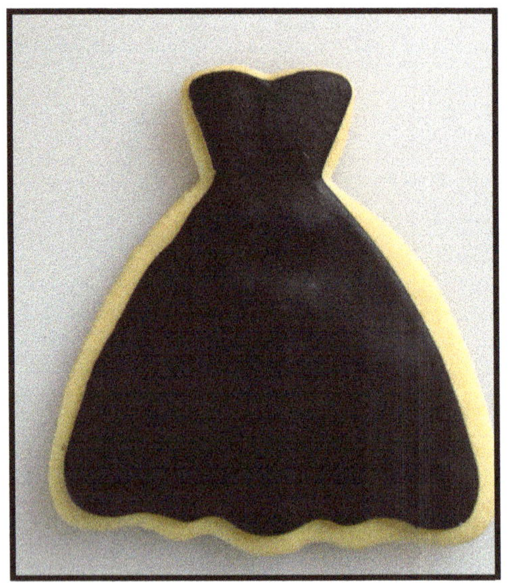
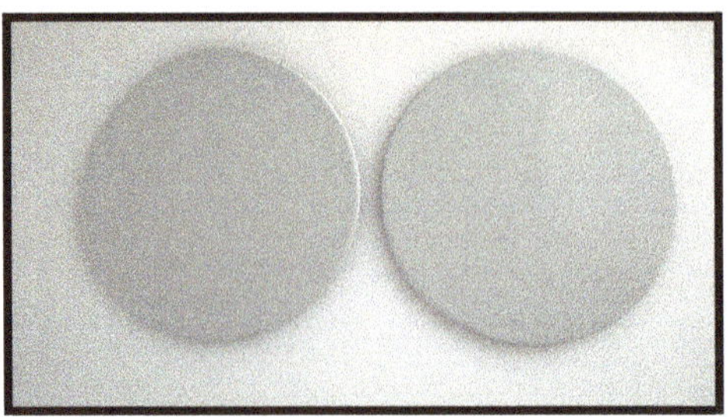
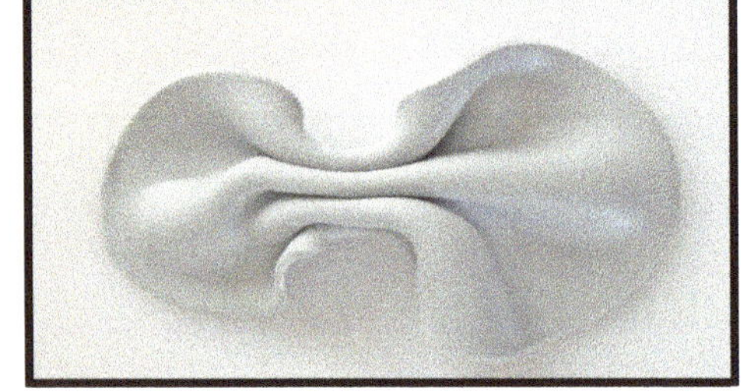
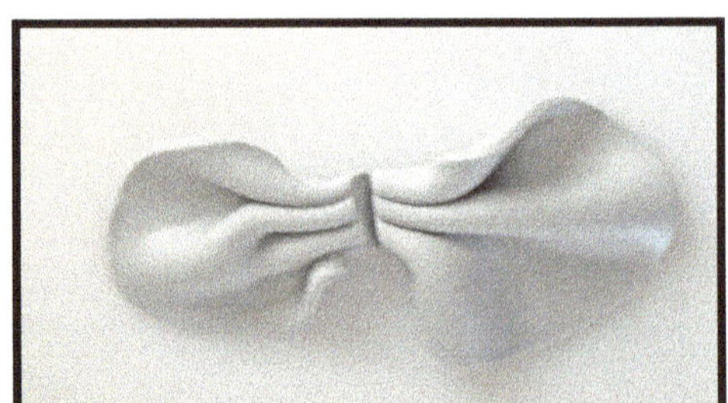
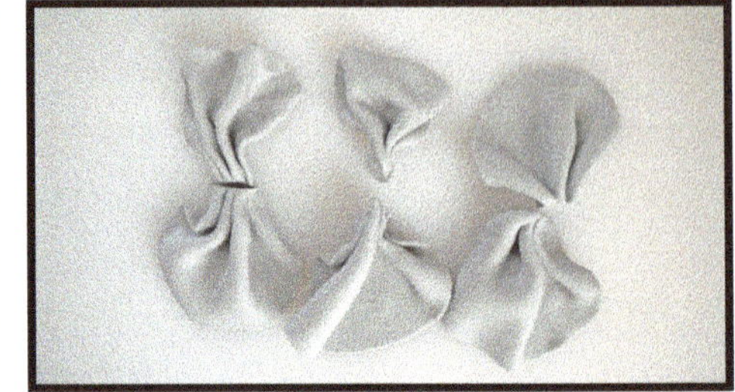

1. Roll out black fondant. Use the dress cookie cutter to cut out the black fondant dress. Use a paint brush to apply a thin layer of piping gel onto your dress cookie. Apply fondant cut-out to cookie, and gently smooth top.

2. Roll out gray fondant. Cut three 4-inch circles. Use your hands to gently fold circles in and out evenly as shown above. There is a center pleat and two end pleats.

3. Use a pizza cutter to cut these pleats in half. Lift up the round edge pleats. Use the pizza cutter to mash down a small part of the gathered sections.

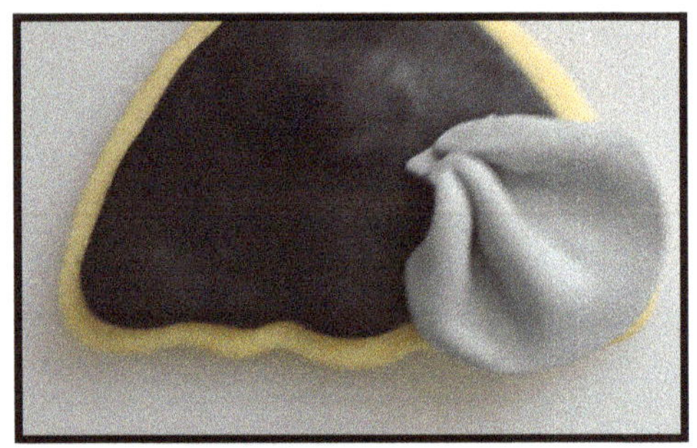
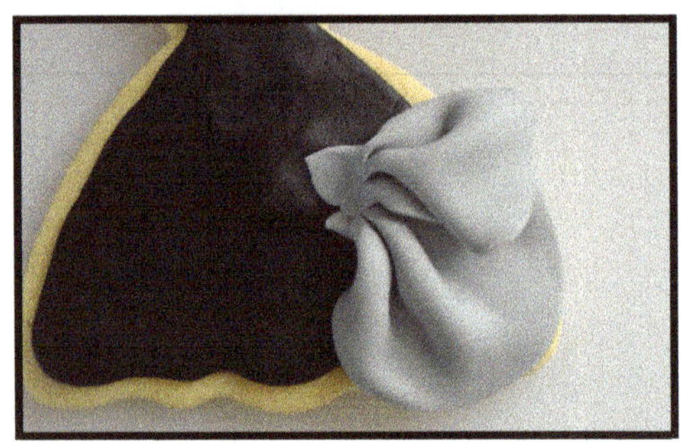
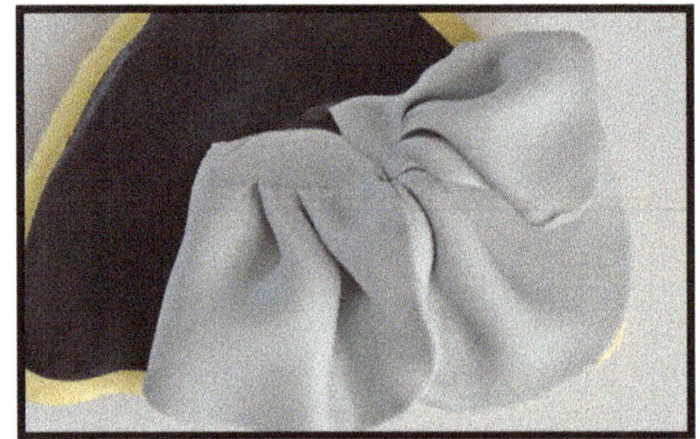
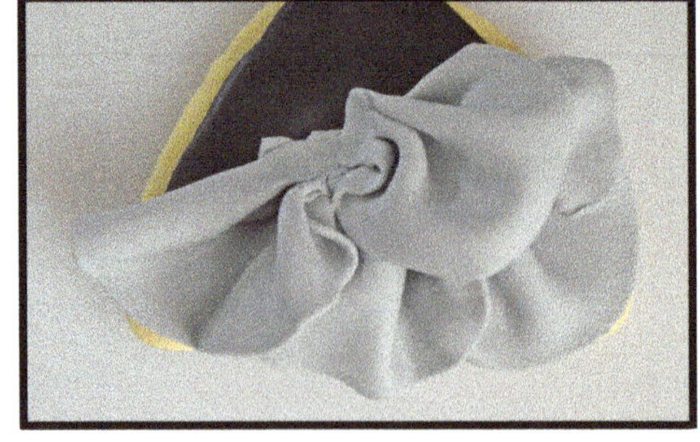
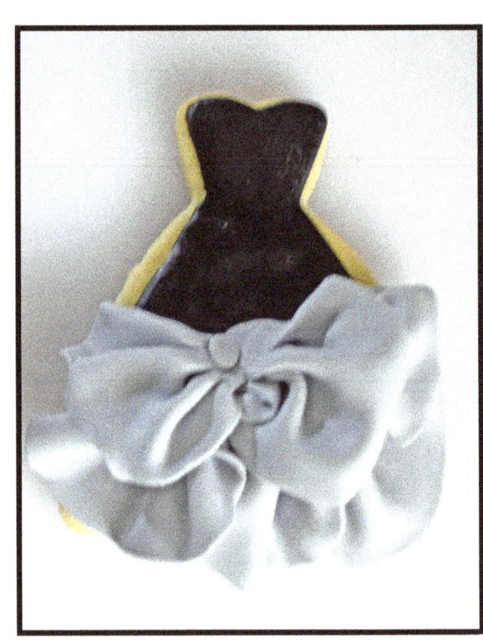

4. Cut away a part of the gathered section as shown and attach to the dress cookie on the right bottom edge. Gently press the gathered section down. Attach second ruffle as shown. Press gathered section down to secure.

5. Attach third ruffle to middle bottom part of dress cookie as shown. Gently press the gathered section down to secure. Lift the ruffled edge up slightly. Repeat with the fourth and fifth ruffles. Gently press the gathered section down to secure. The last two ruffles are facing each other.

6. Use a small piece of fondant to create a circle, and attach with a dab of piping gel at the connection point of the gathered ruffle section. Press down to secure.

Burgundy Swirl Dress Cookie

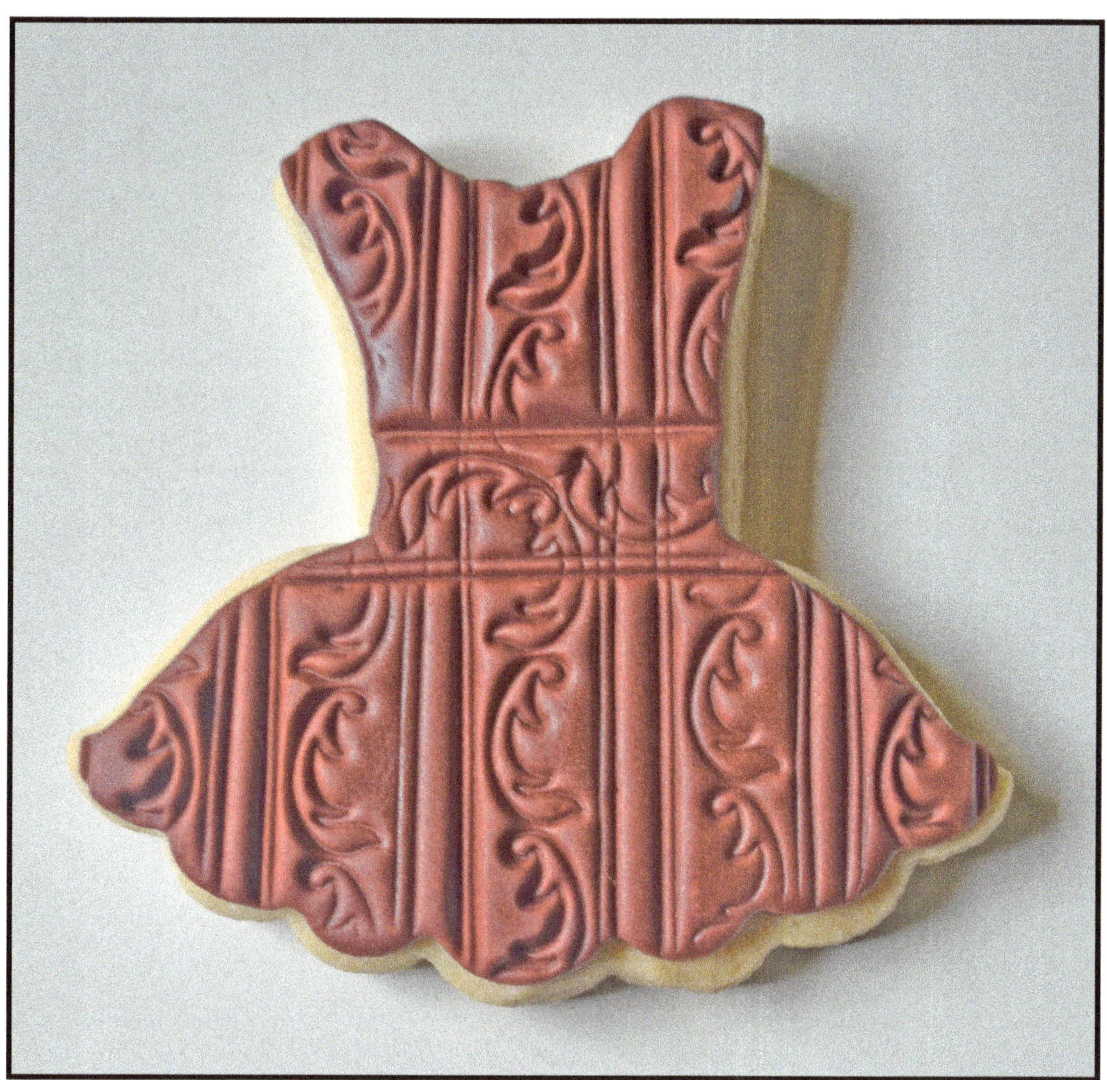

Materials:
- Dress cookie
- 0.7 oz. Fondarific Burgundy fondant
- Piping gel
- Food safe paint brush

Tools:
- Tutu and Dress Cookie Cutter (etsy.com, WhiskedAwayCutters)
- CK Products Ribbon Fondant Cutter Set (Barley and Eyelet)

Use cellophane bag size 4x6 inches to bag this dress cookie.

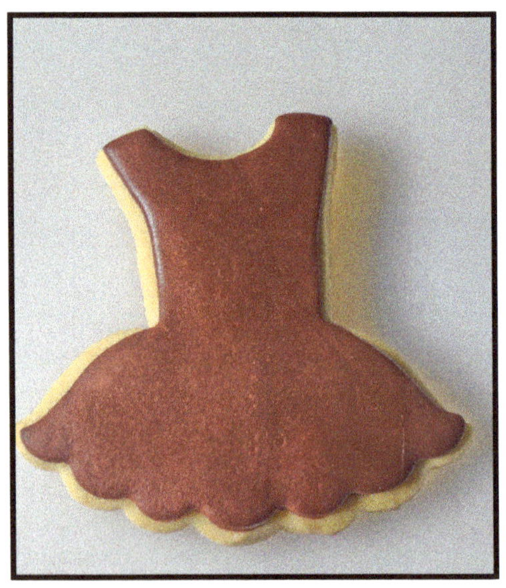 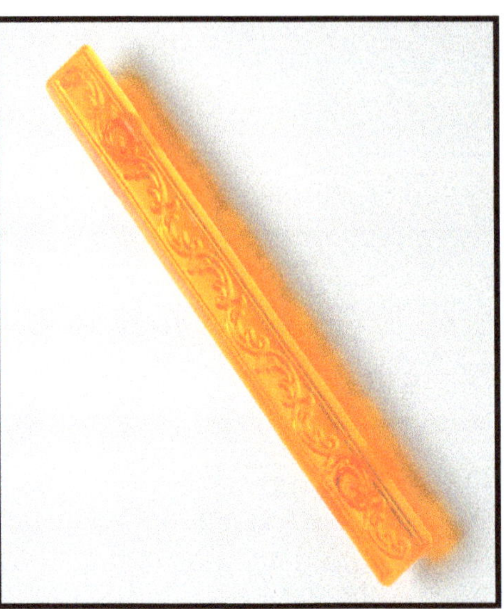 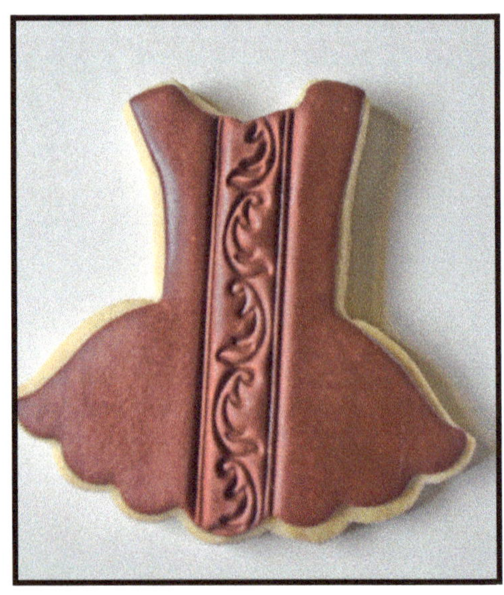

1. Roll out burgundy fondant. Use the dress cookie cutter to cut out the burgundy fondant dress. Use a paint brush to apply a thin layer of piping gel onto your dress cookie. Apply fondant cut-out to cookie, and gently smooth top.

2. This is a ribbon fondant cutter tool that is used to imprint the fondant. It looks like cascading swags with lines on the border.

3. Use this ribbon fondant cutter tool to imprint the fondant dress skirt cookie center as shown.

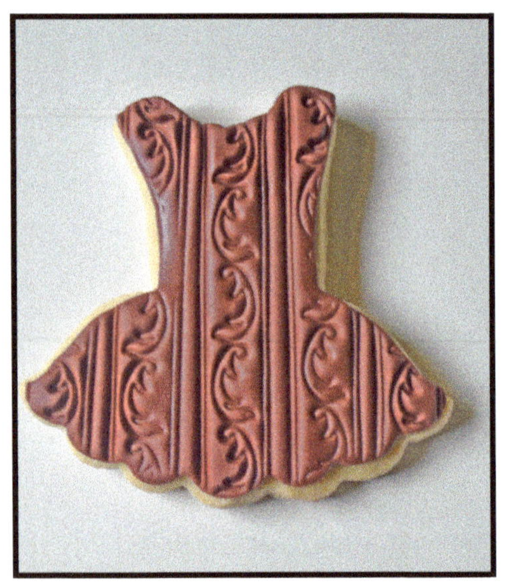 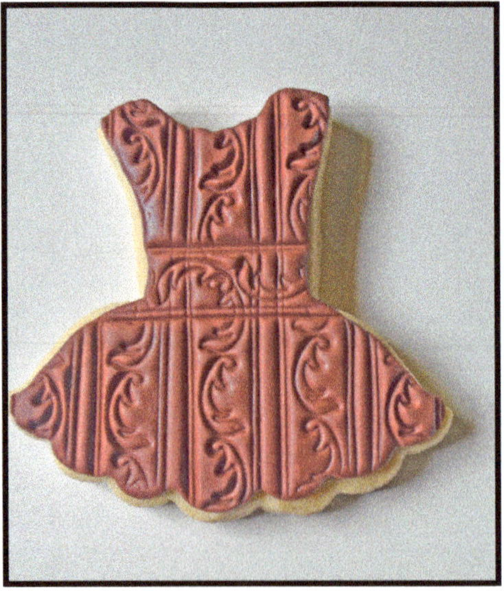

4. Imprint the sides of the fondant dress skirt as shown.

5. Imprint the waist of the fondant dress skirt as shown.

Final Touches

Congratulations! You have finished decorating your fondant dress sugar cookies, and I hope you are excited. Here are some tips for the final touches.

Drying Your Decorated Fondant Dress Cookies

Please allow your fondant-covered dress cookies to completely dry and set overnight so that the fondant design will not mess up when packaging the cookies. If you have a dehumidifier, you can speed up the drying process.

Packaging Your Decorated Fondant Dress Cookies

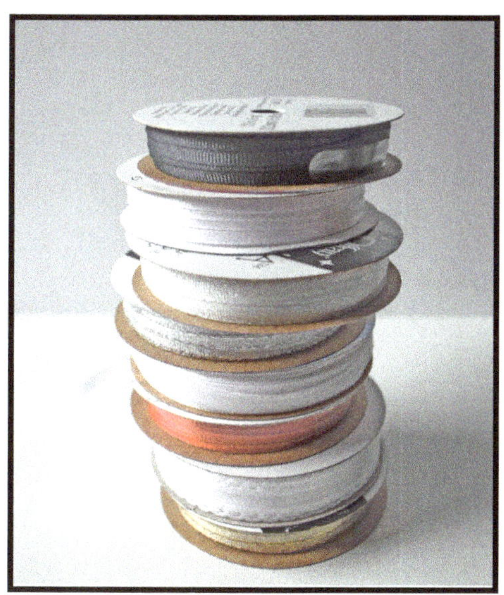
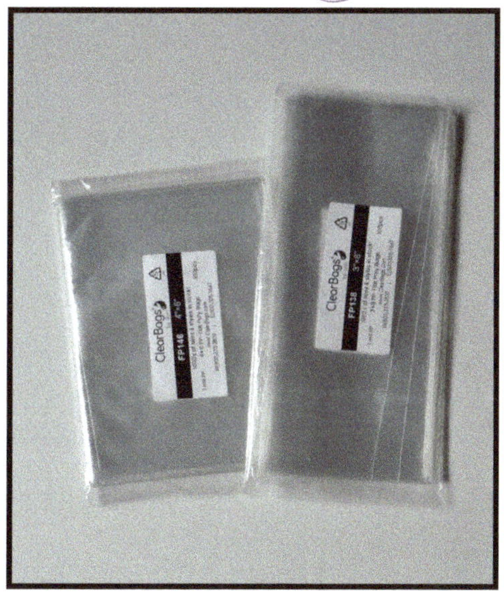
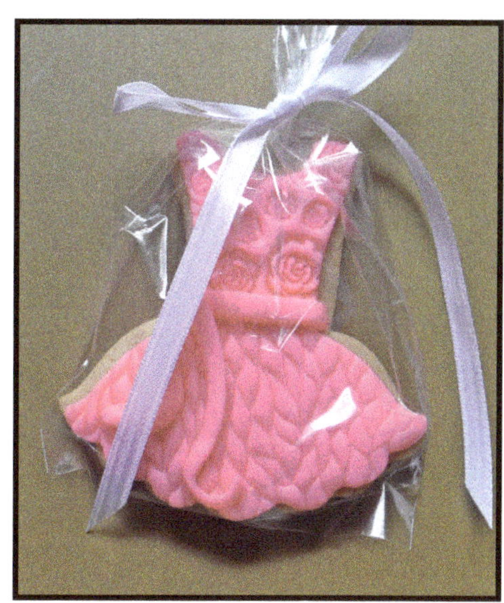

There are many options for packaging your fondant-covered dress cookies.

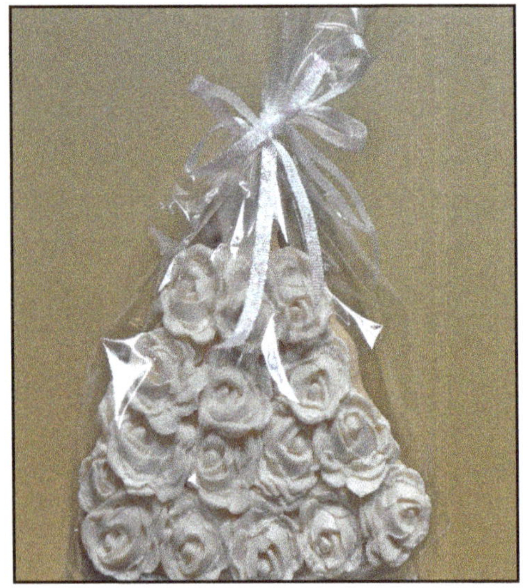 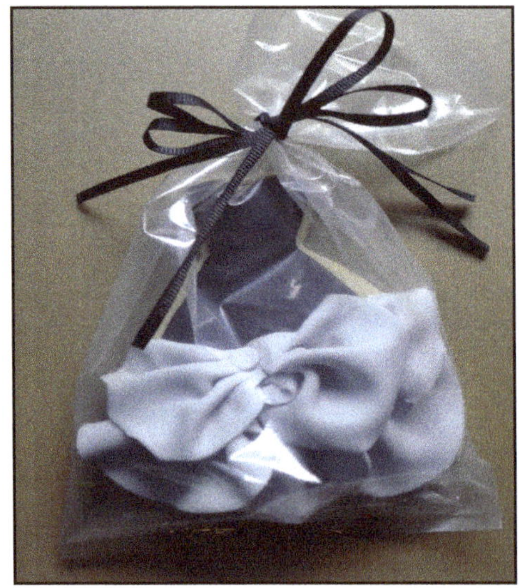 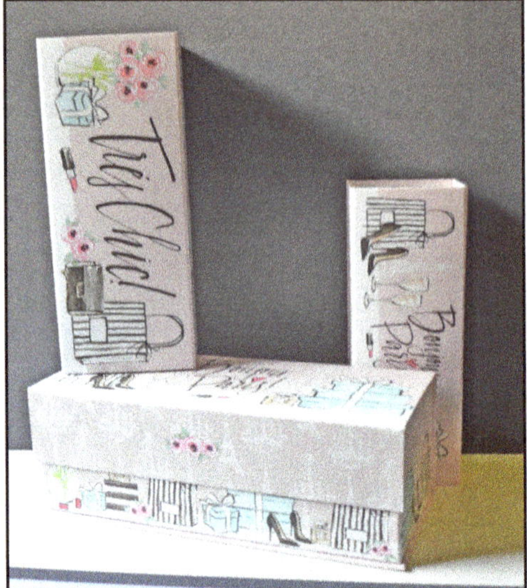

I use ribbon to close fondant-covered dress cookies when I plan to stand them up and display them in a sturdy cake box (that has the top cut off and has been decorated). I tape the cookies closed whenever I place them into decorative boxes. You can place different-sized dress cookies in these decorative boxes. Even though it does not have dresses on it, this box definitely has a chic look, and can be used for your decorated dress cookies. See the picture on the next page of the stacked boxes. This makes a great gift.

Troubleshooting Packaging Problems

Decorated sugar cookie too tight to fit into cellophane bag? Use a microplaner to shave off some of the sides of the dress cookie and try again.

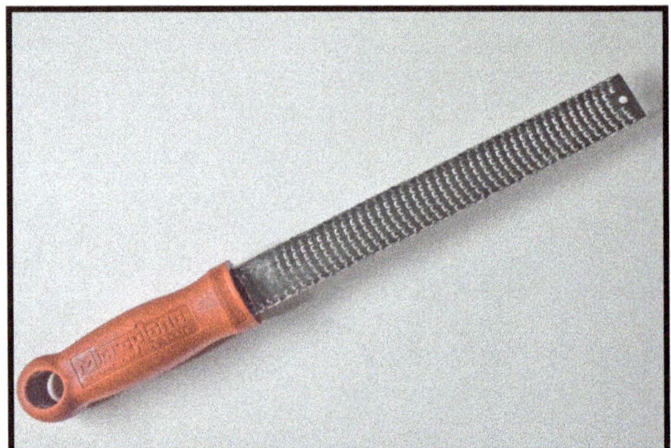

Cannot hold the top of the bag to add the ribbon? Use a binder clip to keep the top together until you add the ribbon.

Displaying Your Decorated Fondant Dress Cookies

There are many ways to display your decorated fondant dress cookies. You can display them on beautiful trays, in decorative boxes, or even create your own decorated containers to place your creations. I have also covered large paper boxes with wrapping paper to match the decor for the party.

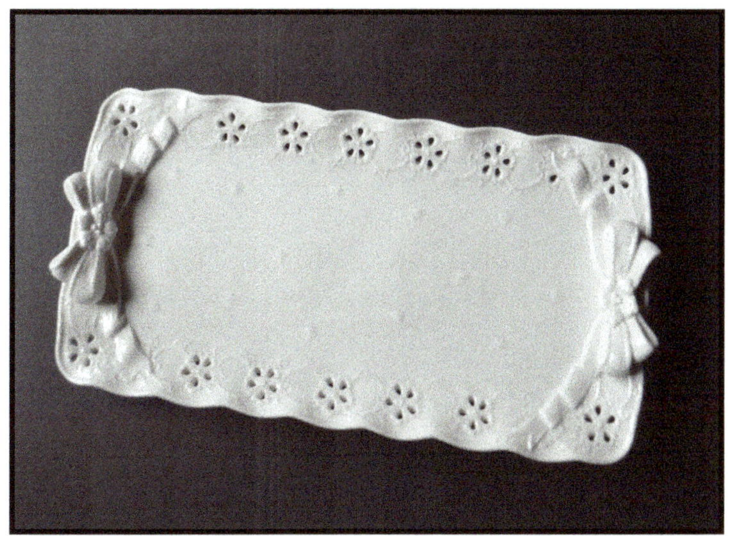

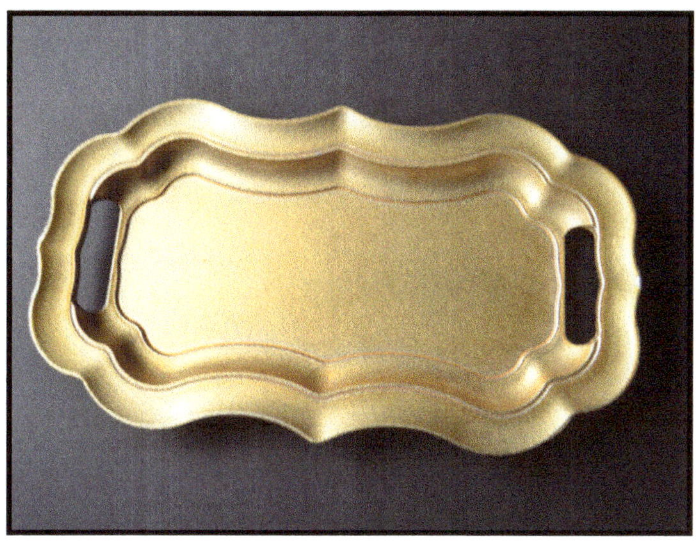

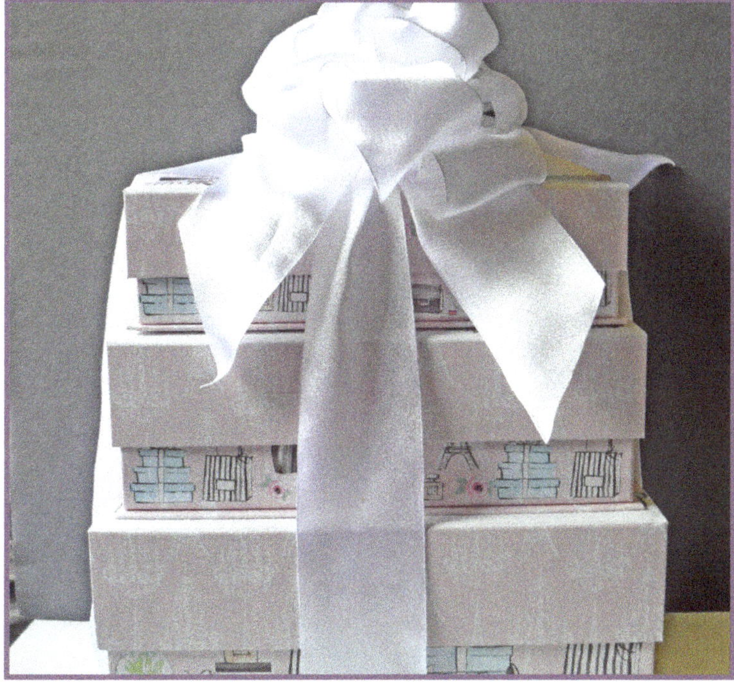

There are a lot of beautiful trays on the market that will make your fondant-covered dress cookies stand out on a table. Have fun mixing and matching trays for different decorated cookies. With trays like this, you may choose not to individually package your decorated sugar cookies. Please make sure to have some cellophane bags on hand for people who want to take their decorated sugar cookies home.

Pictured to the left is the stack of decorative boxes I found at my local craft store. Each box can be filled with different styles or flavors of decorated dress sugar cookies. I recommend individually packaging the decorative sugar cookies before placing them into decorative boxes like these for safety.

Favorite Websites / Suppliers

clearbags.com

Clear Bags has a huge selection of inexpensive cellophane bags to package your decorated sugar cookies. Stock up on popular sizes like 3x8 inches, 4x6 inches, and 5x7 inches.

countrykitchensa.com

Autumn Carpenter has lots of cookie decorating supplies available for purchase on her website.

cynfulcakezbakeshop.com

Cynful Cakez Bake Shop is a new cake, candy and baking supply company in Baltimore, Maryland, and is owned by Cynthia Knox. She has a large supply of unique products ready to ship out to you or you can pick them up.

etsy.com

Etsy has a number of great suppliers who have products you can use in fondant cookie decorating. Please check out Sinful Cutters, Whisked Away Cutters, Bakers Tool Store, and Cookie Cutter Lady. You can tell them that I sent you to them.

franscakeandcandy.com

Sallee McCarthy has everything you need to get started making fondant-covered dress cookie designs. Please tell her that I sent you.

fondarific.com

Fondarific has the best fondant I have ever tasted, and it is easy to use. Each color fondant is a different flavor or you can choose buttercream flavor in many colors. They also have small tubs of fondant you can order.

michaels.com

Has a huge selection of cookie decorating items. They also have a good selection of cellophane bags, ribbon, and boxes to make your decorated dress sugar cookies look special.

shopbakersnook.com

A great website with cake, cookie, and other decorating supplies. Brian Shockley is wonderful. He runs several busy group pages for cake and cookie decorating on Facebook that you should check out.

sugardelites.com

Jennifer Dontz has a new paint line, crimpers, and other products on her website. Sign up for her amazing newsletter. It always contains incredible information and pictures.

waybeyondcakes.com

Mayen Orido has the 12-inch Crystal Clear Acrylic Rolling Pin featured on page 2 in Item No. 3. I love it.

Index

About the Author & Photographer 149

Basic Sugar Cookies 7

Cake Embossers 24
Cake Stamps 24
Cutting Fondant with Cookie
        Cutters 27

D

Dress Cookie Creation Chart 150
Dress Cookie Cutters
  Ann Clark Gown Cookie Cutter
    Gold Stenciled Dress Cookie 45
    Silver Tulip Dress Cookie 93
  Dress Cookie Cutter
    Blue Pattern Press Dress Cookie 79
    Blue Wavy Dress Cookie 41
    Burgundy Butterfly Dress
        Cookies 105
    Chocolate Daisy Dress
        Cookie 131
    Lavender Swirl Dress Cookie 35
    Marbled Swirl Dress Cookie 75
    Peach Smock Dress Cookie 67
    Pink Swirl Dress Cookie 111
    White Flowers Dress Cookie 83
    Yellow Sprinkles Dress Cookie 117
  LILIAO Wedding Dress Cookie Cutter
    Lavender Lace Dress Cookie 89
    Metallic Gold Dress Cookie 97
    Navy Lace Dress Cookie 33
    Orange Lace Dress Cookie 95
    Pink Pattern Dress Cookie 53
    Purple Lace Dress Cookie 101
    White Rose Bow Dress Cookie 37
  Party Dress Cookie Cutter
    Blue Sprinkles Dress Cookie 47
    Coconut Dress Cookie 31
    Green Lace Dress Cookie 57
    Lavender Black Dress Cookie 129

Princess Cookie Cutter
  Coral Blossom Dress Cookie 133
  Coral Rose Dress Cookies 51
  Gold Sprinkles Dress Cookie 121
Susan's Wedding Dress Cookie Cutter
  Purple Roses Dress Cookie 69
The Diane Dress Cookie Cutter
  Black Lattice Dress Cookie 29
  Blue Imprint Dress Cookie 103
  Hot Pink & Black Dress Cookie 55
  Lavender Pattern Dress Cookie 65
  Navy Peach Dress Cookie 59
  Tan Flowers Dress Cookie 73
The Marilyn Gown Cookie Cutter
  Black Sparkle Dress Cookies 43
  Cream Mini Dress Cookies 91
  Peach Bridesmaid Dress
      Cookies 109
  Red Gown Dress Cookie 87
  Silver Cake Comb Dress Cookie 125
  White Lace Dress Cookie 115
  White Lace Gown Dress Cookie 71
Tutu and Dress Cookie Cutter
  Black Mini Dress Cookie 77
  Blue Hearts Dress Cookie 63
  Gold Pressed Dress Cookie 99
  Pink Patterns Dress Cookie 85
  Purple Pattern Dress Cookie 81
  Red Swirls Dress Cookie 39
  Silver Dots Dress Cookie 113
  Yellow Lattice Dress Cookie 127
Wedding Dress Cookie Cutter
  Black Lace Dress Cookie 61
  Gold Strip Dress Cookie 107
  Silver Pattern Dress Cookies 119
Wedding Dress Outline #3 Cookie
    Cutter
  Green Grass Dress Cookie 49
  White Large Roses Dress Cookie 123
Dress Cookie Designs 29
  Black Lace Dress Cookie 61
  Black Lattice Dress Cookie 29
  Black Mini Dress Cookie 77
  Black Ruffle Dress Cookie 139
  Black Sparkle Dress Cookies 43
  Blue Hearts Dress Cookie 63

Blue Imprint Dress Cookie 103
Blue Pattern Press Dress Cookie 79
Blue Sprinkles Dress Cookie 47
Blue Wavy Dress Cookie 41
Burgundy Butterfly Dress
      Cookies 105
Burgundy Swirl Dress Cookie 141
Chocolate Daisy Dress Cookie 131
Coconut Dress Cookie 31
Coral Blossom Dress Cookie 133
Coral Rose Dress Cookies 51
Cream Mini Dress Cookies 91
Gold Pressed Dress Cookie 99
Gold Sprinkles Dress Cookie 121
Gold Stenciled Dress Cookie 45
Gold Strip Dress Cookie 107
Gray Ribbon Dress Cookie 137
Green Grass Dress Cookie 49
Green Lace Dress Cookie 57
Hot Pink & Black Dress Cookie 55
Lavender Black Dress Cookie 129
Lavender Lace Dress Cookie 89
Lavender Pattern Dress Cookie 65
Lavender Swirl Dress Cookie 35
Lavender Tulip Dress Cookie 135
Marbled Swirl Dress Cookie 75
Metallic Gold Dress Cookie 97
Navy Lace Dress Cookie 33
Navy Peach Dress Cookie 59
Orange Lace Dress Cookie 95
Peach Bridesmaid Dress Cookies 109
Peach Smock Dress Cookie 67
Pink Pattern Dress Cookie 53
Pink Patterns Dress Cookie 85
Pink Swirl Dress Cookie 111
Purple Lace Dress Cookie 101
Purple Pattern Dress Cookie 81
Purple Roses Dress Cookie 69
Red Gown Dress Cookie 87
Red Swirls Dress Cookie 39
Silver Cake Comb Dress Cookie 125
Silver Dots Dress Cookie 113
Silver Pattern Dress Cookies 119
Silver Tulip Dress Cookie 93
Tan Flowers Dress Cookie 73
White Flowers Dress Cookie 83

White Lace Dress Cookie 115
White Lace Gown Dress Cookie 71
White Large Roses Dress Cookie 123
White Rose Bow Dress Cookie 37
Yellow Lattice Dress Cookie 127
Yellow Sprinkles Dress Cookie 117

Edible Food Color Spray 19

Favorite Websites/Suppliers 146
Final Touches 143
    Displaying Your Decorated Fondant
        Dress Cookies 145
    Drying Your Decorated Fondant
        Dress Cookies 143
    Packaging Your Decorated Fondant
        Dress Cookies 143
    Troubleshooting Packaging
        Problems 144
Flavoring Fondant 26
Fondant Decorating Tools
    & Techniques 18
    Cake Stamps 24
    Edible Food Color Spray 19
    Fondant Embossers 24
    Icing Tips 20
    Luster Dusts 21
    Paint Brushes 18
    Patchwork Cutters to Emboss Your
        Dress Cookie 22
    Plunger Cutters 20
    Sanding Sugar or Sprinkles on Your
        Dress Cookies 23
    Silicone Lace Fondant Molds 25
    Silicone Molds for Fondant
        Decorations 25
Fondant Troubleshooting 27

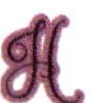

How to Cover Sugar Cookies in
    Fondant 14
    Instructions for Fondant-Covered
        Dress Sugar Cookies with
        Designs On the Cookie 14
How to Use Fondant Right Out of the
    Package 12
How to Use this Book 4

Icing Tips 20
Impression Mats 21
Introduction 1

Luster Dusts 21

Paint Brushes 18
Patchwork Cutters to Emboss
    Your Dress Cookie 22
Princess Cookie Cutter
    Gold Sprinkles Dress Cookie 121

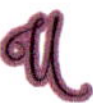

Sanding Sugar or Sprinkles on Your
    Dress Cookies 23
Silicone Lace Fondant Molds 25
Sugar Cookie Recipes 5
    Basic Sugar Cookies 7
    Carrot Cake Sugar Cookies 8
    Chocolate Sugar Cookies 8
    German Chocolate Sugar Cookies 9
    Time to Roll Out Your Sugar Cookie
        Dough 10
    Using Cookie Cutters to Cut Out Your
        Sugar Cookie Dough 10

Time to Roll Out Your Sugar Cookie
    Dough 10
Tools & Techniques
    Cake Stamps 24
    Edible Food Color Spray 19
    Flavoring Fondant 26
    Fondant Embossers 24
    Icing Tips 20
    Impression Mats 21
    Luster Dusts 21
    Paint Brushes 18
    Patchwork Cutters to Emboss Your
        Dress Cookie 22
    Pattern Rollers & Stencils 22
    Piping Gel 18
    Plunger Cutters 20
    Sanding Sugar or Sprinkles on Your
        Dress Cookies 23
    Silicone Lace Fondant Molds 25
    Silicone Molds for Fondant
        Decorations 25
Top Tools for Beginner Fondant Cookie
    Decorators 2

Using Cookie Cutters to Cut Out Your
    Sugar Cookie Dough 10

About the Author & Photographer

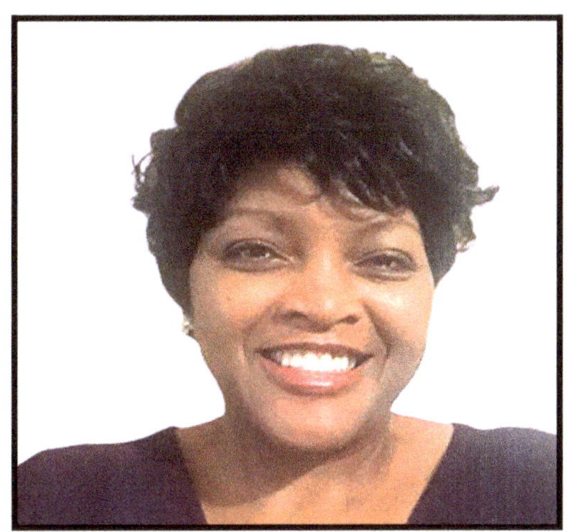

Debra J. Mosely is an avid cake, decorated cookie, and sweet treats designer. Her passion for baking and decorating is clearly apparent when you see how her eyes sparkle when she is teaching others how to decorate using Fondarific fondant and buttercream.

Debra comes from a creative family with talented hands. Relatives on both sides of her family are skilled at quilting, home decorating, cabinet making, carpentry, sewing, and other handmade crafts. Debra currently lives in Selma, Alabama.

For the most up-to-date information on Debra's new book releases, classes, tutorials, or other decorating information, please check out her website at debrajmosely.com. You can connect with Debra online by following her on Instagram at instagram.com/debrajmosely_author.

Please follow Debra J. Mosely on Amazon, and leave a review if you like this **Simple Fondant Dress Cookies** book. Your reviews are important.

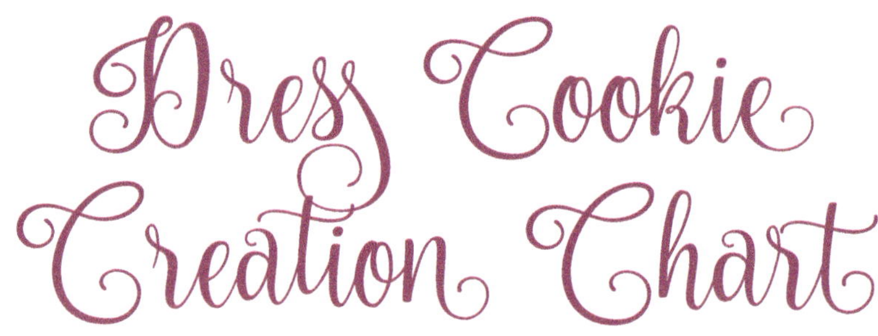

When you want to share cookies with your family and friends, this chart will help you keep track of your cookie gifts. Get your pdf copy of this form from my website – www.debrajmosely.com.

Recipient Name	Cookie Design(s)	Qty	Date Delivered

Recipient Name	Cookie Design(s)	Qty	Date Delivered